A MIND TO CRIME

Also by Anne Moir and David Jessel

BRAINSEX

A MIND TO CRIME

The controversial link between the
mind and criminal behaviour

ANNE MOIR AND
DAVID JESSEL

MICHAEL JOSEPH
LONDON

MICHAEL JOSEPH LTD

Published by the Penguin Group
27 Wrights Lane, London W8 5 TZ
Viking Penguin Inc., 375 Hudson Street, New York, New York 10014, USA
Penguin Books Australia Ltd, Ringwood, Victoria, Australia
Penguin Books Canada Ltd, 10 Alcorn Avenue, Toronto, Ontario, Canada M4V 3B2
Penguin Books (NZ) Ltd, 182–190 Wairau Road, Auckland 10, New Zealand

Penguin Books Ltd, Registered Offices: Harmondsworth, Middlesex, England

First published in Great Britain 1995

Copyright © Anne Moir and David Jessel 1995

Typeset by Datix International Limited, Bungay, Suffolk
Printed in England by Clays Ltd, St Ives plc
Set in 11/13pt Monophoto Sabon

A CIP catalogue record for this book is available from the British Library

ISBN 0 7181 3768 x

The moral right of the authors has been asserted

CONTENTS

PREFACE

A Mind to Crime has its genesis in our previous book, *BrainSex*, which charted the biological brain differences of men and women. The book became a television series, and it was while we were filming in the high-tech neurological laboratories of Professor Ruben Gur in Philadelphia that the idea of an investigation into the roots of crime began to take shape. We were looking at scans of the brains of men and women generated by the new and exciting brain-imaging technology known as PET scans. For the first time, here was a non-invasive method of watching the brain at work – and not just the upper and outer levels of the brain, which conventional scans could reach, but the very secrets of the limbic system, deep at the heart of the brain. The scans showed that brain activity takes place at different levels and at different sites in men and women, even when both sexes are engaged in the same mental task.

Gur turned to us and said, 'You know, that's why men are criminals and women are not. The roots of crime lie in the brain.' But how much, we asked, did scientists actually know about the criminal brain? Gur replied that, like the investigation into brain sex differences, the field was rapidly expanding. As an example of the knowledge being gained, he gave us a copy of a graduate thesis on the roots of juvenile delinquency, which concluded that as well as the well-established social origins of persistent criminality, there were biological factors as well.

This conversation set in motion a three-year trail through many thousands of often almost impenetrable academic studies. Often studies on crime and the brain lay deep beneath the undergrowth of centuries of criminological and psychological theory.

What we uncovered – after hacking back much verbiage – convinced us that academics have a fascinating story to tell, with profound implications for almost every aspect of criminal justice. There really is a mind to crime – indeed, different, identifiable minds to different, specific crimes.

It has not been an easy story to tell, and we have endeavoured to interpret the science without mistranslating it, or oversimplifying it. We are deeply grateful to Professor Katharine Hoyenga who has written, with her husband Kermit, the equivalent academic versions of *BrainSex* and *A Mind to Crime*, and who painstakingly and generously worked her way through the draft to correct our errors and to warn us about over-hasty conclusions. The book is much improved as a consequence. Any errors of fact or opinion are, though, entirely our responsibility.

We would also like to thank the many academics who sent papers and patiently explained the complexities of their work. Their names are too numerous to mention here, but their work is acknowledged in the detailed references at the end of this book. Forgive us when we say, as we repeatedly do, that 'many researchers . . .' or 'most experts . . .' say this or that; our aim has been to make the facts as simple and clear as possible and to credit each statement individually would make for an even more cumbersome book.

We would also like to thank William Moir, consultant and voice of common sense (not to be confused with common opinion). Thanks, too, to Trish Rushen who runs the local library for the village of Aldbourne, Wiltshire, who did a magnificent job of finding many thousands of academic papers from hundreds of different academic journals. Sam Willmott and Debbie Cowan both contributed a much welcome extra hand. Thanks also to Sara Ramsden of Channel 4, who commissioned the television series which reflects some of the areas covered by the book.

The book itself would not have been written without the

viii

enthusiastic support and ineffable patience of our publisher Susan Watt, who let deadline after deadline fall, and asked infuriatingly valid and pertinent questions. Thanks, too, to Anne Askwith, senior editor at Michael Joseph, who contributed her share of excellent suggestions.

We are neither moralists nor criminologists. We know that crime, like all human behaviour, is a vast and complex phenomenon springing from many different sources, all of which interact with each other. We can only present what we believe are new, significant and verifiable discoveries which may lead to a deeper and a truer understanding and fresh optimism – and hope that by doing so others will be able to stand upon our shoulders and get a clearer view.

Anne Moir
David Jessel
1995

CHAPTER I

Science – a Light in the Darkness of Crime?

CRIME IS THE PRODUCT of poverty. Or greed. It is the result of social dislocation, television, the genes or the devil. Choose your decade, and you will find a criminological theory to suit you.

We accept all these as valid explanations for crime, severally or in combination. We think that some people commit crimes because they are bad, because they are desperately poor or because they have grown up in horrendously dysfunctional families – that they commit crimes for any or all of these reasons.

But we also believe – because we accept the findings of clinicians with no penal axe to grind – that many criminals act as they do because of the way their brains are made, or how they function. Every textbook on criminology has dealt with the sociological explanations of crime, but cultural and economic causes alone cannot explain the phenomenon of crime. The past two decades have vastly extended the horizons of knowledge, and we believe that it is time to benefit from that knowledge – the results of the work of endocrinologists, biophysiologists, neurophysiologists, biostatisticians, geneticists and many others; that we must travel to those horizons to seek additional explanations.

This book does not excuse crime. What it tries to do is to explain one aspect of it. The explanation is not comprehensive: there is no magic bullet, chemical or genetic, to solve what is one of the most corrosive challenges to society.

Our objective is to lay out the available evidence; to summarize for the first time for a non-specialist audience what clinical researchers have found about the chemistry and neurophysiology of the criminal mind.

There is now very strong evidence that many criminals – whether violent or non-violent – are likely to have a disordered mind. They are not like the rest of us. There is a chemical or structural malfunction in the brain which time after time can be related to offending behaviour. Moralists will be reassured to know that some people who have these mental deficits can and do struggle successfully to overcome them and lead law-abiding lives; but for them it is truly a struggle and a triumph. Those who fall by the wayside are, quite literally, the weaker amongst us. We are just as open to temptation as they are, but the criminal may lack the mechanisms the rest of us have to resist it. It is difficult to be judgmental about such people when we understand that they have to exercise far greater efforts to inhibit their behaviour than do normal people. For example, many of us may experience a flicker of annoyance at a self-important official or an obstreperous colleague, and entertain for a brief moment the delightful fantasy of giving him a bloody nose; instead, we rise above the situation and congratulate ourselves on our superior, civilized forbearance. For others, though, it is a titanic undertaking to resist the urge to lash out. Many of us may have cast an envious eye as we pass a shop window; for others, the urge to smash it and grab the goods displayed is almost a physical need.

These brain deficits may appear separately or together, act in concert with economic, social or physiological factors, or they may simply be the sole cause. If you have low levels of a certain chemical neurotransmitter in your brain *and* an alcoholic father, your chances of being able to lead a normal life are worse than if you simply had a drunken father *or* a chemical deficit. The degree of damage, the type of damage and the combinations of different damage have been linked to specific and differing patterns of crime. As is to be expected, the more damage there is, the worse the prognosis. The greater the constellation of factors – both biological and cultural – the greater the likelihood of crime.

What scientists are also discovering, as they unravel the

links between brain function and criminal behaviour, is that there is no single criminal type, no single mind to crime, but several. There are different brain patterns for different sorts of crime. The brain structures of the paedophile, the violent criminal and the serial sex killer are different from each other; but among those who commit each specific offence, there are similar abnormalities in the brain. What has become startlingly clear is that there are explanations for 'bad' or 'immoral' behaviour which may stem from abnormalities in the brain's structure or chemistry.

There's evidence of a new understanding of environmental and hereditary influences. 'Environment' is the shorthand to describe the multitude of cultural influences upon us; 'heredity' embraces the complex way that the genes compose the blueprint that makes us all individual. Genetic theory has advanced in sophistication, and we now know that environmental factors can interact with the genes, as it were switching their messages on or off. So you can inherit a predisposition to crime – but you will not necessarily be a criminal. Without that predisposition, you are less likely to take up a criminal career, whatever the environmental temptations. There is no 'gene for crime' (except one – the gene that makes us male) but a whole array of genetic influences. What's more, there seem to be genes that predispose some to non-violent property crime, and genes that predispose others to violent behaviour.

It's like a hand of cards. Just one 'environmental' or 'biological' card won't give you the 'full house' of criminality. A healthy mental constitution can overcome social disadvantage (indeed, in the overwhelming majority of cases it does) and a basic biological deficit in the brain can be tended, nursed, or assuaged by careful and patient treatment. You need a large hand, and strong cards in it, both cultural and biological, to achieve the royal flush of a violent, persistent and criminal personality.

The biggest biologically predisposing factor, as we've already hinted, is gender. Sex is the strongest human distinction: all over the world, the behaviour of women and men is more distinct than, say, the behaviour of a male in Frankfurt is from that of a male in the jungles of New Guinea. Sex difference in crime has been so clear and bright that most studies have been blind to it. The literature on delinquency and crime frequently refers to the fact that boys alone were studied 'as there were too few girls in the sample to be statistically significant'.[1] They do not stop to ask why. But the difference is so large – 89 per cent to 95 per cent of all crime is committed by men – that it cannot be ignored. When it comes to crimes of violence, men have a near monopoly.

Is there something in our culture that is restraining women from such antisocial behaviour? No, the male mind – whether for reasons of evolution or something else – is wired and fuelled to be more criminal. Men are born with a greater number of crime cards up their sleeves, predisposing them to criminality – cards that the female simply does not have. Biology is at the heart of the huge differences between the sexes when it comes to crime. It's partly the story of testosterone, aggression and violence. There's also new knowledge about the power of the hormones – and a dire warning about the trouble we may be in for – from new studies on those who have taken excessive doses of anabolic steroids. These chemicals, taken illegally by some two million juveniles to improve sporting performance, have transformed perfectly normal, mild-mannered young men into rapists and murderers. But hormones, as we will see, are not responsible for the whole difference. All the new evidence shows that men's and women's brains are operating on different neurochemical fuels. They are minds apart when it comes to the potential for criminal behaviour.

We will tell the story of new research into neurotransmitters, the key activators of thought, and how the pattern and concentration of these mind-altering chemicals is different in men and women. The male brain is wired to be more impulsive and sensation-seeking, with a low frustration threshold and a low boredom threshold. The neurotransmitter directly responsible for controlling impulsive behaviour is found at much lower levels in the male brain than in the female. He is less likely to assess the consequences of his action because of the chemical mix of his mind. He is less likely to think of the consequences as he races down the motorway, 'borrows' the petty cash, smashes the plate-glass window or reacts violently to provocation.

But while young men are constitutionally prone to delinquency, only one in fifty will graduate to a life of crime. They have a distinctive set of biological cards. The evidence suggests that we can pick out the 'career criminals' from the crowd through tests that show how the brain is operating; that in these individuals the brain is different from normal. Tests can indicate which child has this criminal potential, and whether the criminality will take a violent or non-violent form; much dysfunction in the brain can be identified at an early age. Studies conducted over long periods, based on clinical assessments of unbiased samples of the population, and conducted 'blind', with no way of predicting the outcome, have shown an astonishing degree of reliability. All children do odd things at one time or another; but a child who holds a juvenile full house of deviant cards is displaying the clearest possible signals of future offending. We ignore them at our, and the future adult's, peril. We can help. We can do something.

In the area of violent crime, we will investigate the different brain patterns involved. We will question the assumption in law that the aggressive psychopath is sane and responsible for his actions. Such a criminal, we will argue, is not responsible for his feelings; he is deaf to them, and to the needs and feelings of others. He lacks the mechanism of conscience. Can we really find someone guilty when guilt itself is an alien concept? Ignorance of the law is no defence – but is a constitutional failure to care about right and wrong at least a cue for clemency? According to one estimate, such people form a large proportion of the prison population. Apart from keeping them out of circulation, there is no long-term benefit in imprisoning them: such people are not deterred or deterrable,

5

because their brain function is such that they do not calculate the consequences of their actions; they lack the mental equipment to experience fear; and they have an abnormality in the pre-frontal (thinking and planning) area of the brain. The latest research suggests that in the brains of aggressive psychopaths the area that creates feelings, and hence our ability intellectually to comprehend guilt, shame and remorse, is disconnected from the more 'thoughtful' frontal lobes. The thinking part of the brain is not being informed by the emotional part, so it lacks the necessary moral education.

Illness, too, can alter the mind and result in violence. Charles Whitman, who killed his wife and children and then shot dead eleven people from the top of a Texas tower block, was suffering the mind-altering consequences of a brain tumour.

Then there is the mind of those whose behaviour changes dramatically, without obvious provocation: the Jekyll and Hyde personality who suddenly flies into unpredictable rages. This man's crimes can be terrifyingly domestic: he is the sort of man who beats up his wife and might even kill her for no apparent reason. In virtually all such cases, the criminal will be found to suffer from an electrical storm in the rage control centres of the animal brain which results in violent and inexplicable changes of mood and behaviour.

In the case of violent women – and child abuse is one area where women rival men in violence – there are complex biological roots. Infanticide is recognized in law as being linked to possible post-natal depression and is a mitigating circumstance, as is premenstrual syndrome. New discoveries show that women suffering from the premenstrual syndrome have a pattern of neurotransmitter abnormalities similar to those of the violent male.

The sexually deviant criminal has a different mind pattern again. The truly sexually deviant mind, where the person is sexually aroused by inappropriate needs, is probably born, not made. The non-violent paedophile has a distinct brain abnormality, a mind lacking the normal pattern for sexual arousal. New brain-imaging techniques called PET scans have revealed an abnormality in the hypothalamus, the area of the brain which controls sexuality, and they also show that such people have an abnormal hormonal balance. The violent paedophile displays a different pattern: he has the same hypothalamic abnormality but, in addition, has abnormalities in the frontal lobes and in the animal area of the brain, the limbic system, echoing those found in the violent aggressive offender. Those rare schizophrenics who kill – and there is often a sexual element to such killings – are now believed to suffer brain abnormalities which are at the root of their delusional paranoia. Again, scientists think that this may be an underlying genetic disorder which is precipitated by some traumatic event.

Rape, the most politically problematic of crimes, is under intense study. Some rapists, especially those who fall into the 'date' rape category, differ little from 'normal' men who keep their sexual impulses under control. Studies show, however, that they are not good at reading or interpreting social cues – that they are blind to body language or misunderstand facial expressions – with the result that they misapprehend situations and think that they are having consensual sex. But the rapist who stalks his victims, planning his attacks, has a different mind. He often has an effeminate personality, and is sometimes homosexual. Studies of this type of rapist indicate a high probability of hormonal imbalance, as well as abnormalities in the sexual control centres of the brain.

This story will not be news to thousands of researchers around the world. All the clues are there. They lie in the intricate folds of the brain, and at the very frontiers of knowledge itself. It is a story which should have dramatic consequences for the way we deal with the problems of crime, how we prevent it and punish the perpetrators. But criminology experts are so engrossed in what they are doing that they do not notice the parallel and complementary research going on around them.

Much of the problem has been in specialization and the

separation of academic disciplines. Criminology is seen as a branch of the social sciences. It would seem as strange to the criminologist to share a laboratory with a biologist as it would to share an electron microscope with a chemist. Anyway, what do biology and chemistry have to do with crime? The idea of innate biological explanations has been treated with suspicion; notions of genetic or biological inferiority are inextricably tarnished by memories of the ultimate social experiment: racial purity through genocide. One of the doyens of criminology, Larry Siegal, recounts how when editing *Criminology* he suggested a chapter on biological and physiological theories of crime but found himself attacked on all sides by his fellow faculty members. One colleague warned him that 'even suggesting a biological basis to crime was politically incorrect, and jeopardized my entire career; this chapter would cause my colleagues to see me as a right-wing zealot.'[2] A more recent academic book which concentrates on the biological roots of crime has been denounced by the critics more because of its 'political danger'[3] than because of any error or inaccuracy. But the perversion of science by political psychopaths does not negate scientific truth.

Just as our first book, *BrainSex*, provoked a horrified response (although it is now accepted as a mainstream text of gender studies), because of the gulf between theorists and biologists, we predict opposition to this book from the existing schools of criminology. Psychology grew up in innocent ignorance of how the brain actually *works*. When science provided the information, psychiatrists, instead of assimilating it, largely ignored it. How many psychologists keep up with the latest medical research into the ever-expanding knowledge of that miraculous and perverse organ, the brain? Perhaps many psychotherapists simply see no necessity to understand neurotransmitter pathways, or to identify the principal components of the limbic system.

Some of those who might be hostile to this book may want to cling to the opinion that crime is simply the result of evil in the world. Others may seek to hold on to theories of social dislocation, and the psychological impact of childhood emotional trauma as causes of crime. Still more may see crime as overwhelmingly connected with economic disadvantage. It might, too, be argued that this dangerous new knowledge (whether it is true or not) will lead us to seek genetic or surgical fixes to crime, that we will be tempted to abort criminality.

There are no such fixes, and there is no such temptation. We do not want to encourage doctors and politicians to play God, to create a crime-free society or even to eradicate society's criminal elements. But there is a wonderful opportunity actually to do something about crime: as a result of this knowledge, we believe that there are some areas where criminals can be treated. People talk endlessly about the plague and disease of crime; there is, properly understood, the chance of a criminal antibiotic in some carefully defined cases. In Sweden, severe cases of premenstrual syndrome are now being treated with great success, using drugs which increase the brain transmitters involved in inhibiting impulsive behaviour. Men, too, with certain violent patterns of behaviour are being treated successfully with drugs; for instance, sex offenders and repetitively violent offenders are responding to treatment.

It's not as if we were overburdened already with answers to the question of crime. Politicians can tweak the figures every which way, and, yes, in some areas crime seems to be flattening out, in others falling, and everything is distorted by the degree of reporting. But taken on any view, crime has risen greatly over the past four decades, and there is no very good reason to believe that the trend will cease. Traditional 'short, sharp shock' treatments may provide a moment of popularity for their proponents, but it is an open secret that such treatment simply breeds fitter young delinquents with a master's degree from the university of crime. 'Softer' approaches (such as probation or counselling) involve an unacceptable investment in time, money and personnel – and have not been proved to be successful. When, as happened recently, a young offender is reported to have been taken on a character-building safari trip to Africa without any very obvious change in his pattern of re-offending, even liberal penologists despair.

We need to think again; we need new ideas and we need new knowledge upon which to base those ideas. Faced with gargantuan costs, public and political panic at crime, and the proven failure of virtually all strategies to curb it, one would expect governments to clutch at even the least plausible straw that promised some sort of solution. Yet solid, scientific evidence, clinically assessed and reported in textbooks and periodicals of unimpeachable authority, goes disregarded. It would be surprising if even one hundredth of 1 per cent of the annual crime bill had been devoted to procuring information which already existed and, we believe, may hold some of the keys to the question of crime.

This knowledge raises a colossal new agenda. What are we to do with our traditional, reassuring moral judgments, and our comfortable assumptions of good and evil? If criminals are crippled, should we punish them any more than we should discriminate against the physically disabled? What should we do with the law's distinctions about responsibility and intent? Is not punishment of the offender the defining social glue – and what shall we find to take its place? Do we dare to treat crime, in the hope that we may not have to live beneath its shadow? Should we prescribe drugs which have a likelihood of success and whose effect would save tens of thousands of pounds per criminal per year – or is there a deep sense that somehow treatment 'excuses' criminality, robs us of some need to punish? And what about the civil liberties issue here: would drug treatment be more of an infringement of an offender's rights than locking him away?

But we believe that the evidence that biology is a central factor in crime, interacting with cultural, social and economic factors, is so strong – as we hope to prove in this book – that to ignore it is perverse. As perverse, indeed, as to cling to the mysteries of astrology long after the astronomer's telescope has opened our eyes to the skies.

CHAPTER 2

Crime on the Cards

SOCIAL AND ENVIRONMENTAL factors are still reckoned as the essential determinants in the search for the key to criminality. But how far can we actually predict criminality from the early influences of home and the circumstances of birth? Which of the following children, dealt different hands by fate, ought we to be most concerned about?

Rick lives on a run-down council estate. His father has a drink problem and is rarely home. His mother, as so often, is the reliable one. She has single-handedly brought up Rick and his two brothers. Rick was sixteen when he first got into trouble with the law. He, along with a group of friends, had a little too much to drink. They smashed up the local playground. 'We were bored,' was the only explanation he could come up with. Rick was fined and warned.

Simon ought to have everything a boy could want: a comfortable home, an environment free from financial worries and the full attention of caring parents. But Simon was a difficult child from the day he was born, irritable, negative and prone to temper tantrums. The problems got worse when he went to school. He never sat still long enough to learn anything. He constantly disrupted the class. His concerned parents arranged special lessons for him. That helped a little, but when he was nine he horrified them by stealing silver from a neighbour. It was when the police brought him home, after they had caught him in the process of removing the booty, that his parents sought help.

Mary was adopted when she was three months old by a comfortably off couple. Guy, her father, had a good steady job on the line of the local Honda factory. She was a strange and distant child given to fantasies. She seemed to find it hard to distinguish them from real life. Mary also had a distinctly cruel streak. She had to be restrained from hitting her younger brother, who was also adopted. Her adoptive mother was shocked and dismayed when she found Mary singeing the fur off the pet cat. Mary was only eight at the time.

James was adopted when he was one month old, by a couple who on paper seemed the perfect parents, after his parents were killed in a car accident. He was a quiet, self-contained, reflective child, and despite little support from his adoptive parents James did well at school. But the adoption agency had been fooled by the well-heeled credentials of the adopting couple. James was two when his father was arrested for stealing £100,000-worth of jewellery from a country house. His mother escaped conviction, even though she had fenced the stolen goods. James subsequently hardly saw his father as he was in and out of prison at frequent intervals.

If poverty and a disruptive home life are the cause of later criminality, there's little hope for Rick. Simon, with all the care in the world, should be all right; and so should Mary, who, with her loving parents, should surely grow out of her strange behaviour. And as for James – literally brought up in a thieves' kitchen – what chance is there for him? But in a world where the wealthy Menendez brothers murder their parents in California, and the comfortable and stable Newall family in Jersey ends up with both parents murdered by one of their sons, can we truly draw any safe conclusions about the role of social, economic, or family factors in predicting crime? Is it not a grimly negative view of the individual power of the human spirit to suggest that children are doomed by their environment? Would any social scientist have identified sports star O.J. Simpson as someone who would be charged with a violent double murder? The so-called predictive powers of social science aren't a great deal better than the tarot pack or the crystal ball.

It's obvious, then, that we cannot predetermine criminality from environmental or social circumstances alone. If man could predetermine criminality, would not totalitarian societies have already prohibited potentially criminal marriages, aborted deviant foetuses, or locked up for ever the infant gangsters? While it would be stupid to ignore social factors in the genesis of crime, we must see them as merely one possible dimension of the phenomenon. Poverty, loss of parents or bad education *may* and *can* contribute to the making of a criminal, but the patent survival of children who have been born poor, fatherless and deprived as pillars of rectitude and models of citizenship proves that other factors are involved in criminality: both negative factors which can turn even the most loved and advantaged rich kid into a criminal menace and positive factors which can protect those who have been dealt the least advantaged hand of cards at birth. If we want to solve the mystery of crime, we should start not with analyses of broken homes and economic hardships, but with the most blatant fact about crime, a fact which any detective would relish, because, at a stroke, half of the suspects can be eliminated from enquiries. And it's nothing to do with broken homes or potty training: it's a blunt, biological fact.

CRIME: THE GENDER CARD

There is a truth about the nature of criminality which is hardly ever mentioned. If theorists were to discover that nine out of ten crimes were associated with the consumption of peanut butter, the phases of the moon, a specific gene or a particular pattern of social or emotional deprivation, our approach to criminology would be revolutionized. Nobel laurels would be distributed, new chairs of Dietary, Lunar, or Genetic

Criminological Studies would be set up in place of existing university departments, and we would soon be looking back on existing psychological or social models as well-intentioned but futile fumblings in the dark.

Yet the fact that nine out of ten crimes are committed by men, that gender is the largest single correlate of crime, and that this fact may be significant seems to have passed most theorists by. Is this because it is too obvious a point to be meaningful, too fundamental a point to be worth addressing? Or could it be that the overwhelming sex bias of crime doesn't fit easily with theories of society, family and psychopathology?

It is a dramatic enough statistic – and to be statistically accurate we must refine the figure to 89 per cent of crimes being committed by men – to deserve rather more attention than it has received in the past. Independent and hitherto unco-ordinated academic studies all over the world, which are beginning to suggest a demonstrable biological input into the causes of crime, are showing that the major biological fact about ourselves as a species is our gender: 'Sex differences in criminality are so sustained and so marked as to be perhaps the single most significant factor about recorded crime'[1] and 'The difference between the sexes is immense and it is universal. There is no known society in which the level of lethal violence among women even begins to approach that among men.'[2]

If 89 per cent of crime were committed by women, our (mainly male) professors and researchers might have begun to develop a theory of crime in which biological, genetic and hormonal factors played a prominent part. But in fact few have asked themselves whether these 'marked', 'immense' and 'universal' differences perhaps hold an important clue to the conundrum of criminal behaviour. As it is, the principal result of the male criminal bias has been simply to exasperate researchers; the literature on delinquency and crime is peppered with such despairing observations as 'there were too few girls in the sample to be statistically significant',[3] or 'all attempts to study female criminality may be thwarted by the difficulty of obtaining a sample of women and girls that is sufficiently large to allow meaningful statistical analysis'[4]. But could this very discrepancy be a clue in itself – in Holmesian terms, the dog which significantly did not bark?

There was, at one time, a suggestion that the growth of women's liberation would reduce the embarrassing divisions. Alarmist analysis did discover an occasional threefold growth in female crime, but closer inspection revealed that the rise was a statistical aberration – a 0.3 per cent rate had become a full 1 per cent. Between the early 1960s and the late 1970s the rate of female burglary increased by between two and three times, but from a very low base: from 2.9 per cent to 6 per cent in the case of burglary and from 3.6 per cent to 8.1 per cent in the case of car crime. The only area where there has been a significant increase in crime committed by women is in shoplifting; but here again this may be the result of a policy to arrest more women. In one study, only 1 per cent of women shoplifters, historically, were actually arrested, compared with 12 per cent of males. Thus sexual equality did not mean that more women suddenly felt liberated to commit crimes, but that those women who did commit criminal acts were being prosecuted equally with men.

Otherwise, the ratio remains virtually static, defying the impact of the decades and their evolving sexual politics. 'The overall female to male percentage of crime across age groups has remained quite stable over the past fifty years.'[5]

Even a study of the most severe crime in the criminal calendar, murder, reveals an actual decrease in the female offending rate. Women were responsible for a fairly static 15 per cent of murders in the United States until the last decade, when the number began to fall, from 2,500 to 1,500 per year; all this, of course, at a time when the male murder rate was rocketing. 'The single most amazing thing about women who kill, or commit crimes of any sort, is that there are so few of them.'[6]

But look at the record sheet of the male. Some surveys suggest that 45 per cent of males in the UK have committed a serious offence of one type or another – a figure that bears comparison with most figures worldwide, especially those taken from Western, urban environments. A detailed study of males in Philadelphia, USA, shows that among those aged between 10 and 18, 35 per cent had been arrested at least once, and 43 per cent had been arrested before reaching the age of thirty. In another study of UK males, 44 per cent had been arrested before reaching the age of thirty.

The police chief in *Casablanca* issues the curt command, 'Round up the usual suspects.' In identifying those likely to commit crime, we have already narrowed the field: men commit most crimes and most men have committed crimes. But we can narrow the focus further: nearly *all* men have committed crimes of one sort or another at a particular time of their lives.

THE YOUTH CARD

Biology has another impact on the likelihood of offending, and it's a blunt one: crime is largely a function of age. Amongst teenage males, criminal behaviour is as natural as acne. 'Crime is an activity carried out by young men in large cities. There are old criminals and female criminals and rural and small town ones, but to a much greater degree than would be expected by chance the criminals are young urban males . . . This is true . . . in so far as we can tell, in every society that keeps criminal statistics.'[7]

Most crime, then, is male, and most male crime is young. Male behaviour is much more associated with age than with any other variable; income, social group, state of the family unit or whatever matter far less in predicting crime than the simple fact of how old the individual may be. Six out of 10 arrests for serious property crime involve youths of 20 years or younger. A random sample of 1,445 13- to 16-year-old boys in the UK revealed that 70 per cent had stolen from a shop, and that 17 per cent had stolen from private premises. The majority had committed offences for which, if caught, they would have been prosecuted. Independent studies strongly suggest that official crime figures actually underestimate the true extent of crime, especially among the young.

But whatever it is about the make-up of the male that biases him towards crime, in most cases it is remediable or reformable. Reassuringly, for parents of wild young men, all the experts report 'a steady decline throughout life of the likelihood of being arrested'[8]. The most common individual pattern is for delinquent behaviour to tail off in severity and frequency before ceasing entirely after the teenage years. Self-report studies show that 90 per cent of males admitted engaging in some form of illegal activity, but, critically, stopped as they grew up.

By the age of 40, criminality has shrunk to a hard, male core: only 7 per cent of property crimes are committed by men over 40, an age group which accounts for only 10 per cent of violent crimes. Crimes of the elderly are largely related to alcohol, and such socially defined offences as vagrancy – although there is, perhaps not surprisingly, a cluster of senior males involved in embezzlement, at a time in their career when opportunities for making off with major sums begin to present themselves.

The pattern emerges of a majority of young males for whom antisocial behaviour and crime, however reprehensible, is somehow constitutional. That shouldn't surprise us. From birth to death, males suffer a constitutional disadvantage: there are more things that go wrong with them. Baby boys suffer higher mortality rates: in their first four years of life the rate is 30 per cent higher than it is for baby girls. By adulthood, the rate can be 400 per cent higher. In the US, males die earlier than females in every age group, ethnic or social category of the population. Men are disproportionately represented in dysfunctional groups from stammerers to suicides. They will be more likely to die in automobile accidents, firearms accidents, falls and drownings – the phenomenon is the same the world over. Crime is, in this sense, just another natural shock that male flesh is heir to.

17

Males invite more opportunities for disaster. The number one killer of 15- to 24-year-olds is accident, the result usually of impulsive behaviour. Nine out of ten arrests for drunken driving involve men. For all our panic about the killer plague, aggression is far more likely than AIDS to cause the death of a young man.

It's a cliché – two clichés, in fact – that boys will be boys, and that it's a phase they all go through. But the problem with truisms is that their very obviousness blinkers us from seeing their significance. Looked at with any degree of objectivity, the facts show that there is a problem in the make-up of young men which takes the form of a propensity towards criminal behaviour. In most cases, either the disease gets cured, or the symptoms can be suppressed, or the malfunction can be recti-fied – take whatever metaphor you want: society or maturity, a sense of punishment or a sense of proportion, will neutralize the problem.

The consistency and universality of the sex divide in crime is enough to convince most scientists that there must be biological factors as well as cultural ones at work.

THE IQ CARD

A child with a comparatively low verbal IQ is more likely to develop a habit of delinquency.

Any talk of comparative intelligence lights the fuse of furious opposition. In these politically correct days it is not possible to conduct an analysis into the link between crime and IQ because it is not thought proper that such an analysis be conducted; because of the fear among some that others may misuse such knowledge, scholarship is held hostage. This is prejudiced thinking, because it presumes that any analysis of the correlation between intelligence and, say, red hair will show the redheads to be dim. The research is not undertaken, which is wrong – and it might, for instance, reveal that redheads are actually cleverer.

But let's bite the bullet. According to those who have actually studied the field, there is a 'clear and consistent' link between criminality and low intelligence. As we will show, there is a difference in IQ between the law-abiding and persistently offending sections of the population. It's time the issue was addressed; the fact that the criminal IQ is generally lower than average has been the guilty secret of the scholars for more than forty years – yet 'the correlation between intelligence and crime has yet to penetrate most of the textbooks or the conventional wisdom of criminology.' Why have they rejected 'what might appear to be a first-class relationship between delinquency and intelligence?'[9] At its crudest, what wonderful propaganda it might be for the young to show that it's not cool to be criminal – it's dumb?

Not all criminals have low IQs: as we will see, the psychopathic offender and various types of fraudsters are not unintelligent and have a vast natural cunning. And we should always be cautious of statistical findings. Critics rightly point out that it is wrong to take one factor in isolation. If, for instance, there was widespread discrimination against redheaded people, to the extent that they were disproportionately denied a basic education, you would expect them to score poorly on IQ tests. Corrections must be made for the distorting effects of SES – higher than average socio-economic status will modify, or reduce, the observed differences in IQ. But it doesn't eliminate them.

A huge study of young people in Philadelphia found that chronic offenders had consistently lower intelligence test scores than those without a police record – as did a large study by Farringdon and West of 400 working-class London schoolboys. In neither case, however, were the results subjected to correction or modification to take account of the sample's socio-economic disadvantage.

But a critical study of 9,000 white offenders in the American state of Tennessee did. Expert researchers took into account the social factors, in particular the status of the jobs and professions of the offenders' parents. The conventional wisdom forecast that once the relative social disadvantage of these youngsters was revealed, it would explain and eclipse their relatively low IQ. In plain words, it would turn out that they were delinquent because they came from poor backgrounds, which also accounted for their low intelligence. But Richard Herrnstein and James Wilson found that, while taking social factors into account certainly reduced the differences, 'IQ was a stronger correlate for offence rate than parental occupational status'[10]. And they believe that there is now enough evidence to make them believe that socio-economic factors are *incidental* to crime, whereas low IQ is 'essential' to producing the persistent criminal.

The blunt, statistical fact is that four decades of study reveal a ten-point gap between the intelligence scores of the offending and non-offending population. The more sophisticated elements of IQ testing reveal that there is 'a cognitive predisposition towards offending'[11] – or, in simpler terms, that the way the criminal mind thinks is different from that of the average mind.

Faced with this inconvenient rebuff, those with a wholly sociological view of crime change tactics to pour doubt over the very nature of IQ testing, claiming that the tests have an inherent bias against the sorts of people engaged in crime. It is certainly true that in the early days testing methodology was fairly crude. But it has since been sophisticated, refining intelligence scores into individual categories. And this refinement has strengthened the evidence of the central role of intelligence levels in criminality.

Back in the 1950s, the father of the IQ test, Wechsler, compared 500 seriously delinquent boys with non-delinquents. Certain factors stood out – body type, personality, attitude towards authority, and a family history of alcoholism or mental disease were among the correlates of crime. IQ seemed at first not to be a factor – the two groups matched in overall IQ. But closer and more sophisticated examination revealed something intriguing: the delinquent children seemed to score well on *performance* IQ – skill in doing things – but fell short when tested on *verbal* IQ. Wechsler even then thought that developing the verbal IQ could help in rehabilitation – an idea which persists in the tradition of convict study and education.

Wechsler's finding is confirmed by a host of subsequent studies. Twenty-one different research projects involving thousands of males and females reveal an average verbal deficit of 7.9 IQ points; the performance IQ was also low, but not as low as the verbal shortcoming. Herrnstein and Wilson have come across an even more intriguing aspect confirming the link between crime and IQ. Recidivists – that is, persistent offenders – were compared with those offenders who committed only one crime and then went straight. If the general criminal population scored lower than the average citizen on verbal IQ, would the recidivists score lower than the one-off offender? They did – though it's fair to report some controversy over this finding, since some other studies have not established the same link.

Other fascinating links emerge – such as the finding that less intelligent people are more likely to commit impulsive crimes. A Californian study – known as the Hirschi study and one of the largest ever conducted – surveyed several thousand junior and high school students. Like the other studies, it indicated that impulsive offending was more a matter of intelligence than class or socio-economic status. Those with low verbal IQ did worse in school, misbehaved earlier and more often and more seriously than non-delinquent children.

But the study also revealed how IQ was woven into the very fabric of behaviour. The students were asked whether they had committed an illegal act. The study then examined police records, school records, intelligence tests and data on family status. Not surprisingly, the study showed that a tendency to break the law was associated with a set of attitudes that could be characterized as unconventional, antisocial, irresponsible and 'present-oriented' – a West Coast neologism presumably meaning a failure to foresee future consequences. There will always be the bright, young mischief-maker whose schoolroom pranks will mark him (almost always it's 'him', not 'her') as a future leader of men; but in general, low intelligence can form part of a self-reinforcing pattern of behaviour; in the young. It can, for instance, lead to low self-esteem, and a corresponding need to perform public, delinquent acts to win respect in the playground – 'I may do badly in class, but I'll bet I'm the only one who dares let off the fire extinguisher.' Again, there will be an interplay between behaviour and intelligence: the less gifted tend to be more impulsive, lacking the imagination to foresee the consequences of their actions. Whoever let off the extinguisher 'didn't think', or, asked why, will – honestly – reply, 'I don't know.'

It should not surprise us that IQ and behaviour are related. These IQ tests are not conducted in some subjective vacuum: they can actually pinpoint specific damage of malfunctioning areas of the brain. A low verbal IQ is, as we will see later, an indicator or marker for critical damage in an area of our brain which mediates behaviour. Low verbal IQ is not going to make your child a criminal – but it is an area of concern, and one where parents and teachers can do something to help.

For the intellectually disadvantaged child, there is also a social spiral of intertwined cause and effect. Failure in the classroom fuels a youthful feeling of unfairness; short-term horizons correlate with low intelligence and favour the kinds of impulsive violent behaviour characteristically committed by offenders with low IQ scores. There do not seem to be the usual internal inhibitions against crime. Moral reasoning, too, is affected by IQ – and in particular by verbal IQ scores. And so low intelligence tips the scale towards crime.

One argument against the IQ link with crime is that only the dim criminal actually gets caught, thus skewing the statistics. There is perhaps an element of truth in this – but not enough to challenge the irrefutable link between crime and low IQ.

THE PERSONALITY CARD

While research has been painting an ever-stronger picture of the link between intelligence and crime, equally striking evidence has emerged that persistent law-breakers have different personality profiles from those who do not offend. Simply put, criminals are different from the rest of us, and that difference – we may argue to what degree – makes them commit crime. Acknowledging and identifying these behaviour patterns may enable us to identify possible future offenders before the emergence of serious delinquency.

Let's leave to one side, for the moment, the question of how far home and social factors affect the psychopathology of the delinquent, and how far temperament is influenced by biological, chemical and neurophysical factors. Evidence from a number of studies shows that law-breakers are psychologically atypical.

Five hundred boys who were in correctional schools for offences ranging from recurrent delinquency to homicide were analysed and compared with non-delinquent boys of the same age and social background. All, in fact, came from slum neighbourhoods. The first trend to emerge was that the delinquent boys tended to come from less well-educated families, where there was a greater history of serious physical illness, mental retardation, emotional disturbance, alcoholism and marital discord. The potentially damaging impact upon personality of any or all of these factors must be considerable. Personality tests of the delinquents against the control sample showed that they were more assertive, unafraid, aggressive, unconventional, extroverted and poorly socialized. The controls were more self-controlled, more concerned about relations with others, more willing to be guided by social standards, and richer in emotional responses, from love through anxiety to despair.

Other studies confirm offenders as psychologically atypical, and suggest that such future offending can be identified in advance. In a study of 2,330 boys, 271 were habitually delinquent by the age of 18. But the important finding was that these boys' future wrongdoing could be predicted. Three years earlier, before they embarked on their delinquent careers, the 271 could be distinguished from the rest either by standard personality tests or by teacher evaluation. They were characterized as emotionally unstable, impulsive, suspicious, hostile, given to petty expressions of pique, egocentric and generally more unhappy, worried and dissatisfied than their non-delinquent matches. By the end of the third grade, these future offenders were already seen by their teachers as less well adapted than their classmates, with less regard for the rights and feelings of their peers, and for the need to accept responsibility for their obligations, both as individuals and members of a group. They were characterized by poor attitudes towards authority, including a failure to understand the need for rules and regulations in any well-ordered social group and the need to respect such controls. They both resented and rejected authority in the school environment. Their overall social behaviour was simply less acceptable, not just to the teachers but to their peers; they had more difficulty in getting along with children of their own age, both in one-to-one contacts and in group situations. They were less willing or able to treat others courteously and tactfully, and less able to be fair in dealing with them. In return they were less well liked and accepted by their peers. They were significantly less likely than their non-delinquent matches to be viewed as dependable, friendly, pleasant and fair.

Another sample was surveyed in Denver, Colorado. This time, the findings went further. Not only was there a psychological difference between delinquents and non-delinquents; there was also a difference of degree between the psychological profiles of the occasional and multiple offenders. The recidivists were more unstable, less sociable and less capable of following rules than the occasional or rare offenders.

But hold on: the problem with this sort of study is that we know the outcome in advance. We shake our heads sadly as the prison doors clang behind the offender and tell ourselves that we always knew that he would turn out wrong. The safest way of establishing the existence of a predictable link is to make the forecasts in advance, before those gates clang, rather than work back from existing offenders to see how the psychological seeds of their wrongdoing were sown earlier; although retrospective studies yield broadly similar results, there is the obvious danger of finding what you are looking for.

A vast British study examined 6,000 schoolchildren in Buckinghamshire. Parents had been quizzed about the existence of symptoms commonly regarded as indicative of emotional disorders. Seven years later, the researchers returned to see how well their predictions had turned out and how many of those who showed childhood problems turned up in court. In this major, classic study nothing was learned about the girls. They were dropped from the study as representing too small a sample of offenders to be statistically valid. But those boys who had been coded as deviant seven years earlier proved to be twice as likely as the others to appear in court and six times more likely to be attending a child guidance clinic. There was a 'direct correlation' between symptoms in childhood and trouble later; the broader the range of symptoms, the greater the risk of delinquency and the need for guidance. Interestingly, those symptoms which foretold delinquency were different from those which foretold the need for help in a clinic. Those who were to become delinquent were more assertive, less shy, more disruptive, from poorer backgrounds and from larger families – with parents who tended to be more than usually absent – than those who were to need help in a clinic.

Not all youthful psychological turmoil is the inevitable precursor of adult crime. What is clear, however, is that an adult sociopath – someone who, in the accepted clinical jargon, suffers from APD or Adult Personality Disorder – is the product of earlier damage; he is invariably an antisocial child who has simply got older. There is no case of adult sociopathy without identifiable antisocial behaviour having manifested itself by the age of eighteen. In boys the symptoms begin well before adolescence – a defiant recklessness, impulsive behaviour, a lack of remorse following wrongdoing. And many who suffer from earlier damage go on to become criminals. One in three of the 400 working-class London schoolboys studied by Farringdon and West and had established habits of delinquency by the age of 21. Two thirds of those youngsters who demonstrated the highest scores of anti-social behaviour became adult offenders.

The idea that patterns of deviant or antisocial behaviour in childhood can be related to patterns in adulthood has, historically, been treated with some scepticism – in spite of the evidence. From 1950 to 1965 the majority of studies have shown significant personality differences between offender and non-offender groups. Research projects from 1966 to 1970 strengthened the case even more, as both the tests and statistical methods became more sophisticated. We are now at the stage, according to Herrnstein and Wilson, where 'since both tests have discriminated between samples of criminals and non-criminals 90 per cent of the time, they deserve special attention.'[12]

The dauntingly-named Minnesota Multiphasic Personality Inventory, or MMPI, is one of the latest tests. Those under scrutiny must respond to some 566 statements describing aspects of their personality, and mark them true or false. Analysis of the results reliably discriminates between the average population and those who suffer from psychopathological problems ranging from hypochondria to schizophrenia. The MMPI has been used since 1947 to predict antisocial behaviour – in other words to predict who is going to break the law.

The first test involved 4,000 boys and girls in the Minneapolis public school system, and charted their progress over two-year intervals. Researchers examined the police, court and social agency records. Once again the study abandoned the task of tracking the girls' progress, because so few appeared on the court, police or social records; delinquency, especially serious delinquency, was confirmed again as predominantly male, with the most delinquent showing the highest scores of psychopathic deviance. Delinquents and non-delinquents scored quite distinctly. Offenders were scarce among those who marked themselves low in areas such as tendency to depression and introversion. The delinquents, however, routinely scored highly in areas which measure hypochondria, psychopathic deviancy and schizophrenia. They also distinguished themselves with high levels of questionnaire invalidity – they cheated a lot, as various skilful trick questions revealed. When, eventually, the survey went statewide, they finally had enough girls to merit analysis; the results showed that delinquent girls had a similar pattern to the at-risk boys. Both demonstrated low scores on scales measuring responsibility and self-control. A lack of conformity, a relative misapprehension of social control, an absence of 'value orientation' and social adjustment all contributed to the offender profile, the typical crimogenic personality.

The test was then extended to cover 26,000 people in ten countries. Across this wide cultural spectrum, 'not only did the scale discriminate offenders and non-offenders in every comparison, but average scores for offenders fell within a narrow range'[13].

Particular levels of intelligence and identifiable and predictable personality traits must, therefore, be counted as two of the high-value cards in the deal that determines criminality. While low intelligence and a particular psychopathology – or even the combination of both – do not pre-ordain criminality, they tilt the odds in its favour.

Yet what do governments do about redressing that balance – about helping those who, as we now know, can be confidently and realistically assessed as being at risk? Why, when we see houses ablaze, do we cry for more fire engines, when we have all the data we need in advance to warn us that there are petrol and matches on the premises, and that the installation of a sprinkler system might prevent catastrophe? Why, when we can assess low verbal IQ and a youthful psychopathology, do we not put the funds we will later spend on locking up these people to better use – such as giving them every support to overcome their handicap?

The cost of juvenile crime in Great Britain alone is seven billion pounds a year. Investing a mere hundredth of that in using this new knowledge would yield incalculable dividends and save immeasurable misery.

CHAPTER 3

The Hormone Card

WE HAVE LOOKED at some of the most common biological factors in criminality. Now let us take a closer look at individual biological influences which predispose an individual to criminal behaviour – which, dealt to us by nature or other misfortune, may make the difference between a law-abiding existence and a life crippled by crime.

One of the principal cards in the pack, affecting male potential for violence and aggressive behaviour, is well known: testosterone is one of a large family of hormones known as androgens, 'male' hormones which play a critical role in contributing to the royal flush, high straight or full house of criminal behaviour.

To understand the role of hormones in criminality, the first question we need to ask is that, given that crime has such an overwhelming male bias, and that the brain is the governing organ of behaviour, are we to expect that the brains of men and women are different? The answer is that they are. They are different in structure and different in their neuro-chemical functioning; and those differences in the brain result in different emotions, attitudes and behaviour. There is still argument about the scale of these differences, but none about their existence.

The brain acquires a sex before we are born, just as the body does. In the early weeks of foetal development, we are sexually neutral; our sexual buds could develop into clitorises or penises. What we are to become is, however, preordained by the action of hormones, and they in turn are instructed by parental chromosomes.

Hormones are small molecules which act like a key to

interpret or unlock the coded instructions contained in our genes. Theirs is the responsibility to execute the genetic blueprint unique to every individual. Until fifteen or so years ago, it was believed that hormones could not cross over into our brains and influence our behaviour; we now know that they can, and indeed are, in the beginning, the very engineers of our brain structure, directly affecting the membranes, enzymes and electrical activity of nerve cells even before birth, and laying down the wiring diagram for the fantastically intricate web of our neural network.

Hormones are engineers, acting on the instructions of genes. We are each the product of forty-six genes. Forty-four of them come in identical pairings. The forty-fifth and forty-sixth, however, the sex chromosomes, are different – they even look different under the microscope. A girl is the result of a pair of X-shaped chromosomes. A boy is the result of one X chromosome, paired with a Y-shaped chromosome.

The Y-chromosome is the tiny trigger for a very limited number of genetic instructions. But its action is crucial in making the male. It starts a chain reaction on the other chromosomes, switching on the male aspects of other genes, including the ability of the foetus to synthesize the mind- and body-altering chemicals for a family of hormones known as androgens. Testosterone is the best known of these and is popularly known as the male hormone – although there is in fact a whole array of such hormones responsible for creating maleness. We must not, however, speak too glibly of 'male' or 'female' hormones. Testosterone, in fact, actually needs to be chemically converted before it becomes active. A further complication is that androgens can quite easily transmute into oestrogens or oestradiols, which are usually thought of as 'female' hormones. And, as a final complication, oestrogen is actually one of the principal hormones responsible for arranging the foetus into a masculine pattern. But, with those qualifications, it is essentially the presence or absence of androgens which makes for our male or female identity, so for simplicity's sake we will use the term 'androgen' to cover that family of

29

hormones that makes for maleness. A normally developing female has all the same potential masculinity in her chromosomes, but without the detonator of the Y-chromosome this latent maleness is never triggered and she retains the basic female template.

At six weeks from conception, the male and female foetuses look identical. But at this point the future male, under instruction from the Y-chromosome, starts to produce this set of androgen hormones which instigate the instructions on the genetic blueprint to build a boy-shaped baby instead of a girl-shaped one. The hormones cause the genital bud to become a penis and lay down a distinctively male pattern in the brain. (Why a male brain needs to be different is another matter, but presumably evolutionary demands have left their mark.)

In the absence of the male hormones, a female body develops, with a female brain structure. The female pattern is nature's matrix. All men are, in this sense, converted women, remoulded in the womb – exactly the reverse of what medieval theologians believed, that women were incomplete men.

The first clue about the power of the hormones came from animal studies. Unlike the human mammal, where the transformation occurs before birth, in the womb, baby rats are born in a very immature state, effectively with their brains and bodies unformed into either a specifically male or a female pattern – that development comes later. This has allowed scientists time to intervene, to manipulate the hormones and to see what happens as a result. A genetically male baby rat, deprived of androgens after birth, develops not into the male as specified on the genetic blueprint, but into a female rat, in appearance and in sexual behaviour. A genetically female baby rat, injected with male hormones from birth, develops into a male rat – it looks and behaves like one, and has male organs. What the studies indicated was that – broadly speaking – the more male hormones the immature brain was exposed to, the more male the resulting pattern of behaviour; the less exposure to male hormones, the more female the behaviour. At the extremes of hormonal dosage, too high or too low, the picture becomes less clearly causal – but in principle, the neuronal architecture of the brain is organized into a male or female pattern by the chemical impact of the hormones.

The same is true of the process with rhesus monkeys, where development takes place, as it does with humans, in the womb. Scientists have learnt how, with a cocktail of hormones administered at different strengths and during different stages of gestation, to choose virtually any model of animal behaviour, such as male monkeys who don't like to be one of the boys, or females who engage in uncharacteristic rough and tumble. Of course, we are neither rats nor monkeys. But we do share the same material that makes up the brain and its chemicals. The function of the human mind is much more complex, but how we transmit messages across the brain network is no different in the rats than it is in humans.

The evidence is now overwhelming that the human brain and body acquire a sex in the womb. Some unfortunate individuals have been exposed to an accidental imbalance of hormones in the womb, which gives them a 'wrong' sex for the body they inhabit and the genetic identity they have inherited. For example, a developing baby girl may be exposed to male hormones, or a developing baby boy may not receive the adequate hormonal input. So it comes about that a genetic (XX-chromosome) female will be born looking like a normal boy, the dormant, potential maleness innate in every female having been triggered into action. It can happen in reverse: the XY-chromosome genetic male may be born a girl because some critical absence of male hormone, or an inability to respond to androgens at a crucial time of development, means that the male genes have not been switched on.

So what is it that – hormonally speaking – goes wrong in such cases? Some babies exposed to an excess of male hormone in the womb are the product of a condition known as Congenital Adrenal Hyperplasia or CAH. This occurs in about one in a thousand births, and has been extensively studied worldwide. An enzyme normally produced by the adrenal gland, whose

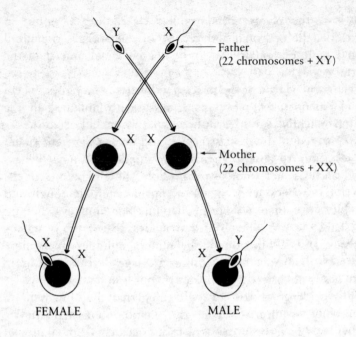

Normal genetics sex determination

job it is to break down androgen hormones, is missing. So the androgens, no longer neutralized, build up in the body and, especially where the developing baby is a girl, significantly affect the child's development. The androgens that build up in this female foetus are the same as those that the male foetus produces, which mould his mind and body into the male pattern. So it comes about that a genetically XX female will be born looking like a normal boy. They are physically male, though internally they still have female sex organs (and so are capable of having children). In most cases, the amount of male hormone is at low levels, and they are only partially masculinized externally, and are corrected surgically soon after birth.

This exposure to male hormones/androgens during foetal development colours their later behaviour. The girls, though brought up as girls, behave like little boys. They are more active, aggressive, interested in things rather than in people. As they grow older they show little interest in clothes, make-up, romance and jewellery. They are to be found climbing the trees or playing ball with the boys. Their mental skills, too, are affected. These girls have better spatial skills (recognized as an area of male advantage) than the average girl; they are better at tackling the mystical complexities of higher mathematical theory, and tend to be career-oriented, competitive and self-assured. And single.

Then there are the rare cases of XY males, who do not develop the necessary receptor sites for the androgens. Without receptor sites, the cascade of male hormones cannot switch on the child's genetic maleness. Such males default to the female pattern. They are born looking like girls, and they behave in a characteristically female manner. Neither mind nor body has been exposed to the effect of the altering androgens.

Others who are born after a hormonal malfunction are boys who, *in utero*, were exposed to lower than normal levels of androgens. This may often be the result of a genetic abnormality which gives them an extra female chromosome; instead of being XY, they are XXY. They are born looking male, but the male hormones during foetal development are abnormally low, as are the second wave of male hormones which come on stream at puberty. These boys are much more feminine in their behaviour. They are much happier playing co-operatively with the girls than competitively with the boys. Whereas the masculinized CAH girls were better at maths, the feminized XXY boys are better than their male peers at all the language skills (an area of known female advantage), and suffer in tests which demand spatial ability. They are less aggressive and competitive than the average male.

There seems to be an optimum level of androgens that create maleness, the absence of which makes for the female. Very low levels of male hormones make for a more female flavour to behaviour, higher levels a more male flavour. It is not a consistently direct relationship – very high levels of male hormone may not make you excessively more male, since all the available receptor sites may already have been switched on, and any excess simply goes to waste; it's rather like watering a plant – an optimum degree of watering will make it flourish, but flooding it with water won't make it any healthier – or like taking vitamins, when massive doses simply pass through the body without imparting any massively extra advantage over and above the recommended dose.

The first studies into the effects of hormones on behaviour restricted themselves to traditional sex-role patterns. But since then the studies have become more sophisticated. More recent investigators into brain chemistry have found that other, subtler behaviour and attitudes are influenced by those hormones to which the foetus is exposed in the womb. Could such factors provide some explanation for delinquency and crime?

One of the most marked sets of sex differences lies in the three areas of aggression, dominance and hostility. In many hundreds of studies, covering societies worlds apart in terms of class, colour and culture, it has been proved that the male of the species has more of all three of these personality traits than are present in the female.

Again, it's from animal studies that we know how the foetal hormones in the womb influence all three of these characteristics. Exposed at an optimum level to androgens, the resulting individual will have a greater than average degree of aggression, dominance and hostility in later life. 'The evidence leads one to conclude beyond any doubt that androgens can alter the mammalian nervous system in ways that increase the probability of offensive aggression.'[1]

The evidence for humans, this time, does not rely so much on natural, hormonal malfunction or accidents of nature. In the 1960s and 1970s, many thousands of women were given doses of hormones during difficult pregnancies. The hormones were strictly neither male nor female, but they mimicked the effects of naturally occurring hormones of both genders. The children of these women have now been extensively studied. Those girls who were exposed to male-mimicking hormonal substances emerged as far more aggressive and assertive than

34

their sisters who were not exposed to the drug. Boys exposed to female-like hormonal doses showed the comparatively mild and less aggressive behaviour patterns associated with girls. 'There is little doubt that circulating levels of testosterone during foetal stage have profound organizational influences on the brain of human and non-human primate males. These effects include an increased readiness to engage in aggressive behaviour.'[2]

We also know that, beyond aggression, there is a wide range of general behaviour patterns which are sexed in the brain; they alter the way men and women approach the outside world, and this in turn alters the balance between men and women – and the chances that they will have trouble with the law.

Neighbour disputes are one of the most frequent causes of violence and criminal assault. People who have lived next door to each other in apparent harmony and tolerance are capable of volcanic explosions of anger and resentment if, say, a hedge overlaps a boundary by a couple of inches. For instance, this very scenario has led, in a celebrated British case, to shots being exchanged; and it's not only the Englishman who has an aggressively defensive attitude to his domestic castle.

In animals, the amount of space we feel we need around us has a lot to do with how hostile we feel and how we respond to others. (In pre-Second World War Germany, Hitler played on a whole nation's feeling of cramped frustration in his appeal for *Lebensraum*.) In animals this is called spacing behaviour, and it includes procuring, marking, patrolling and defending the chosen space. The space may immediately surround the defender, in which case it is called 'personal space', or may be fixed geographically with or without prescribed boundaries, in which case it is called 'territory'. It seems broadly to be the case that this behaviour is linked to status and dominance – the higher a male is in the hierarchy, the more space he has and the more vigorously he feels the need to defend it.

Throughout the mammalian world, the male is more likely

to establish and defend both personal and territorial space. In the case of the rat, those that have experienced the optimum levels of androgens in the womb have a correspondingly greater need for their own space. Further up the mammalian scale, it is men, rather than women, who form gangs to defend their particular territory, leading to violence between gangs all over the world. An obvious example is a flashpoint in a football stadia, when fans (usually predominantly male) of one team colonize a particular area, and woe betide the supporters of the rival team who penetrate that rowdy, crowing territory. Indeed, the very act of crowing – whether it's a cock marking out his space, or a crowd establishing their loyalties by provocative chants – incites and invites aggression.

Other innate differences between the sexes – differences originated and triggered by hormonal activity – include a difference in the tolerance of pain. Human studies usually consist of a volunteer submitting to an ever-intensifying degree of pain until he tells the experimenter that the pain is too severe to endure. Although women often regard men as the most terrible hypochondriacs, cry babies and cowards, all tests show that males tolerate more pain, on average, than females, and that the difference is evident in the very first few weeks of life. This isn't simply manly stoicism; the male brain is actually wired up and organized to increase the nervous system's tolerance of pain.

This physical phenomenon, too, has its effect on delinquent behaviour. If young men feel less pain, they will tolerate more extreme forms both of danger and of the consequences. They won't be put off and they won't learn from their mistakes. Maybe the reason why the philosophy of 'spare the rod, spoil the child' never really worked is that boys' comparative tolerance means that no amount of chastising can really be successful.

There is good evidence that boys do not learn from their mistakes as successfully as girls. Scientists have dubbed it 'retarded acquisition of aversive conditioning' or RAAC, which refers to the tendency to continue behaving in a particular way in spite of significant punishment. Experiments such as showing a rat some food and trying to teach it that if it chooses food A rather than food B it will get a nasty shock indicate that the more male hormone the animal is exposed to, the more punishment it will take. The same seems to be true for us; three human studies indicate that males are more RAAC prone than females. Boys are less likely to be deterred by punishment than the girls; they simply won't learn.

Another sex difference involves the sensation of fear. A dose of foetal male hormones makes the subject considerably less prone to the emotion of fearfulness. Research into adults shows well-documented evidence of this sex difference, males experiencing less fear than females. Again, the evidence suggests that foetal androgens are involved; exposure to them at a critical stage of development somehow organizes the brain to respond in a less fearful manner when confronted with a threat. The males will stand and fight; whereas a girl is more likely to withdraw from a threatening situation. Two studies on newborn infants seem to show that males are less likely to display emotional fear responses to strangers than females.

So the sex difference – as expressed in behaviour – starts early, well before society (that universal explanation and scapegoat) has had the chance to stick its oar in. Even at this early stage it is possible to make a rough prognosis of the children who are going to grow up 'difficult'. Babies are naturally social creatures: they display a desire to win the approval of others and they like being loved – and expect that love, under reasonable circumstances, to be forthcoming. Shortly after birth, babies can be classified into 'easy' children – those who adapt well to the kaleidoscope of new experiences to which they are exposed, who are cheerful, regular in body function and sleeping habits – and 'difficult' children – those who are listless, unresponsive, demanding, unpredictable over feeding, wakeful and liable to scream at the slightest change in their routine. Psychologists point to a tacit dynamic of mutual and self-reinforcing anxiety, as the babies pick up their parents' nervousness, and common sense says there must be some truth in that. But there is also a biological explanation: most of these difficult babies are likely to be boys, and the more foetal androgens they are exposed to at the time their brains are developing in the womb, the more difficult they will prove to be.

For the inherent aggression of the male to achieve its full potential, one other chemical condition has to be satisfied by the hormones. The potential for aggression is defined before birth; the fulfilment of it comes with puberty. For this aspect of personality to reach full expression, a second rush of male hormones is necessary at the point of sexual maturity. Interestingly, these two points of human development – before birth and at puberty – mark the twin high-water marks of hormonal activity in the human species.

This second flood of hormones, at puberty, is sudden and dramatic. Men find themselves supercharged with up to twenty times the amount of circulating androgens as in women. But women experience a directly contrary chemical effect: the female hormones which come on stream at puberty, oestrogen and progesterone, smother and neutralize the small amount of naturally occurring androgens produced in women by the adrenal gland. (Here again, we need to make a slight qualification: oestrogen at some levels may make some women more aggressive.) Thus at puberty, while men experience greater feelings of aggression (caused by the rush of androgens), women's aggression is being damped down, probably by progesterone.

When hormone levels plummet, shortly before menstruation, women may feel irritable, irrational and emotional. Studies show that the worst feelings occur when the hormone levels are going through rapid changes. In those women who show dramatic changes in mood, evidence links menstrual symptoms to depression, alcohol use, accidents, suicidal and violent behaviour. In most women mood swings are minimal, a monthly inconvenience. In a few, however, the effect is dramatic and debilitating, and has lately been recognized as a syndrome which can be, and needs to be, treated. Severe cases can result in a dangerous lack of competence, for instance in driving, piloting aeroplanes or, at the extreme, in criminal actions; these women, as we will see later, have a brain wired in a manner to make them susceptible to criminal behaviour.

In men there is a relationship between the amount of androgens circulating in the blood and the level of aggression. But it has proved to be difficult to draw a direct and clear correlation. That's partly because 'aggression' is not a specifically identifiable behavioural activity; and also because androgens are not the only hormonal players involved. A further complication is that it's not just the action of the hormones which affects the brain – it's the nature of the brain itself. But scientists are beginning to unravel those complexities.

First, they are beginning to understand the interplay between the hormones and the brain. The androgens in the womb set the wiring of the brain to respond to the second burst of testosterone that occurs at puberty. Puberty is a time of great physical, emotional and behavioural change; that's because the sex hormones are once again binding on to those receptor sites – just as they did in the womb – which were ordained during gestation. Once the hormones lock on to the receptor sites, they again set off a chain reaction which switches on the genes, the blueprint for the body, leading to the physical and mental changes which boys experience at puberty. Girls, of course, experience these changes too, but a different set of hormones causes a different set of physical responses.

What's going on is a subtle and only partly understood process, whereby it is necessary for enzymes in the brain and other target organs to convert hormones into an active form before they can have their full chemical effect. The higher the concentration of enzyme – and this, too, seems to be determined in the womb – the more sensitive the body and brain are to the hormonal effect.

Until recently, researchers had not recognized the complexity of the hormonal influence. They tended to overlook the wide range of androgens – produced in the testes and the adrenal glands – and the interplay of the enzymes. They measured, in the main, simply the effects of one androgen, testosterone. As a result of this inevitably limited approach, their results were often inconsistent: some studies were finding links between testosterone and aggression, others not. We now know that to understand the proper link between male hormones and aggression we must study the wider range of the family of androgens, defining those active hormones which prove to be specifically linked to aggression; and if we do that, we find a clear link between male hormones and aggression.

Aggression is a broad term, which we need to analyse in separate categories. The most potent catalyst for intermale aggression in animals is the presence of another male threatening home territory. This activity is found exclusively among males and is not usually fully developed until puberty. (Lionesses will defend their cubs, but their aggression is maternal – they are not stirred into aggression by the mere presence of a stranger on their home patch.) There is a clear correspondence between intermale aggression and the territorial 'gang' ethos of human juvenile criminality. Sexual aggression is related to the hormones and their seasonal flux: in seasonally breeding species, testosterone, sex, aggression and sexual aggression are all bound up together. In humans, incidents of rape tend to peak at autumn, the same time of year that male hormone levels are at their highest. As for aggression as a function of impatience and irritability, in a recent study investigating provoked and unprovoked aggression, researchers have found a positive relationship between circulating androgen and aggressive behaviour. 'High levels increase the probability that the boys will initiate aggressive destructive behaviour ... by making them more impatient and irritable ...'; '... high levels of androgen in puberty made the boys more impatient and irritable, which increased their readiness to engage in aggressive behaviour of the unprovoked and destructive kind.'[3]

Studies from cultures as diverse as a Swedish Borstal and the hunter-gatherer society of the Kung bushmen reveal a similar pattern of male adolescents being prone to irritability, aggression and delinquency. And all the time the picture is becoming clearer. For instance, it's not the crude level of androgens that's significant – more hormone doesn't necessarily mean more aggression; what makes the difference is the level of 'free' circulating androgen, free in the sense that it is available to work its effects on the receptor sites in the brain. In the case of the Kung bushmen, a distinct relationship has been established between the levels of free or active androgen (and other male hormones, or androgens, produced by the adrenal gland) and experiences of rage, anger, inadequate control of compulsive behaviour and low toleration of frustration – all personality traits that are well known precursors of impulsive, violent behaviour.

The impact of androgens on the personality is far-reaching. Legal advocates who address the court have higher levels of free androgens than their desk-bound colleagues behind the scenes. Vicars and social workers have the lowest levels. High androgen levels are linked with high achievement, through single-mindedness and ruthlessness. There is, however, an optimal level for androgen-linked success; with too much male hormone, there is the chance of resultant antisocial behaviour which can inhibit advancement. A tenacious advocate will succeed; an advocate who behaves like a bull in a china shop will not.

When it comes to the quality of personal relationships, one researcher believes that high levels of androgens can actually poison a marriage by the potent mixture of high sexuality and aggression. Far from having a high and fulfilling degree of marital sex, men with high male hormone levels, a study has revealed, are less likely to marry, and, if married, more likely to leave home and indulge in extra-marital sex, more inclined to experience what is described as 'a lower quality of spousal interaction' and more likely to throw objects at their wives than men with low levels. The recurrent link between high androgens and aggression, or antisocial behaviour, seems to mean that high-achieving men may carry their contentious, hostile and ruthless behaviour into their relations with the opposite sex.

The same researcher has even linked androgen levels to the

facial expression: men with high levels of androgens smile less than those with low levels. A further study of 5,000 military veterans and 400 college students found a link between high androgen levels and drug and alcohol abuse. The correlation was most acute in people in lower socio-economic groups. This would seem to offer a bridge between the biological and cultural schools of criminology, suggesting that we are to a large extent the result of our hormones, but those of us with social advantages are better equipped to attenuate their malign influence. The duke can write a stiff letter to *The Times*; the dustman has fewer opportunities to sublimate his spleen.

Androgens seem to be allied to a certain callousness, verging on the psychotic. The higher the hormonal levels someone has, the less inhibitions he or she has about inflicting pain, the less guilt he has about indulging in antisocial behaviour. This is bound up with a lack of empathy – the ability to imagine, and in some sense to experience, the pain of others. The less sensitive you are to the distress of others, the more likely you are to inflict suffering, which you do not in any sense share or feel as your own: 'the painful consequences of an aggressive act through the vicarious response of empathy should function as inhibitors of the instigator's own aggressive tendencies.'[4] The relationship between empathy and aggression is a strong and stable phenomenon – and androgens are a critical part of the equation. In this light, it is not surprising that – in all studies that have been conducted, and in all common experience – women, who have lower levels of androgen, show more empathy. Some studies have established a link between adrenal levels of androgens and antisocial behaviour in women, but even what male hormone there is may be neutralized, or masked, by the effect of the female hormone, progesterone. After the menopause, however, when the mitigating effects of female hormones are gone, women may become more aggressive and assertive.

Thus androgens, which are what adolescent boys are made of, are a significant cause of male aggression. Girls, on the other hand, who are blessed with twenty times less androgen, are far less likely to be aggressive.

Hormone levels affect men and women in other ways. Scientists have identified a link between high male hormone levels and an appetite for sensation-seeking, searching out novel and exciting situations and predicaments. Such a pursuit of sensation can encompass sky-diving, bungee-jumping, mountaineering; experiments with drugs, hedonistic extrovert behaviour involving drunkenness and orgiastic sex; a restlessness and boredom with routine. These people court danger; their passion for novelty and experience is insatiable; their anxiety mechanisms just don't seem to be activated in the same way as those of more responsible people. While men are likely to fit this description – the impact of androgens again – we all know of exceptions. And maybe we can explain them, too: perhaps those doughty elderly matrons who, having lived lives which were a model of decorum, cast off their inhibitions and set off on expeditions round the world, to the exasperation of their families who regarded such undertakings as monstrously irresponsible, did so because their natural androgens, unfettered at last by female hormone, were coming into their own.

(Intriguingly, scientists have discovered one particular group of girls who to some extent share this male attitude to sensation-seeking. Animal studies involving twins of each sex revealed that the females had masculinized brains – the effect of prenatal hormones. Would the same be true of human twins? What researchers found was that girls who had a brother for a twin were much more inclined to be adventurous sensation-seekers than those who had a twin sister. The softer sciences of psychology and sociology will ascribe this to a kindred spirituality, girls subconsciously modelling themselves on their adored male twin. This doesn't quite explain why the male twin fails to model himself adoringly on his sister. It is more likely, surely, that both twins were exposed to male androgens in the womb, so that the sister's very personality – at least in terms of adventurousness and sensation-seeking – mirrored that of her male sibling.)

There's one more dimension to the complex jigsaw of aggression and hormones: the link to age. Most impulsive crimes – which include the sudden lashing out, the act of vandalism, the rash devil-may-care attitude to drink and driving – are committed by males under twenty years of age. Androgen levels peak at the age of eighteen and from then on maintain a steady decline. Although it's not a simple relationship – there is other biochemistry at work especially in the brain, apart from the free or active androgens – one study which measured levels of dominance and anger against the levels of active androgens circulating in the blood found that as men got older, this anger and ambition to dominate subsided.

But if there is a link between hormones, men and innate aggression, does the link extend to include criminal behaviour? Is there an extra, hormonal card in the hand dealt to the criminal mind? The answer, it seems, is yes.

A number of studies of institutionalized delinquents show a consistent link with high androgen levels. Forty young inmates, aged between 14 and 19, were tested. They were all serious, multiple offenders. Compared with a non-offending sample, the delinquent youths had distinctly higher androgen levels. Those with the highest levels were more than usually assertive, extrovert, sensation-seeking and more verbally aggressive; they were also less neurotic.

The most carefully constructed testing has been done in Georgia by Professor Dabbs. He, too, has found a correlation between male hormone levels and violent offending. Dabbs tested the saliva of a group of offenders for free androgen (a particularly accurate measure of free androgen levels, since only the free androgen molecules are small enough to pass through the saliva glands). Of the eleven lowest-scoring prisoners, nine had committed crimes which had no element of violence in them. Of the eleven highest scorers, ten had committed crimes involving violence. It was also interesting to see how the inmates rated each other: those by general consent reckoned to be the toughest also turned out to have the highest androgen levels.

The link between violence and androgen also appears in a study of rapists: those who introduced an element of non-sexual violence were found to have higher levels than those whose violence was confined to the sexual act itself. Another study of a group of persistently offending adolescents showed higher androgen levels than a group of normal boys of the same age and same stage of puberty; those who had committed armed robbery had higher levels than those who had committed less aggressive crimes. We believe – and in later chapters we will provide the scientific evidence – that a constellation of social and biological factors goes towards the creation of a propensity for crime; none of these factors, of itself, will be decisive and determining, but if destiny deals the individual the extra ace or king of high androgen, the chances are greater that he will be a violent offender.

We have made the point repeatedly that crime is an overwhelmingly male pursuit; and, as the reader will have gathered by now, that we believe strongly that there is a biological constituent to crime. These two points reinforce each other when we come to the study of crimes committed by women under the abnormal influence of hormones. The idea that women become less competent or rational as a consequence of the fluctuation of their hormones according to their menstrual cycle is not a new discovery. The effects of the menstrual cycle were recognized in the courts in 1845, when one Martha Brixley stood charged with the murder of her employer's children. There was no apparent motive and no attempt was made to escape the consequences of her act. Martha was acquitted on a plea of insanity due to 'obstructed menstruation'. In the same year Ann Sheper was charged at Carlisle quarter sessions for stealing a fur boa; she also was acquitted on the ground of 'temporary insanity from suppression of the menses'. In 1851 Amelia Snoswell was charged with murdering her baby niece and she, too, was acquitted on the ground of 'insanity due to disordered menstruation'. Lombroso, the Italian criminologist, observed the connection in 1894 when he reported that of 80 women arrested for 'resistance to public officials' 71 (89 per cent) were menstruating.

In 1890 a French physician, studied 56 Parisian shoplifters, of whom 35 (62.5 per cent) were menstruating at the time of their offence. He listed the terrible effects: 'kleptomania, pyromania, dipsomania, homicidal mania, erotomania, nymphomania, delirious insanity, . . . jealousy, lying calumny, illusions, hallucinations and melancholia'.[5] Of 156 women offenders in a 1961 study, 49 per cent had committed their crimes during the paramenstruum, defined as the last four days before menstruation. An investigation of 50 consecutive female London prison admissions in 1980 showed that for women charged with crimes of violence (including murder, manslaughter, grievous bodily harm, arson and criminal damage) 44 per cent of their crimes were committed during the paramenstruum. Looked at the other way, if crimes were evenly distributed over the 28 days of the cycle you would expect to see 3.6 per cent of crimes on any one day; but nearly half of all female crime is committed during the four days preceding menstruation.

Whatever the wishful thinking of those who hold that we have conquered our own biology, the evidence is now overwhelming that changes in mood and behaviour are linked to the hormonal fluctuations of the menstrual cycle. In a recent review of all the studies the conclusion was that women the world over suffer from a similar pattern of symptoms. Around 40 per cent suffer very mild physical and psychological symptoms – so mild as to have little or no effect upon the women concerned. But between 2 and 10 per cent of women suffer severe symptoms. It's this group that yields interesting evidence in the study of female crime.

Over many years, Katharina Dalton has treated many thousands of women suffering from premenstrual syndrome. Dr Dalton is convinced that irrational mood swings are due to the sudden fall in progesterone just before the onset of the period. And between 44 and 50 per cent of female crimes are committed just before or on the day of menstruation. Significantly fewer crimes are committed when a women is ovulating and during pregnancy – when progesterone levels are at their highest.

In today's highly charged atmosphere of sexual politics, this connection between hormones and female crime presents something of a minefield. Some women resent the idea that they can be depicted as 'endocrinological cripples' and so denied responsibility and advancement. Other women believe that if men were subject to a similar disadvantage (the effect of the menstrual cycle on examination results is acknowledged) compensatory legislation would surely by now have been passed by our male legislators.

Not all hormones arise naturally in the body. Scientists have found intriguing – not to say disturbing – evidence of the effect of artificial hormones, particularly when used or abused in quantities well over the recommended level. Many athletes and body-builders take anabolic steroids, to boost muscle mass. These steroids mimic the effect of androgens, male hormones – but they are even stronger and more potent than their natural counterparts. Research into otherwise normal men and women suggests that taking anabolic steroids promotes aggressive and violent behaviour. In a very small number of cases the chemicals can contribute to the emergence of a psychotic personality; in both Europe and the US a defence of insanity has been pleaded in trials involving crimes committed by people taking anabolic steroids. Hostility, aggression and resentment rise in direct relation to levels of steroid intake. Steroids also seem to have an effect on raising the motivation for suicide.

A 1988 study examined the cases of 41 body-builders and football players who were taking steroids. The associated physical problems – such as acne, testicular atrophy, hair loss and a deepening of the voice in both men and women – were dwarfed by the apparent psychological havoc wreaked. Of the sample, 22 per cent showed severe behavioural problems and 12 per cent showed psychotic symptoms. The chemical effect on the brain can be speedy and dramatic: within two weeks of being prescribed steroids for impotence, a salesman suffered from depression, feelings of guilt, and visual and auditory hallucinations. A seventeen-year-old male body-builder who illicitly obtained steroids spent six months haunted by depression, paranoid ideation and 'audible thoughts'. Other users suffered paranoid delusions – in one case that the user's friends were stealing from him; or delusions of grandeur – another believed that he could pick up a car and, singlehandedly, tip it over. Many described 'pronounced euphoria and grandiosity, believing that nothing in the world could hurt them' – such as the man who deliberately drove a car at 40 m.p.h. into a tree and asked a friend to videotape it. Two developed paranoid jealousy over their girlfriends. One driver became enraged because the driver of the car in front had left his directional signal flashing; at the next stop light, he jumped out and smashed the windscreen of the 'offending' driver. A 22-year-old construction worker took two courses to help in the body-building he was trying. At first, he noted increased irritability and confusion, and had difficulty sleeping. On the second course he became worse. He suffered the delusion that his mind was influencing pictures on TV, and promised to introduce a friend of his to God. Luckily, he went to the doctor and was treated to block the drugs. He recovered and has never taken steroids again. Most of those in the study had no history of previous psychiatric problems. These moods only occurred while they were on steroids. In all cases, the symptoms abated when they stopped taking the steroids.

Other scientists are doubtful about this study for two reasons: first, it simply describes what it finds, rather than producing crisp statistical correlations. That's largely because the researchers did not have enough subjects willing to come forward and present themselves for interview. Another reservation is that no one has been able exactly to duplicate the findings in laboratory conditions. One explanation may be that the steroid abusers are using doses up to one hundred times stronger than those ethically tolerable in experimental conditions.

If steroids affect behaviour, it seems likely that they can also promote what we identify as criminal behaviour. Again, the evidence is anecdotal. Horace Williams was described as kind, considerate and a regular churchgoer. He was proud of his body and had embarked on a course of anabolic steroids. Over a period of months, friends began to grow concerned at a dramatic change in this previously mild-mannered young man. He became aggressive, argumentative and impulsive. One night he went joyriding in a car and picked up a hitchhiker. The night ended with Williams murdering his passenger. For the first time in legal history, the effect of anabolic steroids was pleaded in mitigation.

Nothing in all this research into hormonal roots of offending behaviour excuses violent, unprovoked aggression. But it surely explains much of it. What is clear from all the studies is that the biology of crime involves a complex interaction of chemicals; the hormones themselves can act directly on the brain, but they can also interact with other chemicals in the brain, the so-called neurotransmitters that allow the brain to send messages and control behaviour. The criminal mind frequently contains abnormal doses of androgens, but, as we'll see, for a mind to be criminal it's necessary to add a further ingredient to the recipe.

CHAPTER 4

The Chemical Card to Crime

CULTURE AND BIOLOGY both make a contribution to criminal behaviour – and just as there are a thousand and one social factors involved, so there is a variety of ways in which the physical workings of the brain conspire towards a criminal outcome. The brain, as we have seen, acts under the influence of the hormones, and the male brain seems particularly susceptible to that influence. But hormones are only part of the story. How gender, chemistry and crime combine is the next part of the mystery that scientists have begun to unravel. Before we can understand what's different about the brains of those who show a criminal pattern of behaviour, we first need to know how the normal brain operates and understand its dynamics, what fires it up and damps it down. 'By studying the brain, specifically by studying the process and functions of the nerve cells of the brain – we may come to know things that are fundamental to our understanding of ourselves, including who we are ... The excitement in neural science today resides in the conviction that the tools are there at last to hand to explore the organ of the mind.'[1]

While hormones influence the broad behaviour pattern, it's the neurotransmitters – chemicals controlling the flow of electrical messages in the network of nerve cells – that are responsible for the instigation of specific actions. Neurotransmitters essentially allow the various areas of the brain to communicate. Understanding how our own brains work is a fascinating but complex endeavour, for each control system or transmitting system interacts with another. Behaviour is the consequence of many layers of activity in the brain.

The more we unravel the strands of our new knowledge of

the brain, the more we will discover how the male brain is intrinsically more specifically wired and fuelled for aggression, impulsiveness, antisocial behaviour and crime than is the female brain. This doesn't mean that all men are criminals, of course; it's simply that they have a far greater potential for criminal, aggressive and antisocial behaviour programmed into them. Put another way, it takes a far greater effort of will for a man to behave well than it does for a woman. This may sound like a piece of saloon bar reasoning – but there is a scientific basis to this excuse for male shortcoming.

Research is now uncovering a whole new area of sex differences in the chemistry of the brain. The male brain is driven by a different chemical mixture of fuel than the female brain. This mixture drives the male to explore the world in a physical way rather than through his perceptions; it makes him want to dominate rather than negotiate, to seek sensation and to take risks rather than to accommodate, passively and contentedly, his situation. That is what, historically, has made men challenge the oceans, the galaxies, their rulers, the church, conventional wisdom. For good or ill, they have been the agents of change – while women's role has been to manage the change, civilize the change, pick up the pieces that lie shattered in the course of change. It is also what makes man an awkward animal, often an antisocial one, and sometimes a being whose behaviour even a male-dominated society brands as criminal.

The brain is one mass of interconnecting single nerve cells, or neurons, forming a giant network. Some of these cells form strands, or fibres, which in turn are combined into large trunks or cables responsible for actions and activities in the various specific areas of the body. The messages from our eyes, for instance, all enter the brain through two large crossed trunks, the two optic nerves. Every organ in the body has at least one large outgoing cable of nerve cells. This cable keeps the brain informed about the general operating state of the organ – it is our internal telemeter. The brain analyses these messages and then sends out instructions via the outgoing cables.

But what are these messages – how are they sent, and what code are they written in? We now know that the general principles for communications are very similar everywhere in the brain.

The single most important constituent of this massive and intricate network is the nerve cell or neuron. The neuron has two different sets of wires, or projections, that extend from the main body of the cell. There is usually one single projection, called the axon, which carries the outgoing messages. The other projection is more prickly and branches into a collection of dendrites (the word is derived from the Greek word for a tree, dendron) which carry the incoming messages.

It is through these projecting extensions that the nerve cells talk to each other. The extensions do not actually touch each other: there is a tiny gap between them. The gap is known as a synapse, and communication between the cells occurs only when the correct chemical messengers, or neurotransmitters, are released by the nerve cells into the synaptic gap. It is the bridging of the gap by the neurotransmitters that promotes the conversation between the nerve cells – just as an arc of energy springs across two electrically-charged rods – for it creates an electrical flow of activity between the nerve cells, sometimes between many thousands of them. The messages take the form of an electrical flow, just as a telephone call is the result of infinite variations in electrical impulse.

Indeed, we can measure the level of brain activity by monitoring the level and the flow of electricity in the brain as it travels down the wires of the brain networks. The electrical nature of this communication means that we can tweak human behaviour by electrically stimulating certain parts of the brain to create different sensations. Electrically stimulating a certain area of the limbic system, for instance, will create a feeling of anger; stimulate another area, and the volunteer will experience a sensation of pleasure. The activation of the neurotransmitters, in the synapses of the nerve cell networks, carries the

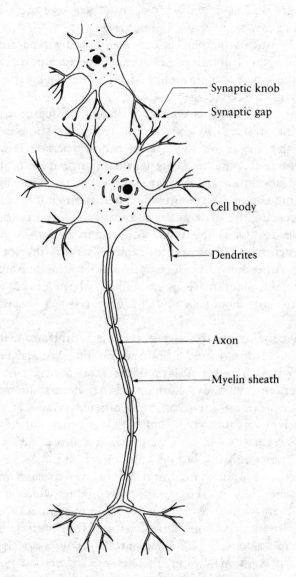

Synaptic knob

Synaptic gap

Cell body

Dendrites

Axon

Myelin sheath

The geography of the nerve cells

messages that, say, let us marvel at the genius of Michelangelo or tell us that we have stubbed our toes.

Our thoughts and perceptions are caused by the activity of a relatively small number of neurons. Experiments with volunteers show that a single event taking place in a single nerve cell is enough to create the sensation of touch. Studies in rats, monkeys and humans concluded that a conscious sensation could be produced by concerted activity in just four neurons. It doesn't take a lot, then, to change our perceptions, or, in more formal language, 'What we desire or need or feel may be related to subtle changes in the chemistry of our brains.'[2]

Brain scientists are pioneers in a new frontier. They have yet to agree on the geography of the new territories they are discovering. As in the Wild West, authority is in a state of flux; each scientific prospector-explorer stakes different claims to the ownership of wisdom in this exploration and exploitation of the inner space of the mind. All we can do here is present a snapshot of the ever-changing state of knowledge and debate.

What is clear, however, is that these neurotransmitters, the powerful chemicals in the brain which influence and facilitate the actions of our bodies and the thoughts of our minds, interact with the body's hormones. They in turn interact with other neurotransmitters, of many different kinds. Hormones themselves can mimic the action of the neurotransmitters as well as regulate them, so it's a highly complex equation which scientists are only just beginning to unscramble.

Some four hundred neurotransmitters have been discovered. Researchers have shown by various techniques which networks in the brain produce which neurotransmitters and what stimuli they respond to. The different neurotransmitters become active in response to different outside stimulation. Some respond to emotional stimulation; others to motor commands from the brain. The response of the network depends on the type of neurotransmitters which the neurons, individually or collectively, are capable of manufacturing. The various neurotransmitters have specific pathways in the brain and control different aspects of behaviour. Thanks to intricate and minute research all over the world, we now have a rough neurotransmitter map of the brain.

But before we study this basic route lay-out of our newly-discovered territory, we should acquaint ourselves with the simple, underlying, physical geography of the brain. Before we study the roads, let us see what cities, lakes and mountain ranges they connect.

The brain is a massively complex organ, but as Caesar did with Gaul, we can divide it into three parts – known to brain scientists as triunes – and study those functional parts particularly in relation to criminal or antisocial behaviour.

Think of these three parts as three different electrical circuits. One looks after the lights. The second is connected to the power points. The third, let us say, looks after the heavy domestic equipment in the basement. (The analogy isn't exact: at home, the electrical supply is generally constant, and the wires it travels along are standard, whereas subtle differences in neurotransmitters and neurons produce different effects – but it will do for the moment.)

Think of the three areas of the brain as three layered circuit boards with messages passing back and forth. The number one layer, the cerebral lobes, or hemispheres, lies at the top of the human brain. These lobes are covered by a network of nerve cells, known as the cerebral cortex. This is our 'thinking cap' and the area which distinguishes us from other animals – for it is here that the functions of thought, consciousness and language are found. It is the control centre for our responses to the outside world. The frontal cortex and the cortex in general are, not surprisingly, the most developed in the mammalian kingdom.

The number two layer just below that, but intimately connected to it, is the limbic system. It is known as the animal brain, because other mammals also possess this system. The limbic system, variously called the 'emotional' and 'motivational' brain, is the centre of feelings such as anger, rage, sadness and love; medical students find it easy to remember

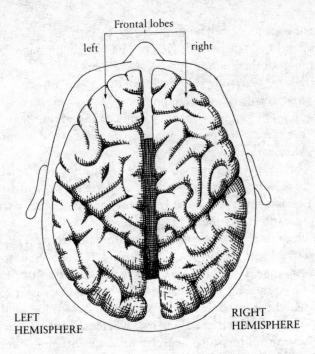

The cerebral lobes, or hemispheres: the thinking cap

it as controlling the four Fs – fear, fleeing, feeding and . . .
sexual appetite. The limbic system implements our gentlest as
well as our wildest reactions.

The limbic system is all-important to much of the behaviour
we will be discussing. It manages – or fails to manage – the
whole range of our emotional reactions, and conveys our raw
feelings to the more thoughtful cortex for processing. It is
responsible for the physical accompaniment to strong emotional feelings, such as the shaking of the knees when afraid,
the dry mouth. The limbic system in lower animals as well as
in humans is also closely associated with the olfactory senses,
which may account for the emotional effect produced by many
smells, and demonstrates the interconnectedness of sensation –
the taste of Proust's madeleine biscuit stirring up whole vol-
umes of reminiscence. Although the limbic system is more like

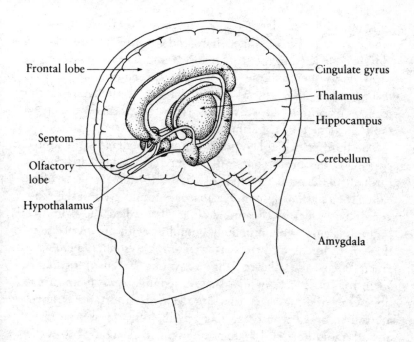

The limbic system, or animal brain

an interconnecting set of separate circuit boards, we will, for the most part, be talking of it as a single structure; but each component may provide one of the individual cards that contribute to criminal behaviour, so we should briefly outline their functions.

A small area, the hypothalamus, is important to our sexuality – and we will come to know this area well when we discuss the sexually deviant criminal. It lies very close to another part of the brain that is part of this story, the amygdala. It lies deep in the forebrain, a walnut-wrinkled mass of grey cells. This area is active in the production of aggressive behaviour. Twenty years ago when psychosurgery was in vogue, surgeons would destroy this part of the brain to rid a patient of uncontrollable rage. The problem was that this also destroyed much of the patient's interest in life. It also seems to be fundamentally involved in the generation of the emotions – whether we feel love, anger, hate and so on. The amygdala is closely connected to the frontal cortex and is crucial in communicating to the thinking brain what the emotional brain is feeling; it is also crucial to our ability to understand the feelings of others. As we will see, this area seems often to be faulty in some types of criminal minds.

The third principal layer of the brain, lying below the limbic system, is the brain stem. All incoming messages are routed through the central terminal of the brain stem. This is often called the reptilian system, because it is found even in the most antediluvian classes of animal. It is also called the primitive brain. It seems to be intimately bound up with our response to the environment and acts as a filtering system. There is a crucial area called the reticular activating system (*reticulus* is Latin for 'little net') which sieves incoming sensory information. Only the messages that are deemed important or novel are routed onwards for treatment by the rest of the brain. It is our alarm and arousal system; unless it rings the bell to wake up the rest of the brain, the brain will take no notice of what is going on. This is an area of the brain which, among some criminals, seems to operate differently than it does in normal people; we will return to it later.

So, there's our rough geography. But, as we've claimed, there are subtle differences in the brain's make-up between men and women.

The first area of difference involves the limbic system, which deals – among other things – with crises. The limbic system isn't dependent on instructions from the 'thinking' cortex – it has an autonomous mind of its own. The animal sides of our nature emerge when the limbic system decides to take things into its own hands and operates free of the reins of the rational brain. In some people, the effects of alcohol cut out the rational processes of the cortex, and the limbic system takes control – a bit like the lunatics taking over the asylum.

It is in the limbic system and the brain stem (the activating

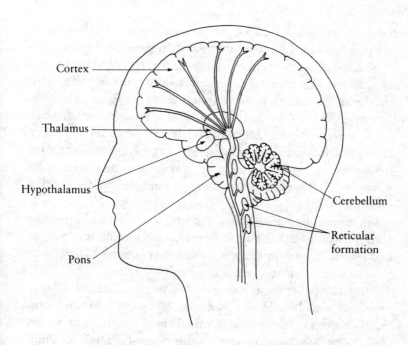

The reticular formation or activating system

or arousal system) that we find the neurotransmitter pathways, which are intimately involved in the control of all our emotional and motivational behaviour. They are vital to human neurological well-being, and, on the basis of their chemical structure, are commonly divided into two groups: the catecholamines and the indolamines.

There are four major monoamine neurotransmitters. The first three are dopamine, norepinephrine and epinephrine, known as catecholamines. They are chemically very similar, and are involved in similar actions and motives. They are the fuel of the brain, the activators of the neuronal pathways. The fourth is serotonin, which works mainly in the opposite direction to the others. If the others are the fuel, or the gas, of the brain, serotonin represents the system's brakes. It is an inhibitor of neuronal activity. Just as how well the brakes work is vital to safe driving, so, as we shall see, the efficacy of serotonin is central to the question of antisocial behaviour.

Serotonin, or 5-hydroxytryptamine, often abbreviated as 5-HT, is one of the major transmitter substances in the parts of the brain that control motivational and emotional behaviour. Serotonin is involved in the control of a wide range of behaviours, such as food intake, anxiety, depression, pain sensitivity, and, most importantly for our story, aggression and impulsive behaviour. Serotonin seems to have a general property of inhibiting or toning down our waking behaviour, and it promotes sleep.

But the really significant thing about serotonin is the way neurotransmitters link the three areas of the brain: the activating area in the brain stem, the limbic system and the frontal cortex or thinking area of the brain.

The limbic, or animal, brain, we know, can make its own primitive, impulsive decisions, but is kept under control by the cerebral cortex, the more rational part of the brain. But control can only be maintained through good communications, and that's the specific job of the neurotransmitter serotonin – to link the emotional, impulsive limbic system to the sensible, civilized cortex. As long as those pathways are fully operational, as long as the brakes are working properly, with an optimum amount of available serotonin, there will be healthy and normal communication between the two areas of the brain. In one sense, the more transmissions there are between the rational part of the brain in the cortex and the emotional brain in the limbic system, the more rational – and less animal – our behaviour will be.

ABNORMAL SEROTONIN

Neural pathways and brain chemicals are well beyond the examination of the microscope. They are molecular in size, and correspondingly hard to measure. Scientists are always looking for what they call a 'marker' – a substance which can be found in the bloodstream which can indicate the presence, absence and levels of neurotransmitters in the brain, and which is comparatively easy to measure. Luckily, there is a marker in the bloodstream for neurotransmitters. It's called monoamine oxidase (MAO), an enzyme which reacts with the chemicals found in neurotransmitters. Levels of MAO roughly reflect the ability of the brain to maintain and control neurotransmitters.

Low levels of the MAO family of enzymes in the blood are usually and broadly a measure of low levels of serotonin in the brain. Low levels of MAO are linked with sensation-seeking and impulsiveness – the same behaviour which results from low serotonin levels, when the irrational, animal, limbic part of the brain is less well connected to the rational parts of the cortex. What's puzzling is that abnormally high levels also seem to produce the same behaviour. In most people MAO levels hover within an optimum range for efficient brain functioning. People with unusually high or low levels 'appear to exhibit less socially desirable behaviour and consequently are more anxious and hostile compared to those with intermediate MAO levels'.[3]

So the brains of people displaying hostility and antisocial behaviour are like vehicles with faulty brakes – cars out of control. Could serotonin, the braking mechanism, hold one key to the question of crime, violence, and antisocial behaviour? Can aggressive behaviour, and its extremes, be unravelled at the basic level of brain chemistry? Is the reason why the accident-prone male of the species is much less likely to assess the consequences of his actions simply the chemical mix of his mind?

Nothing in the emerging science of brain chemistry is simple. Scientists don't understand all the pieces of the puzzle. But the study of serotonin is already producing intriguing results. Animal and human studies suggest that low levels of MAO – reflecting low serotonin levels – 'may decrease the individual's ability or motivation to maintain his or her self-control . . . [they] are associated with irritability and tendencies toward impulsive responses to environmental conditions.'[4]

We each have a specific, and constant, level of these chemicals in our bodies until the ages of around 23 to 25. In both sexes the levels of MAO gradually rise with age – so women become even more capable of controlling impulsive behaviour, and men calm down, as they get older. Meanwhile, the most interesting and exciting result comes from comparative measures of these two chemicals between the sexes. Across the mammalian spectrum, females have consistently higher levels of both serotonin and MAO. The difference in humans is particularly marked: 'In healthy normal humans ... males had, on average, just under 52 per cent of the serotonin levels found in females.'[5]

If we have understood the function of serotonin correctly, this must suggest that the female brain is more 'in control' of itself than the male brain, where the impulsive limbic activity is under less restraint from the rational cortex. The finding mirrors experience: girls are less likely to do impulsive, thoughtless things.

There is also evidence that a dysfunction with serotonin – or 5-HT – levels is at the heart of offending, aggressive and suicidal behaviour.

The first clues came from animal studies, where the levels of 5-HT were deliberately suppressed. Regardless of which animals were used, the reduction of central 5-HT activity increased aggressive behaviour. The laboratory workers then tried the experiment in reverse: they stimulated the production of the animals' 5-HT by injecting them with specific chemicals. Effectively, this treatment blocked the aggressive behaviour. What this means is that we can manipulate aggressive behaviour by varying the chemical cocktail in the brain to alter the levels of serotonin. We can put animals more or less in control of themselves.

There was one particular aspect of aggression that researchers found particularly interesting. Apart from studying the generation of aggression in general, they studied what would happen to the animals under provocation or in circumstances of deprivation – the aggressive response to adverse stimuli.

What they found was that diminished central 5-HT activity appeared to lower the threshold at which an organism ordinarily responds aggressively to adverse stimuli. 5-HT seems crucially involved in the control of irritability, the level at which tempers – and control – are lost.

The next stage was to move to human studies – and infant human studies in particular. Blood taken from the umbilical cord was assessed during the first three days of life. MAO, we remember, is the enzyme which acts as a 'marker' for serotonin. What emerged from the study was that children with low levels of MAO, therefore with low levels of serotonin, were more restless and less consolable, when upset, than normal babies. They also slept less and cried more and were – a refreshingly down-to-earth term to find in a clinical study – less 'cuddly' and less emotionally stable.

The research team believe that such behaviour is a key indicator for antisocial behaviour in later life. When they looked at a group of boys between the ages of six and twelve they found that those diagnosed as suffering from ADD – attention deficit disorder – had significantly lower levels of serotonin. Could this be influencing their impulsive and inattentive behaviour? Another study confirmed that low levels of serotonin are not confined simply to those children with ADD; across the whole range of behavioural problems and conduct disorders, from hyperactivity to oppositional defiant disorder (ODD) – every parent can imagine what that is – low levels of serotonin manifested themselves. Children with aggressive, impulsive behaviour patterns have a reduced number of serotonin binding sites, compared to children in control samples. A two-year-old's tantrum may be the direct result of serotonin deficiency. The good news is that, while all two-year-olds have tantrums, most will have calmed down by the age of three or four; nature remedies the defect, or nurture, possibly, mitigates its worst expression.

But that didn't happen in the fascinating case of Mary.

Mary had been adopted at birth into a kind, caring and

affluent middle-class family. At the age of twelve, her adoptive parents began to worry about her behaviour. She was averagely intelligent, but seemed to have a cruel streak in her. It came out in the way she treated her pets, cramming them into ever more confined spaces. While she played with a young bird, she was observed throwing it into the air to try to make it fly until it died of exhaustion.

On a test she came out with a 99.9 per cent score on the subscale measuring aggressive and cruel behaviour. She was tested for serotonin markers, and found to have low levels. A subsequent follow-up at the age of fifteen showed that she was being held in a detention centre for the offence of passing bad cheques. Her conduct disorder symptoms had increased in variety and severity: Mary had made a number of suicidal gestures, such as lacerating her wrists – a type of behaviour frequently found in association with low serotonin levels.

Cruelty to animals – and there is another study of a boy with low serotonin levels who killed the family cat – is known to be a predictive risk factor in later aggression towards humans. Low serotonin levels are common to a whole range of antisocial behaviour – from childhood conduct disorders such as restless and uninhibited behaviour patterns, through sensation-seeking, impulsiveness and drug abuse to a high probability of criminality. There is a clear link with what yet another study has described as 'general aggressiveness and sudden feelings of anger and frustration'.

These studies suggest that the effect of serotonin is not just as an aggression control mechanism, but that it has an overall control over misconduct, so that low levels trigger aggression more easily in those who are naturally aggressive – perhaps those with high testosterone – while in naturally milder individuals the effect is simply a failure to inhibit their better moral instincts, so they trick, cheat or steal.

Given that serotonin keeps our more primitive instincts in

check, by connecting our impulses with our reason, it follows that the lower your levels of serotonin, the more impulsive your behaviour. Abnormally low levels lead to impulsive violent behaviour – as in the case of the television character, hotelier Basil Fawlty thrashing his broken-down car with a branch and compulsively cuffing his hapless waiter.

Using various techniques, scientists have measured the levels of serotonin in men and women, criminals and non-criminals. What they have found is that men have lower serotonin levels than women, and that criminals have markedly low levels. A large number of studies into the crime–serotonin link suggest that a lack of serotonin may mean a comparative lack of control over your impulses – you're exceeding the speed limit because you have defective brakes. Or, in more measured academic parlance, 'a decrease in impulse control might be related to the biological trait of serotonergic activity.'[6]

This information obliges us to ask if we can really call a mindless offender 'mindless'. If there is, in fact, something wrong with the offender's mind, is it as pointless to punish such a man as it is to thrash a car which has a mechanical malfunction? Could serotonin be another of the clues to the overwhelmingly male character of crime? Men on average start out in life with levels of serotonin that are half those of women. So an abnormally low level in a man is, compared with that in a woman, a very low level indeed.

What's clear, however, is that in serotonin the scientists are convinced that they have found at least one biological factor contributing to criminal, aggressive and violent behaviour.

Some of the clinching evidence comes from a study of violent offenders in a Finnish forensic establishment. They were classified by impulsive or non-impulsive violent offences. This time the scientists looked for the tell-tale by-products of serotonin. The impulsive violent offenders, tested by the American Medical Association's diagnostic bible as having an antisocial personality disorder, also demonstrated significantly reduced levels of serotonin by-products compared with the paranoid or non-impulsive offenders. This confirms our suspicion that low serotonin correlates more with *impulsive* aggressive behaviour than with aggressive behaviour in general.

The Finnish study looked at thirty-six male murderers, and under the test which diagnoses 'intermittent explosive disorder' or 'antisocial personality disorder' identified those whose crime had involved a sudden, explosive and impulsive outburst of aggression. These had significantly lower levels than non-impulsive offenders. Nearly half of them had also made suicide attempts – such as the self-laceration we have already seen as being linked with low serotonin. This is consistent with other findings linking low levels of serotonin with impulsive violent behaviour and histories of attempted suicide.

Again, the link seems to be with impulsiveness rather than simple aggression – a point that's strengthened when you study people who set fires. Arson is a destructive, but basically non-aggressive, crime – the violence is not usually directed against people.

Daniel was three when he started playing with matches; he seemed to be fascinated with fire. It was when his mother caught him making a bonfire of his wooden bricks that she began to worry about him. He was also very difficult to control. He would just run off and do things without thinking – such as running out into the street for a ball without taking any notice of traffic. Boys will be boys, she consoled herself; but when Daniel went to school the problems grew – he was always getting into trouble, not just because he would not sit still but also because he kept lighting fires in the school cloakroom. As he grew older his compulsion to light fires began seriously to frighten his mother, and she took him to see a psychiatrist – but to no avail. Eventually the impulsive fire-raising took a serious turn. At the age of fourteen, Daniel set fire to a school in Liverpool, causing damage estimated at £80,000. He was convicted of arson, and placed under a two-year supervision order where he had to attend a juvenile justice centre for a treatment programme including a fire-awareness course. Daniel is improving but he still has a fascination with fire; if he has too much to drink he still finds the urge to set a building alight almost uncontrollable.

We cannot tell what factors were involved in that wide spectrum of fascination with fire. But what we do know is the result of a study into the serotonin levels of other fire-raisers. Levels of serotonin were the same as for those involved in violent, aggressive crime; the common factor in both groups was the failure to inhibit impulsive action. Further, the study found the lowest serotonin levels among the arsonists who had the most consistent history of impulsive behaviour; non-impulsive violent offenders had intermediate levels and people in control samples had the highest levels.

And just to add a further evidential ingredient to the chemical brew of crime: there are also a few preliminary studies which suggest that women suffering from premenstrual syndrome – which, as we have seen, increases their propensity towards crime – also have lowered levels of serotonin, so causing a double drive towards impulsive behaviour.

Perhaps the most dramatic part of the chemical search for the roots to crime is also the easiest to understand. It concerns the relationship, in some individuals, between serotonin, crime and glucose. Serotonin seems to affect impulsiveness and over-reaction because when there is an imbalance in the neurotransmitter levels it seems to translate into an imbalance in the body's ability to maintain the right levels of glucose in the brain.

Low glucose levels involve the triggering of a complex biochemical process. They increase the levels of the neurotransmitter norepinephrine. This has the effect of making us more active. In one way this makes sound, survival sense: we're hungry, so we get up and do something about it. In another way, however, it can make for antisocial behaviour, as one consequence of low glucose levels is that they make the emotion-processing limbic system more reactive to outside events. Put at its simplest, we get more irritable when our blood sugar is low, and in some people this reaction reaches extremes.

What researchers have found is that in those violent impulsive people with low serotonin levels their feed-back mechanisms which control blood sugar levels – the thermostats, as it were, that keep the levels of glucose constant – are abnormal. If they have not eaten they are more susceptible than are normal people to impulsive behaviour. Young habitually violent males classified as suffering from APD – antisocial personality disorder – as well as intermittent explosive disorder and aggressive conduct disorder all display symptoms of hypoglycaemia, or low blood sugar. During tests to see how they reacted to glucose, some were found to secrete abnormally long-lasting supplies of insulin, the hormone that controls sugar metabolism. The hypothesis is that some people burn up their sugar to an unnatural degree, with the result that they are constantly on the edge of irritability or impulsiveness.

Among these individuals, who crave sweets – or alcohol – and have high insulin/low blood sugar levels, are people who have manifested antisocial behaviour and impulsive, aggressive acts, and arsonists. The activity is more pronounced when glucose levels are at their lowest.

In a study specifically of arsonists, the more frequent the offender the lower the blood glucose nadir was found to be. In general the arsonists displayed a low level, below 3 ml of sugar per litre of blood; those who had committed three or more offences showed the lowest levels of all. In another study violent offenders, too, displayed low glucose levels. Clinical evaluation of a group of impulsively violent patients revealed that those with high levels of insulin showed a greater incidence of antisocial behaviour. High insulin meant that sugar was metabolized at an abnormal rate. The group also suffered sleep disorders and showed abnormal patterns of brain activity.

When scientists looked at that family history, they found in these high-insulin patients a consistent propensity towards impulsive, violent behaviour. Relatives recounted an early onset of aggressive, antisocial behaviour, including lying, stealing, abusive language and alcohol abuse. Most clearly fulfilled the diagnostic criteria for ADD – attention deficit disorder. They often had fathers who exhibited a history of violent behaviour, typically precipitated by drunkenness, and an inability later to recall the event. So – and this perhaps ties in with findings we shall see later about heredity, alcoholism, and low serotonin – a tendency towards hypoglycaemia may represent a familial or even heritable trait of some impulsive male offenders.

Other research links low blood sugar to serotonin deficit. Lack of serotonin output in the forebrain, the suggestion is, causes a lesion which disturbs sleep patterns and the metabolizing of glucose. The effects of low serotonin seem to match a lot of what we know about low blood sugar – that it directly lowers the threshold for impulsive, violent behaviour, and disturbs day and night activity rhythms, producing feelings of unease and depression. Serotonin seems to have a link with the control of insulin secretion: low serotonin = high insulin = low sugar = aggression. The exciting, if tentative, proposal is that treatment of these individuals with medications which increase their serotonin levels may help to stabilize blood sugar levels, reduce the hunger for alcohol and prevent aggressive outbursts.

Thus glucose/serotonin is a powerful card in our metaphorical hand of cards which are needed to create a criminal propensity. Alcohol/serotonin is another. All research points to the colossal influence of alcohol in virtually every branch of crime. Drink obviously has a disinhibiting effect, loosening the moral constraints on behaviour – but it is now possible to be more precise about what exactly is going on. There is now a large body of research which shows that low serotonin, the neurotransmitter involved in inhibiting impulsive behaviour, is intimately linked with the need for alcohol; further, alcohol seems to have a more intense effect on those who already have chronically low serotonin levels. It's a lethal spiral: such people have a stronger thirst for alcohol, and it does them greater damage.

At first, alcohol raises serotonin levels: people feel mellow, easy-going and the brakes are on – there's no impulse to do anything dramatic. But as the euphoric effects wear off, an intricate feed-back mechanism takes effect and serotonin levels fall. Those with already low serotonin levels find that those levels fall further still, until the danger point is reached and exceeded. It's at this point that anger and violence are triggered. Further, with these desperately low levels, the alcoholic seeks to drink more, because – to begin with at least – alcohol will bring the serotonin levels up, only to plunge again later. In one sense, the alcoholic is trying to medicate himself for his depressive, aggressive and suicidal feelings. He is seeking to take a drug – drink – to remedy the low serotonin levels which cause these feelings; but the drug works for only a short time, and has the desperate mid-term side-effect of lowering the levels further still. And when the levels fall, the power to inhibit ourselves falls as well. At its most innocent, this results in us doing things of which we are heartily ashamed the next morning, as we recollect hazily, and through a thumping hangover, what we got up to the night before. But for people with constitutionally low serotonin levels, the outcome can be much more aggressive and violent.

In many studies of the link between crime and drink abuse, the majority of impulsive violent offenders fulfil the diagnostic criteria for alcohol abuse and are found to have committed their offence under the influence of alcohol. The precise relationship between crime, serotonin and alcohol has yet to be quantified, but the fact that there is such a link seems, to scientists at least, to be unarguable.

There is one more new and fascinating twist to the serotonin story – which brings together the social and biological schools of criminological thought. It now appears that the levels of this critical chemical can be affected by social factors. According to a 1994 study, measures of stress in rats, such as their reaction to electric shock, deplete serotonin in the amygdala (the part of the limbic system active in the production of aggressive behaviour). And the social isolation of male mice (who, presumably, don't like being lonely any more than do the rest of the mammal kingdom) lowers their serotonin and increases their aggression. People, too, seem vulnerable to the same effect; a study of girls whose fathers left home through desertion or divorce showed that in their cases the serotonergic activity in the brain decreased. Common sense tells us that such girls would feel depressed; but this information gives us a clue to the chemical process which mediates that emotion.

If outside events can negatively affect our neurochemistry, could they also affect it positively? And suppose a wonder drug was found which actually increased serotonin in those with seriously depleted levels? Surely this would be a contribution to lessening the danger of future offending by these people – neutralizing one of the key cards in the criminal deck. Well, there is a product on the market, whose adherents – and in the USA they number millions – regard it as a miracle drug. It works by specifically increasing serotonin levels, by preventing the neurons from removing the serotonin from the synapses where it is making the electrical connections work. The drug is called Prozac, and for anyone with a mild depression it seems to lift it and make them feel good again. As we will see later, a number of different treatments have been tried on those with low serotonin levels; for the moment, it is enough to say that any biological intervention in trying to understand the roots of crime, and minimize the chances of future offending, has to take serotonin levels into account. It raises, of course, vast medical, ethical and political problems. But crime itself is a vast and frightening problem. If we have a means to affect the incidence of crime, and to lessen the chances of an individual developing into systematic criminality, we ought to discuss it. To discuss it, we ought to know about it. There must surely be room, among all the political rhetoric and sociological theory, for a bit of clinical science.

Constitutionally low serotonin levels aren't the only way in

71

which the brain structure and chemistry of men and women is different. As significant as what inhibits antisocial action is the physical reason why such antisocial ideas occur in the first place.

The key to this seems to lie in what it takes to stimulate us. Most of us find our attention and interest engaged in the day-to-day challenges and satisfactions of life. But for a few, this isn't enough. Normal stimuli just don't keep their brains ticking along. They need stronger stuff. Take, for instance, the confession of this arsonist, M.Y., who admits that he is

fascinated by fire. I can understand why our ancestors worshipped fire, why it was so important. I love its incandescent beauty. I was an absolute arsonist, a little kind of Nazi – I burnt down my father's library: my mother came down one day, horrified to see me in the act of book burning, and literally the whole fireplace was filled with books, smouldering and blazing away. Fire still haunts me. I was once in Los Angeles, getting off the freeway at the Sunset ramp, and suddenly looping the loop: I'd been rammed so hard by a drunk driver that my gas tank ruptured and the whole car blew up. And by chance there was a newsreel crew taking five at a little café near by, and they filmed me standing in front of my car going up in flames – it was spectacular, and it was shown on the news; it's probably one of my best performances . . .

It's a question of what scientists and researchers call arousal. A clue to its importance comes from realizing that the brains of men and women are different. The very structure of the male brain makes his interest hard to arouse, his attention span short, his boredom threshold low and his perceptions of danger blunt – and this difference fundamentally alters the approach men and women take to life. We'll also discover that just as there is a difference between men and women, so there is also a difference between criminals and law-abiding citizens in what it takes to stimulate the murky recesses of the mind.

There is a crucial group of neurons, or nerve cells, which spread through the brain stem and into the mid-brain, with connections to all the key parts of the brain. That critical communications network is called the reticulus, or reticular formation. It's also called the reticular activating system, or RAS. It is net-like, not only in terms of communication, but also because it acts as a sort of sieve – filtering out the important messages from the unimportant ones, and passing them on for action to the relevant parts of the brain.

It's a network which grows with experience. As children, we may be worried by the swish of a curtain in the night, the creak of an unaccustomed floorboard. The RAS tells us to wake up, and it switches us on to a state of alert. As we get older, we realize that the swish is just the action of the nighttime breeze, the creak just the sound of the house settling, and the RAS doesn't bother to wake us up. The crash of a breaking window is, however, a novel and unexpected sensation, in which case the RAS will set the alarm bells ringing.

Continuing the bedroom example: it is usually the woman who wakes up at the sound of faint and unaccustomed sound, while her partner remains submerged in slumber. That's because the female RAS is more sensitive, more easily switched on, better programmed to alertness. Extensive studies on the male brain have shown that males need greater levels of stimulation, call it curiosity or interest, to activate the brain. Man's greater sense of adventure is in fact a symptom of this mental sluggishness. He gets bored with his surroundings, because he finds it harder to become aroused by them, so he goes off in search of new sensations. Danger may lie ahead, danger which a woman would be alert to, but to which men are comparatively deaf. And there's no satisfying this male hunger for new sensations; novel signals or sensations soon, with the male, lose their capacity to excite: men in combat, for instance, soon learn not to wince at the sound of a gunshot. The need for stimulation in males is obvious in small boys: they seek stimulation by climbing trees, and they climb higher and higher – literally oblivious to the increasing danger. Indeed, it is the increase in danger which drives them on, as the fun of the lower branches loses its effect and the thrill of the higher branches beckons.

Think of a male brain as rather like a jaded palate, which needs spicier and spicier food to satisfy and stimulate it; think of it as a drug addict, ever more quickly sated by sensation, ever hungrier for new stimulus. (Indeed, that is why those with high sensation-seeking behaviour also tend to be those who experiment with drugs.) This pattern is laid down in the womb by the action of androgens on the evolving brain.

We can actually see this happening in the laboratory, when the brain is wired up and volunteers are exposed to a barrage of different sound and sight sensations, loud bangs and flashing lights. In Philadelphia, Dr Ruben Gur can display the sex difference on television monitors; using PET scanning techniques, which produce a colour picture of brain activity, he can demonstrate how the female brain is much more 'busy' than the male brain, reacting to these stimuli. If you present both males and females with a verbal or mathematical pattern, the male brain perks up a bit – but to nothing like the basic level of the female brain. A female brain at rest is actually busier than a male brain engaged in problem-solving. The male brain gets bored, and needs to skip on to a bigger, better, noisier, flashier, sexier conundrum.

In the case of the criminal, and especially the violent offender, we discover that he is even less easily aroused than the average male. Normally, those flashes and bangs would be logged by the cortex, or thinking cap, and would pass on messages to the lower areas of the brain informing them of the developing crisis. But just as the normal male brain needs more alarm signals than the female, the violent male needs more such arousal than the average male.

Most men simply could not behave in the same way as a violent criminal, because in most people there is a sort of tripswitch. Too much stimulation creates too high a level of anxiety and unpleasant feelings, causing the ordinary person to be deterred from the pursuit of too much danger. One of the reasons why most of us will not get into fights or rob banks is because we know that we would be terrified to do so. Those extreme sensations – which the violent criminal seems to need and to be able to cope with – would trigger too many anxiety messages back to the thinking part of the brain. So, in the analogy of the boy up the tree, he would want to keep climbing, to gather the excitement of new sensations; but, having reached the top, he wouldn't jump, because his reason tells him (via the network of the brain) that the sensation of falling would be exhilarating, but the sensation of landing would be painful.

The criminal brain can't make that distinction. The violent mind can tolerate the execution of many cruel and vicious actions because the violent brain can tolerate those high levels of arousal and anxiety, and takes them in its stride. The rational, moral and intellectual filter that most of us have, the RAS, has considerably wider mesh in the criminal brain. Indeed, there is evidence that criminals entertain, but discount the unpleasant consequences of their actions. Terrible actions do not register as terrible to that sort of mind. Remember the appalling massacre of the Holocaust. Most of us cannot even imagine being part of the SS mass execution squads, whose most frequent complaint was of sore shoulders caused by the recoil of their rifles during so many shootings of naked men, women and children. Were these men morally deficient – or simply lacking in the normal, mental mechanisms necessary to inform them that such actions were inhuman and vile?

There are chemical methods of displaying the comparative inertia of the male RAS and the consequent links between that and the criminal mind. The chemical adrenaline is well-enough known to have become part of the layman's vocabulary. Most people know that it is secreted when we are faced with a challenge, a threat, a danger. The more adrenaline in the blood and urine, the greater the stress we are reacting to. A series of studies has demonstrated that those individuals with less adrenaline circulating in their urine and bloodstream tend to be more aggressive and destructive.

At first, this seems to run counter to our idea of adrenaline pumping up, or psyching up, the personality. Surely high adrenaline should make people 'hyper'? In fact, the opposite is true. High adrenaline shows that alarm bells are ringing in the arousal system. The alarm bells trigger the adrenaline, which in turn will tell you to avoid risk and danger. In other words, high adrenaline will make you want to take yourself out of an aggressive situation. But if you don't have much adrenaline, you are deaf to those alarm bells; you press on regardless, with your dangerous or antisocial actions. Perhaps that's why a study of highly aggressive school bullies revealed clearly lower levels of adrenaline than that in their meeker peers – those with the sense, and the adrenaline, to run away. What emerged was that high levels correlate with feelings of anxiety, apprehension and inadequacy ('Here comes the bully, he's stronger than me, let me get out of here!'), while low levels correlated with impulsiveness and aggression ('What the hell, why not beat up this policeman, I don't care about the consequences, I won't feel any pain').

Studies show that the conventional psychological wisdom – that bullies are motivated by an underlying lack of self-esteem – simply is not the case. What's more likely to be the case is this. A boy with typically low levels of cortical arousal suffers from a stimulus hunger, a sort of craving for sensation. He becomes easily habituated, and therefore easily bored with his environment. Strong stimuli are not experienced as unpleasant and to be avoided – rather they can be exciting and engaging. The cycle becomes self-reinforcing: a child in a deprived community with nothing to do, and no hope of creative stimulus, satisfies his hunger for sensation and novelty by an ever-increasing spiral of danger and impulsiveness. As he grows older, he associates this satisfaction with the acting out of antisocial behaviour. He has, indeed, become dependent on it in stronger and stronger doses. It's no use offering this boy a jigsaw or a bicycle – he'll get bored; it's no use offering him a dinghy or a skiing holiday to 'let off steam' – the novelty soon wears off. He can be satisfied only with wrecking the regatta or crashing down the off-piste suicide runs. There's been fury (some of it synthetic) about the way social workers tried to help a persistent delinquent by taking him on safari in Africa. The intention was excellent – after all, it's cheaper than a custodial sentence which, as we'll discover, is counter-productive; but it was never going to work so long as the boy in question (now old enough to be safely behind bars in an adult penal institution) had this craving for sensation.

The bully may grow out of his childhood craving for aggression and ever more exciting sensation, either because his physiology settles down, or because social factors are strong enough to suppress his instincts. He may, on the other hand, become one of that small percentage of difficult boys falling into one of those categories that we have discussed – those suffering from conduct disorder, attention deficit disorder, or hyperactivity. Whatever definition researchers use, it is overwhelmingly the case that the excessively difficult child, who starts getting into trouble with the law at a very young age, and is involved in persistent misconduct, is plagued by this abnormal level of arousal – and needs to compensate for it by behaviour which we define as antisocial.

It is, of course, one thing to say that a violent offender requires more arousal than the average person, but it is possible too that he actually seeks out situations and behaviours which will produce this arousal. Just as people who join the Army or the police, or even those in the Army who volunteer for particularly hazardous missions, may be identifying a need in themselves, could it be that people with low arousability are actually drawn towards potentially dangerous, risky situations, where an act of violent crime may be perpetrated? Extraordinary acts of courage are a hair's breadth away from extraordinary acts of folly and recklessness.

As we delve deeper into the brain, other techniques confirm our finding of this low arousal in criminals. Using electroencephalograms – EEGs – the level of electrical activity in the brains of violent criminals has been studied. Particular attention has been paid to the theta activity, which denotes drowsiness and has a direct link with brain arousability.

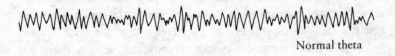

Normal theta

Abnormal theta

EEG brain activity scan

The higher the theta activity occurring in the cortex, the harder the brain is to arouse or activate. Theta activity in offenders is high: therefore their arousability is low. Meanwhile the alpha levels, denoting how relaxed or not as awake someone is, are related to high testosterone; high testosterone goes with low alpha activity, which in turn relates to the low arousability of the brain. So in the brains of these criminals we have a fascinating chemical and physical prescription for violence – high androgens which we have identified as hormonal dynamite, plus the fact that it takes a very large explosion to stimulate their brains.

In Sarnoff Mednick's study of 600 children with no delinquency records, the boys and girls were given waking and sleeping EEGs several times before the age of seventeen. Twelve years later the Swedish police records were examined, so that scientists could cross-reference early EEG patterns with later offending. You will probably be able to forecast the result: the average offender had a distinctive EEG at the original testing, even though over six years separated the test from the crime. Offenders had atypically slow brain wave rhythms of a type associated with low arousal and abnormal patterns of sleep. Another study of 129 Danish males confirmed the correlation between theft and atypical patterns of arousal.

That major study of Los Angeles children also measured the effect of noise on the brain. A loud noise stimulated a brain wave whose amplitude is labelled as N2. N2 is related to general arousal – it measures how much noise is necessary to produce a given mental reaction. Hyperactive children needed a bigger noise to stimulate them than did normal children – but delinquent hyperactive children needed the biggest bang of all.

David Farringdon measured the pulse rate among the 400 at-risk children between the ages of 8 and 24 he studied. Pulse rate is thought to be linked to low autonomic reactivity (a measure of arousal) and the findings suggest that there is an association between low rates and bad behaviour in school. Boys convicted of violent offences had a significantly lower pulse rate than unconvicted youths. Farrington shares the frustration of those who cannot understand why so many students of crime turn their backs on empirical, clinical evidence; 'criminology has been dominated by the sociologists since the Second World War, and most of these sociologists are hostile to research on biology and crime.'[7]

Yet the research is all there, waiting to be taken into account. For instance, we can tell that those with APD – antisocial personality disorder – have lower measurements of skin conductivity than normal people. Tests measure how sweaty the subject gets under stress, by passing a weak electric current between two electrodes. The skin conductivity in those with APD is low because outside, stress-making stimuli do not have the same arousing effect as they would on normal people. This makes a nonsense of lie-detectors, or polygraph tests in the case of the psychopathic offender: he can beat the lie detector because he does not feel anxiety when he lies – he is not aroused by the questions. Many studies have found that criminals are less likely than other people to exhibit symptoms of stress when threatened with impending pain. And there is evidence that, once put under stressful conditions, criminals recover more quickly, reverting to their previous low level of arousal: 'criminals may exhibit a brain functioning pattern that insulates them to an unusual degree from punishing aspects of their environment.'[8] Which must tell us something about the deterrent and rehabilitative effects of prison . . .

We have seen that the danger flags are raised long before the age of adult, criminal responsibility. The phenomenon we have identified with hyperactive children – they are not over-active because they are over-stimulated, but because they find it so difficult to gain satisfactory stimulus from normal activity – has been enough, in the past, to drive parents and teachers to despair. But this needn't be the case. At last we know what is going on in those troubled little heads.

And, having diagnosed the problem, very possibly we can do something about it, long before the child gets into serious trouble with the law. The most frequent treatment is, para-doxically, with stimulant drugs. That's because studies of hyperactive children have revealed that they suffer from subopti-mal RF values – inadequate arousability of the reticular forma-tion. The child can't engage with the task in hand, seeks something different to do, and then gets bored with that. Stimulant drugs make the RF system more alert and responsive to the matter in hand, thus making it less boring, creating less appetite for different stimulation. The most effective treatment so far identified is Ritalin, or amphetamine methylphenidate; on two thirds of children this stimulant has a notable calming effect. Even caffeine has also been known to work. That's because the effect of these stimulants is to make the reticular formation and its peripheral neural support structures more alert and sensitive to incoming information. It takes less, then, to engage the attention and the interest. The attention does not wander from the blackboard to such an extent, or seek the alternative and greater excitements of mischief.

The biological evidence keeps rolling in. For instance, corti-sol is a steroid, which is produced by the adrenal cortex. This is produced following the first adrenaline rush if the stress stimulus is prolonged, so it is also a measure of arousal. By measuring cortisol traces in the salivary gland we can assess the degree of alertness, or wakefulness, of the brain. Children with high incidence of conduct disorder have low levels of salivary cortisol. Low levels are also associated with high aggression and habitual violence, and the indications are that such behaviour in children may predict later, adult offending. The same is true of adrenaline secretion: youths aged between 18 and 26 were found to have conspicuously lower levels of adrenaline secretion at the age of 13, compared with the levels of a group who did not go on to offend.

And further biochemical evidence is there for the investigating. The neurochemicals involved in the process of arousal are the catecholamines mentioned earlier. The principal neurotransmitter pathways for brain arousal are provided by noradrenaline/norephinephrine. High norephinephrine correlates with high impulsiveness, irritability and extrovert behaviour. Low levels of norephinephrine are associated with introversion; subjects are less stimulated, react less. We do not yet know how, if at all, norephinephrine and serotonin interact, but the suspicion is that high levels of anger-inducing norephinephrine and low levels of inhibitory serotonin make an explosive chemical combination. Add testosterone (one of the family of androgens, or male hormones) and the blue touch paper lights.

The chemistry of our brains, then, fundamentally influences our behaviour. And central to that behaviour is what it takes to keep our brains aroused, involved, engaged. For most of us, nature takes care of the balance. But we have seen that there are others to whom nature has not been so kind. After all, what does it take to arouse the young person whom nature has left below par? Well, drink works pretty well. And the search for new sensations – a couple of Ecstasy tablets will help. No drugs available? Well, a dustbin hurled through a shop-window induces a gratifying result. This young man has an abnormal need for stimulation which impels him first towards a psychopathology which involves misbehaviour and mischief, and may later lead to crime. In this respect it is worth making the point that modern Western society is the ideal hothouse for juvenile delinquency. Those elders who complain about the comparative advantages of the younger generation miss the point entirely; it is precisely those advantages – peace, safety, education, welfare, freedom from hunger and want – that drive the young male to acts of apparently motiveless delinquency. The older generation had wars, faced genuine risks, went hungry, had to get on their bicycles to cross the country in search of work – changes and stimuli that fed the appetite for sensation which only could arouse them. Today, the routines of school, the commuter routines of work, the routines of domesticity fail to satisfy the male mind. That explains why petty pilfering is rife in an age of affluence, and vandalism flourishes in an age when we strive for a prim, municipal utopia. Vandalism isn't mindless – it's the consequence of minds hungry for sensation.

There are social solutions. Some boys who steal and wreck cars can be rehabilitated by being put to work mending old vehicles – the activity, presumably, providing the stimulus they need. But that sort of replacement activity is not going to work as a universal panacea. We can't channel the aggression of every young man by making him a professional boxer. But it is a significant beginning to acknowledge the fact that we are who we are, and do what we do, largely because of the chemical imperative of hormones and neurotransmitters in the brain.

CHAPTER 5

The Criminal Brain: Damaged Goods

So we know that there are various chemical inputs which contribute to the formation of criminal intent, and the failure to resist the criminal urge. To summarize the story so far: high testosterone, abnormal levels of neurotransmitters – especially inhibitory serotonin – have a clear, clinically defined effect. What's also important, it seems, is a low level of brain arousal, a failure to be engaged or interested in the normal stimuli of life, with the corresponding need for bigger, bolder, rasher challenges. It's rather like the person who says he needs a couple of drinks just to feel normal.

At this stage, the reader will know more about the nature of the genesis of crime than any of the politicians or civil servants who agonize about it.

But that's not the whole picture. There are other factors which predispose people to criminal acts, which tilt the balance, or stack the odds, or add another high card to the royal flush of criminality. Certain abnormalities in the brain function have been well documented by clinical researchers, but are hardly acknowledged by criminologists and are positively a closed book to politicians and to most lawyers and judges. Yet the presence of these abnormalities almost certainly increases the likelihood of offending; we include the qualification 'almost' because the exploration of the brain is at a comparatively early stage, but we believe that future findings will only confirm and elaborate what most experts now believe. We also believe that different abnormalities may result in different forms of criminal behaviour. The purpose of this chapter is to demonstrate that while brain damage or abnormality in the functioning of the brain clearly affects individual behaviour in various ways, one of those ways is to increase the likelihood of violent, aggressive, persistent and remorseless crime.

Brain surgery has achieved a mythic status among the public. The brain surgeon has become synonymous with stratospheric levels of intelligence; the phrase 'You don't have to be a brain surgeon to realize [some glaringly obvious fact]' underlines, in a backhanded manner, the awe in which we hold those who delve in the mysterious crevices of the brain. The brain is, indeed, complicated; it has been rightly described as the most complex living structure in the universe. But we shouldn't let that worry us; we can simplify the picture without distorting it. Let's keep that simplified map of the brain in our own minds, split as it is into three main processing areas.

At the top is the cortex, the thinking cap which deals with language, reason and the higher thought processes. You play chess with the cortex. Below that, the limbic system, or animal brain, which deals with our emotions and our motivations: 'I really *want* to play chess with this highly attractive partner,' or 'I really want to *get even* with this chessboard rival.' And finally, the reptilian brain, including especially the reticular activating system or RAS which puts us in touch with our environment and filters out irrelevant information: 'I will stop playing this game of chess because the house is on fire, as I know from the fact that my respiratory system is inhaling noxious and acrid fumes.' All these three brains are, and need to be, connected: we need to know how to play chess, we need to want to play, and we need to stay alive to play.

Let's start with the cortex, the thinking bit. Most people will be familiar with the brain's design: its two hemispheres, left and right, looking rather like a shelled walnut, are the principal division of the human brain. Each hemisphere sub-serves the most complex human functions, from voluntary (as opposed to reflex) movement or interpretation of sensory input (making sense of the world about us) to helping us to learn, speak, understand foreign languages or solve problems. These hemispheres are covered by a layer of tissue called the cerebral cortex. In humans the cortex is deeply wrinkled, or furrowed. Rather like a rucked-up blanket, this furrowing has the effect of increasing the overall volume of the brain – the surface area of the brain is estimated at 1.5 sq ft/0.13 m². The two cerebral hemispheres are almost completely separated by what is called the longitudinal fissure – the gap between the two halves. The hemispheres are joined by a few tracts called commissures, the biggest of which is the corpus callosum – a central bundle of cables, the telephone exchange connecting most of the subscribers in each half of the brain.

There are regular patterns to the fissures, so we have some reliable landmarks in this strange world. We already know about that central divide, separating left from right; there's a further subdivision caused by deep grooves called sulci which serve to split the brain into four functional areas called lobes. These lobes are named either to describe what they principally do, or to describe where they are. The frontal lobe is, unsurprisingly, at the front of the brain. Its job is primarily to control our motor functions, and it also co-ordinates the other three lobes.

We can further divide the frontal lobe, covered by the frontal cortex, into the fore and aft sections – the front section being referred to most commonly as the prefrontal cortex. This bit of the cerebral machine regulates the ability to plan, organize behaviour methodically, and keep our emotional reactions under control. Other normal functions of the frontal lobe include sustaining attention and concentration, abstract reasoning and concept formation, identifying goals and objectives, and programming and setting in motion a series of actions necessary to achieve the objective. The frontal cortex also keeps an eye on our own behaviour – it is that part of the brain that, in Robert Burns's words, helps us 'see ourselves as others see us', deterring us from unsuccessful, inappropriate or impulsive actions, as well as helping us to adapt to changed circumstances. These are commonly called the 'executive' functions, which govern our reaction to how our actions are judged by others, our response to punishment, and our ethical and moral conduct. The frontal cortex does not do all this in

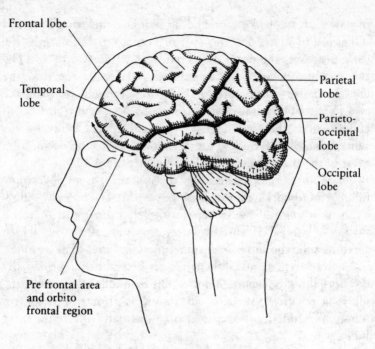

Frontal lobe

Temporal lobe

Parietal lobe

Parieto-occipital lobe

Occipital lobe

Pre frontal area and orbito frontal region

The cerebral cortex, or thinking cap

isolation: it interacts with adjacent brain systems, gathering sensory information, processing it and feeding it into its decision-making process before putting its plans into operation. There is a further subdivision of the frontal cortex that is important to our story: the orbitofrontal cortex is an area which seems to be intricately involved in our sense of moral reasoning and sense of right and wrong. It is positioned just below the eyes and is intimately linked to the limbic system and the amygdala, which generates what we experience as feeling and emotion.

Just behind the frontal lobe is the parietal lobe. Its principal job is to assess and organize our sensory information. The occipital lobe sits right at the back of the brain, and its sole job is to process visual information – what we see with our eyes. Down the side of each hemisphere – brush your hands

86

through your hair just above the ears and you will be a mere skull's width away – are the temporal lobes. Each temporal lobe's primary responsibility is for hearing and speech. The back portion of the temporal lobes seems to play a part in integrating and acting upon information received from other parts of the brain, including the limbic system, as well as the regulation of behaviour; in that respect, it seems to duplicate some of the functions of the frontal lobe. But the most significant role of the temporal lobe seems to be an almost metaphysical one. It seems to be where we develop a sense of ourselves in our emotional context, and is concerned with the processing of our emotions and our instincts. It manages our gut reactions to physical and emotional changes in our circumstances. It is very much the centre of our feelings about who we are and how we relate to other people. We suspect that when our hearts break, they break in the temporal lobe.

In relation to emotion, the left and right hemispheres seem, in general, to have different roles. Ideally, they seem to work in a delicately balanced partnership: the right side of the brain receiving and acknowledging emotions, and the left side of the brain processing and managing those emotions, acting as a check to inhibit inappropriately emotional behaviour. It's the left side that tells us that some particular personal or domestic crisis is not the end of the world, that helps us keep things in proportion: that tells us, in other words, not to cry over spilt milk. The left side represents in effect the brake on our emotional responses. Damage or a malfunction on one side has the effect of accentuating the power of the undamaged side – in other words, damage to the inhibiting left side of the brain will give a freer rein to the emotions perceived by the right. Both hemispheres are involved in the processing of verbal and non-verbal information, but the left side plays a bigger role in language functions, especially in speech output. In contrast the right side plays a greater role in processing and organizing visual, spatial and tactile information.

The hemispheres, then, have different roles, and different powers; but neurophysiological studies consistently confirm

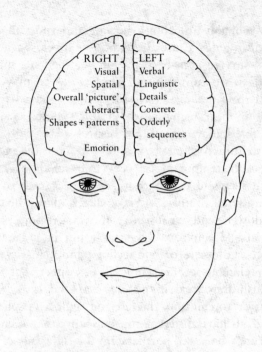

RIGHT | LEFT
Visual | Verbal
Spatial | Linguistic
Overall 'picture' | Details
Abstract | Concrete
Shapes + patterns | Orderly
 | sequences

Emotion

The general geography of the brain

the existence of another factor – a dominant hemisphere. In nearly all right-handed people (96 per cent) it is the left hemisphere which dominates. In 65 per cent of left-handers, it's the right hemisphere which dominates. So for most people (since most people are right-handed) the left hemisphere – the less emotional, organizing and regulating side of the brain – is the dominant one.

There's not only a difference in function and dominance, but also, apparently, a difference between the left and right sides of the brain in the way they approach their respective tasks. The (usually dominant) left hemisphere processes information in a methodical, orderly and sequential manner. The non-dominant right side takes a holistic or overall view of the information. The right side sees the wood, while the left side sees each individual tree. The predominance of the left hemisphere is probably an evolutionary phenomenon; mankind has had to distinguish cause and effect, and the sequencing of events, to survive. Our progress is largely due to the fact that we see how we can sustain ourselves in the future by not eating all the seeds available, but reserving some to plant in the earth to bear fruit in due season. Man is distinguished from the other animals, after all, by his sense of time.

Just as the two different halves of the brain have different functions and responsibilities, so it seems that there is a subtle difference in the balance of the neurotransmitters between each side of the brain. The right side (holistic, emotional) is more endowed with norepinephrine and serotoninergic neurotransmitters, which play a key function in the arousal and inhibition of the emotions. The left side (methodical, sequential, strong in language) is more influenced by the dopaminergic neurotransmitter, which governs selective attention and concentration, helping to exercise a restraining, regulatory role on that emotional right brain, inhibiting the impulses and attitudes and actions deemed undesirable by society.

Most of this interplay between the hemispheres is conducted through the central telephone exchange of the corpus callosum, the main neural link between the two sides of the brain. Without this link we'd be in trouble, because we would have no idea of what was going on with the left side of our bodies; the right brain controls the left side of our bodies, and needs to pass that information through the telephone exchange to our centres of self-awareness which are in the left brain.

Some researchers have concluded that the uniquely human phenomenon of conscious self-awareness may be largely localized to the left side of the brain, where of course the language skills are known to be centred. At the same time, they believe that ideas which originate in the emotional right side reach consciousness only when they are telephoned through to the language-dominated left side. This raises an intriguing and hotly debated theory about the nature of the regulatory, inhibitory role the left brain plays: that, with its verbal and memory assets, it actually 'talks' the impulsive and emotional right side of the brain out of extreme and impulsive actions; that we need to crystallize our feelings into verbal form in order to manage them. When there's trouble on the line, and there's poor contact between the hemispheres, the impulses have free rein.

Making things even more complex is the fact that the brains of men and women are different. The organization of the brain, and the lay-out of its functions, are different in men and women. Women, broadly speaking, have their brain functions scattered more widely between the two hemispheres, and have many more connections between the various sites, giving them the advantage of being able to make associations between ideas which – to men at least – seems almost magically intuitive. Men have their brain functions in much more compartmentalized little boxes, giving them the advantage of being able to focus on a subject. As we outlined in *BrainSex*, women are better equipped to read body language and emotional clues. For a start, they see and hear better than men do, and have better-tuned senses. They hear the emotion in a voice because they pick up the slight changes in volume and tone to which the man is literally deaf. Since they have a brain that has better internal connections and communication, the emotional right brain is in better contact with the verbal left brain. If it is true that we only fully understand our own emotions when we put what we feel into words, then women by nature are better equipped to understand true feeling and not just their own feelings; significant differences in intuition and empathy for others have been found between men and women; women really can feel another's distress more acutely than can men – something else militating against hurting another person, be it physically or financially.

(There is another interesting difference between men and women. Across the spectrum of mental disadvantage, men are substantially more at risk of brain abnormality – perhaps because of the 're-wiring' process which converts their brains from the female pattern with which they start in the womb.)

From the study of brain damage, and its effects on behaviour, we can begin to gain an insight into the abnormal brain and its links with criminal activities. Epilepsy is a particular case in point. There is nothing criminal about epileptics; it's not even a mental illness, merely a severe neurological dysfunction. But investigation into epilepsy has – literally – opened the brain in a way which helps us to understand deviant behaviour. Some studies of epileptics found that when the area affected lay in the left side of the brain, the damage was sometimes associated with sexual deviation and schizophrenia. Could this mean that the regulatory mechanisms in the left brain had been knocked out, giving free rein to the impulsive side of the individual's nature, while at the same time destroying the cognitive areas – thus promoting schizophrenia, which is, above all, a failure of the cognitive systems and of the differentiation of reality from illusion? It was also discovered that when the damage was in the right side of the brain, where the emotions are stored, the result of this wound was severe manic depression: either because the intact left hemisphere could not govern the right, or because its control messages could not be received.

Phineas Gage, a railway worker, had a large metal rod blown through his skull, as a result of an accident at work. He survived, but damage to the frontal lobes transformed him from a good husband and a likeable and reliable worker into a violent, unreliable and thoroughly unpleasant individual. More recently, in 1968, a helicopter pilot aged thirty-eight crashed into the mountains. He was unconscious for three or four weeks, and within a year of his waking up, his personality had completely changed. Before the accident he had been a perfectly normal, happy personality, with no history of mental problems or any trouble with the police. After it, however, he was a model of psychopathic behaviour, showing no guilt, shame or remorse for the appalling damage he wrought. He left his wife and children and embarked upon a string of different relationships with other women. He could no longer hold down a job, and wandered from town to town, consistently outstaying his welcome. He would cheat and lie, but could still be very charming – as ruefully attested by the many people who 'lent' him money which they never saw again. The helicopter accident had caused severe damage to the frontal and temporal regions of his brain.

There is also the evidence from early brain surgery, however crude. Lobotomy was a process that essentially cut the pathways between the lobes. It was an attempt to put the uncontrolled, emotional or violent part of the brain in exile, isolating it from those parts of the brain which might put such violent emotions into action. Thousands underwent such operations, even though surgeons were operating in the dark; no one really understood the underlying mechanisms of the brain.

There were two principal medical outcomes of this treatment: thousands of patients ended up as emotionless zombies, and doctors began to acquire an understanding of the functional features of the brain. They found, for instance, that when the frontal lobe was isolated, the patient lost the power to look critically at the results of his actions; he couldn't identify or correct mistakes, or verify that his actions were following the prescribed course. On the credit side, the operations resulted in a marked lowering of anxiety or neuroticism and an increase in inappropriate euphoria. Unable to plan or identify critical decisions, there seemed less to worry about. The patients' arousal levels dropped as well. They became less inhibited and tended to get on better socially with other patients. The barriers, in every sense, seemed to have come down.

But other barriers seem to have fallen as well: for instance, some patients with frontal lobe damage on the right side of the brain showed increased anger, aggression and sexual deviancy – the control mechanisms had been cut out. Those with damage to the left side showed little mood change. It is from such a study that we suspect that something in the prefrontal cortex controls and disciplines behaviour, is critically responsible for our power to discriminate, regulate and verify complex behaviour, and enables us to form and carry through plans and intentions. It also seems to hold in check our impulsive, antisocial and sensation-seeking tendencies – including those in the sexual sphere.

But the experts were beginning to dig deeper, and distinguish more specific damage-related behaviour. They looked at damage in the orbitofrontal region, which is the point in the brain where the cortex meets the limbic system – where the rational mind meets the mind's emotional and sensory monitoring and filtering relay station. Damage at this crucial point would mean that there was a break in the chain of mental communication from one level of the brain to the other; the sensory information was being evaluated by the limbic system, but was not getting through to the area responsible for analysis. The orbitofrontal region was unable, then, to 'learn' that certain actions can have unpleasant consequences. The very principle that actions do have consequences is at the heart of moral development; but if a fault in the apparatus fails to school the system, it is not surprising that a heartfelt code of moral conduct is not learned. Criminals may know – intellectually – the difference between right and wrong, but if that knowledge is not accompanied by the necessary feelings and experience, they do not, and in a sense cannot, care.

The behaviour of patients with damage to this area of the brain supports the hypothesis: this broken link was accompanied by a lack of self-control, emotional outbursts, dramatic changes of personality, indifference to or loss of normal guilt, shame or remorse, greater impulsiveness, sexual, aggressive and psychopathic behaviour, and periodic disorders such as mania and depression. The tides of emotion were not being held back by the floodgates of reason. The limbic system was not being regulated by the cortex.

While damage in this area seems to affect our emotions, damage in another area threatens other specific rational processes. Patients with lesions in the prefrontal cortex were studied, and their behaviour monitored. The conclusion was that damage in this particular site compromises our ability to form plans and intentions; it means we cannot work out the consequences of our actions. Massive frontal lobe lesions lead to a loss of foresight, and of the capacity to sustain an intellectual process of thought. People thus affected can't reason in the abstract. Their strategic and tactical senses go by the board. Their attention wanders to a far greater extent than happens normally with people who have not suffered the same damage. They can't concentrate and are not motivated to do so.

Damage in yet another area, the temporal lobes – along each side of our heads – also produces different behaviours, according to exactly where the damage occurs. While the frontal lobes seem to regulate and control our plans and actions, the temporal lobes, as we have said, seem to be related to our own self-awareness and consciousness. The temporal neocortex at the top of the temporal lobes integrates all the incoming sensory information and relates it to what we already know – our memory. So if we see a car coming as we cross the road, we compare the speed of the car with our existing knowledge of the time it takes to cross the road, and pass on the result to parts of the brain dealing with executive actions and bodily motor controls.

Since the temporal lobes are also the headquarters of language, and since, when we think, we think in language, if we get an injury to the left temporal lobe we find it hard to understand the written or spoken word; we find it hard to write, to remember words or conversations, and to follow sequential narrative or logical argument. We may develop epilepsy and suffer from delusions and auditory hallucinations – 'hearing voices', a common symptom of schizophrenia.

Damage to the right temporal lobe has a different effect. It makes it hard for us to recall visual and spatial information, to appreciate the actions of our own bodies (a sense called kinaesthesia) and to discern the qualities of music such as pitch and tone. Mood is disturbed, and there will be experiences of *déjà vu* and its less well-known cousin *jamais vu* – a powerful sense of unreality or depersonalization accompanied by a feeling that one has never before seen what is being perceived, even though it may be a perfectly normal and routine domestic situation.

The temporal lobe surrounds the nut-like amygdala – and other structures of the limbic system – which is associated with emotions such as aggression, anger, love and regret. Aggression and psychosis have been reported in a high percentage of patients with epilepsy localized in the temporal lobe. These patients suffering from lesions in the temporal lobe display unpredictable outbursts of emotion in response to minor frustrations: in the study 40 per cent needed hospital treatment and 47 per cent were viewed as psychopaths – a broad definition meaning that they displayed deeply antisocial behaviour, seemed callous, and had no regard to other people's feelings. The suggestion, then, is that the temporal lobes, as well as the left frontal areas of the brain, have the task of regulating and controlling the emotions nurtured in the amygdala; damage to them means that aggression is off the leash.

So how does all this fit in with our juvenile offenders, those with conduct disorder, attention deficit disorder, hyperactivity and all the other differently designated behavioural problems which are such powerful indicators of later adult criminality? Many certainly display the same sort of disorders as would result from some of the brain damage outlined above. For instance, the inability to govern actions, resist impulses, learn by mistakes or understand the consequences of actions, and failure to plan ahead or accommodate their behaviour to changed circumstances, have all been noted under the different definitions of childhood misconduct, and have all been identified as the consequence of specific brain deficits. The big question is, to what extent are they connected; is this bad behaviour the result of a brain which is not working or of one that is functioning in a normal manner?

The answer is crucial. All the evidence suggests a strong link between dysfunction in the brain and criminal behaviour. All adults diagnosed as having antisocial personality disorders were once children with conduct disorders or behavioural problems, and began their criminal careers at an early age. So did underlying, innate brain deficits doom them to a criminal career? Is the root of crime not so much badness as – however you define the term – madness?

Many researchers think so; they believe there is 'substantial evidence for the significant role of brain dysfunction in the genesis of violent criminal behaviour'.[1]

In 1971 Professor Lorne Yeudall, a clinical neuropsychologist working in Canada, undertook a major study into the relationship between psychopathology (the scientific study of mental disorders and the way they manifest themselves in behaviour) and neurological functions (the mechanism of the brain). Two thousand offenders were subjected to neurophysiological tests. These were described as habitual criminals who had not responded to efforts to rehabilitate them, and who in consequence had not even tried to 'go straight' and so returned, time after time, to gaol. What became startlingly clear was the high incidence of deficit and dysfunction in the frontal and temporal regions of the brain of these patients. The consistency was staggering: brain damage was identified in 90 per cent of the 2,000. The principal finding was damage to the frontal lobes, resulting in either depressed, apathetic and indifferent personality disorders or aggressive, impulsive antisocial personality disorders – the precise outcome depending on the exact site of the impairment.

Small wonder that these prisoners had not responded to efforts to rehabilitate them if they were already the prisoners of their own brain deficits.

Since then Yeudall and a host of researchers have discovered further evidence of a link between a characteristic behaviour pattern and damage to the frontal and temporal regions of the brain. In many instances the misconduct manifests itself early on in life – and bears 'a rather striking resemblance to the behavioural traits of the persistent criminal'. Many factors can cause such neurophysical damage. It can be the result of genetic inheritance, prenatal complications, actual head trauma, convulsions, or a disease called limbic encephalitis. And since, as we know, the brain is intricately interlinked, damage to one section has an effect on other sections; disconnection between the three levels of the brain can result in a host of behavioural problems.

This, researchers like Yeudall and Flor-Henry believe, is the genesis of much criminal behaviour; episodic violence or sexual deviations, they believe, are fundamentally rooted in neurobiology, the result of disturbances in one or more of the brain systems. Damage to the regulatory left brain may – the picture is still confusing – lead to the dominance of the impulsive right brain – yet damage to the right brain can also lead to an excess of right-brain impulsiveness as well as depression.

Experts believe that the criminal die is cast during childhood; by adulthood it is too late to intervene. They are also convinced that, with the proper diagnostic tools, such future, habitual offenders can be – and have to be – identified in their earlier years. The internal damage – brain dysfunction on maybe only a minimal scale – must be identified, before the external damage to society is done. In a later chapter we will suggest how the manifestations of such underlying dysfunction can be recognized early.

A whole battery of neuropsychological tests, developed over the years with people who have recognizable brain damage to very specific areas, is available to find out whether or not the brain is working as it should. These tests have proved to be a very accurate measure of an underlying brain dysfunction. That's why we can be confident in – as well as disturbed by – the results of another neurological examination of convicts in 1988, which found that the presence of brain abnormality was one of the strongest predictors of 'impatient assault'.

You meet a lot of men like Harry F. in gaol. During years spent in the prison gymnasium he has tautened his body to a whipcord, with a sinewy leanness. There's nothing obviously menacing about him, but it's clear that the other inmates give him a wide berth. No one wants to get into an argument with him – because Harry F. is dangerous in an argument. Fury erupts – seemingly – from nowhere. The slightest frustration can ignite his wrath and aggression. Anything to hand – a pool cue, a chair, a fire extinguisher, even once the keys of a prison officer – serves as a weapon. When released, his pattern of offending is consistent: he cannot hold down a job at best because of a lack of persistent application, at worst because through boredom, frustration, a misjudged comment or an apparent slight he will lash out and assault his boss or his workmates and trash the factory.

His problem can almost certainly be categorized as 'impatient assault' – so prison, by definition a catalogue of curtailed freedoms and frustration, is the very worst environment for him, compounding his frustrations. We would not treat a hay-fever sufferer by locking him up in a room with an artificially high pollen count. Yet that's exactly what we are doing to Harry F.

Highly violent schizophrenic patients, when compared with a non-violent schizophrenic control group, showed a greater degree of neurological and neuropsychological damage. The same syndrome was observed with mentally subnormal offenders: those with a history of violence displayed greater brain damage than those without. A group of psychiatric in-patients was examined for the presence of frontal cerebral lesions; such damage, accompanied by a history of seizure, was among the strongest predictors of violent behaviour.

Other investigations have shown that adult violent offenders have more neuropsychological deficits than those who commit crimes against property. A study of a sexual sadist, comparing him with other sexually aggressive and non-aggressive offenders, found specific brain abnormalities. (We will devote a specific chapter to sexual crimes later on.)

Thus a clear link is emerging between brain damage and criminality. An Israeli researcher who has been studying the violent and criminal mind for many years is convinced that the overwhelming problem with violent criminal offending lies with left brain damage. As we know, the left brain normally controls the emotional and impulsive right brain, and when damaged it leaves the right brain without its normal control mechanisms. Left-handers, he argues more controversially, are more prone to criminal behaviour. Since the left side of the body is controlled by the right side of the brain, a left-handed person has a dominant right brain. Israel Nachshon's argument is that the more the right brain dominates the personality, the more the subject will be at the mercy of his or her own impulsive, emotional behaviour. The evidence of one survey is that left-handers constituted 65 per cent of those arrested – way out of proportion to their representation in the population. The complication here is that in some left-handers the functions of the brain hemispheres are transposed – so that while the right hemisphere may be dominant, it is, in fact, the rational hemisphere rather than the seat of impulses and emotions which it is for right-handers.

So far we have concentrated on damage to the major, exterior blocks of the cortex, the frontal and temporal lobes. It's time to go deeper.

We have seen that the limbic system – brain level two, below the cortex and above the reptilian functions of the brain stem – is a group of interconnected brain structures that are involved in the regulation and generation of a number of emotional behaviours – including the flight, feeding, fighting and sexual motivators. Our feelings of fear, love, hate and so on are all generated within the limbic system in response to the incoming sensory messages which it receives.

Within the limbic system, the amygdala, a large nut-shaped structure with intimate links to both the temporal and orbito-frontal areas of the brain, is one of the key areas where malfunction can be linked to aggressive and violent behaviour. Stimulation of the amygdala in animals produced different behaviours, according to the precise region stimulated: in one area it would produce aggression, in another the reaction of flight and fear. Another area seemed to be the general site of aggression; closer investigation revealed that the basolateral region of the amygdala was responsible for defensive and protective maternal aggression, while in the centromedial amygdala was to be found the trigger for competitive aggressive acts. In cats, fear, flight and aggression responses were all found in separate and distinct parts of the amygdala.

Operations to remove the amygdala in monkeys resulted in a marked change in temperament. They became altogether less belligerent, while also becoming less terrified of objects which hitherto had been a cause of fear. There were some unexplained side-effects, such as a new tendency to eat inappropriate things and an increase in unusual sexual behaviours, as well as the loss of the ability to recognize familiar objects; but overall the operation was characterized by a general reduction in emotionality – including anger and fear – and an increase in sociability and sexuality.

The area seems to be the major site for fear and anxiety, in humans as well as animals. Removal of the amygdala has proved to have an effect on the behaviour of aggressive and violent people. Episodic treatment or wholesale destruction of the amygdala both result in a marked reduction of aggressive behaviour – an outcome which lobotomy cannot achieve.

One of the most graphic ways to investigate the brain is the PET scan, which shows up the degree of electrical activity going on. (High activity shows up as red, low as blue, and there is a whole spectrum of colours in between.) The American expert Ruben Gur did a PET scan study on a man who underwent a dramatic psychological change from a loving husband to a rapist and murderer after a car accident. The scan shows a deeply damaged amygdala. 'When I saw the scan it made my hair stand on end,' he said. He testified in the court hearing that the man was in the grip of emotions too powerful and alien to control, but the man was convicted and given a death sentence.

Another key area is the hypothalamus. This is a small but vital structure sited at the base of the brain under the thalamus.

In its central position, with connections to the entire limbic structure, it is known to be involved in many different areas of brain activity; but for years it has been regarded as the brain's emotional centre. The hypothalamus is an essential, biological determinant in our personality. Along with other limbic systems it organizes behaviour that is essential to survival: feeding, sexual behaviour, fighting, fleeing and emotional reactions connected with these behaviours. It is also one of the sites for intrinsic reward and punishment systems discovered by self-stimulation studies where the subject learns how to procure pleasurable sensations; and it exerts control over the pituitary gland, which in turn regulates the endocrine system, including the sex hormones. Selective destruction of the hypothalamus also reduced violence, just as it did in the amygdala, indicating that these two areas play an important part in violent and hostile behaviour. Damage to the hypothalamus can interfere with or destroy activities essential to survival; in rats, destruction of the lateral section of the hypothalamus prevents them from eating and drinking. It destroys not the ability to eat or drink, but the motivation to seek sustenance.

A healthy personality clearly depends on an intact, functioning brain. The more damage to the brain, the greater the psychiatric disturbance. That was about as far as we could go, until the explosion of research into the brain, and its links with offending behaviour. PET scans have advanced the science exponentially, because we no longer need to use invasive techniques; by stimulating the subject in differing ways, we can see what area of the brain is activated, so making the graphic link between behaviour and brain function through direct investigation of the basic physiological and biochemical processes of the brain.

PET scans represent a vast advance even over the comparatively modern electroencephalograms or EEGs; scans of four violent patients revealed cases of brain abnormality which had not been picked up by the old EEG technology. Two of them had a history of repetitive acts of violence, including rape, homicide and arson; neither of them showed any comprehension of the ethical implications of their behaviour. PET scans revealed that they had damage in their frontal lobes. The frontal lobes, as we know, are involved in abstract reasoning and problem-solving; damage in this area would seem to accord with a failure to grasp moral and ethical implications of actions. Scans on the other two showed defects in the cortex, which were more marked in the left hemisphere. Again, both subjects had demonstrated repetitive violent behaviour, but differed from the other two in showing intense emotional arousal and lack of control. That would square with the failure of the controlling left brain. They sometimes had no recall of the violent incident, and the event was followed by repentance and depressed feelings. When the moment had passed, they still had their moral faculties intact.

In the past, the tools were not sophisticated enough to make clear and consistent correlations. But now we can confidently say that all these investigations into brain damage show that it is clearly associated with that small proportion of offenders who cause most of the problems – the chronic, recidivist, often purposelessly violent criminal. He is one of that 6 per cent of offenders who, according to one study, perpetrate 55 per cent of crime. He is the man who is statistically most likely to have abnormal brain function, and where biology will be found to be at the root of his violence. The cerebral mechanisms involved are still being unravelled; but his damage is almost certainly to be found in either the frontal lobes – controlling executive functions – the temporal lobe or the limbic system, where the emotions are stored and moderated.

It must be said again that there are many, complex routes to violence – cultural, biological, physiological and psychological. All may in some way contribute to each other – for instance, psychological motivation may be the result of the interplay between biochemistry, neurophysiology and social environment. There is no one explanation. But the findings we have outlined cause us to ask, once again, whether some of these 'mindless' violent offenders are, quite literally, out of their proper mind. Are they really in a position to exercise the self-restraint that prevents most of us committing a hot-blooded act of aggression?

Any dysfunction in the frontal lobe, temporal lobe, cortex or limbic system can lead to violent, impulsive behaviour. Our brains are designed to receive and process information, and to formulate appropriate responses. Any misconnection, short-circuit or structural damage results in corrupted reactions. At present, scientists still have much to learn about what precisely goes wrong, but a picture is emerging. The same criminal offence can be caused by a host of different brain deficits. But fascinating new discoveries have shown that different types of damage are associated with different sorts of criminal behaviour. Problems in the frontal lobe or limbic system can be clearly linked to violent, impulsive and apparently callous, unthinking behaviour; temporal lobe damage is also associated with violence – though, as we will see, it can be associated with sexual deviancy. Damage of less severe degree in the frontal lobe and sometimes in the language area of the temporal lobe can be linked to persistent criminality. The next question – which we will explore in the next chapter – is this: could all categories of crime – from infanticide to serial sex killings – be clearly linked to specifically different types of brain damage?

CHAPTER 6

Born and Made?

JUST AS NO SINGLE card can win a game, so being dealt, by nature, one unfavourable biological card is not enough to condemn the recipient to a life of crime. Hormones, neurotransmitters, brain structure and malfunction all contribute. And they have something else in common: they, in turn, are all influenced by genes. We may literally inherit the unsought legacy of the chemistry and biology which makes us criminal.

Thirty years ago two baby boys were adopted at birth by different families. They lived entirely apart; they neither saw each other nor even knew of each other's existence. The only thing they seemed to have in common was that they were both adopted into similar, working-class Ohio households. But when investigators began to research into the fate of the twins they found that there was an astonishing number of other similarities. As children in their separate schools both had liked mathematics but had been poor at spelling. Both worked part-time as deputy sheriffs, had holidays in Florida and drove Chevrolet cars. Both had dogs called Toy and had married women called Linda. Both had divorced and both had remarried women called Betty. One named his son James Allan. The other had his son christened James Alan. Both like mechanical drawing and carpentry, have almost identical drinking and smoking patterns and chew their fingernails. Both suffer from haemorrhoids, and have identical pulses, blood pressures and sleep patterns. Both inexplicably gained ten pounds in weight at the same time, and suffer from 'mixed headache syndrome'. They did, however, have different hairstyles, and one expressed himself better in speech, while the other was better in writing.

The coincidences are eerie, and you would expect to read

about them in a sensationalist newspaper or a cheap magazine; but they are in fact the product of a major scientific investigation into the outcome of adopted twins. This Minnesota Study of Twins Reared Apart – MISTRAL – one of scores of such research projects – has the principal purpose of helping us disentangle those traits that are conditioned by our environment from those, if any, with which we are born. Clearly, in an investigation into the biological roots of crime, twin studies are essential.

Few contemporary criminologists would argue that anyone is a 'born criminal'; most believe that there is a subtle interplay between what we are and what we make of that, between the person we are born as, and the forces of fate, destiny, environment, family, society or opportunity which mould or modify our identity. Even the famous Italian physician, Cesare Lombroso – the nineteenth-century father of criminology, who is often mocked for his physiological theories – accepted the influence of parents and society. Although Lombroso believed that the criminal was the product of a genetic constitution, and that criminality could be indirectly inherited through contact with 'degenerates' such as the insane or alcoholics, he also considered poor education to be one of the contributory causes of crime. In his later writing he concluded that one third of offenders were doomed to criminal careers from birth, while the rest were the product of external factors. The work was echoed in England, where Charles Goring studied 3,000 convicts and concluded that their criminality was the product of genetic forces rather than the abuse of free will.

Lombroso's methodology was suspect – we now know that it was based on a highly unrepresentative sample which included many mentally ill people. But at least he began the process of bringing a scientific, empirical and statistical model to criminology, and in shifting the debate away from the moral and religious arena.

Unfortunately, the more scientific knowledge unfolded, the more complicated the moral perspectives became. As knowledge grew about genetic inheritance, for instance, so did anxiety that unscrupulous regimes would use that knowledge to seek to abort the criminal foetus, castrate the criminal father or sterilize the criminal mother. As the Nazi period was to show, such anxieties were not groundless. The mentally ill, after all, were the original candidates for the gas chambers in the quest for racial purity. But the fact that science can be perverted and put to evil uses does not invalidate the science itself – it simply reminds us of the responsibility that knowledge brings.

The growth of projects like the Minnesota twins study provides some fascinating insights into the power of genetic inheritance. The study investigated every aspect of the life histories of twins who had been separated at birth – their medical histories, physiology, tastes, psychological inclinations, abilities and intelligence. Each pair was subjected to six days of intensive testing.

Whereas the two boys we described at the beginning of the chapter had been raised in roughly similar families, the backgrounds of twin brothers Oskar and Jack couldn't have been more dissimilar. Oskar Stohr and Jack Yufe were born in Trinidad of a Jewish father and German mother. Shortly after birth, Oskar was taken back to Germany and raised as a Catholic by his mother; his adoptive grandmother had strong political sympathies and converted him to Nazi ideology. Jack, meanwhile, stayed in the Caribbean, where he was raised as a Jew. Both, naturally, lead very different lives; and yet both wear wire-rimmed glasses, both have moustaches, both like spicy foods and are absent-minded. Both think it's funny to sneeze in front of strangers; both flush the lavatory before using it, read magazines back to front, dip buttered toast in their coffee and store rubber bands on their wrists. Both are domineering towards women – even though Oskar was raised by women and Jack grew up among men.

Bridget and Dorothy were identical twins who only met each other for the first time after thirty-eight years apart. They, too, grew up in very different sorts of families – yet, when at last they came to know of each other they found that they had named their sons Richard Andrew and Andrew Richard, and their daughters Catherine Louise and Karen Louise. Each had manicured hands, wore seven rings, carried two bracelets on one wrist, and a watch and a bracelet on the other. No one suggests that Dorothy and Bridget had a gene which commanded them to wear seven rings. But what they certainly had was a gene, or a collection of genes on different chromosomes, which contributed, for instance, to producing attractive hands and fingers.

Then there were the so-called 'giggle sisters' who developed, quite independently, the compulsion to laugh at virtually everything. They also shared identical ways of coping with stress, by ignoring it, and avoiding conflict and controversy – a psychological trait which is classically regarded as learned behaviour. This emotional and psychological overlap in twins is well attested. They are frequently found to share the same or similar phobias, and suffer comparable depressions. Even twins who had been brought up in very different emotional environments – one disciplinarian, the other warm and loving – both showed similar neurotic, hypochondriacal traits. Features such as aggression and altruism seem also, strangely, to be inherited. The overall finding of the Minnesota study was that the social or domestic environment generally plays a modest role in the determination of personality traits.

So – crime apart – the evidence suggests that personality and tastes are to a degree inherited or hereditable. This won't please the social scientists; it never has. There is still a widespread suspicion of explanations which rely on or incorporate genetic explanations for behaviour. But we believe, on the basis of a mass of scientific research, that a genetic process – probably involving the interplay of a number of combining genes – contributes to personality – including criminal personality.

But first, what exactly do we mean by personality, and how do we measure it?

There's good reason to be suspicious of a scientific attempt to rationalize something as elusive as personality. Over the centuries there have been widely differing theories. The Greeks believed that emotions were sited in particular organs of the body. The Elizabethans believed in a constant flux of 'humours' – such as the sanguine, choleric, melancholic and phlegmatic. Another problem is that in our desire to dissect behaviour and personality, we are too anxious to compartmentalize; most people, for instance, are neither extroverts nor introverts, but ambiverts, people who are a bit of both.

To satisfy the thesis that aspects of personality can be inherited, a trait needs to be consistent, continuous and stable in the particular individual. It should also be capable of being linked with a particular area of the nervous system and there should be an equivalent to be found in other animal species.

Attempts to simplify the human spirit are never easy, but there is growing support for defining personality on five major criteria, or 'five robust factors'. These are:

1. Extroversion/dominance: is the subject dominant or submissive, talkative or taciturn, candid or secretive, adventurous or cautious, sociable or reclusive?
2. Agreeableness/aggression: good-natured or irritable, jealous or generous, mild or headstrong, co-operative or negative and aloof?
3. Conscientiousness: fussy or careless about tidiness, responsible or undependable, scrupulous or casual, persevering or a quitter?
4. Emotional stability/neuroticism: poised or nervous, calm or anxious, composed or excitable, hypochondriacal or confident about well-being?
5. Culture: artistically sensitive or insensitive, intellectual or unthinking, narrow or broad, refined or crude, imaginative or straightforward?

It's a crude division, and other researchers have subdivided *ad infinitum*; adventurousness, for instance, can be broken down into four sub-factors – thrill-seeking, experience-seeking, disinhibition, and susceptibility to boredom. Or fearfulness can be refined into fear of small animals, and then further into fear of specific animals. Anxiety can be divided into fear of failure or fear of being seen to fail. But, as a useful working model, the five-way division has proved to have remarkable durability. Rather like the primary colours, we can mix the various factors to produce shades, tones and different colours – hence dominance mixed with hostility can result in the bully. In the same way, one characteristic minus another yields a different result. Scientists distinguish between 'additive' effects, when many similar genes combine to increase a particular effect, and 'non-additive', when a random combination of different genes creates an unpredictable outcome. The influence of dominant or recessive genes means that traits can be neutralized or mitigated. Just as dominance plus hostility added up to a pretty nasty combination, a gene for agreeableness instead of hostility will result in a less unpleasant outcome. Dominance plus agreeableness might make you a charming persuader – a good salesman, perhaps.

Different mixes cause different interactions, which makes it hard to find consistent traits in families – brother and sister, for instance, will have different blends of genetic input. That's where identical twins help explain genetic inheritance, because they share all their genes identically. They are also likely to have been brought up in a similar fashion; so to make sure that we are not confusing cultural or social factors with genetic ones, we have to compare them with ordinary (fraternal) twins, who, while sharing the same upbringing, do not share identical genes. In 1929, nine twin studies found that identical twins are twice as likely as fraternal twins to be similar with regard to criminal activity. The largest study showed evidence that identical twins are three times more likely to be alike than fraternal twins – suggesting that there is some shared genetic characteristic which may increase the risk of both being registered for criminal behaviour. The results have been criticized because studies have shown that identical twins are more likely to be treated alike than fraternal twins, so the identical nature of their upbringing may have some influence.

Another way of extracting and identifying the influence of inheritance is by studying the behaviour of adopted children compared with that of both their adopting and their natural parents. The more the adopted child takes after the biological parents, the greater the inheritance quotient, whereas the more he or she takes after the adoptive parent, the greater the influence of upbringing.

A key Danish study set out on the track of the elusive 'criminal gene' by seeing what happened to the children of criminal or non-criminal natural parents, adopted by criminal or non-criminal families. A study of 5,483 adoptions in Copenhagen showed that the rate of criminal behaviour of the adopted sons of criminal fathers was considerably higher than that of boys whose fathers had no criminal record. One crude statistic among several Danish adoption studies is that of those adoptees who came from criminal families 50 per cent acquired a criminal record, yet out of those adoptees who came from non-criminal families only 5 per cent deviated from the straight and narrow. Other studies, particularly involving property crime, show a close association between antisocial behaviour of adoptees and biological parents. It's that sort of finding that makes Mednick and others believe that there is 'a solid case for the involvement of genes in . . . deviant human behaviour and criminality'[1] – that some biological characteristics, which may play a part in causing involvement in criminal activity, can be inherited. The picture emerging from all the adoption, twin and family studies means 'that we should take seriously the idea that some biological characteristics can be genetically involved in causing a person to become involved in criminal activity.'[2]

The picture comes into sharper focus when the criminal or non-criminal background of the adopting parents is taken into account. A two-decade investigation of 14,427 children yielded the following results:

Parental background	Criminal outcome
Neither adoptive nor biological families involved in crime	13.5 per cent of sons had criminal records
Adoptive families involved in crime, but not biological	14.7 per cent of sons had criminal records
Biological parent had criminal record, but not adoptive	20 per cent of sons had criminal records
Adoptive and biological families involved in crime	24.5 per cent of sons had criminal records

This study was mainly looking at non-violent property crime, and found no discernible link between violence and heredity, unless the mental health of the biological parent was taken into account: biological parents who had a drink problem or who were schizophrenic were more likely to have violent offspring.

Something else also came out of the survey: the persistence of offending seemed to have a biological dimension, too. Chronic offenders – and they are the ones that matter, since 4 per cent of the adoptees accounted for 70 per cent of the crimes committed by those in the survey – were more likely than others to have biological parents who had multiple convictions. As the report concluded, 'This extremely high rate of convictions among a very small number of adoptees whose parents were multiple offenders suggests genetic predisposition plays an especially important role in their criminality.'[3]

There's even a fascinating hint from the studies that the very type of crime may have a hereditary component. The adoption data from various studies suggests that petty property criminals have a genetic predisposition distinct from that of violent offenders. The likelihood of an inherited factor involving property crimes is 78 per cent, and that of crimes against people 50 per cent.

But the genes do not act in isolation: hormones play their part. One study concluded that genetic factors lie dormant until the hormonal tides of puberty come into play; that criminality in parents is more strongly associated with delinquency in their offspring after puberty than before. Again, non-criminal behaviour may be genetically inherited which of itself leads to criminal behaviour. Alcoholism, for instance, may be an inherited trait – and the link between alcohol and crime, which we have already explored, is too blatant to need stressing. One of the best predictors of antisocial behaviour in the adoptees sample is having a biological relative who is either antisocial or alcoholic.

Class, also, seems to be a complicating factor. One controversial finding was that children born to parents from a lower social class had the highest rates of criminality – no matter what type of family they were adopted into.

There's widespread acknowledgment that 'the interaction between genes and environment appears to be crucial.'[4] The sort of home you grow up in, and the values that surround you, obviously play their part. But the conclusion of one leading researcher is that 'evidence from family, twin and adoption studies strongly suggests that genetic factors do have a role to play in understanding crime. While some studies favour genetic influences and others maintain that environmental factors exert greater force, there is overall general agreement that there is an interaction between genetic and environmental factors which is crucial.'[5]

Let us now review those factors which we have already found to be significant in determining criminal propensity, and see if they have a genetic dimension.

We have seen low intelligence linked to criminal behaviour – and the evidence here is that IQ levels are in large part inherited. Twins adopted into separate homes were studied, and found to have similar IQs. This may, of course, have to do with the fact that social workers try to place children in similar homes, or that the adopting class is characterized by similar, shared educational values and attitudes. Nevertheless, the MISTRAL study concluded that environmental factors cannot explain the coincidence of IQ parity. In particular, reading disabilities seemed to have a genetic component.

The individual levels of testosterone, and the androgen family of hormones, can also be passed on genetically – another way in which the potential for aggression or violence may 'run in the family'.

There was also the matter of low brain arousal. Nearly two hundred electroencephalograms – EEGs – studied the brain patterns of identical twins, who are monozygotic, the product of the same original maternal egg. The investigation focused on traits which are known to be inherited, influenced by the genetic process. This, and other studies, confirmed that identical twins had almost identical brain patterns. And the same is true of the arousability of the reticular formation, that crucial process which, in some unfortunates, is so deadened that they need more and more extreme stimuli – including the thrill that delinquency can bring. The extent of arousability varies from individual to individual, but the latest research shows that it has a definite genetic component – possibly in conjunction with hormones.

The closely-related phenomenon of low serotonin levels, too, is influenced by heredity. Low levels of this chemical messenger result in a decrease in control over our impulses, leading to uncontrolled aggression – and this firmly biological link with criminal offending is a stable, inheritable characteristic in all primates, including man. Serotonin levels vary enormously between individuals – by a factor of up to twelve – and the actual genetic geography is complex; several genes at various loci are believed to be involved. Sex-linked genes seem to play the leading part in setting the serotonin levels.

Perhaps the biggest advance in this area comes from the work of a Dutch team at the Department of Human Genetics at the University Hospital, Nijmegen. They have examined MAO, the enzymes which metabolize serotonin, dopamine and norepinaphrine and which act as chemical markers for serotonin. Recently a mutant of the MAO family of enzymes has been identified in several males who suffered borderline mental retardation, and who also displayed high levels of impulsive behaviour including aggression, arson, rape, voyeurism and exhibitionism. The females of the family had normal intelligence. The key seems to lie in damage to the X chromosomes in the area which controls the genes for MAO-A and MAO-B, which, though carried by the women, is only 'switched on' in men. Broadening out the implications, the suggestion is that impulsive behaviour, a constituent of crime which is the direct result of abnormal serotonin levels, may be the result of a genetic deficiency.

We are merely on the threshold of genetic understanding – but it would be perverse to overlook the evidence of a genetic contribution to many of the circumstances which predispose to crime. And some of those turn out, as we will see, to be surprising.

But what about the brain dysfunction/damage which, in the last chapter, we have seen so closely related to criminality? Does that, too, have a genetic component? In one very obvious sense, the answer is yes – because being born male is a matter of genes, and being born male is, in respect of crime, a severe disadvantage.

Those brain abnormalities which cause behavioural and temperamental disorders which lead to a greater likelihood of conflict with the law are often the result of prenatal damage. This effect is not strictly genetic, although there is a gender difference here again. Men are much more likely than women to suffer such damage. The reasons for this are not well understood, but the hypothesis is that since the basic blueprint is female, and it's the addition of androgens or hormones that creates the male, there is more scope for things to go wrong.

If the child has survived undamaged while in the womb, the next obstacle to surmount is birth itself, when the danger of brain damage leading to a mind to crime is just as great. A number of studies indicate that birth trauma, be it lack of oxygen or forceps delivery, is predictive of later impulsive criminal offences; delinquent children are much more likely than normal children to have suffered some form of perinatal damage, and in serious delinquents (those incarcerated in penal institutions) the damage is greater than in offenders who are not locked up. Studies on women who were ill during their pregnancies or who had difficult births are predictive of a higher level of aggressive behaviour in their children. The evidence suggests that central nervous system damage makes it harder to control impulsive behaviour.

This was demonstrated in a study of more than eighty juvenile delinquents at a regional correctional school who were compared with non-incarcerated delinquents of the same age and social class. The average number of offences in the first group was twelve, compared with an average of two among the others. Of the 'hard' group, 36 per cent had committed violent offences such as assault, threatening behaviour, arson and robbery compared with 6 per cent of the non-incarcerated group. The seriously delinquent children were found to have suffered a difficult birth – particularly those who were violent. Other cultural and social disadvantages aggravated the situation, as the survey found when it examined the correlation between violence and parental neglect; if the child had been removed from the mother during the first year of life, this mix of brain damage and neglect was even more predictive of violent crime than either neglect or brain damage alone.

This has led to the conclusion that there are 'identifiable biopsychosocial factors'[6] which combine to contribute to violent delinquent behaviour. Coming from an emotionally deprived home, such as would be characterized by neglect, is one such factor. Damage to the central nervous system – damage that weakens self-control in early life, leading to impulsive, violent offending in later life – is another. If you are also neglected, it is much more likely that this behaviour is expressed, given that such a child usually has not been taught the social norms of conduct. There is a clue here – which we will go into more deeply later in the book – as to how we can seek to remedy some of the disadvantages of those who are born with an innate vulnerability to crime.

Other studies indicate that inherited characteristics and pre-natal influences can also affect a child's antisocial potential. A random sample of 9,000 children in Copenhagen, followed up over a period of years, showed that those who had suffered prenatal or perinatal stress were much more likely to be aggressive and indulge in bullying at or by the age of eighteen. The damage, typically the result of problems such as hypoxia (severe lack of oxygen), may be related to later neuropsy-chiatric disturbances such as schizophrenia, impaired intelli-gence or achievement, attention deficit disorder and reading failure. Directly or indirectly, complications in pregnancy or childbirth may lead to behavioural disorders and delin-quency.

What is strange is the degree to which pre-existing physical injuries – some of them blatant – seem to have been overlooked by the medical authorities at the penal institution where the study of incarcerated young offenders took place. Among the boys, whose average age was fifteen, there was a high preva-lence of head and face injury, incidence of seizure and other neurological problems such as fainting, epilepsy and blackouts; 90 per cent had suffered a major accident of one form or another, 85 per cent had suffered severe head injury and half had experienced perinatal problems. The serious delinquents were much more likely to have sustained severe head and face injury than the less serious. Especially violent children had more prenatal difficulties, accidents and injuries than did their less violent incarcerated peers. The question is, does delin-quency increase the chances of injury, or does injury increase the chances of delinquency? The authors of the study suggest that a combination of early trauma to the central nervous system, parental psychopathy and social deprivation is respon-sible for subsequent serious delinquency. But there is certainly 'increasing evidence that there is an association between ad-verse medical events, particularly those affecting the central nervous system, and serious behaviour disorders including delinquency'.[7]

Among the constellation of factors which predispose a child to a criminal career, the influence of the family is powerful. The fact that we have concerned ourselves primarily with biological sources of criminal offending does not mean that we ignore the traditional, social explanations; it is just that we approach them on the same, statistical basis – and statistics and studies yield evidence which shows the relevant and relative influence of the family in the formation of delinquency.

The interaction between parent and child is critical in the development of the child's sense of conscience, self-control and responsibility. Much depends on the sense of attachment between parent and child, and the child's desire for parental approval. These help to shape the child's ability and inclination to take account of the more distant consequences of present actions – the development of a conscience, an internal constraint against certain actions which could call down parental disapproval.

That's not to say that everything depends on the nature of the interaction between mother and child. Babies may come into the world morally neutral, but we have seen that they display from the moment of birth an underlying psychopathology; that they come with minds of their own, and with their minds to a large extent already made up; that they can be classified into easy or difficult children; and that there are also innate sex differences. Quite independent of family influences, the difficult children may develop as withdrawn, irregular in habit and tearful, inactive or subject to tantrums; 70 per cent of such children will later develop behavioural problems needing psychiatric help, while only 18 per cent of the 'easy' babies had such problems. The fact of a constitutional, innate personality is also demonstrated by blind studies of identical twins; observers did not know which twins were identical (monozygotic) and which merely fraternal twins, but simply by observing similarities of temperament they knew which children were which.

The evidence is strong that, given this innate personality, a failure to bond with the mother causes great developmental harm, and that the absence of warmth and the lack of an intimate and continuous relationship leads to later behavioural problems including depression and delinquency. This is a bland enough statement of conventional social wisdom, but it has some factual rigour behind it. Much research has been done retrospectively on children raised in orphanages. Some children survived the experience better than others – and researchers asked why. They found that in almost every case where the children developed healthily they had lived with the biological mother in the first year of life. Another finding was that children placed with foster parents were more likely to form a bond with them if they had been in the orphanage for less than three years. Any longer, and the fostered infants seemed less capable of developing a sense of right and wrong, the need to observe rules and the ability to form lasting relationships. The studies showed that children with a strong sense of attachment grew up with greater self-esteem, while those with weaker bonds would show more impulsive, aggressive behaviour.

What a child is born with, and how the child develops a bond, clearly impact upon each other. A naturally difficult child may prove harder to hug, teach, enfold – especially by families who are under pressure already from the influence of poor housing, poverty, or domestic strife. Such a child inherits a double deficit. A poor outcome is not inevitable, but more likely.

Most of us, according to a prevailing theory of social control, would be delinquent if we were not taught the importance of approval, reward and punishment. In the early years – and it is between the ages of one and two that a child begins to develop a crucial sense of self – the parents (or lack of them) are central to the inculcation of such notions – or the lack of them. It is the parents who can influence the strength of the rewards for good behaviour, by helping the child to want approval, and by making that approval contingent on good behaviour.

Most research suggests that punishment in itself may not affect the behaviour of the child; it may even have an adverse effect. If the punishment is not logical, straightforward and consistent it may merely confuse the child. Investigators compared families with problem children and families with no delinquency or antisocial behaviour. The families differed not in whether they punished their offspring but in the manner in which punishment was meted out. The problem families did not know how to punish; they were less likely to state clear rules and to punish violations of those rules. The rules were altered or abandoned in an unpredictable manner, and punishments were random and episodic – such as a sudden slap in the middle of a conversation with others. The findings suggest that an irritable parent who does not discipline effectively tends to produce aggressive children, while the children of an indifferent and ineffective parent have a tendency to thieve.

In 1937, the University of Cambridge, Massachusetts, began a colossal, long-term study to predict delinquency. It selected 650 boys. Half were chosen because their teachers or social workers thought it likely that they would become delinquent, and the other half because they were considered to be normal boys. The study began at the age of eleven, well before any members of either half had committed delinquent acts. The objective was to test the efficiency of counselling on delinquency. The boys were randomly assigned to treatment/control groups. There was little evidence that counselling worked; the real, accidental value of the study was what it revealed about the relationship of delinquency to family background.

Eighteen years later, the great mass of records was analysed blind – that is, none of the analysts knew which of the boys had been convicted of a crime and which had not. The result, though, was startlingly apparent: children who were then revealed as delinquent were twice as likely to come from homes where parental discipline had been rated, all those years ago, as erratic or lax. Delinquents were also more likely to come from homes that were quarrelsome than from those where there was an affectionate atmosphere. Of the boys who came from families which were not only quarrelsome, but also had erratic discipline, 25 per cent were found to have been convicted of crimes. A principal factor seemed to be the attitude and conduct of the mother.

The big London study of 400 at-risk boys found much the same: that persistently delinquent boys had had parents who were cruel, neglectful or passive where discipline was involved. We already know from that study about the link between persistent delinquency and low IQ; here was another element stacking the odds in favour of delinquency. The full catalogue, the royal flush of criminal predictors, were, according to Farringdon and West, low IQ, a large family, parental criminality, low income, and poor childraising practices.

Evidence that divorce or single-parenthood contributes to criminality is less clear-cut. For more than half a century, juvenile delinquency has been blamed on the harmful influence of parental absence. In the 1920s, boys at New York state reformatories were compared with boys in normal local schools; the delinquents were found to be twice as likely to come from families where one of the parents was absent. Other American, as well as British, studies produced similar results – single-parent families were more common among incarcerated delinquents than among a random sample of the population. So convincing was the data that by the mid-1960s Senator Daniel Moynihan issued a call to encourage stable, two-parent families among American blacks as a contribution to crime prevention. Although this dramatic intervention – multiple heresy by today's politically correct standards – forced the issue on to the agenda, several of the resultant studies failed to show that parental absence made much or any difference to crime among blacks – or whites. A British study followed its subjects over a thirty-year period, and found that while children raised in broken homes were more likely to become delinquent, the results were not consistent. A study of 1,400 London children established no link. A comprehensive review of 18 different studies indicated that 7 of them found greater delinquency in homes headed by the mother, 4 found a lower criminal outcome, while the remaining 7 were inconclusive. That makes sense; there is no constitutional reason why a single-parent family should be more stable than a family where the parents are continually at war – indeed the Cambridge study suggests that quarrelsome families produce twice the number of delinquent boys, and several other studies have indicated that living in discordant homes with two parents could be more damaging than living in homes with more stable, solo mothers.

Even so, there does seem to be some sort of a link between single-parent families and the emergence of antisocial behaviour or variants of conduct disorders. In the UK more five-year-olds live with one parent than with both biological parents or a combination of natural and stepparents. Many of these five-year-olds have been reported as 'antisocial'. An unusually high level of delinquency has been identified ten years after the trauma of a parental divorce; and truancy is twice as rife among young people brought up in fatherless homes as in families with the normal complement of parents. The same seems to be true of drug abuse. And yet this is a prime example of where statistical and social sciences collide; alcoholism, poverty and lack of education are all inextricably bound together, and to tease out a specific strand of criminality from this skein of social, economic and familial deprivation is a confusing and possibly misleading undertaking.

The clearest conclusions we can draw from the Cambridge study are also the broadest – and they also conform to common sense. Discounting all the variations in family structure and social groupings, what seem to matter above all in delinquency and social behaviour are the mother's competence, the father's involvement in and interaction with the family, and the climate of discipline and control. Mothers with a low level of competence, weak family control, alcoholism on the part of the father – as well as the criminality of the father – all contribute, according to the survey, to the risk of delinquency. All this interacts with the question of broken homes; intact families offer no protection against the risk of delinquency when parental control is weak, whereas it was only in two-parent families that parental alcoholism tilted the scales towards juvenile delinquency.

On the specific subject of child abuse, there is a consensus among social workers that an abused child is likely to grow up to be a child abuser. Many studies – including an eight-country survey in New York which studied the court records of several thousand children – of such offenders, especially the more violent, show that they were exposed to highly abusive parents. Shaking and striking a baby not surprisingly can lead to brain damage, creating, in turn, a violent and impulsive individual. But the results are uneven and inconsistent, possibly because of the definition of abuse itself – is it mental, physical, sexual, or a combination of all or some?

If a question mark hangs over that, and many other areas of research, we should not be surprised. Science's exploration of these questions is only just beginning, and has been impeded by the presumption that genetics, biology and neurochemistry have no place in the study of crime. The lesson of this chapter is how difficult, and how wrong, it is to deny either the cultural or genetic roots of crime. They are intricately, and still to a large extent inexplicably, bound up in each other. And, as we will see, there may be social means to undo some biological damage, as well as chemical measures to mitigate the worst effects of the hands of cards that nature, family or fate have dealt us.

CHAPTER 7

Thieves, Cheats, Liars and Fraudsters

WE'RE FAMILIAR, THEN, with the various biological cards which fate, heredity or accident can deal us. As we have said many times, no single card will doom us to a life of crime; it takes a combination of cards. What is intriguing is that – as far as we can tell from a growing body of evidence – different combinations of cards seem to play their part in determining different sorts of persistent, chronic offenders. In this and subsequent chapters, we move from what the scientists believe goes on in the criminal brain to the criminals themselves. As we do so, we will discover startling examples of how the science which we have unravelled translates into criminal behaviour.

THE THIEVING MIND

This is the story of three thieves. At the time of writing, they are all at large, although one of them has a trial pending and is resigned to spending the next three years in gaol. The first of our villains is Jim R.

Jim R. lives in Gloucester, but speaks with a hint of the lilting Welsh that is his native accent. A minor speech impediment makes it sometimes hard to follow him. He is a thin, ferrety individual, with a certain charm. He says he took to thievery at a very early age. 'I was on my way to school, and I walked past a greengrocer's shop. It was locked, but I could see the key was inside, in the lock. I remembered a film where they'd slipped a sheet of newspaper under the door, poked the key out from the outside so that it fell on the paper, and then carefully pulled the paper out with the key on it. I stole a pineapple. Pineapples were rare in them days. The next day I did the same. The third day I took a pineapple and a couple of quid from the till. Next day, I saw they had stopped leaving the key in the lock . . .'

It was a habit of life which Jim found it hard to grow out of. He progressed, acquiring a reputation for genius with locks. As such, he became an essential member of several burgling gangs. These days, their habit is to head south for a few score miles until they reach a plush part of the countryside, and then spend the night on a tour of houses, entering by broken windows and taking small, portable items. Jim parks the gang's vehicle about a mile away from the scene of activity, and then returns to it with the night's takings. Occasionally he stashes the booty in a hedge and comes back next day to collect it.

Jim has a son, Terry, of whom he despairs. He doesn't see much of him, being separated from the boy's mother. But Terry seems to be following in his father's footsteps. 'It's cars with him,' says Jim. Night after night, Terry and a couple of school-age pals maraud around the overnight car parks. They open cars with speed and clumsiness, crudely carving out the locks. Radios, tapes, anything of value is quickly seized. Terry just can't resist taking the sports car left with the key in the ignition for five minutes while its owner nipped into the local store. It's not as if he was planning a crime when he left home – 'It just sort of happens,' he says lamely. Terry's escapades are not financially rewarding; the few pounds he might pocket from an opportunistic snatch are hardly worth the risk of youth custody – but Terry doesn't think like that. He never even contemplates the possibility of being caught.

But if Jim is worried about Terry, that's nothing to his concern about Dennis M. Jim used to go burgling with Dennis M., but now refuses to have anything to do with him. That's because of the last three times they went out. Jim has always prided himself on his cat-like stealth. It is a different matter with Dennis M.: he used to make a point of terrorizing his victims. 'He'd go into their bedrooms and shine a torch into their faces,' says Jim. 'He'd put on an Irish accent and pretend to be a terrorist. He particularly liked to frighten old women – sometimes I think he picked them out specially. Once he took a gun with him, and pistol-whipped an old dear. I thought he'd killed her – and he said he wished he had.' That was, as Jim puts it, 'out of order', a degree of violence that was out of Jim's league.

All these three characters exist, and although they all participate in what is loosely called non-violent crime, their methods, means and motivations are all different. As we'll see, each of them has a different 'hand' of biological and social factors which accounts for their differing behaviour. And if you think that Terry's behaviour isn't all that different from his father's, there is an important distinction: reassuringly, Terry isn't necessarily set on a criminal career.

The criminal we are most likely to encounter is the one that science – so far at least – knows least about. We are very unlikely to be the victims of murder, rape or kidnap. What is likely to happen to us, with sickening inevitability, is the violation of our homes, our vehicles and – less frequently – ourselves as we are mugged on the street corner. All surveys show that most offences are relatively trivial, a non-violent corpus of crime involving minor damage to property and thefts of small sums – burglary, car theft, shoplifting. (Fraud and white-collar crime we will come to later.) Most, too, are unplanned, opportunistic. One survey found that 25 per cent of adult offenders and 40 per cent of juvenile offenders had no intention of robbery when they left home – the opportunity simply presented itself. The fast-growing phenomenon of drug-related or alcohol-related crime is not robbery for gain as such but the seizing of opportunities on the street to appease the imperative of need. This in itself presents a suggestion for a major reduction in crime: remove the opportunity by better security.

Sadly, the blunt statistics show that very few of the perpetrators will be caught. The clear-up rates for burglary, robbery and car theft are around 10 to 15 per cent both in the UK and in the USA. That means that the burglars studied have been a somewhat skewed sample – they're the small proportion of villains who are actually caught, the ones that come to the attention of the police and the social scientists. Even so, enough is known to be able to distinguish the separate behaviour of different sorts of thieves and the reasons behind it. Reasons, of course, are not excuses, but they ought, once understood, to help us to better understand the phenomenon of crime – and, maybe, to find ways to confront it.

The first thing is obvious enough: we're talking about the male of the species here. Of those in the US arrested for burglary, 93 per cent are male; the same figure applies to motor theft, arson, larceny and shoplifting and is roughly the same throughout Western industrialized nations. As we have seen, men have an underlying chemistry card making it more likely that they will come into conflict with the law. This, as we know, is particularly true of young men: they have not yet learned to keep the impulsive side of their brains under control, and they don't want to; they relish that thrill of excitement that comes from challenging authority. The excitement is as important as the monetary rewards.

But, as we have also seen, most young men do not go on to become career criminals. Terry is not necessarily going to become a career villain like his father. What he's doing is, to some extent, perfectly natural for his age, and the wiring of his brain. The hand that biology has dealt him may consist of perfectly normal cards. It's just that at the moment he does not have the equipment to acquire and metabolize the moral lessons of reward and punishment. It doesn't help, of course, that no one is trying to inculcate such lessons, but even if they were, Terry, like most male teenagers, would be almost constitutionally deaf to them. Comparative inadequacy in language means that the message simply doesn't get through as well as it does with girls. Constant and consistent messages, reinforced with practical examples and punishments, would largely overcome the problem, though they might provoke an overreaction. But for the many children who are the product of dysfunctional and broken families, at loose in the amoral urban sprawl, poor and with a desperate poverty of expectation, such lessons are few and far between.

Conventional wisdom is that the bent sapling grows up into a twisted tree. So why do most children, in fact, grow up straight? The controversial finding is that parental influence counts far less than we hope or fear.

A vital study into this area followed children from poor homes. It compared the criminal outcome of neglected children, abused children and children from normal, albeit disadvantaged, homes. Those children who had been neglected, rather than abused, started their criminal career very early, and there were twelve times more chronic offenders in the combined abused/neglected children than among the 'normal' controls. But the key finding was that these factors had no influence on adult offending. The children from normal homes were just as likely to become adult offenders; indeed, those few who did offend as youngsters were more likely to grow up into adult criminals than their abused or neglected comrades. The most significant predictor of chronic criminality is when the activity begins at a young age (9 or 10) and if it is persistent.

What are we to make of this? It seems obvious that the neglected children are unlikely to have the same degree of moral guidance about right and wrong as the normal sample. So why, in the long run, do things turn out well? Most, as we know, turn their backs on crime by the age of eighteen. The point is that in the end the children do learn. In spite of parental neglect, the normal mores of society percolate through. The majority of youthful, unreceptive minds mature into ones that can, thank goodness, receive messages and absorb them. They have minds so constructed that in the end they can learn right from wrong.

But while Terry, whatever his wildness now, may not necessarily go on to a career in crime, there is a minority of minds which are so constructed that – whatever the moral input in youth or thereafter – simply do not accept the message. And they're the ones who do go on, like Jim, to careers in crime.

As we have seen, innate in the brain, there is a constellation of biological factors which environment and upbringing may mitigate, but be powerless to neutralize. The best upbringing in the world may not be able to tame a mind which is born to resist the 'normal' codes of society. Herein lies the answer to the riddle that has puzzled sociologists and politicians for so long: if poverty is a cause of crime, how come not all poor people grow up criminal, while some of the most privileged – and well brought-up – children grow up to be villains? The fact is that poverty is not a cause of crime in itself, though obviously it represents a spur and a motive to a mind which is already predisposed, through personality, neurochemistry, genes or hormones, to crime. All these factors – a different mix, a different shuffle, in all of us – make us uniquely more or less likely to offend. What the latest research is showing is that those who will go on to become career criminals have a different hand of cards from those of us who are non-criminal; and that the non-violent criminal's hand is different from that of his violent counterpart.

So let's take a closer look at Jim, who has been in and out of gaol for a series of house thefts – 'an occupational hazard', as he puts it. He sees nothing wrong with what he does – it's just another job to him. Burglary is generally characterized by little if any confrontation between perpetrator and intended victim, and Jim's burglaries are no exception. Given the choice and an appropriate exit, the typical burglar would most often choose flight rather than fight. Rarely does even the unskilled burglar enter premises if he knows that someone is home. Jim is different in one respect: most households are broken into during the hours of daylight, but Jim likes working at night, which is usually the preferred time for the burglary of commercial premises. Jim is just as horrified by the violence of his erstwhile partner in crime, Dennis M., as any law-abiding citizen would be. He is, in fact, something of a physical coward. Fifty now, he's wondering if it is time to retire. He's not as agile or quick on his feet as he used to be – and the other day a farmer he was burgling loosed off a hail of shotgun pellets at his fast-retreating form.

Talking with Jim, we can work out which of the biological cards that predispose to criminal behaviour he holds. There's a clue, of course, in that speech impediment; Jim's trouble with expressing himself is a likely sign of a low verbal IQ and of a brain that is not functioning as normal. He was easily bored at school; his frustration took the form of disruptive behaviour or simple truanting. That's exactly what's happening, now, with his son Terry who, like his father, does well at practical tasks – for there's nothing wrong with his spatial IQ (his ability to work in three dimensions and solve mathematical problems that require this sort of skill). But neither father nor son has displayed any childhood signs of cruelty. They don't pull the wings off butterflies, or taunt kittens. Neither has been a playground bully. Neither has ever had a taste for exotically gruesome literature. The more violent Dennis – terrorizer of the elderly – was always something of a terror himself; his record of juvenile offending includes seemingly random acts of cruelty to the very young. He also seemed to delight in shooting squirrels with an air-pistol, laughing at them when they were maimed and in agony.

Low verbal IQ is usually found in chronic offenders, both violent and non-violent, though, as we will see, there are some exceptions to this – such as the psychopaths and serial killers whom we will be meeting in later chapters. There is a consistent difference in the degree. Violent offenders have a lower IQ than the offender population as a whole. Conversely, studies on non-violent offenders show a higher IQ than the offending average. What we can surmise is that somehow that internal dialogue which we may call conscience or reason takes place less well in some people, who may as a result take a more antisocial attitude to life; and that the more meagre the dialogue, the more antisocial – that is, violent – that attitude may be.

What about that other identifiable culprit, abnormal hormones? That's something else which marks out Jim from Dennis, and which will help determine which path young Terry will take. A whole range of studies indicate that violent behaviour is associated with high levels of male hormone, the aggression hormone, in both males and females. Crime is – in most cases – an act of aggression, whether it be trespass or theft, but it has been determined – by R. T. Rubin among others – that those who had committed armed robbery had higher rates of testosterone than those who had committed less aggressive crimes. James Dabbs's study of free testosterone measures confirms that those inmates with higher levels were more often those convicted of violent crimes; the levels were most striking at the extremes, where 9 out of 11 inmates with the lowest testosterone levels had committed non-violent crimes, while 10 out of the 11 inmates with the highest levels had committed violent crimes. Plasma testosterone levels have been found to be higher in those men who had committed violent offences than in non-violent offenders.

So the lower the IQ and the higher the testosterone the more likely it is that criminality takes an aggressive, violent form. But we know that there's a third biological factor: the chemistry of the brain is a major card in the pack.

Is there an identifiable abnormality in the serotonin levels of our trio of thieves? Serotonin, as we saw, is the messenger that inhibits impulsive behaviour, the chemical brake on our impulsive, runaway selves. Those with abnormally low levels of this neurotransmitter are characterized by much more impulsive and violent behaviour. Our guess would be that the juvenile pineapple thief, Jim, had low levels for his age. Most of us, at least most of us who have been boys, have teetered on the edge of theft, shoplifting or ringing the fire brigade with hoax calls – it just feels such an exciting thing to do. At the last moment, most of us just about hold back. (This seems to be far less of a problem with girls, who, on average, have constitutionally higher serotonin levels and better behavioural brakes as a consequence – although those with abnormally low levels for their gender do display impulsive behaviour.)

This may be the card that young Terry has, to his misfortune. Maybe it is a stage of his biological development which time will put right – but if it turns out that he has a constitutional deficit of serotonin, his impulsive behaviour will persist and grow in severity. His father, Jim, the 'honest' burglar, does not act on impulse; he cases the joint, calculates the odds. He does what he does for a living. But Terry acts on impulse. His father would never steal that flame-red Ferrari – so easy for the police to trace – but Terry has to have it.

So should criminals run the Serotonin Defence? M'lud, it wasn't me, it was my brain chemistry – oh yes, and my low verbal IQ and high testosterone? On one level, it's a ludicrous idea. Yet it does leave us with a problem: we can't claim that a person 'should have known better' (like the rest of us) if he is constitutionally less capable of knowing better and restraining his behaviour.

The impulsively violent criminal has this card of low serotonin too; but, as we will see, what form this impulsiveness takes depends upon a whole range of other biological cards in the pack. Low serotonin levels denote impulsiveness rather than aggression *per se*.

What's likely, if we can trust the research that has been conducted on criminals, is that in all three cases – Jim, Terry and Dennis M. – their brains are flickering, as it were, on low wattage. We have here the manifestation of low arousal. We have seen that cortical arousal is vital to a sense of well-being, and for offenders, in everyday life, there just doesn't seem to be enough of it. The offender needs bigger and more exciting stimuli to make life interesting. He needs more sensation than the rest of us.

All of the chemical effects of arousal, be they from the hormones or the neurotransmitters, leave tracers, so we can test the degree of arousal involved – and there is a total consistency in the results. A clear negative relationship has been observed between the level of adrenaline (produced when the Reticular Activating System sends a message to the thinking cortex) and attitudes to unprovoked aggression or destructive behaviour; the more aggressive the youth, the lower the levels of adrenaline excretion. A study of fourteen highly aggressive bullies showed that they had clearly lower levels than in more kindly boys – and aggressive bullies and those that show cruel and violent behaviour are the types that are more likely to be violent in adulthood. No one's accused Terry of being a bully; impulsive, yes – but he's not necessarily going to grow up like Dennis, his father's erstwhile aggressive accomplice.

Research has shown that individuals differ markedly in both threshold and habituation levels of activation in the alertness regulating system. Non-aggressive individuals have low thresholds – the anxiety mechanism is activated quite easily. The opposite is true of violent individuals. So there's a dual arousal process going on here: all criminals have low arousal (hence their need for the kicks of criminality) but the careful, planning criminals are those whose anxiety-arousal is more easily evoked. That explains why Jim gave up burgling with Dennis M.; it was all right in the beginning, when Dennis would come along on Jim's meticulously planned nights of nefarious thieving, but when Dennis M. started terrorizing and assaulting his quarry, Jim's anxiety was aroused. Those whose anxiety alertness is easily turned on are very unlikely to commit high-risk, uncalculated crimes. So the more underaroused on both these factors you are – needing excitement to get your arousal system going, and being comparatively numb to the signals of anxiety – the more likely you are to be a violent, vicious individual. If you are underaroused on the stimulation area, but more easily aroused in the anxiety section of the brain, the less likely you are to commit an impulsive, risky, spur-of-the-moment crime. You're more likely to be an 'honest burglar' like Jim.

Every day we are discovering new aspects to the chemical and biological inputs to the criminal mind. It is for others to assess the exact degree to which these things determine criminality, the exact balance between sociological and clinically quantifiable influences. But factors like education and chemistry are not, in fact, separate: low arousal is directly related to the capacity to learn. The fascinating hypothesis which now intrigues the scientists is this – that a low or slow-reacting arousal system impedes the criminal's capacity to recognize and so avoid the unpleasant side-effects of offending behaviour.

As we suggested, most of us, when confronted with a potential danger, will recognize the situation, be automatically stimulated to react to it, and try to avoid it because we know how unpleasant the consequent feelings of anxiety are going to be. So, in almost Pavlovian terms, we quickly learn to associate retreat from over-stimulating situations with a diminution of anxiety. But with the criminal, or among those with a low and consequently slow arousal system, everything takes a lot longer: there isn't the instant and easily learnt lesson that putting the brakes on impulsive behaviour will lessen the feelings of anxiety and fear.

We have established that we learn the difference between right and wrong, ideally, by studying the example of our betters, and modelling ourselves upon them. But the history of morality suggests that it is a predominantly negative lesson. Most of the Ten Commandments are expressed in negative form. Most statements about moral behaviour which are critical for everyday activities are negative and inhibitory: don't tease your sister – if you do you'll go to bed early. If you've got a fully-functioning autonomic nervous system (the system that controls heart rate, breathing and all the things we do automatically) the following process occurs in the mind, albeit not quite in such dispassionately scientific language:

1. I'd quite like to tease my sister.
2. Last time I did this, I experienced being sent to bed.
3. This involved a degree of television deprivation.
4. This is not an agreeable prospect. It causes me anxiety.
5. I can neutralize the anxiety by abandoning the plan to tease.
6. I am rewarded for this by the dissipation of my anxiety.

The reduction of fear and the inhibition of aggression become intertwined. But those who have a low sensation of fear and anxiety cannot experience this self-reinforcing experience of learning. If you don't have the mental equipment to become anxious at the prospect of a sanction, deterrence ceases to have any relevance. People are not deterred by a prospect which does not – cannot – cause them fear.

But there is still another factor involved in the making of the criminal mind. What's almost certain in the cases of our criminal threesome of Terry, Jim and Dennis M. is that there is an underlying abnormality in the functioning of the brain. The degree of abnormality, and the exact areas of the brain involved are different in the violent and non-violent minds. So far, the methods for measuring and detecting those differences are relatively unsophisticated – but it's a field where researchers confidently expect a significant enlargement of our knowledge.

Already, scientists have conducted tests for neurological impairment – brain damage – on a group of offenders with similar social backgrounds. Some, however, had a history of unpredictable and aggressive behaviour – rather like Dennis M., the burglar who turned nasty. The others had no violence in their background – they were thieves, conmen and perjurers. Both sets had a degree of brain damage, but in all 31 of the tests conducted, those with a violent background had more pronounced and severe impairment. The pattern of damage was not only greater, but it was subtly different from the damage of the violent group. And the damage can be identified early: in a study of 99 adolescent offenders, 83 per cent of the males and 86 per cent of the few females showed an abnormal neurological profile. If Jim is really worried about the outlook for Terry, maybe he should submit his son to similar tests.

The research team then split the group into those who had committed violent and non-violent crimes. The violent group were found to have greater damage to the dominant lobes of the brain; 100 per cent of them showed greater frontal damage, and more temporal and anterior lobe damage than the non-violent group. Corresponding EEG abnormalities showed further differences between the two groups – predictably, with those whose behaviour was characterized by motiveless and random violence the graphs traced a higher incidence of abnormality. In this group the pattern was more profound and more severe, suggesting a disturbance in the limbic system (the animal brain where rage and anger are generated) as well as elsewhere. Pulling together a host of studies shows that five times more violent than non-aggressive individuals have abnormalities which manifest themselves on EEGs. The more impaired the brain is, the more difficult it is to put on the brakes; the violent criminal has fewer or weaker braking mechanisms, and brain dysfunction makes it harder for the thinking part of the brain to apply them.

There was some abnormal functioning to the prefrontal lobes of non-violent offenders – though not to the same degree as in the aggressive criminals – which suggests a failure to plan, or perhaps to put together actions with their consequences. Again, when we look at the theories of learning, we learn to control our emotions via the left verbal brain putting into silent words what we feel. If the verbal side is impaired, it will not function so well in the moral learning process. With an intact verbal system, or one that is working at top pitch, the child will learn the moral signals more effectively than if the brain is below par, when learning at all levels becomes more difficult.

Maybe this is where some of the problem starts in childhood – Jim, Terry and Dennis always found it hard to connect punishment with their misdeeds. There seemed no logical connection. To misbehave, and to be punished, were two separate events, seemingly unconnected by cause or reason.

There's still one more card to add to the hand that makes us criminal, or, if criminal, violent or non-violent. There is a genetic dimension to crime, and to types of crime.

Caution is obviously needed; the gene story is hugely complex, with many different types of gene involved. And genes themselves can be turned on or off as a result of external factors – genetic information is not always acted upon, just as architect's blueprints do not all necessarily turn into buildings.

That's what gives us all our unique personalities, outlooks and behaviour – inconvenient as it may be for the scientist – plus of course the extra complication of how we are brought up, how our peers behave and what we see on television.

So much for the academic Health Warning about genetic generalizations; even so, we saw in Chapter 6 that many of the researchers into this field feel that it is indeed possible to attribute a percentage to the influence of environmental and genetic factors. And a Swedish researcher who has performed extensive twin research studies believes he can produce an even more sophisticated assessment – claiming to be able to put a figure on the likehood of violence in the offending pattern, or to predict the mathematical genetic predisposition to property crime.

Christiansen's twin data assesses that when burglary and theft run in the family, the influence of the genetic factor is some 78 per cent; that doesn't mean that 78 per cent of the sons of thieves will in turn become thieves, but that if they do become thieves, then the trait is 78 per cent attributable to heredity. There's a 54 per cent heredity factor in aggressive, assaultive crime. Those Stockholm adoption studies we saw in Chapter 6 also suggest that there is a genetic element to petty property criminals – and a different and distinct genetic input for those who commit crimes against the person.

So it's good and bad news for Terry: he has a strong chance of inheriting his father Jim's trait of burgling, yet there does not seem to be any inherent violence in the family.

There's a fascinating dimension when it comes to female crime. It's generally agreed that there is more cultural, social and environmental pressure against women taking up crime than there is in the case of men. So when there was a study of girls who had been adopted into good homes – and who nevertheless went on to display antisocial traits like thieving – scientists were especially interested in what sort of biological parents the wayward women had had. In fact, female adoptee property criminals had a higher percentage of biological parents who were property criminals than did the men. What seemed to be happening was that a more concentrated genetic input seemed to be necessary to overcome the cultural conditioning that militates against female criminality.

Another aspect of gene studies looks at recidivism and the chronic offender. As we know, a very small number of offenders commit a disproportionate number of crimes. Jim admits to over two thousand separate burglaries, and Terry is a one-man crime wave in himself, considering the number of cars he has broken into. The chronic criminal, it seems, has more criminal genes than the one-off offender; he has been found to be three times more likely to have a biological parent with three or more convictions. So crime, to a degree, runs in the family – even families where father and son have no contact with, and often no knowledge of, each other. A mere 1 per cent of this group accounted for 30 per cent of the crimes, leading the author of the study to conclude: 'This extremely high rate of convictions among a very small number of adoptees whose parents were multiple offenders suggests genetic predisposition plays an especially important role in their criminality."

Jim, our non-violent burglar, was adopted, and by good parents. They had been warned by the social services about his behaviour, but were nevertheless appalled by his antisocial and disruptive conduct. They were late in realizing that he was having learning difficulties at school; they thought he was just a bad boy. Bad blood, they put it down to. They did not know or understand that Jim had a real deficit in his brain – among other things that's what was causing his speech impediment – and that brain damage and chemistry were predisposing him to behave as he did. His real father was 'known to the police' with a long history of convictions – though none of them, interestingly, for violence. This is important to Jim's genetic inheritance, for the work done in this field shows that what exactly you inherit does influence the nature of your offending.

The genes constitute a constellation of characteristics, which combine, and interact with the social and familial environment. They can also have a direct influence on the chemical balance of personality. For instance, individual differences in testosterone can be inherited – many studies show this. Jim does not have high testosterone levels, which may serve to keep his son on the non-violent side of the line. As we know, testosterone can be directly related to behaviour: the more you have, the uglier and more aggressive, less sympathetic the outcome. We also know that arousal levels, and EEG brain patterns too, have a strong hereditary component. This is another clue in the genetic puzzle of crime – for low arousal and abnormal EEG activity is, as we have seen, inextricably linked to sensation-seeking, most often of an antisocial nature.

Again, we have established that serotonin levels in the brain control impulsive behaviour. These levels are in turn controlled by an enzyme called monoamine oxidase, whose function is controlled by the genes. This enzyme too appears to have a genetic component.

Our personalities, themselves to a large extent genetically inherited, interact with the whole array of our behaviour. Criminals are different from the general population in that convicted prisoners nearly all have a distinct and more accentuated psychopathology, displaying, among other things, higher degrees of schizophrenia and hypochondria. The more deviant on the test scores, the more serious the behavioural problems, the more serious the crime, and the poorer the prognosis for the future.

Our fundamental genetic inheritance – our gender – also plays its part. Men traditionally score higher on measurements of dominance, coldness, hostility, quarrelsomeness, while women rate higher on tests of submission, altruism, ingenuity, warmness and agreeability. The male attributes – none of which are going to determine criminality in themselves – clearly add weight to any pre-existing criminal propensities. The submissive and hostile poles of character seem to have an additive effect, combining with impulsiveness and irritability. A person with many hostile genes and few warm agreeable ones is more likely – given the wrong circumstances – to have his underlying neuropathology triggered by a provocative situation.

What we can say – so long as we accept the studies that have been conducted – is that personality assessments, and the measurement of inherited genetic characteristics, can differentiate the violent from the non-violent criminal, your Jims from your Dennises. While Jim and Dennis have a lot in common – they are both, after all, amoral, incorrigible rogues – they each have an array of individual personality characteristics which bias the hand nature has dealt them towards a more or less non-violent form of offending.

This whole biological drama is played out against the back-cloth of our environment; again, it must be stressed that although we now know of neurophysical and chemical factors contributing to the formation of the criminal mind, it would be as fatuous to ignore the importance of social factors as it would be futile of the sociologists to turn their faces against the evidence that science is providing. Nature and nurture are not two competing, exclusive explanations for behaviour. As we said in our once controversial, and now accepted, book *BrainSex*, the two are the tides and winds that influence the course of our human voyage, each causing us to set our sails, and alter our bearings, in a multitude of varieties.

Female offending, as we know, is more or less a footnote to the study of the criminal mind. It is so rare, compared to male offending, and the study samples of offender so small, that the statistics have to be approached with some caution. Nevertheless, a composite picture emerges – and, since we have no one individual case study in mind, unlike those of Dennis, Jim and Terry, we will have to create a composite female offender.

We'll call her Jane. She has a string of convictions for petty thieving, shoplifting, and possession of marijuana. Her offences seem to be committed on impulse – she never anticipates the consequences of her actions, which do not bring her any relevant financial gain. In a way, she's very like Terry – an opportunist criminal who cannot resist immediate temptation. The chances are that there is a genetic effect here. Adoption studies have shown that there is a stronger link between the criminality of biological mothers and their adopted daughters than there is in the case of fathers and sons.

There are a few professional shoplifters – or boosters as they are known as – including the woman who literally trades on the promise of Marks and Spencer to make full refunds of faulty goods by stealing them, damaging them and taking them to the refund desk. And there are the older women who, for reasons no one can adequately explain, deviate just once from a law-abiding habit of life, and who are overcome by remorse and shame. Lady Isobel Barnett, the British television celebrity panellist of the late 1950s, was one such who committed suicide over the shame of stealing a can of fish. It is widely recognized that the menopause can cause uncharacteristic offending behaviour; the condition results in a lowering of serotonin levels, with a corresponding fall in the capacity for impulse control. Progesterone indirectly boosts serotonin, so when this female hormone tails off, serotonin levels fall too. Testosterone, whose effects are masked by normal female hormone, lowers serotonin levels, so when, with the menopause, female hormone levels fall, testosterone is given fuller rein, contributing further to low serotonin levels. Low serotonin is also associated with depression – another factor commonly linked with atypical behaviour such as once-in-a-lifetime shoplifting.

Hormone replacement therapy has successfully remedied the problem, even in the extreme case of one 56-year-old married woman who had a history of shoplifting every day for fourteen years. She would wake every morning with the compulsive need to go out and steal. There was a simultaneous feeling of repugnance at the thought, but she would always give way to it. She would invariably steal useless things, such as baby shoes, even though she had no baby. She said she wished she were 'chained to a wall' to stop her giving in to the temptation to steal. Such extreme measures were not, in the end, needed: hormone treatment succeeded in raising her serotonin levels.

In fact, chemistry will probably come to the aid of Jane. She is likely to end her criminal activities when she has her first baby, and if she thereafter goes on the pill. Progesterone, the hormone of pregnancy, increases serotonin levels, leading to greater contentment and less impulsiveness, a trick of nature designed to make sure that mothers do not rush about doing crazy things that might endanger the baby's life. The pill Jane will take after pregnancy is a mix of progesterone and oestrogen, which will act together to maintain the hormonal balance. The responsibility of family too has its impact – the thought of the separation from her baby involved in a gaol sentence is unbearable – but serotonin itself helps her to imagine the consequences of her action.

There is not, as yet, a similar pill for men – at least not one which can be confidently recommended. In their case, time alone has the answer. As readers of *BrainSex* discovered, as the sexes grow older they come to resemble each other more, as the contending hormonal tides begin to ebb. It seems that, indeed, with age comes wisdom, at least for certain types of crime. Only 7 per cent of property crime is committed by people over 40 years old, and the same is true of vandalism and drink-driving offences. Partly it's a learning process – the message eventually getting through that there are better things to do with one's life – but biology is intimately bound up in the process too. As men age, two key criminal cards fall out of the pack. The enzyme marker for serotonin levels, monoamine oxidase, starts to increase substantially around the age of 24 – exactly the point at which the figures for impulsive theft begin to drop. And male hormone levels begin to tail away from their peak at the age of 18, reaching their lowest ebb at fifty.

According to the governor of a long-term-sentence gaol, where part of the prison is being converted to a criminal geriatric ward, 'as they grow older, the armed robbers realize they're not going to be so nimble on their feet, they're not going to be leaping in and out of getaway cars.' The tragedy is that for some the lesson is learnt so late: one reason for the need for geriatric accommodation is that many of the prisoners, seeing old age approach, have no desire to be free; gaol is the only real life they know, and they have very little option but to end their days behind bars. Jim, never likely to attract a long custodial sentence, anyway, shudders at the thought. In any case, burglary is beginning to lose its excitement. Plodding across a frosty field at dawn, after a night's slim pickings, he often wonders whether or not it's time to pack it all in. His testosterone is ebbing, the cautious chemical of serotonin is in fuller flow. His cortex – his rational mind – is communicating better with the animal brain. The same process is most likely to be the saving of Terry. In his late twenties, he will find the desire for the red Ferrari less irresistible. The impulsive chemistry of his brain will be cooling down. He may even, as Jim hopes, get himself 'a good girl' – somewhere else to spend his male hormones.

We have seen that the criminal mind is a complex mix of biology, and that life, experience and the passing of time all affect that cocktail of chemical, physical, and genetic influences. But how far can – or should – we seek to neutralize those influences, insofar as we are able? If we can identify what's going on with Terry, should we simply cross our fingers and wait for his thirtieth birthday, or for Miss Right to come along? Could earlier identification of Jim's learning problems, and corrective effort on his verbal IQ, have steered him away from a life of crime? We have the means to study tell-tale neurophysical patterns which can help to identify people predisposed by genes, or brain damage, to become chronic offenders – those with an abnormally unresponsive autonomic system, slow brain wave activity, neuropsychological deficits, biochemical abnormalities and a number of behavioural signs of impulsivity, and poor school performance. Should we be using this knowledge to help them?

We study these people enough when they are in prison – indeed the overwhelming mass of the data comes from the study of convicted offenders. But such studies are only of academic interest unless we apply our new knowledge to the as yet uncriminal, as yet unconvicted. We offer remedial classes in mathematics or language for those who find it hard to tackle those subjects; but we are doing nothing for children who seem to have a constitutional incapacity to know the difference between right and wrong, impulse and control. Are we so fearful that this knowledge could be abused that we dare not contemplate using it positively, creatively, and to society's – and the individual's – benefit?

CHEATS AND LIARS – DISHONEST OR DISORDERED?

We may have a sneaking admiration for the confidence trickster – as long as we are not one of his victims – but the common view of society is that such fraudsters deserve punishment. If they are canny enough to commit frauds of Byzantine complexity, presumably they know well enough what they are doing. They have calculated the risk. They know the score. And, society believes, we are entitled to punish them when we find them out, whether they sell the non-existent time-share villas, or cajole the life savings out of a widow, or even make criminal use of a stolen credit card. Not many tears were shed when the popular jockey, Lester Piggott, was jailed for tax evasion.

The term 'white-collar crime' was coined by Edwin Sutherland in 1939; it was defined as violation of the criminal law committed during the course of their occupational activities by persons of upper socio-economic status. These acts are recognized by the law as harmful, often affect large numbers of victims, and are usually the result of wilful and intentional behaviour – although the stealing of my employer's electricity to write this paragraph could equally well count as white-collar crime. Like that crime, much goes unreported. Companies cover up. Our culture condones certain dishonesties. A television producer was once driving past the walls of Wormwood Scrubs prison, and remarked to his colleague, 'There are people in there for stealing what we fiddle on expenses in a week.' He was right. Cheating on expenses is often tacitly condoned as an unofficial form of overtime or bonus. Once condoned, it is hard to put a limit on it. If it gets thoroughly out of hand, organizations often prefer to dismiss the offender rather than to bring a criminal case, in the course of which the offender might implicate any number of his colleagues, or even his superiors.

Fraud is commonplace, widespread, and major. More money is lost by fraud in the financial institutions of the City of London than in the whole annual 'take' of robberies and burglaries throughout the UK. Forty per cent of 56 large corporations reported at least one fraud costing over £50,000. The average company fraud in London involves sums of nearly £2 million. In the collapse of the Bank of Credit and Commerce International (BCCI, a.k.a. the Bank of Cocaine, Conmen and Impostors), something between 5 and 15 billion pounds seems to have evaporated. The collapse in the US Savings and Loan (S. & L.) business is reckoned to cost the taxpayer one trillion dollars – more than the cost of the Vietnam war.

Criminologists have often wondered why this kind of crime, more widespread, more serious and more damaging to society than common crimes like robbery, burglary or theft, is not regarded as seriously or punished as severely. Partly it is a matter of history, class and status; the courts do not like sentencing PLU – People Like Us – to the sordid confinement of the prison cell. Can – society is inclined to feel – a bank president who has embezzled bank funds really be classed as a common criminal? Even if he is, he usually gets sent to an 'open' prison, where the regime is typically less austere, and where he can often continue his mercantile career by use of the prison telephone. Perhaps, too, our lack of outrage is due to the feeling that we are not personally threatened by it – robbery, burglary and theft are perceived as far greater personal violations than are the acts of an embezzler.

Nevertheless, such acts are antisocial. And we know that being antisocial in a criminal sense carries a whole array of biological cards. Is the opposite true – are the honest blessed with an absence of such handicaps? What makes for a huckster, what for a Mother Teresa? Are morals a matter of culture, conditioning, education? Is there a hereditary dimension to being a saint or a sinner? Or is dishonesty, too, in any way the result of that range of chemical and neurological abnormalities of the brain which we have been able to associate with the cruder forms of crime?

Research on androgens and testosterone levels is beginning to yield a clue. Ministers of the church, for instance, have low levels, according to a study of seven occupations. Those with high levels are more selfish. Actors, a somewhat egotistical breed, were found to have high levels. Most fraudsters are larger-than-life characters, dominant, flamboyant and devil-may-care. Do they also suffer, perhaps, from low serotonin levels – and the consequent failure to resist the temptation of the easy, immoral fix in exactly the same way as the impulsive handbag snatcher, or the hooligan vandal?

The first, most obvious biological factor is the gender card. Women in business are more honest, less greedy; given a chance of renting a car on expenses, for instance, they tend to trade down to a more modest model, whereas men take every opportunity to trade up to a plusher, sportier car. Women tend to stay within the daily allowance, whereas men tend to push it to the budgetary limits. The difference between the honesty of men and women shows up in the official crime statistics, and, as we shall see, there is a biological basis to this disparity in gender honesty.

But apart from this obvious criminal gene – the gender chromosome – is there a type of mind which flouts the rules of honesty more flagrantly than the rest of us? Do those who ruthlessly rip off shareholders or the little old ladies suffer from the same brain chemistry and functional deficits as the other criminals we have identified? After all, the fraudulent mind, like other criminal minds, suffers from the problem of not discerning right from wrong – or not caring about the distinction.

This seems to be the case from a study of men convicted of embezzlement. Most did not see what they had done as criminal; they had a false self-image, maintained by adjustment of the facts – they managed to convince themselves that they were just 'borrowing' the money and would soon return it. As one subject put it, 'I figured if you could help yourself and replace it and not hurt anyone, it was all right.' Most said that they would not have committed their offences if they had thought of such activity as theft.

The same rationalization – that no one suffers, so no crime has been committed – is frequent in white-collar crime. When a Westinghouse executive on trial for price fixing was asked if he thought his behaviour was illegal, replied, 'Illegal yes, but not criminal ... I assume that criminal action means hurting someone, and we did not do that.' The same rationale is put forward by workers caught stealing from their employers – the company can afford it, it is an unofficial reward for work, pilferage is a 'morally justified addition to wages'. Other excuses are that 'everyone's doing it'; the plea in mitigation is, 'I did nothing more than what is accepted business practice. If I bent the rules, who doesn't? If you are going to punish me there are many others who should be in the dock.'

Central to the question of honesty is the quality of altruism. Defined as the opposite of egotism, it is the quality which makes us perform an act of kindness to another person, with no hope of personal benefit. In recent years social scientists and biologists have become particularly interested in altruism, although the two groups approach the subject from different angles.

The sociologist believes that a number of factors influence this behaviour: empathy (an emotional response resulting from awareness of another's emotions), society's expectation of how people 'should' behave toward others, social learning and various subjective factors.

Biologists, however, find themselves confronted with a bit of a puzzle. Altruism runs counter to evolutionary theory, in which we are all, genetically speaking, out for ourselves, and in which the weaker brethren go to the wall; survival of the fittest does not square with lending an altruistic, helping hand to the unfit. Yet it is not uncommon for animals to share food, help provide for another's young, raise the alarm and defend others against predators – all deeds done on behalf of others, often to the disadvantage of self. There are social insects, such as honey bees, ants and wasps, which frequently sacrifice their own lives while defending their group against the attack of intruders. Some female birds protect their young by feigning injury, offering themselves as a vulnerable sacrifice to draw the predator away from the nest. In this sense, altruism can underwrite survival, because the spreading of prosocial genes aids the cohesion of the clan. Thus acts of altruism can be genetically selfish. Termite soldier ants spray their enemies with a glandular secretion which fatally entangles both themselves and their enemies; but the genetic pay-off here is that they protect their female kin, who possess 75 per cent of the all-important gene pool.

It is understandable enough to help your own kith and kin – but what about altruism towards non-relatives? Do animals calculate that a contribution to the well-being of others will be repaid in the long run? Do men and women behave charitably because they think that such acts enhance their social standing – such as captains of industry giving money to political parties in the hope of knighthoods – or because they gain prestige, which will increase their chances of attracting a mate? There is some genetic evidence of inherited altruism – but the findings are not conclusive. Even so, and even if much apparently altruistic behaviour has a selfish motive, there is little doubt that mankind does have a biological potential for prosocial behaviours; even a one-month-old infant will become distressed when it hears another child's cry. The infant cannot display altruism as such, but is it exhibiting an innate empathy – the ability to experience, albeit at second-hand, the feelings of others?

It's an important question, because empathy/altruism seems intimately bound up with the individual's moral stance. They are all tied up with the capacity to anticipate and feel the hurt that someone might feel as a result of one's own wrongdoing – and indeed the sense of guilt that one would experience oneself.

Those who have studied empathy believe that there is a

strong link between it and the formation of moral principles and judgments. Learning what is right and what is wrong comes, according to this theory, from the sense of anticipated, vicarious distress. Put simply, what happens is this. A child does something wrong; the parent is angry and upset; the child experiences these emotions, which are distressing; and so learns not to repeat the wrong which led to such a distressing outcome. If a child is unable to feel the disapproval or upset of a parent – even perhaps if the parent does not seem to be upset – the child will experience no pain and distress, and the motivation to avoid wrongdoing will be the weaker.

Empathy has a special relationship with aggression; if your levels of empathy are high, you won't cause other people pain and suffering, because you would be inflicting a proportion of that pain on yourself. Most normal children, if they hurt another child and make it cry, will experience the distress as their own and will, in consequence, be less likely to do it again.

A multitude of studies in the 1970s illuminated the link between high empathy and low delinquency. In one, children were played videotaped stories about other children – some of them happy, some of them sad – and the young audience's reactions were then analysed. Typical tapes involved scenes of children winning races, experiencing pride, getting a new bicycle, being frightened by a sudden noise, losing a pet or moving to a new and strange neighbourhood. Each video built to a climax, and then the children were interviewed about their own feelings. Overall, the girls responded with slightly more empathy than the boys did, and seemed to learn the social norms more quickly. With the boys, the degree of their empathy correlated very strongly with their cognitive skills – such as command of vocabulary, reading skills, comprehension and spatial perspective taking.

These results suggest that empathy is closely connected to low verbal IQ, which we know to be connected with crime.

And there is a genetic dimension to altruism, too. Many aspects of our personality seem to be inherited, including things like sociability and gregariousness, which are known to be intimately linked to altruism: sociable children are more likely spontaneously to help others than unsociable types. The traits of hostility, altruism and aggression also have several genetic components each, and can have an additive effect; the more of the relevant genes a person possesses, the greater the predisposition for the trait that person will have.

The arousal card figures large in altruism/empathy, too. Since empathy is often defined as an emotional response to the perception of another person's feelings, those who need a greater deal of stimulation will be correspondingly more deaf to other people's feelings. As we know, men need much more stimulus to arouse them, as do those who are antisocial – which is possibly the reason why the sexes differ in their ability to conform with society's rules. Women have a brain that feels – more than men's – much of what others feel, be it pain or joy, and the knowledge of the pain that can be inflicted on others militates against the commission of the deed – whether it is the defrauding of pensioners or the sabotage of a company and other people's jobs through embezzlement. Morality, then, is to an extent a function of brain chemistry.

The inhibiting influence of empathy, of course, means nothing to the psychopathic mind. This mind stands out from the rest of the minds to crime in one major way. Psychopaths are totally callous, without any guilt or ability to feel remorse. They do not care about the norms of society, so without compunction break all and any rules that get in their way. Not every con-man is a psychopath, but fraud is a crime almost designed for the non-violent psychopathic mind.

In the public mind, the term psychopath evokes images of a wild-eyed serial killer. In most cases, nothing could be further from the truth. The psychopath is just as likely to be the pillar of local society, the life and soul of the party, the dazzling charmer. Because of the pulp-fiction image of the psychopath, many researchers shrink from using the word, and there is much argument over its proper use. But Robert Hare in

149

Canada has spent a lifetime studying psychopaths, and feels that with careful diagnosis the term is a perfectly valid one.

What is clear from his and other research is that there is a personality profile that is psychopathic, which is common to serial killers, the chronically violent offender and the non-violent personality alike. For psychopathic violence to occur, additional cards are necessary to complete the hand. These cards are not present in the hand of the non-violent psychopath.

And, according to Robert Hare, there's a disturbing number of such people inside and outside gaol. He says that they are people that we all meet in everyday life 'and we have all been deceived and manipulated by them.' Their hallmark is a stunning lack of conscience. 'Psychopaths are social predators who charm, manipulate, and ruthlessly plough their way through life, leaving a broad trail of broken hearts, shattered expectations, and empty wallets. Completely lacking in conscience and in feelings for others, they selfishly take what they want to and do as they please, violating social norms and expectations without the slightest sense of guilt or regret.'[2]

Hare has developed a checklist of personality traits which allows him to identify the psychopathic personality. It is a list of classic behaviour patterns common to all those with a psychopathic personality, whether it be violent or non-violent. An individual has to fit all of the following to qualify as a psychopath:

Glibness/superficial charm
Grandiose sense of self-worth/egocentric
Pathological lying
Lack of remorse or guilt
Shallow emotions
Callous/lack of empathy
Failure to accept responsibility for actions

Self-centred and callous, totally lacking the power to experience another's feelings or to form warm emotional relationships with others – the very qualities that allow us to live in civilized harmony – these are the people, in Hare's view, who make up a major proportion of the world's 'serial killers, rapists, thieves, swindlers, con men, doctors who have lost their licences, wife beaters, white-collar criminals, hype-prone stock promoters, gang members, disbarred lawyers, drug barons, and unscrupulous business people.'[3]

Such a person's egocentricity makes him see himself as the centre of the universe, with a grossly inflated sense of his own importance. This superiority justifies his breaking of other people's rules. A truly Hitlerian sense of the unimportance of the *Untermensch* is revealed. Psychopaths often come across as arrogant, shameless braggarts, opinionated, domineering and cocky. Nevertheless they appear charismatic to some people. They are seldom embarrassed by legal, financial or personal problems, seeing them as temporary setbacks, the result of bad luck or an unfair, incompetent system. This applies to the non-violent and violent psychopath alike. The flawed newspaper baron Robert Maxwell displayed many of these character-istics.

Their lack of remorse manifests itself in a stunning lack of concern for the effect of their actions. Much of this is associ-ated with a total lack of empathy – the inability to think or feel themselves into the soul of another person – although they are intellectually capable of thinking themselves into another person's mind. Such people are indifferent to the rights and suffering of family members and strangers alike. If they do maintain ties with family, they see them as chattels, seeming to be more interested in the inner workings of mechanical things than the mechanics of relationships. Such criminals parasiti-cally bleed people of their possessions, their savings, their dignity. An especially appalling class of offenders turn to running old people's homes, farming the elderly as a cash crop, treating them worse than cattle – but these are mercifully a tiny proportion of a generally caring profession.

All this is masked in a general plausibility, a glibness and superficiality. Psychopaths are often witty and articulate, amusing and entertaining conversationalists. They are at the centre of their anecdotes, which invariably cast them in a good or heroic light. Effective at presenting themselves, only the most finely attuned judge of personality can detect their inherent insincerity; there is an element of the play-actor, rehearsing his lines.

Deceit and manipulation are central to the psychopathic character. Psychopaths are totally unconcerned when caught out in lies – lies often told for no apparent motive. They will unblinkingly change their story to accommodate a necessary correction. Some observers get the impression that psychopaths are sometimes unaware that they are lying, others that they are consciously proud of their skill.

But Hare believes that there must be a second set of factors, taking into account the actual behaviour of the subject, and the inherent instability of his lifestyle. These include:

Need for stimulation/proneness to boredom/need for
excitement
Parasitic lifestyle
Poor behavioural controls
Early behaviour problems
Lack of realistic, long-term goals
Impulsiveness
Irresponsibility
Juvenile delinquency
Revocation of conditional release

Hare claims that this Psychopathy Check List (PCL) is very accurate at predicting criminal behaviour, and insists that it is important to distinguish the true psychopaths more precisely from the mass of violent criminals. We need to distinguish them from the others because of the damage they do and the fact that their condition, once they reach adulthood, is incurable.

Psychopaths are not a homogeneous group; and psychopathy is not a sharply defined entity, but rather the product of a number of deviations from the common dimensions of personality. But the 'true psychopath' demonstrates a cocktail of all the behavioural ingredients, in subtly differing degrees, of the characteristics and actions described above.

Plausible, charismatic, intelligent and utterly ruthless, the psychopath feasts on the opportunity fraud provides. As one of Dr Hare's subjects confesses, 'I wouldn't be in prison if there weren't so many cookie jars just begging me to put my hands in them.' His cookie jars were pension funds, stock promotions, charity fund-raising drives and timeshare schemes. He was convicted of selling forged corporate bonds. 'They are fast talking, charming, self assured, at ease in social situations, cool under pressure, unfazed by the possibility of being found out, and totally ruthless. And even when they are found out, they carry on as if nothing had happened, often leaving their accusers bewildered and uncertain about their own positions.'[4]

White-collar crime is lucrative, the chances of being caught are relatively low (Britain's Serious Fraud Office has provided a dismal catalogue of prosecution failures in major cases) and the penalties are often trivial. Society colludes with the psychopath in apparently minimizing the seriousness of the crime; a bank robber may be sentenced to twenty years, but the businessman, lawyer or politician who defrauds the public of millions may even walk away with a fine and a suspended sentence, usually after long legal delays, manoeuvres and compromises.

Frank – a usefully misleading name, implying a candour which was totally alien to his nature – was a specialist in balance sheets. He also fitted Hare's checklist to a T. His scheme was to apply for a succession of jobs as an accountant to various small companies. He did the books well, and conscientiously – and once he had won his employer's confidence, a large chunk of funds would go missing. So would Frank. Often, the companies were too embarrassed to report the theft, but eventually the police caught up with him. Gaol made no difference: each time he had completed his sentence he would go off and 'borrow' from another company into whose trust – and books – he had wormed his way. Frank's charm and manipulative ability meant that he served the minimum of his sentence. He was in his fifties when he finally came out and decided to go straight. This time he was taken on by a prisoners' charity, who were well aware of his background. He did them a wonderful job, and kept his hands clean for a whole year. Then the charity realized that it was missing £30,000 from its books and that Frank was missing too.

All the clues should have been there, in Frank's early patterns of behaviour. As a young lad at school he was always thinking up ways to make money, always borrowing from his best pals for schemes that he said would double their investment. Of course none of them worked, and gradually his friends grew to realize that Frank rarely delivered. He started taking money from his mother's purse when he was four years old – a penny here and a penny there, just enough for her to think that she might have spent it. But then when she did not notice he began to take larger and larger sums, until finally, when he was five, his mother realized who was stealing from her. She tried and failed to curb the stealing and the lying. Frank started stealing from shops at the age of eight, and soon learnt a smarter tactic – to change the price-tags on the goods he 'bought'. He was in constant trouble with the police, but none of what he did had any violent component to it. No one, in Frank's reasoning, ever really got hurt.

Many psychopaths are incorrigible, shuttling between gaol and their next swindle and back to gaol again. Others manage to cut gaol out of the equation, staying just the right side of the law, but using their callousness, ruthlessness, egocentricity and manipulative skills to build a financial empire. With such people, the line between genius and evil is a thin one; the shady deal comes in many different shades. 'If I were unable to study psychopaths in prison,' says the Canadian Richard Hare, 'my next choice would very likely be the Vancouver stock exchange.' Their grandiosity convinces them that they need not play by society's rules, like the New York millionairess jailed for tax evasion who said that 'only the little people pay taxes'.

They need not necessarily fall foul of the law. The corporate psychopath, although an uncomfortable workmate, can rise successfully through an organization, even though those nearest to him realize that he is a liar, a bully and a fraud. 'David' is a case in point. He first attracted attention for irregularities in his c.v., which he managed to brush aside. His constant tirades at company meetings and verbal abuse to those in inferior positions won him no friends – but he managed to convince those higher up the corporate ladder that his tantrums were evidence of creative genius, his aggression and backbiting manifestations of a commendable ambition. Thus his manipulation and lack of integrity have actually helped him proceed up the corporate ladder. Whether we hear more of him or not depends on the success with which he keeps this side of the law.

Psychopaths' lack of remorse or guilt goes with a confident ability to rationalize their behaviour or divorce themselves from responsibility for the havoc they wreak on other people's lives. In some cases they deny that anything happened at all. The few studies of embezzlers show that, to a man, they considered what they had done as a mere loan which they had unfortunately been prevented from repaying. Because they have no sense of guilt, psychopathic conmen have no sensation of fear. Because they have no real concept of right and wrong, they can lie with the fluency of a preacher. They can charm the birds out of the trees, and the dollar bills out of the most prudent bank account, and have not the slightest compunction about doing so. In their book, it would be criminally foolish *not* to exploit the gullibility of others.

'Brad' comes from a respected professional family. His younger sister is a lawyer. Three times married, with a love of fast cars and expensive apartments, a cocaine user and inveterate gambler, Brad has been serving a four-year sentence for a breach of trust involving millions of dollars. He took the money from the trust accounts of several clients and even defrauded his own family members by forging cheques on their accounts. When caught, he said that he had only borrowed the money to cover a temporary, if drastic, reversal on the stock exchange; naturally, he would have paid back every last cent, plus interest, if the officers of the law had not clumsily intervened. As a teenager, the writing was on the wall. Although he did well at school academically, and was considered bright, his parents frequently had to bail him out when he was arrested for vandalism, bullying or, on one occasion, sexually assaulting a twelve-year-old. He went to law school, where he was caught with drugs, but neatly sidestepped the problem by claiming they were someone else's. He was released on licence, but promptly broke the terms of his parole. He has no sense of remorse – there is an insurance fund, he says, to recompense his victims – and as for himself, he regards his prison sentence as having settled any outstanding account. In his interviews with Dr Hare, Brad came across as very pleasant and convincing, like so many: 'Given their personality it comes as no surprise that psychopaths make good impostors. They have no hesitation in forging and brazenly using impressive credentials to adopt chameleon-like professional roles that give them prestige and power. When things begin to fall apart, as they usually do, they simply pack up and move on.[5]

A case in point is that of a Vancouver man who posed as an orthopaedic surgeon, performing a number of operations, including some quite difficult ones. He lived a lavish life, and was a regular at local charity galas and high-profile events. He had sexual relations with several of his 'patients'. When evidence of botched operations inevitably surfaced, he simply decamped, leaving behind an embarrassed medical community and a number of physically and emotionally damaged patients. A few years later he turned up in England and was arrested and goaled for posing as a psychiatrist. At trial, it emerged that he had also posed as a social worker, a police officer, an undercover customs agent and a psychologist specializing in marital problems. He received a short sentence and is now free. What or who he is presently claiming to be, we do not know.

Usually flagrant abuse of trust is involved – for trust and loyalty do not figure in the psychopath's moral vocabulary – as in the cases of therapists who exploit their patients, fathers who sexually abuse their children, priests who use their status to mask their seduction of choirboys. 'I just take what's available,' said one of Hare's subjects, who had been convicted of sexually assaulting his girlfriend's eight-year-old daughter.

In a very literal sense, psychopaths do not have feelings like the rest of us. Studies show that, like other criminals, they lack the normal mechanisms of arousal which ring alarm bells of fear in most people. They lack any concept of empathy. Confronted with trial and danger, their skin does not sweat and become clammy like the skin of normal people. Few studies have been conducted on the brains of fraudsters, but those that there are show that the psychopathic fraudster has a brain in which the frontal lobes – concerned with conscience, guilt and remorse and where our morality resides – are disconnected from the limbic area, which generates these feelings. Indeed, the very latest research, using modern technology to examine the brains of non-violent psychopaths, measured the reaction of the group to a number of words. Some of these words were neutral, nonsense words, while others – like rape, death, murder, cancer – carried strong connotations. The individual under study was connected to an EEG, to measure brain activity, and did a test on the computer at the same time. He had to judge, as fast as possible, if the word was a real or a nonsense word.

EEG patterns show where and how this discrimination takes place. In normal people the neutral words are assessed in the parietal region, a basic language-processing centre at the back of the brain, and activate only this area. But the emotionally-loaded words trigger other areas of the brain, in particular the frontal lobes, where each emotional connotation is being checked for its significance against memories from the past. For instance, the word 'cancer' will trigger associations with friends, families, fear, death or sorrow.

But if the same tests are done on people who are diagnosed as psychopathic by Hare's checklist, the emotionally loaded words are processed on a much more superficial level, like the neutral or nonsense words. The psychopath does not distinguish between the recognition of emotional words versus neutral words. For him, no matter how emotional the word, the EEG brain pattern was the same – unlike a normal individual's; the psychopath did not make emotional connections with the words. This suggests that the psychopath does not process information – and feelings – like the rest of us.

Hare teamed up with another psychiatric researcher in New York, Johanne Intrator. She used a new technology known as SPECT, which combines the picture of the brain's structure and geography provided by magnetic resonance imagers with the record of brain activity supplied by PET scans. SPECT examined normal and psychopathic types while engaged upon the word test described earlier. What emerged was a dramatic difference.

In normal individuals, neutral words activated only the back of the brain and the emotional words activated both the back and the frontal lobes. In the psychopath the emotional words registered only at the back of the brain, in the same way as the non-emotional words. They were fully aware of the meaning of the words, but did not hear the emotional music.

Another Canadian researcher has found a similar pattern. Psychopaths have emotions – they get angry, like the rest of us – but they cannot express them in terms of feeling; ask them what guilt is, and they find it an alien concept. The amygdala generates the emotions, but these emotions make no contact with the thinking part of the brain, the frontal lobes, to put those feelings into words, or even to suggest corrective alternatives. They know the difference between right and wrong, but the difference does not matter. This disconnection in the brain makes it hard for the psychopath to understand or imagine the pain of other people; he has no feeling of disquiet or disgust about his actions.

Honesty and greed are influenced, then, by the chemistry and structure of the brain, with the psychopath displaying the most dramatic and identifiable damage. The problem is that those characteristics of ruthlessness and dispassionate decisiveness are the very qualities which will propel him to positions of power, influence and trust which he can abuse, exploit and betray.

CHAPTER 8

Mindless Violence?

IN ONE OF those Victorian gaols that really *look* like a gaol – a dour, mock-Gothic castle of a place, with clanging doors and echoing landings – the governor surveys his domain. He is nearing retirement, and a lifetime in the prison service has blunted the liberal ideals with which he entered it. 'I realize now,' he says, 'that my job is mostly to warehouse thoroughly nasty pieces of work, providing a penal dustbin for people who are beyond rehabilitation.' The prison chaplain demurs – all souls are capable of salvation, he maintains. But somehow we feel that his own faith is somewhat stretched.

In what may seem a stunning statement of the obvious, the most violent inmates of the world's gaols are classified as suffering from 'antisocial personality disorder' or APD. This is a somewhat self-fulfilling definition, since one of the factors which contributes to this diagnosis is the fact that they have a prison record for violent crimes. In statistical terms, APD is at the root of 55 per cent of crime. In blunt terms, we are talking about thoroughly unpleasant, violent behaviour, for which there seems to be no excuse.

There does, however, seem to be a lot of it around. An American epidemiological study of more than 19,000 citizens of St Louis identified a lifetime prevalence of APD in 7.3 per cent of males. The figure for females was 1 per cent. Projected against the adult population of the USA, that adds up to 8.87 million men and 1.27 million women capable of thoroughly unpleasant, inexcusable violence.

Among this antisocial aggressive group researchers now think that there is an even more dangerous sub-set of psychopaths. How the numbers break down – even whether or not we can categorize the psychopath as a distinct group – is a matter of guesswork and debate. Some estimate that 90 per cent of APD subjects can be classified as psychopaths. Another eminent expert believes that the true psychopath is a small percentage of the violent types, but represents a large percentage in the population, given that not all psychopaths are necessarily violent – they include, for instance, the callous, cheating mind we have already met. The outstanding characteristic of psychopaths is a total lack of guilt or remorse. They can do the most terrible things without feeling a pang of remorse. They have no constraints – nothing that the rest of us would call conscience. One estimate is that 20 per cent of male and female prison inmates can be classified as psychopaths.

In examining the biological and chemical roots of violence, we will be referring to both categories of violent criminal – the antisocial personality disordered and the psychopathic – and we will discover that there are identifiable differences in the origin and expression of their violence.

Violence is a fact of prison life – but the psychopathic prisoner stands out, committing more than twice as many violent and aggressive acts both in and out of prison as other criminals. We all of us are capable of violence, the moment provocation goes beyond our control and we lash out. It doesn't happen very often, and afterwards we feel foolish and ashamed. Most of us, at least, feel that way, even some violent criminals. But for a few, violence is almost routine, and shame is an irrelevant emotion. Diagnosed violent psychopaths have typically committed more offences, received more prison sentences and spent more time in prison than other violent criminals. They are twice as likely as normal offenders to reoffend, and the likelihood of committing further violent offences upon release is triple that of other offenders. As for their victims and their crimes, a study has shown that the normal violence of non-psychopathic criminals occurs in the course of a domestic dispute or a period of intense emotional upheaval; the violence of the psychopath more frequently occurs during the commission of a crime or during a drinking bout, or is motivated by revenge or retribution. Two thirds of the victims of normal criminals are family members or friends; with the psychopath two thirds of his victims are strangers.

These people have lived with violence for a long time. There is not a simple cure, because there is not a simple diagnosis; their violence is not a single pattern, but countless combinations of many different ones – and each of these patterns, in turn, reacts with the other cards in the hand, the cards of genes, personality, mind chemistry and brain function. As we know, the psychopath is in a class of his own when it comes to feeling – a strong clue that there is a specific dysfunction in the brain which sets him apart from the mass of APD criminals, most of whom are capable of some remorse, some regret.

The violent psychopath has the same checklist of personality factors that apply to the fraudulent conman and is extremely skilful at concealing his behaviour. Robert Hare's checklist again helps us to distinguish the violent psychopath, whose condition 'casts the longest shadow in terms of future social deviance' from the general mass of the aggressive and antisocial. We are familiar with the catalogue:

a lack of guilt, loyalty or empathy; an incapacity to form deep or meaningful interpersonal relationships; a failure to learn from experience or punishment; profound egocentricity and superficial charm; persistent antisocial and criminal behaviour without any evidence of remorse for the harm done to others; and a predisposition to aggression particularly under the influence of alcohol.'[1]

Thus the natural role of the psychopath, almost by definition, is criminal. That impulsiveness, that lack of internal control, the absence of the pricking voice of conscience or concern for others' feelings, all these are the ingredients of violent criminality.

Few women would seem to figure among that catalogue, but the female psychopath, though three to four times rarer than the male, is likely to show the same indifference to the suffering of others and to exhibit even stronger antisocial attitudes, although is less likely to resort to actual violence. There is a suggestion that women psychopaths seek out their male equivalents to commit crimes – like the child-killing duo of Myra Hindley and Ian Brady, who tortured their victims before killing them and burying them on the Yorkshire Moors. Even after years of imprisonment, and a concerted campaign to prove to the public that she represents no danger to them, Hindley is capable of joking, 'I don't know why they call me the Moors Murderer – I've never murdered a Moor.' Such insensitivity to the families of her young victims is a classic psychopathic trait. Brady accepts his fate and acknowledges his condition.

The psychopath baffles us, because his is a mental disease which wears the mask of sanity. The severe psychopath may seem to enjoy robust mental health. Psychopaths are not disoriented or out of touch with reality, as may be the case with schizophrenics. They do not suffer the delusions, hallucinations or distress that characterize most other mental illnesses. They are rational and aware of what they are doing, and the law accepts that their behaviour is the result of choice freely made. The Moors Murderers were not acting on the instructions of mystic voices. They knew what they were doing, and the consequences of it.

The psychopath intellectually knows that what he has done is wrong; it's just that he does not care about it. Many violent inmates express no regret for the appalling injuries they have inflicted. They feel justified in their actions. 'He was asking for it.' Since the expression of regret is necessary for parole or release on licence, many psychopathic offenders soon learn to display a synthetic regret. Inside, the denial or self-excusing continues.

There is very little appreciation of the emotion, for instance, of fear. Indeed, it is this failure to feel the terror which they are inflicting on others which makes it possible for them to do what they do, and which helps us distinguish them from the normal, nasty-piece-of-work APD criminal; the APD is usually sparked into a violent act, losing control of himself, whereas the psychopath takes his opportunities coolly as they arise.

One rapist, high on the psychopathic checklist scores, said of his victims, 'they are frightened, right; but don't you see, I don't really understand it. I've been scared myself and it wasn't unpleasant.'[2]

Indifferent to the feelings of others, they are also possessed of a glibness that allows them to charm and to manipulate their victims – and the system – alike. One 24-year-old murderer recounted his life on video for the benefit of forensic psychiatrists. In the video he described how he had left home at 8, started flying at 11, and achieved his pilot's licence at 15. A whole catalogue of personal triumph followed. It was all untrue.

Given this emotional poverty among psychopaths, they can appear cold and dispassionate. For them, sexual arousal takes the place of love, sadness is equated with frustration. Laboratory experiments using biomedical recorders have shown a lack of the physiological responses normally associated with fear – significant when we remember that the threat of punishment is a powerful motivator of behaviour. One psychologist described the psychopath as one who 'knows the words but not the music.'[3]

The merely antisocial and aggressive APD type may lack guilt and remorse in comparison with the non-criminal population, but not to the same extent and not to such a degree as the psychopath. And there is some interesting new biological evidence to suggest why this may be the case.

James K. faced the electric chair after the particularly brutal double murder of an elderly couple. He says he does not remember what happened or what triggered the shooting, which occurred during the course of a robbery. As a boy, he had a history of violence at school, but, significantly, it was not the cruel manipulative type; he had a short fuse, and got into a lot of fights, but never inflicted deliberate suffering on animals or his weaker brethren. He had been prescribed Ritalin, in an attempt to rectify his under-arousal and his chemical need for kicks.

As he got older the violence got worse, especially when fuelled by alcohol; for the naturally impulsive, drink is particularly dangerous since, as a depressant, it further weakens what brakes there are on behaviour.

Yet James K. was capable of remorse, and not, it seemed, the synthetic remorse that the psychopath might display in order to escape the horrors of judicial execution. Professor Frank Woods conducted a PET scan of his brain and discovered a classic pattern associated with antisocial personality disorder, but distinct from the condition of the psychopath. While in the psychopath there is a disconnection between the emotional limbic system and the thinking orbitofrontal cortex, James K.'s connections were intact. What he had, however, was specific damage in the amygdala, which was capable of generating an instant and furious storm of rage – responsible for the 'short fuse' in the playground, and the 'red mist' of uncontrollable anger which led to the murders. Guilty of the crime, yet capable of genuine remorse, James K. escaped the electric chair.

The problem with identifying what Hare calls 'true psychopaths' lies in the very nature of the sample studied – prisoners. Inmates are mistrustful of outsiders – especially academics – and, as long as research relies on self-report criteria, they are likely to pull the wool over the eyes of their well-intentioned investigators. One study using a battery of self-report tests concluded that one particular individual was caring and needed only the psychological equivalent of a warm hug. He turned out to be a callous killer. Another inmate has become so skilled in filling out the Minnesota Multiphasic Personality Inventory, the MMPI, that he has a complete set of booklets and score sheets, and runs a profitable enterprise coaching fellow inmates in how to fill in the test in such a manner as to improve the chances of parole. A third decided to portray himself as anxious and depressed, and produced an MMPI profile suggesting mild depression. He was given Valium, which he then sold to the other inmates. It's hard to resist

Hare's conclusion that the literature is 'cluttered with studies that purport to be about psychopathy but have little to do with it.'[4]

The most obvious expression of psychopathy is the disregard and criminal violation of society's rules, which, while shared by those identified as APD, is much more consistent and intense. But many psychopaths either avoid detection or avoid incarceration, by dint of their charm or their chameleon camouflage, the only evidence of their misdeeds being the wreckage of the lives they leave behind them.

The total pattern of the psychopath's personality differentiates him from the normal criminal. Aggression is more intense, his impulsivity more pronounced, his emotional reactions more shallow. His guiltlessness, however, is the critical distinguishing trait. The normal criminal has an internalized, albeit warped, set of values. If he violates these standards he feels guilt.[5]

The nature of the psychopath is an area fraught with differing views, even of definitions, and where the battleground of nature versus nurture is fiercely fought over. The best evidence is that there is a biological component to the condition – although environmental factors play a necessary part as well. The conventional view is that the answer lies in some traumatic psychological event in childhood. But for every adult psychopath from a troubled background there is another with an apparently warm and nurturing family life; and most people who have had appalling childhoods do not become psychopaths. In brief, in the words of a leading researcher, 'I can find no convincing evidence that psychopathy is the direct result of early social or environmental factors.'[6]

The evidence of childhood, however, provides one clue to help us distinguish the psychopath from the 'normal', violent offender. All violent, antisocial adults have one thing in common – they were violent, antisocial children. American clinicians believe we can identify such people from their early actions. By the age of fifteen, they will have been involved in at least three of the following categories of misdemeanours: truancy, expulsion or suspension from school, delinquency, running away, lying, substance abuse, thefts, vandalism and fights. After the age of eighteen the individual will exhibit four or more behaviours from the following: inconsistent work patterns, inability to function as a responsible parent, unlawful activities, inability to maintain an enduring attachment to a sexual partner, irritability and aggressiveness, failure to honour financial obligations, impulsiveness or failure to plan ahead, repeated lying and recklessness with a motor vehicle.

The young psychopath, too, will have been involved in this sort of behaviour – but with one, critical difference. Robert Hare believes that his checklist includes the extra dimension of the psychopath, even in childhood – the callous and unfeeling nature of his behaviour.

> Jason has a record of breaking and entering, theft and assault on younger children. This began when he was six. Now a veteran of thirteen, he robs the homeless, especially 'faggots' or 'bag women'. Jason explains his philosophy. 'I like it. My fucking parents really freak out when I get in trouble. I don't give a shit as long as I'm having a good time . . . Other people? You want the truth? They'd screw me if they could, only I get my shots in first . . . One guy I got in a fight with pulled a knife and I took it and rammed it in his eye . . . he went around screaming like a baby. What a jerk.'[7]

Hare thinks that all the distinctive signs can be evident at a very young age. One mother wrote to him in despair, 'My son is always wilful and difficult to get close to. At five years old he had figured out the difference between right and wrong – if he gets away with it it's right, and if he gets caught it's wrong. From that point on it has been his mode of operation. Punishment, family blowouts, threats, pleas, counselling and a run at a psychology camp haven't made the slightest difference. He is now fifteen and has been arrested seven times.'[8]

Many fear to pin the label of psychopath on to a child; but Hare believes that clinical experience and empirical research clearly indicate that the raw materials of the disorder can and do exist in children. 'Psychopathy does not spring unannounced at adulthood.'[9] Such children are inexplicably different from normal youngsters: more difficult, wilful, aggressive, and deceitful, harder to relate to or get close to, less susceptible to influence and instruction and always testing the limits of social tolerance. In the early years the hallmarks are persistent, almost routine lying; apparent indifference to the feelings of others; defiance of parents or teachers; petty theft from other children; persistent aggression and bullying; a record of truancy; absence from home; a pattern of hurting or killing animals; early experimentation with sex; vandalism or fire setting.

Else, a very attractive and sweet-looking girl, was six when she deliberately took the brakes off the family jeep and nearly ran her father down. Always a strange child, she never showed any signs of guilt. She would lie and steal without compunction. Else was always in trouble at school – she would think up schemes and persuade all her playmates to go along with them, but it nearly always ended up with Mary winning all the sweets and toys, having duped her friends. It was after the second time she set the car to run down her father, and in school tried to amputate the fingers of her classmates with a cigar cutter, that her parents admitted that she was different from other children. She was also fascinated by fire, and was continually terrifying her parents as they would catch her inside the house with a little fire burning in the sitting-room or in her waste basket. The family stopped keeping pets for fear that she would torture them; she had set fire to previous pets, seriously injuring two of them.

Michael's violence, physical and verbal, appalled his mother; 'I was disgusted by the things that would come out of his mouth.' There was no problem with his other brother and sister until Michael disrupted the entire household. He could never settle, never sleep. Once he could walk, he became uncontrollable. He had a violent temper ... and tantrums. His mother was aware that he was sexually active from a very young age. By five she found that she could not let him in the bathroom with her – he was too curious and she could see him 'looking her over in a sexually overt way'. A dreadful bully at school – he would viciously kick other children – he never seemed to feel guilty about hurting people. As he grew stronger, he turned his violence on to his own mother. He threatened to kill both his sister and his brother – and the threat was taken seriously. Michael was unable to control his anger and rage, and attempts to discipline the child were fruitless, since disapproval went ignored. All the family bears the physical and emotional scars.

We will meet Else and Michael again, because their story is an important argument in favour of identifying such youngsters as psychopaths; for it is only through this diagnosis that steps can be taken to remedy their condition – just as Else and Michael were helped, and are now leading virtually normal lives.

Most children do fairly dreadful things at one stage or another of their lives, and many researchers believe that the very idea of a child psychopath is inconceivable. Psychiatrists distinguish the hard cases – like Else and Michael – from the run-of-the-mill, hyperactive mischiefmakers as suffering from conduct disorder (CD), or, sometimes, attention deficit disorder (ADD). Even so, a diagnosis of conduct disorder is not enough by itself to suggest an inevitable criminal adulthood. Most adult psychopaths met the criteria for CD when they were young, but the reverse is not true: most children with CD will not grow up to become psychopaths – it takes other biological cards in the hand.

Many of the professionals – doctors or teachers – who encounter such children are loth to label them with a condition generally reckoned to be untreatable in adults. Hare acknowledges that it is no light matter to apply psychological labels which may become a self-fulfilling prophecy. Many prefer to tackle the individual manifestations of the problem, such as stealing or bullying, through a behavioural approach. There is a reluctance to believe that such behaviour is anything more than an exaggeration of normal behaviour – all children are manipulative to an extent – or the result of poor parenting or inadequate social conditioning.

But a recent study at two child guidance clinics in the USA examined a group, mostly male, aged between six and thirteen years, referred for a variety of emotional and learning problems. Each child was assessed using the psychopathy characteristics already described in Hare's psychopathic personality checklist. And the research team identified a subgroup with the same pattern of interpersonal features and socially deviant behaviours that characterize adult psychopaths. Many people could not imagine how two children under the age of ten could abduct and murder the baby James Bulger in Liverpool. But in the case of at least one of the children, there were familiar and classic signs matching the psychopathic checklist, such as persistent truanting, thieving and torturing of animals.

Other studies of violent criminals in a sample of juveniles show that those with an early and long history of offending turn out to be the most violent, confirming the significant indicators as truancy, running away from home, initiation of fights using weapons, forced sexual relations, cruelty to animals or people, vandalism, fire-setting, lying and stealing. Such children grow up to become the truly violent criminals. Indeed, every study confirms that early violence and cruelty is a sure sign of violent trouble to come.

But if we can identify such children at such risk – and Hare believes his checklist is virtually foolproof – why don't we do more to catch them early, apply some form of first aid before they come, irretrievably maimed, to court? And we can go further than identify them – we can begin to understand the causes of the problem.

Psychopathy emerges from a complex and poorly understood interplay between biological and social factors. It is based on evidence that genetic factors contribute to biological bases of brain function and to basic personality structure which in turn influence the way an individual responds to and interacts with life's experiences and the social environment.[10]

THE CARDS OF VIOLENCE

So what is it in the biological hand of cards that makes for the violent psychopath and the similar though distinguishable antisocial personality disordered, or APD, violent type? What clues do we have to those 'biological bases of brain function'? What cards make up the fatal flush of the violent offender, whether he be the coldly calculating psychopath or the explosive, impulsive offender?

Some of those factors will be common to the violent and non-violent offender. The IQ factor operates with the antisocial personality disordered type too – the lower the verbal IQ, the more likely it is that the offender will be a repetitive, violent offender. All studies, interestingly, show that non-violent offenders have a higher IQ than violent ones.

But the IQ picture is more complicated when it comes to the psychopath. Those psychopaths, it seems, with low intelligence commit the more violent aggressive crimes, but there is an exceptional group of highly intelligent sadistic psychopaths, most of whom are sexually deviant serial killers and whom we will encounter in a later chapter. Indeed, many psychopaths, as we have seen, have a strong verbal plausibility; so low verbal IQ is a prerequisite not for every psychopath, but simply for those who are extremely, and impulsively, aggressive.

Both the repetitively violent types, the APD and the psychopath, hold the card of hormonal abnormalities. Once again, the familiar story: unsurprisingly, the hormone of aggression is involved. We're already familiar with the finding that plasma testosterone levels are higher in those men who had committed violent offences than in the other men. Those who had committed armed robbery, for instance, had higher rates of testosterone than those who had committed less aggressive crimes. The levels were most striking at the extremes; 9 out of the 11 inmates with the lowest testosterone levels had committed non-violent crimes, while 10 out of 11 inmates with the highest levels had committed the violent crimes. Three groups of prisoners studied over a period of seven years and found to be aggressive and socially dominant had higher levels than prisoners in the control group. The most violent rapist, who had inflicted the most physical injuries during the rape, had higher levels than all other groups of rapists as well as the groups of controls and child molesters.

The conclusion must be that a high level of circulating testosterone leads to a readiness to respond vigorously, aggressively and assertively to provocation and threat. The most potent 'provocation' for intermale aggression is the mere presence of another male on home ground. So we should not be surprised that in the modern city the presence of testosterone is so volatile – a case of biology and the environment interacting to produce violence.

In females, the levels of male hormone are present, but lower. Nevertheless, they have their effect. A study of 84 undergraduate females showed that those who were deemed to be the most stereotypically feminine had the lowest testosterone levels. Those endowed with a high level of masculinity had higher levels; they described themselves as robust, impulsive and resourceful. Those with low levels picked the adjectives civilized, rational, helpful, practical, worrying and serious. While women, as we know, commit less violent crime than men do, women who commit violent crimes may have more testosterone than those who do not.

The urge for excitement has complex underlying neurological and biological explanations, but what is clear is that the high sensation-seeking nature of the criminal is also linked with the high testosterone levels. Studies show that the higher the testosterone the higher the sensation-seeking. Testosterone levels are also associated with a lack of inhibition. Testosterone is also part of the story of why, as men age, and hormone levels fall, they are less prone to violence.

There's also the familiar criminal factor of low arousal. The psychopath and the APD aggressive type show a pattern which indicates abnormally low levels of arousal; the mechanism which keeps us awake and gets us interested in what is going on around us, the little net or reticular formation which filters information and decides whether or not a stimulus is worth reporting to the higher levels of the brain is somehow denser for the violent psychopath. For him, a stimulus has to be extra strong for the brain to take notice; and novel, too – the brain of the psychopath and APD type soon becomes 'habituated' to the stimuli. The violent types all seem to have a very low boredom threshold. The violent mind can carry out very violent acts because the brain is only being stimulated to the extent where the action is perceived as normal. Terrible actions do not register as terrible to that sort of mind. It is as if the violent criminal can only hear the music when the volume is turned deafeningly high.

But the lack of arousal goes deeper in the psychopathic violent type.

They have, as we have seen, a strange emotional coldness. Normal, professional villains feel less anxiety than normal people, but they are not totally devoid of emotion. They fall in love, are proud, jealous, sentimental. For the psychopath, these feelings do not exist. And while APD types may show little emotion other than outbursts of anger, they do not have the same utter emptiness of feeling as the psychopath.

This extra card of low arousal is a telling one, powerful by the very absence it signifies. Psychopaths do not get emotionally aroused; though their violent behaviour may look like emotion, it is more motivated by a lack of care than is the explosive type of rage found in the APD type. The APD types have a low emotional boiling point, leading to inappropriate and aggressive reaction to minor provocation. In the psychopath, the same overreaction is totally dispassionate. If someone happens to annoy them, they must be dealt with . . .

Researchers have developed tools to measure this iciness, based upon physiological responses the body has when it becomes emotionally aroused, whether by fear, joy, love or hate. When our autonomic nervous system – our fear, flight or fight mechanism – is aroused we feel nervous, we start to sweat, our mouths become dry, our heart rate accelerates. For most of us these feelings are unpleasant. We seek to avoid them, and learn to avoid the situations that stimulate these feelings. But there is plenty of evidence that the psychopath has a very low autonomic nervous system response. The Nazi war criminals tried at Nuremberg went relatively calmly to the gallows.

One standard measure of psychological alertness is electrical conductivity of the skin. Small changes in stimuli – even a train of thought or emotion – may produce transient rises in skin conductivity. It is all part of the 'fight or flight' mechanism. As mentioned earlier, when something frightens us, part of that reaction is sweating, a signal of our fear or anticipation of pain. Perspiration increases the electrical conductivity. The phenomenon is at the heart of the so-called 'lie detector' tests. Studies of aggressive psychopaths show that they have a lower level of natural conductivity, and lower spontaneous fluctuations. Thus lie detection tests are least effective with the very people we most want to catch lying. Their hands do not become clammy.

One clue to the nature of a psychopath's low arousal may lie in an experiment conducted on a group of prisoners. They were shown a series of numbers, one to twelve. When the number eight was reached, said the experimenter, they would experience an electric shock. The non-psychopathic criminals showed strong electrodermal responses as the sequence of numbers approached the dreaded number eight. In other words, their nervous anticipation resulted in measurable clamminess. But the psychopaths showed little or no such anticipation, until, that is, just before the fatal number.

Other tests were conducted on prisoners just before they were due to appear in court for trial. Catecholamine levels, which mark the arousal levels in the blood, were found to be understandably high in normal prisoners as the day of judgment approached. But the psychopaths, to judge from their arousal markers, seemed to experience no such sensations. It was almost as if they were unconcerned about their fate.

Psychopaths do what they do, breaking every canon of civilized or human behaviour, because they are more or less impervious to fear and anxiety. They do not learn, as the rest of us do, techniques to avoid turmoil and distressing situations, because they have no spur of pain or distress.

Could it be, then, that the psychopath, because he has no fear, and feels no dread of sanction, is incapable of learning a sense of right and wrong? Does he simply lack the physical apparatus which, in the rest of us, provides our own aversion therapy? We learn by our mistakes, and by punishment, and we learn to anticipate, or at least imagine, the way punishment will make us feel – so we do not transgress. But the psychopath has a link missing from this chain. He cannot imagine the wrong he is doing, nor is he daunted by the fear of the penalty – he knows about it, intellectually, but he does not feel it in the way the rest of us shiver at an anticipated punishment. The psychopath, in brief, is deaf to the forces of society's moral training, whether those forces are parental, from his peers, or from authority. He has little aptitude for experiencing the emotional responses of fear and anxiety that are the mainsprings of conscience. In most of us, early childhood punishment or disapproval laid down a lifetime's association between social taboos and feelings of anxiety – we learn by experience: but what happens when you are incapable of appreciating the experience? As far as deterrence is concerned, a sort of moral amnesia rules. No penalty has the slightest effect in barring the psychopath from his chosen gratification.

To psychopaths, responsibility for others is an alien concept. One prison inmate of twenty-five who had more than twenty convictions for dangerous driving had killed a pedestrian in a case involving criminal negligence; asked if he would continue to drive he shrugged and said, 'Of course ... it takes two to have an accident . . .' The tiny proportion of AIDS rapists who force unprotected sex on their victims have, in the overwhelming majority of cases, been found to be psychopathic.

The non-psychopathic, APD offender, has, as we will see, a similar problem with moral understanding; his anxiety levels are lower than those found in non-offenders, but in his case, as opposed to the psychopath, the problem seems to lie in an inability to apply the necessary brakes to behaviour.

All repetitively violent offenders hold one set of cards in common – they have a distinctive brain chemistry. We're by now familiar with the phenomenon of low serotonin levels, a card common to the hands of all criminals, violent and non-violent alike. This results in impulsiveness, but whether that impulsiveness expresses itself in violent or non-violent action depends on the interplay with the individual personality. While the APD offender may lash out in disproportionate overreaction, the psychopath, with his emotional detachment, will impulsively take whatever course of action will supply him with the necessary gratification; most psychopaths explain their actions by saying 'I did it because I felt like it.'

One example cited is the man who was walking to a party one night and decided to buy a case of beer. He had left his wallet at home. Some blocks away from home by now, he didn't want to walk back, so he picked up a heavy bit of wood and robbed the nearest gas station, seriously injuring the attendant.

Psychopaths live with no coherent sense of the future, changing their plans frequently – as the fancy takes them. They display no concern about what tomorrow will bring, nor about what they have done with their lives.

Typical behaviour comes from another psychopathic inmate, who made a telephone call to his wife from the prison pay phone. She told him that she would not be able to visit this weekend as she could not find a sitter for their children. So he would not get the cigarettes and food he had requested. 'You fucking bitch,' he yelled down the phone. 'I'll kill you, you whore.' Seconds later he was laughing and joking with the other inmates, and could not understand why he was punished for verbal abuse.

There is a hair trigger to psychopathic violence; but it is different from the heat of the normally aggressive prisoner. As Hare says, 'when they "blow their stack" . . . they know exactly what they are doing. Their aggressive displays are cold; they lack the intense emotional arousal experienced by others.'[11] An accidental bump in the canteen led to one inmate beating another senseless. The attacker then stood back in line as if nothing had happened. When asked to explain his actions, he said, 'I was pissed off. He stepped into my space. I did what I had to do.'

The APD violent offender may manifest the same behaviour, but in his case it is likely to be the result of low serotonin and, as we will see, an inadequate control mechanism. Study after study indicates that lowered levels of serotonin contribute to impulsiveness, disinhibition or lack of control. Violent offenders with explosive or antisocial personalities represent the most extreme serotonin deficits. Low levels don't produce aggression *per se*, but they increase the tendency to respond aggressively to provocation. A connection has been established between low serotonin levels in young adults and a childhood history of behaviour which typically includes lying, stealing, killing a pet or fire-setting. The most disruptive children, whose disruption includes cruelty to other children, are the ones with the lowest serotonin levels, and have been found to be the most likely to progress to adult violence.

The violent types have a royal flush of chemical cards predisposing them to violent outbursts. Violence is likely to persist, until age begins to damp down the general biochemistry of the body and the criminal activities of the antisocial offender and his violence diminish. The serotonin levels increase as he ages, so increasing the brakes on his impulsive nature. But the violence of the psychopathic type tends not to decline with age; it is believed that some psychopaths continue to the day they die, getting better at avoiding detection, but remaining the same egocentric, shallow, manipulative and callous characters.

There is no 'gene for crime', but there is evidence of a genetic input to antisocial personality disorders. The APD types seem to have a cluster of personality traits that make them more prone to express violence. They tend to be more hostile, less 'affiliative' – meaning they seem to care less about relationships. As for the psychopath, as we have seen, he has a very distinct pattern of personality characteristics that make him stand out from the rest of us – lack of guilt, inability to feel what others feel, a cold and hostile profile.

All these characteristics have components that are inherited, and they are all related to our body chemistry. Low serotonin is linked to impulsiveness, and serotonin levels can be inherited. Twin studies have shown that sensation-seeking, one of the core characteristics of the psychopath, and a classic manifestation of low serotonin, is a substantially inherited characteristic. Aggression is not a single behaviour factor, but a combination of irritability, impulsiveness and hostility; but these have a common causal origin in serotonin – and an 80 per cent heritability is one estimate for MAO, the chemical marker for serotonin levels. Social and cultural influences, the study concluded, 'account for little'.

Other twin studies indicate that APD is inherited 'epistatically', in other words that it is produced by a very specific pattern of a number of different genes interacting with each other to produce this type of personality.

Also influencing APD is the gender card which, again, is a matter of genetics. The evidence shows that women 'need' much harsher environmental conditions to become antisocial than do men.

A dramatic illustration of the claimed existence of a genetic dimension to crime is provided by the case of Stephen Mobley.

Stephen Mobley is an armed robber and a murderer. He faces the electric chair, but his lawyers say that because he comes from an identifiably long line of robbers, rapists and killers he cannot be held fully responsible for his actions. They argue not the existence of a criminal gene – merely that a build-up of genetic propensities to crime is bound to influence the behaviour of the man at the end of the line. His father told the court how Stephen 'just couldn't develop a value system or a conscience'. He had trouble since schooldays, lying, stealing and destroying property. The family tried to help, sending him away for specialist treatment, but nothing seemed to work. All the psychiatrists could discover was that he had 'never internalized a true value system . . . he does not have loyalty to anyone, including parents.'

The classic definition of a psychopath's lack of remorse, lack of conscience, lack of loyalties. The jury – in all senses – is still out on the argument that Stephen Mobley inherited his disordered hand of cards from his relatives – from the five close relations who had spent time in gaol for robbery, drugs, and murder? Or from his great-grandparents, including a great-grandmother, Cora Mae, described as 'lacking the ability to tell right from wrong'?

But while there are strong hints of a genetic dimension to violence, science can now offer further biological facts to explain the phenomenon. We can actually find a neurological explanation for that lack of conscience, failure to learn from our mistakes or society's disapproval; and here again we find a difference between the violent antisocial personality disordered type and the psychopathic type. It seems to be the result of an identifiable brain dysfunction.

Study after study of repetitively violent types has indicated problems in a whole variety of brain areas from the frontal and temporal lobes to the limbic system – especially in the rage control area of the amygdala. Blind tests, based on anonymous brain scans, resulted in criminals being distinguished from the non-criminal 87 per cent of the time. We know that brain damage in the frontal lobes, the limbic system or both results in a brain deficient in the normal control systems – the brakes on behaviour are faulty. The violent APD offender, in every study, has been shown to have this sort of abnormality; all have damage to the frontal, temporal or limbic system in one or every combination. The violent psychopath also has this card – but he has an extra dimension of brain abnormality, and one which we have already seen in the non-violent psychopath. In the psychopath the brain mechanism that generates feeling, the limbic system, is not connected to the frontal cortex, the area which is involved in learning from the consequences of our behaviour. This explains why the APD offender, however nasty a piece of work he is, is capable of remorse, while the psychopath is literally detached from the pain he causes. According to one report 91 per cent of psychopaths showed significant neuropsychological dysfunction in the left frontal lobes.

'The level of evidence is substantial,'[12] one scientist concludes. Other studies of behavioural changes following localized brain damage show that impulsiveness and lack of the normal capacity for reflective delay, and the classic features of the psychopath – impulsiveness, apathy, aggression, egocentricity, incapacity for normal affection, absence of conscience, lack of insight, impaired foresight, inability to learn from experience, poor judgment, untruthfulness and absence of normal sense of fear – are all associated with damage in the prefrontal regions of the brain.

Eliza's delinquency career started at the age of 10. By the time she was 17 she had been arrested twice for assault with intent to kill. Her three adult offences were aggravated assaults. She was of high to normal intelligence, but she would often lie and show no reaction when her inconsistencies were pointed out to her. She would manipulate her parents and steal from them, never showing remorse if she was caught out.

What had tipped her into these extremes of childhood delinquency? Doctors discovered that at the age of six she had suffered a head injury due to a car accident. There was a second head injury two years later, whose cause is unknown. The original injury may have left Eliza with some of the basic personality characteristics typical of the psychopath, – for instance the lack of remorse – while the second may have prevented the self-control she might otherwise have exercised on her naturally destructive, remorseless personality.

In the violent mind, the pattern is not necessarily of observable organic brain damage. It is what researchers call brain dysfunction – the sort of dysfunction that would normally be caused by physical damage, but which does not in all cases seem to spring from any obvious trauma.

With the use of magnetic image resonators, we can scan the brain's anatomy – but we need more sophisticated tools yet. EEGs traditionally examine activity in the cortex or thinking parts of the brain, but with the revolutionary new tool of PET scans to look at the function of the brain and to measure the electrical or biochemical activity within it we can eavesdrop on every corner of the brain, and its basic physiological and biochemical processes.

What's beginning to emerge – and PET technology is scarce and expensive – is that in violent criminals, although there may be no structural damage as such, part of the brain may malfunction under stress – rather like a computer which seizes up or crashes: the chips themselves look just the same as before but the activity has somehow ceased. And there seem to be several distinctive 'chip' failures which contribute to the card for violence, and the violent psychopath in particular.

One specific abnormality is interesting: scans of psychopaths show a set of abnormalities in several basic cognitive functions involved in the processing of language. Speech is usually housed on the left side of the brain, and linked to emotion, but in the psychopath verbal processing seems to be more a right hemisphere function – divorced from feeling, and more associated with action. Does this account for the psychopath's use of language to manipulate others, rather than to express real feelings? Could it also account for the phenomenon of 'semantic dementia' in psychopaths, where words seem to have no personal meaning – a disorder that goes beyond conventional, deliberate lying. The evidence also suggests that psychopaths exhibit some strange speech patterns. The evidence has also led some scientists to the theory that psychopathy is a deep-seated form of memory loss – they can tell lies and blatantly inconsistent stories because they have 'forgotten' almost immediately the truth of what they are saying.

We have already noted how low arousal permits the psychopath to commit dreadful acts with no sensation of fear for the consequences. But the most dramatic brain card, and one that in the end explains much of the psychopath's behaviour, remains that disconnection between the feeling brain and that area of the brain involved in learning the lessons of conscience. Conscience, if it has a home, lives in the lower portion of the frontal lobes (the dorso-orbital area). In normal people, it is connected with the structures of the emotional brain. The psychopath's total lack of conscience or guilt is related to the fact that his fear responses are disconnected from the planning part of his brain. They are not shackled by a nagging conscience. Any action, from petty theft to bloody murder, is thus permissible. Violence is simply an instrument to be used to satisfy a simple need such as sex or power. There is no regret at the damage done. Indifference springs from a mind incapable of the emotion, or of connecting the act with the result.

A psychopath has damage, too, to the temporal lobes, where our sense of identity is normally housed. So, psychopaths may be able to distance themselves from the acts they perpetrate. The temporal lobes also include some of the limbic regions in the anterior portions, where our fear and rage are housed. EEG studies of psychopaths show a consistent pattern of damage to this key emotional control centre of the brain, but PET scans have discovered damage which the EEGs did not pick up.

The types of dysfunction are legion. They all result in

different behavioural problems, and the more you have of them the more violent, uncontrollable and incurable the condition. The greater the range and depth of impairment, the greater the degree of violence. The more the brain is functionally abnormal, the less possible it is for the brakes of the frontal cortex to be applied. The cerebral mechanisms involved are still being unravelled; again, we are very much at the frontier of science. But consistent echoes are being returned from this exploration of inner space.

A biological and chemical approach to the problem of crime is sometimes criticized for representing a simplistic analysis, grasped at in desperation because neither the public nor politicians can solve the social problems which environmentalists believe are at the root of crime. The science is not simple, nor are the solutions; but we cannot ignore the evidence. Already, what we know about the biological and chemical roots of violence, from neurotransmitter levels to brain damage and dysfunction, represent a severe problem for the moralist and the penologist. How free is our will, when our internal mechanisms deny us the concept of conscience? How should we be punished, when our actions are in great degree beyond our control?

CHAPTER 9

The Violent Mind: Not Their Fault

THERE IS A third type of violent offender, apart from the APD and the violent psychopath. Once again, his behaviour is caused by underlying biological reasons. A true Jekyll-and-Hyde personality, he is: he appears perfectly normal most of the time – but is prone to sudden outbursts of violent behaviour. Such people hold a biological hand of cards that differs substantially from those of the psychopath and those diagnosed as suffering from antisocial personality disorder.

THE EXPLOSIVELY VIOLENT MIND

There is a class of violent offender who is capable of acts just as savage as the psychopath's, but who nevertheless retains the full ability to show remorse and regret. He has the conscience which the psychopath lacks. He often has no recollection of his actions – particularly if alcohol has been involved, which it often is, since this class of mind is more susceptible to alcoholism than is the case in ordinary people or, for that matter, non-violent offenders.

It's called intermittent explosive disorder, episodic dyscontrol or limbic rage. Prisons are full of people with this problem which, because of the historic poverty of prison medical services, and the fact that part of the illness is the subject's apparent complete normality, is under-diagnosed. The tragedy is that these people are easily treatable and in most cases would have no problem in taking the medication necessary to keep them under control. When they are out of control, however, there is a fit of unbridled rage, where they are capable of inflicting severe injury or even death.

Jason has been in and out of prison all his life, each time as the result of injury that he inflicted on drinking buddies. There was one night that they all remember. They had been drinking and just talking about the usual things – sport, work, the wife. Without warning or apparent provocation Jason tipped up the table, scattering the glasses on the floor. He grabbed a broken glass and started brandishing it, yelling blasphemous abuse at the friends he'd been sitting calmly with only a moment before: they all deserved to die, and he was going to see to it personally that they did. His friends tried to restrain him – and one paid the penalty by receiving a serious cut to the throat. Jason was arrested about a mile from the pub. He asked why the police were detaining him. He had absolutely no memory of the incident. This defence cut no ice at trial. In prison his fellow inmates have learnt to keep clear when the rage begins to come upon him.

An estimated 2–3 per cent of the prison population is represented by people like Jason. They do not have a long history of other offences; theirs is not the familiar graduation from childhood stealing, through adolescent car crime and so on. Their offences are almost always associated with an unpremeditated outburst and consequent injury, usually to an acquaintance or family member. Once again, the gender card comes into play, for this syndrome is much more common in men than women. Yet, as we'll see, women who do fall into this category have the same hand of cards as the men.

One night Agnes set fire to her own home. Her children and husband were asleep indoors. She'd taken a can of paraffin and distributed it over the hall at the bottom of the stairs – probably the most lethal place to set a fire, for a stairwell acts as a funnel, causing a raging firestorm. Her husband nearly died, choking on the sooty smoke. He reluctantly agreed with the police charge of attempted murder. For years he had suffered from her unexplained, tempestuous behaviour; in a way, he hoped that the charge would 'bring her to her senses', or at least ensure that she was given proper medical help.

Both Jason and Agnes have the personality range of a normal person. Their emotional and general arousal levels are normal. But in the hand of violence they hold two major cards, involving the structure of the brain and the chemistry of its operation.

There is a particular form of epilepsy which we can see at work in the explosively violent offender. Epilepsy is not a psychiatric disorder but an expression of neurological damage involving an excessive discharge of electrical activity in the brain. Most epileptics, of course, do not express violent behaviour, but when, in those who have this particular form, this happens in the temporal lobe, there is a sudden and inexplicable alteration in mood. This is almost certainly because of a fault in the regional connections with the limbic system (which generates and controls our emotional responses). The electrical brainstorm cannot be controlled by the higher processes of the brain. All types of epilepsy are more often found among the criminal population than the population at large, and this type is no exception. Also known as psychomotor seizures, the occurrence is ten times higher than would be expected in a normal sample of the population, according to a study of 400 violent prisoners.

The syndrome is not as pronounced as classic epilepsy – there is no occurrence of fits – and the electrical activity happens at a barely detectable level of discharge, which is one reason why it has so often been neglected or overlooked. Unlike mainstream epilepsy it does not show up in the form of abnormal electrical activity in the cortex or the upper part of the brain, but can be identified only if deep probe electrodes are used, passed through the nose so that the deeper regions of the limbic system can be measured.

Doctors at Tulane University, New Orleans, pioneered the exploration of this syndrome, as part of a search for the roots of aggression and schizophrenia. Electrodes were left in the subjects for six weeks and the subject, monitored and measured while engaged in various activities. Eventually, the doctors managed to distinguish covert discharges, which correlated with violent behaviour. They called this episodic dyscontrol.

Most of the people who demonstrated this condition were seemingly normal personalities, who would become aggressive with very little reason. It would take only a mild trigger to produce this abnormal electrical discharge. In a small but significant group of people who show explosively violent behaviour, the explosion comes from within the brain, specifically from the limbic system and the amygdala (which controls – in normal circumstances – anger, hate and other emotional responses). What seems to be happening is that the brain itself generates a form of miniature epileptic fit. An electric storm in the rage areas spreads to the rest of the brain, resulting in apparently unprovoked, unfocused violence, including serious assault and particularly violent rape.

In a different version of the same syndrome a defect in various areas of the limbic system can have a similar outcome; the affected patient has the sensation of feelings that occur in a vacuum – there is no reason or cause for them, but they have been generated internally by this glitch in the system. The mechanism for processing emotions has produced a rogue emotion of its own and it cannot control its own creation. These patients show random outbursts of rage or violence. A high degree of EEG abnormality shows up when depth probes are used to monitor the limbic area, but what it is that causes this sort of electrical storm is not well understood. There is, however, strong evidence that the tiniest amount of alcohol can set off the random electrical activity; it may take very little for Dr Jekyll to transmute to Mr Hyde.

A clinical examination conducted on a large group of men who had behaved in an inexplicably violent manner showed that 94 per cent had neurological abnormalities or dysfunctions in their brain. Most had never seen a doctor before, and didn't realize that they had a problem that was medical rather than psychological. They thought they just couldn't control their temper – and, of course, in a very literal sense they were right.

Unlike the other violent minds we have seen, this is the only brain disorder from which these minds suffer. There is nothing like the extent and degree of brain damage that we have seen in the APD offender and the psychopath, and there is none of the latter's icy and callous lack of remorse – there is no structural disconnection between the conscience and the feeling sections of the brain; after a limbic rage, they deeply and bitterly regret their actions. As a result, many seek help.

There seem to be two causes of this syndrome. The damage may be innate, or it can develop as a result of damage to the limbic system from a head injury or from viral attack. Children from abused families are particularly vulnerable to this sort of damage. When you hit a child round the head, you are not only inflicting psychological damage; when that child subsequently exhibits inappropriate behaviour, the causes may well be physical. Thirty-six per cent of those with dyscontrol syndrome were found, in one study, to have developed it after a brain insult, often resulting in a tumour in the limbic system.

One man underwent a devastating personality change after brain surgery. He set fire to his house, but the court was able to recognize that the action had been taken during an epileptic-type seizure. He was hospitalized, treated with anticonvulsant drugs and made a good recovery. In all such cases treated by his consultant drugs seem to have controlled the syndrome. Other, and familiar, cards may be involved in people with this disorder – they may share with the APD offender and the psychopath a problem with low serotonin levels, which aggravate the condition; but low serotonin levels are only a problem when associated with other negative personality or brain factors, and these people have neither the brain damage nor the personality of the antisocial or psychopathic violent offenders.

This sort of seizure is one cause of 'criminal' behaviour which can be treated, and prevented. Imprisonment, unless it helps to bring the syndrome to the notice of well-informed doctors, seems a more than usually inappropriate response.

There is a specifically female dimension to other periodic bouts of violence. As we saw in Chapter 3, women are cursed with a card unique to their sex which can result in displays of violence, usually referred to as premenstrual syndrome or PMS (the latest name is LLPDD, or late luteal phase dysphoric disorder). Some women are perfectly normal for most of the time, but suddenly, regularly and disastrously run emotionally amok. It affects only some 3–4 per cent of women, but the associated violence can take the form of serious assault or even murder.

Nicola's story is a classic case. She was a cheerful and outgoing twelve-year-old, with her sights set on a professional career as a dancer. Her problems began a year later, when she changed, in her own words, into 'a monster'. She became depressed and irrational in her behaviour. Sometimes she despaired of living. Her weight increased dramatically; even if she had still been interested in dancing she would no longer have been capable of doing so. She was abusive to her parents, attacking her mother with a kitchen knife. It was only when she set fire to the house that she came to the attention of the authorities, but unfortunately it was the police, and not the doctors, who intervened. Nicola was arrested and charged with arson and attempted murder. She was sent to Holloway prison.

Over the past decade, public and health-care interest in PMS has increased, and the syndrome has been used as legal defence. As we saw in Chapter 3, there's a long history of the problem. Strangely, for all the discussion the syndrome has attracted, very little detailed work has been done. We know of no PET scans of women to investigate the phenomenon. Clearly there is a striking similarity to the features of episodic dyscontrol syndrome in the cases of women who may suddenly shout or scream, throw knives, or, in the case of one woman studied by Dalton who regularly tried to kill her boyfriend during the premenstruum by strangling him as he slept. The woman in such a situation 'is powerless to think coherently or act rationally or consciously ... she has no insight into her condition or her actions and any awareness she may have left is only that once menstruation halts the bad dream will go away. It is in that nightmare state that violence can erupt and endow the woman with phenomenal physical strength, although she will have no idea of the damage she may be doing with it. It is an irresistible impulse that directs the action.'

Yet such behaviour can bring a woman into conflict with the law.

Whether or not PMS, or any aspect of it, can be classified as a mental illness is a matter of much debate. It is probable that some women with a fragile mental balance may have it upset as a result of the physical stress of monthly fluctuations. Several surveys have demonstrated increased psychiatric admission during the premenstrual phase – 47 per cent of admissions, in one study, occurred during the critical phase, and a third of admissions, whether for acute depression, suicidal attempts or schizophrenia, occurred within four days of the onset of menses. The fluctuation of the hormones may topple the balance of sanity in several ways – by exacerbating or kindling an underlying psychiatric disorder, or by synchronizing disorders so that they correspond with a particular phase of the cycle.

What new studies are suggesting is a neurochemical dimension to the problem; it seems that in the normal woman with no underlying psychiatric problems, acute PMS is the result of an hormonal effect on the now familiar impulse inhibitor, the neurotransmitter serotonin.

During a woman's cycle, progesterone and oestrogen levels are constantly rising and falling. It is at the premenstruum stage, when both oestrogen and progesterone are falling rapidly, that changes in mood and behaviour occur. The pattern of crime, too, corresponds with the sudden drop of progesterone – it's during this short time period, usually 4–5 days, that problems occur. As we have said, between 44 and 50 per cent of female crimes are committed just before or on the day of menstruation, when progesterone is at its very lowest. (These studies also show that significantly fewer crimes are committed

Days	Phase	Oestrogen	Progesterone
1–4	menstruation	low	absent
5–8	early postmenst	rising	absent
9–12	late postmenst	high	absent
13–16	ovulation	falling	low
17–20	early luteal	rising	rising
21–24	late luteal	high	high
25–26	premenstruum	falling	falling

when a woman is ovulating and during pregnancy, and when progesterone levels are at their peak.)

Progesterone is a hormone which directly affects mood. Chemically it is equivalent to a sedative, and is sometimes prescribed as such. It makes one feel calm and content. When natural progesterone drops suddenly, just before the period starts, the effect is like withdrawing drugs from an addict; the mood is suddenly and dramatically altered. Part of the reason is that progesterone levels are indirectly linked to levels of serotonin; and, as we know, low levels of serotonin are linked to depression and to impulsive behaviour. So when progesterone levels plummet, it is understandable that the effects can be drastic.

There is a simple, and in recent trials 100 per cent successful, fix here as well, although it is so far only available in clinical trials; PMS symptoms can be mitigated by the use of a chemical which blocks the way neurons use up serotonin, or by a treatment which simply enhances serotonin production. These tests on the effectiveness of serotonin now give good reason to believe that it is low neurotransmitter levels which lie at the heart of the PMS problem.

The male hormone, testosterone, also seems to play a part. A study of women with severe PMS showed that they had higher free testosterone circulating than in a control group. We have seen that progesterone, roughly speaking, has a neutralizing effect on testosterone, so low progesterone is likely to result in higher levels of this aggression-provoking hormone. It's an intricate relationship – but what's clear is that all sex hormones influence the brain neurotransmitter serotonin networks.

PMS also seems to be affected by diet. The syndrome is particularly sensitive to low blood sugar. Dr Katherina Dalton, who over the years has treated many thousands of PMS sufferers, is convinced that the irrational mood swings are due to the sudden fall in progesterone just before the start of the period, and that the severity of the mood swing is critically influenced by diet.

Optimum levels of blood sugar are maintained by a self-regulating mechanism. If excess sugar enters the system and the blood sugar level rises too high, insulin is released and the excess sugar is passed out through the urine, thus restoring the blood sugar level to its optimum range. But if blood sugar levels are too low, then the lower regulating mechanism comes into action with a spurt of adrenaline which serves to release the sugar stored in the body's cells.

During the premenstruum, the trigger mechanism changes, especially in sufferers from PMS. The adrenaline burst is fired more frequently, especially if there has been no carbohydrate consumption. You can see what nature intends – to keep energy up at a critical time. Unfortunately, adrenaline has an important side effect – it blocks the transport of progesterone into the cells. So, when PMS sufferers go too long without carbohydrates, the adrenaline prevents the uptake of progesterone by the progesterone receptors. Most of us get ratty when we are hungry – but with the PMS sufferer the effects can be violent. Dr Dalton has found that in every case where one of her PMS subjects committed murder, she had not eaten for 6–7 hours before the irrational outburst occurred. She counsels the taking of many, small and regular carbohydrate snacks.

The debate ebbs and flows among women as to whether the recognition of PMS is acceptable; but our view is that it cannot be right that it is very often a matter of chance as to whether a woman who commits an act of violence in such circumstances is sent to prison or to a hospital – especially when the condition is treatable, and the treatment routinely effective.

Dalton is convinced that PMS does have the redeeming

feature that 'once it has been correctly diagnosed and proper treatment instituted a return to normal health is assured'.[2] She has herself treated over a thousand 'criminal' PMS cases successfully with progesterone. It is, she says, 'a category of explosive violence with an identifiable cause which responds admirably to the correct treatment ... restoring the woman to a normal useful life as a law-abiding member of the community'.

A generous-spirited young man whose girlfriend was prone to attempts to strangle him kept a chart of the occurrences, and took her to see Dr Dalton. The diagnosis of PMS was immediate, and after progesterone treatment the aberrant behaviour stopped. They are now happily married. A young balletomane, Nicola, was also rescued when her father took her to Dr Dalton. She discovered that every downturn had corresponded with the onset of the cycle. At Nicola's trial for murder, a kindly and understanding judge said that she could go free; she was ill, and needed treatment. Progesterone treatment was supplemented with a special diet to iron out the extremes of glucose levels. Nicola still has to take pills to keep her internal chemistry in balance, and will have to do so for the rest of her life.

Some studies, involving the use of placebos, which look like real drugs but have no active ingredients, have questioned the efficacy of the Dalton treatment. The failure to replicate her findings may be the result of the small number of the sample tested, or a confusion in diagnosis with menstrual distress – different from PMS, and not improved by progesterone treatment. But a successful new treatment is an indication that she is on the right lines. The suggestion now is that the underlying problem may be those low serotonin levels – progesterone may not be the answer *per se*, but since progesterone raises serotonin levels progesterone treatment may achieve the same result.

A Scandinavian researcher took a group of women who suffered from severe PMS, but who had no underlying psychiatric problems. He then split the group into two, giving one a placebo, and the other Clomiparamine. This is a drug which, in the jargon of the scientist, is a 'powerful serotonin reuptake inhibitor'. It works by preventing the neurons from removing the serotonin from the synapses, where the electrical connections are made and broken. So the inhibiting messages persist, without losing their power. The result is that low doses of Clomiparamine effectively reduced premenstrual irritability with virtually 100 per cent success. It's another part of a large body of clinical and experimental research suggesting that many of the symptoms of PMS, including poor impulse control, depression, anxiety, sleeplessness and carbohydrate craving may be the result of low serotonin levels.

So it seems that in this particular violent mind there is merely one rogue card – and one which can be trumped with a single chemical remedy. One shivers to think of all the years women have served in wretched prison cells for reasons science has taken so long to identify and cure. There can be no excuse today for a failure of the law, once it has satisfied itself that PMS is genuinely to blame, to realize that violent acts springing from this cause are not a matter for punishment but for care.

EXPLOSIVE VIOLENCE: THE MENTALLY DISTURBED

Not all such explosive violence is so easily contained; much is the result of mental derangement.

Strictly speaking, the law does not hold the mentally disturbed responsible for their actions. The criminal is someone who freely exercises his choice to behave in a way society decides is unacceptable. But as any visitor to prison soon realizes, the inmate population contains a large number of people who have not been capable of exercising that choice, because they are mentally ill.

The legal basis of insanity as a defence goes back to the nineteenth century, and an attempt by a man called McNaghten to assassinate the Prime Minister, Sir Robert Peel. He missed, but killed Peel's secretary. The defence successfully argued that the defendant was suffering from a persecution complex about

Peel, that he had lost control and had been unable to resist his paranoid delusions. He was found not guilty 'by reason of insanity', a decision which gave rise to the McNaghten Rules, incorporating the defence that if the accused does not know the nature or quality of his or her actions, or does not know that those actions are wrong, he cannot be held to criminal account.

Over the years those rules have been modified, but there is a basic problem in this medico-legal overlap. Mental illness is not defined in the Mental Health Act. All depends on medical opinion. The psychiatrist is the one who decides whether an individual is sane or mad. In practice mental illness covers a wide variety of diagnostic categories – psychoses, schizophrenia, affective disorders, anxiety, hysteria and so on. The diagnosis of a mental disorder is inevitably sometimes a subjective judgment.

> The case of the Yorkshire Ripper is an instructive one. Peter Sutcliffe murdered a number of young women, most but not all of them prostitutes. He claimed to be acting on the instructions of 'voices'. The jury was asked to decide whether or not four psychiatrists were right when they diagnosed Sutcliffe as mentally ill. The jury decided they were not, and convicted Sutcliffe of his consciously committed crimes. He was found guilty of murder and sentenced to life imprisonment. Three years later Sutcliffe was transferred to a special hospital . . . because of his mental illness. He is a paranoid schizophrenic. Unless something developed while he was in prison, he always was.

Several studies have looked at the profile of mental disorder in the offender populations. A 1978 study of two English prisons concluded that 34 per cent of 149 inmates could be diagnosed as showing a moderate, marked or severe level of psychiatric disturbance. A more recent study estimates that 31 per cent of prisoners can be regarded as psychiatric cases, compared with a figure of 14 per cent for the general population.

Of those, 30 per cent were diagnosed as psychopathic, a condition, as we have seen, which the law does not accept as a mental disturbance. If you exclude them, and the mentally subnormal, about one in eight of the prison population can be considered mentally ill. They shouldn't be there. Lack of psychiatric resources, and a general lack of priority in penal issues, are the only reasons why they are – wrongly – there. Given that we are dumping the mentally ill into the community without adequate provision, it will be a politically uphill task to argue that the hospitals should be not closed, but used to harbour and treat the mentally ill 'criminal'.

The figure for those who have committed violent offences contains a significantly high proportion of the mentally disturbed. A study of lifers in a London prison found that over two thirds appeared to have some form of psychiatric disorder. Depression and personality disorder were the principal conditions, but as many as 10 per cent were psychotic, almost certainly schizophrenic. And the same diagnosis applies to those in special hospitals who have been involved in serious offences; schizophrenia is the most commonly identified illness, although it should be stressed that in general schizophrenia is not necessarily accompanied by violence.

The first problem with anatomizing the schizophrenically violent mind is that schizophrenia is a cluster of illnesses, not all present in any one patient. Patients are distinguished by disturbances of thought, perception and to some extent movement. Most hallucinations are of heard 'voices', giving instructions or commenting on behaviour, but some may be visual or tactile. Emotion tends to be flat and expressionless, or inappropriate – such as anger without provocation or laughter at misfortune. Motor disturbances can take the form of facial grimaces, or complete catatonic states, where the subject is immobile for hours. Paranoid schizophrenia takes the form of delusions of persecution, where personal, significant threat is perceived in the actions of (uninvolved) bystanders.

While schizophrenics commit the same proportion of non-violent offences as the sane criminal population, sufferers are responsible for a much greater number of violent crimes. A study of male schizophrenics in 1990 reported that their rate of violent offending was nearly four times greater. In another study of inmates of a special hospital, nearly three quarters of those who had killed their mothers were suffering from schizophrenia. The attempt to integrate the mentally ill back into society through 'care in the community' suffers from the rare, but highly publicized incidents of schizophrenics committing random murder. A case which mercifully did not end in a death was the attempt by Ian Ball in 1986 to kidnap Princess Anne in the Mall. He was armed with a gun and acting on the instructions of mystical 'voices' which had to be obeyed. Fireraising is a common theme in schizophrenics. One woman babysitter was initially praised for her efforts to rescue two children from a fire which started in the airing cupboard. It was later discovered that she started the fire herself, and she was jailed for life, after being described as having a 'compulsive fascination for lighting fires'.

The typical schizophrenic is characteristically introverted, indifferent to praise or blame, emotionally cold, subject to unusual perceptions and delusions, and with an odd speech pattern. Unlike the psychopath, he does not – cannot – wear the mask of sanity; his behaviour is palpably abnormal. And although the publicity is out of proportion to the number of such violent incidents, the fact remains that schizophrenics are more likely to commit violent offences than other disordered groups – or, of course, the general population.

But a more intriguing fact, according to those who have studied the pattern, is that schizophrenia may not be in itself the cause of the violence; for a schizophrenic to manifest violent behaviour, he has to have some other cards in his hand – the cards of violence.

But there's not necessarily a simple cause and effect at work here. Although some researchers believe that over 80 per cent of offences committed by the psychotic are attributable to their illnesses, medical opinion today is that the condition of mental disturbance provides the possibility of a violent outcome – but whether or not violence is committed depends on other biochemical and neurophysical conditions.

Once again, we find that low arousability plays its part. Tests on the autonomic nervous system in a group of schizophrenics showed that half of them displayed little or no skin reaction when experiencing a sequence of physical and verbal challenges. The normal resting state of their arousal mechanisms was considerably lower than the average. So we can expect that half of them seek and need the same sensations – risk, danger – which have been found to characterize other, normal offenders with low arousability.

Once again, too, we find that those schizophrenics who have exhibited violent behaviour have comparatively low serotonin levels, although not enough work has yet been done in this particular field to produce telling statistics.

It will not come as any surprise to those familiar with the litany of causation that there is a specific brain dysfunction in schizophrenics which affects the temporal lobe, a specific cause of hallucinations. Injury to the left temporal lobe results in the disturbance of the way we receive, express and understand language; and auditory hallucinations, those familiar 'voices', are well documented results of left-brain damage. Indeed, schizophrenia is above all a cognitive disorder. Brain scans also suggest that schizophrenics may have damage in frontal areas of the brain associated with motivation, emotions and concentration. Taken together, this damage presents the sufferer with a world where his perception and response to it is deranged; a friendly handshake can seem like a threat, to which violent assault seems the only response. And this inability to respond accurately to a stimulus, say the researchers, also affects the ability to distinguish right from wrong – the legal *sine qua non* of guilt.

A few decades ago, in the days when our environment and culture was the reason for everything, few would have thought that there was a genetic dimension to schizophrenia. Today, the results of twin and adoption studies have led scientists to believe that they have identified a specific gene responsible for the condition. But it seems that the picture may be more complicated; identical twin studies indicate that someone with the average genetic make-up of the schizophrenic has a one-in-two chance of developing the illness, so other factors must be involved. One of these may be brain damage; if a child suffers birth trauma leading to brain damage (possibly because of lack of oxygen or a forceps delivery) the incidence of schizophrenia, among families with a genetic predisposition, increases.

EXPLOSIVE VIOLENCE AND THE DEPRESSIVE

Another category of violence is found in the mind of the depressive. Again, these people often lead normal lives, until disrupted by a one-off disturbance, or sometimes cyclical disturbances.

Depression is more than merely the blues. Major depression is characterized by an overwhelming feeling of self-blame, guilt and worthlessness, disturbance of the appetite, long periods of lethargy, and recurrent thoughts of death and suicide; 8–10 per cent of men and 18–23 per cent of women will experience clinical depression at least once in their lives. One person in a hundred suffers bipolar or manic depression – when the condition is accompanied by a manic phase of furious physical activity, long periods without sleep, an overweening sense of self-importance and extreme irritability.

The link between depression and crime is a difficult one to make, but there do seem to be some causal connections; there are the obvious tragedies, for example, when an individual becomes convinced that life is hopeless and before committing suicide kills the children and other members of the family. In 78 cases of murder followed by suicide, 28 of the offenders were found to have been suffering from depression at the time of the catastrophe. General, violent incidents in the home setting are associated with depression – the depressive simply seems more likely to resort to violence when the domestic going gets tough.

Another study of the criminal careers of 26 patients with depression showed the pattern of one single violent offence after a hitherto blameless life. Most of them were committed for wounding their wives or girlfriends; only four of them ever reoffended. This does not suggest any causal link between ordinary depression and crime. But bipolar or manic depression is something else. According to one scientific source, people who experienced manic depressive episodes represented the second largest category of arsonists after schizophrenics; another believes that fire-setting during the manic state may be more common than is generally acknowledged.

Once again, there seems to be a chemical dimension to depression. And, almost predictably, in study after study low serotonin levels have been linked to depressive illnesses. So, depressed and repetitively violent individuals have the same card – yet the behaviour of manic depressives is different from the persistently violent offender. Could it be, then, that there's another brain factor at play which influences the particular manner in which this serotonin deficit is expressed in different individuals?

One clue may lie in the discovery that brain dysfunction in the depressed mind is quite different from that found in the repetitively violent mind. The violent brain, as we have seen, has damage localized in the left hemisphere, the more rational side of the brain. Those who suffer from depression have damage on the right side, the emotional hemisphere of the brain. The difference can be distinguished with 100 per cent accuracy.

EXPLOSIVE VIOLENCE – THE TRIGGERS

In all the violent minds we have described there is another common card. All these individuals are excessively sensitive to the influence of alcohol – much more so than ordinary people. There is also a link between drug abuse and these types of mind.

We do not need scientists to tell us that these substances increase the probability of bizarre and violent behaviour. It's not just that four out of five drivers responsible for road accidents are affected by alcohol; violent crimes like murder and serious assault are also strongly influenced by drink and drugs. One study found that 83 per cent of violent crime is associated with alcohol. Wife-battering is linked with alcohol in 93 per cent of cases.

Alcohol does not lighten and enhance the mood – it is more like a sedative. We are not brighter and wittier when we are drunk; in fact we have largely lost the critical faculty which usually tells us we are being boring. Alcohol is a general, non-selective central nervous system depressant, damping down activity in all nerve cells within the brain. We know that it also lowers the levels of serotonin in all of us, so reducing the ability of the frontal lobes to keep the animal limbic system in check. The result is a loss of inhibition and the possibility of uncontrolled emotional outbursts. In some, this can lead to physical aggression, criminal damage and assault, reckless driving, disorientation and decreased judgment.

Critical, however, is the link between alcohol and the disordered brain.

Studies show an enormous overlap between people classed as APD – antisocial personality disorder – criminal acts and substance abuse. This overlap raises various questions. Does an antisocial personality dispose one to substance abuse? Does the use of drugs and drink aggravate pre-existing conditions, by eliminating extra inhibitions? Or does the abuse of substances actually have a specific chemical effect on a brain which is already dysfunctional?

The evidence is growing that, first of all, the cards in the hand of those with damaged minds make it more likely that they will turn to drink and drugs; and that, second, their brains react in a different way to the effects of drugs and alcohol. What is, for most of us, an occasional resort which cheers us up can, for the psychopath or those with APD, become a compulsion, and, through a genetic and neurological mechanism, result in violent behaviour.

Those people who are prone to episodic dyscontrol syndrome can have seizures triggered by the smallest amount of alcohol; a tiny stimulus may be all that is necessary to unleash the electrical storm in the emotional centre of the limbic system. In those who suffer from this 'hidden' form of epilepsy alcohol can precipitate totally uncharacteristic behaviour; they may experience black-outs, visual disturbances or dramatic changes of mood and personality.

Another link between alcohol and crime in the disordered brain affects those with low arousability. The low arousal that characterizes the criminal and especially the low emotional arousal of the psychopath also makes them more susceptible to the desire for a drink. The low-aroused brain craves a mechanism to spur it into sensation. This happens through the mediation of drink. It is also why these people crave other new experiences like trying various drugs.

Then there is the fact that in many of the violent minds serotonin is already at a lower than normal level. The alcohol depresses it even more so they are even more impulsive and violence-prone than normal people.

Blood sugar levels are also implicated. Those with low levels crave sugar – and may find that alcohol satisfies the craving. This may explain why a large proportion of APD types also have severe drink problems and are often addicted to alcohol. It may well be an attempt to medicate themselves out of an abnormal or irregular sugar metabolism. Low glucose, as we know, leads to irritability and impulsiveness, to which alcohol seems to be the answer. But it is only a temporary solution, and indeed it aggravates the problem, because after this artificial boost it almost immediately depresses the body's glucose production still further. Violence in association with alcohol usually occurs at the end of or just after a drinking spree.

Violence, APD and explosive rage seem to be further associated with drink addiction through a genetic link. Twin studies show a 50 per cent chance of inheriting the condition, the severity and frequency of it. A Swedish study looked at those adoptees who had criminality in the family; the children whose biological parents were criminals had a tendency to property crimes. But those who had both alcoholism *and* crime in the genes had a tendency towards violent crime.

But it all depends on the type of alcoholism, or, more

specifically, who inherits it. Most adoptees whose biological parents were alcoholic developed alcoholic tendencies, but only one type inherited the aggressive behaviour associated with it. These were the males who adopted it from their biological fathers, quite independently of the alcoholism – or lack of it – in the adopting family. Such people were ten times more likely to develop an early onset of alcoholism associated with antisocial behaviour leading to repeated encounters with the law. They're the troublesome, rather than the merry drunks. And there's a link to inherited low serotonin levels: 54 out of 58 violent offenders showed a history of alcohol abuse, and 35 of those had lower serotonin levels than those without alcoholic fathers. The genes can put you more at risk for craving extra alcohol, and for being more adversely affected by it.

Exactly the same factors of sensation-seeking and low arousal can make us more vulnerable to the temptation of drug abuse. The association between childhood conduct problems and substance abuse is well established. Studies find a link between drug abuse and an excess of early sexual behaviour, poor school performance, low aspirations for academic achievements, truancy, stealing, non-conformity with parents' rules and association with other deviant children. Fifty per cent of children will have tried marijuana by the age of 18. (Twice as many men are likely to have a problem with drug abuse compared with women.)

The link between crime and hard-drug addiction is harder to quantify in brain terms, because it is often the need to get money to feed the habit, rather than the drug itself, that causes criminal behaviour. As a result, heroin addiction is most commonly linked to property crime. But looking beyond the mere criminal symptoms of the addiction, we find that the desire is essentially one of satisfying the perceptions; hard drugs reduce pain and produce euphoria, a relaxed feeling of well-being and indifference to stress. Later, the drug produces a sedative effect, and sometimes sleep – with vivid, pleasing dreams. The appetite for food and sex disappear.

What happens chemically is that the drugs overcome, and

take the place of, the endorphins or natural opiates of the brain which help kill pain and can provide a feeling of euphoria. Endorphins are a small chain of proteins with neurotransmitter properties which are responsible for the transmission of messages from one brain cell to another regarding the perception of pain, stress and emotion. Receptors, designed to process this information, are concentrated in the brain stem (which is responsible for natural pain-killing reaction), the medial thalamus (deep pain) and the spinal cord (dampening incoming pain signals), but most are found in the limbic system, that headquarters of emotional behaviour.

The high that comes from taking drugs results from the fact that they increase the normal effect of endorphins. But among those who become addicted, the natural supply of these transmitters goes down. This presents no problem as long as the artificial intake is sustained – but once the drug supply dries up, or becomes scarce, the individual begins to feel – acutely – the loss. The brain is no longer producing its own endorphins, because the heroin has suppressed their production. The addict then experiences pain and anxiety – with the result that he desperately seeks more of the drug.

We've seen in Chapter 3 what happens with anabolic steroids; and crack, too, the major drug in run-down inner cities – even in the school playground – can produce violence, especially with prolonged use. Freud called cocaine a 'magic drug'; it produces euphoria and feelings of competence. Physiologically, it constricts the blood vessels, increases the heart rate, raises blood pressure, dilates the pupils and increases body temperature; psychologically it elevates mood, and produces euphoria and alertness, while reducing fatigue. It's a social drug, in that it enhances confidence, friendliness and calmness, while reducing inhibition. At the same time, cocaine is known to be one of the most powerful chemical rewards in the brain – stronger even than heroin. Long-term use of cocaine leads to aggression, mistrust and violence.

The drug PCP, known on the street as angel dust, has resulted in unpredictable and distressing effects.

A drug dealer in Gloucester, Willie Wiltshire, died after a fight with two low-level criminals. Wiltshire had been taking PCP and alcohol. The combination led him to unprovoked violence – lashing out with a crowbar. After a few minutes, the rage subsided, only to flare up again. In the end, the two others defended themselves, with fatal results – Wiltshire died of wounds, and the two others were found guilty of murder, even though they sent for an ambulance for their 'victim', who was thereafter in the hands of either the medical or the police authorities.

PCP was first marketed as Sernyl – an analgesic for humans and animals. It was quickly removed from the market because of the side effects of delirium, confusion and hallucinogenic schizophrenic symptoms, sometimes lasting days or even weeks after use. It is both a stimulant and a depressant; depending on dose, it affects primarily the limbic system (which is responsible for emotional behaviour) and cortical areas (responsible for higher intellectual functions). Chemically, it mimics the neurotransmitter dopamine, which is involved in attention and concentration. PCP binds to nerve endings on dopaminergic terminals, or it blocks the reuptake of dopamine, decreasing the number of binding sites. In either case the symptoms are conceptual disorganization, violent behaviour and hallucinations, which, in the final analysis, result in a seizure of the nervous system; the mental computer crashes. It also affects serotonin levels in the same way as alcohol, initially raising them, and then leading to catastrophically low levels as drug use declines.

Amphetamine use has led to murder, by making chronic users become irritable and suspicious and subject to paranoid delusions; but at present, no basis has been established for a relationship between amphetamine abuse and violent behaviour. Overall, however, enough evidence supports the notion that drug use directly precipitates criminal acts, other than the criminal acts necessary to procure the wherewithal to buy the drugs in the first place.

Over the last ten years, our understanding of the effects of substance abuse on brain functioning has been revolutionized by imaging techniques. We can now see the extent of the damage, what happens during intoxication and why people get addicted. Cocaine is especially toxic to the human brain and produces stroke-like damage. Users experience biochemical changes in their brain which causes dysfunction in the cortical circuit centres; this leads to impulsiveness and lack of control. Marijuana and alcohol have a similar effect. The normal inhibitory functions are short-circuited. Most chronic alcoholics or drug abusers cannot tell you why they are addicted – it is not pleasurable, but they cannot control their impulses.

Do drug users choose to put themselves into a criminal category because of innate biological needs? And, once there, does substance abuse enhance that pre-existing biochemistry of crime? And if it is largely a matter of sensation-seeking, sensation hunger, oughtn't we to think of satisfying that hunger by serotonin, rather than leaving matters to the free, criminal market? There's no easy answer to the question, but the failure even to address the biochemical roots of crime is fatuous. Well-meaning social remedies, or tough penal attitudes, are of secondary significance compared with the available knowledge of how the dysfunctional brain actually works.

Violence casts too dark a shadow for us to ignore the actual remedies which, at least for some violent offenders, now exist.

CHAPTER 10

Family Violence

ONE OF THE quietest prisons in Britain – it is often the last posting for governors before retirement – is in Portsmouth. It is small and scrupulously clean, and the very low turnover of staff and inmates makes for an almost village-like sense of continuity. The atmosphere is relaxed. Some prisoners breed small birds, who flit tamely around the cream-painted landings. Some prisoners, as they grow old, lose any desire to re-enter the world beyond the walls. The prison is opening a geriatric wing, so that prisoners can enter old age and die, peacefully, among their life-long friends.

Many have been convicted of murdering their wives.

Most murder (as we will see in the next chapter) is a family affair, and the high incidence of spouse murder should not surprise us. Just as most road accidents occur close to home (because that's where, statistically, we most often are), so most murders are likely to be among those we are closest to, and with whose lives we are most intensely involved. Few of us feel very strongly about killing the Secretary-General of the United Nations, for instance, but our nearest and dearest may, occasionally, feel such a motivation when we leave the bathroom floor wet.

The incidence of violence itself within the family is troubling. We are more troubled these days not because there is more violence, but because the violence has become more acknowledged. Pioneers like Erin Pizzey, who opened the Chiswick Battered Women's Refuge, brought a taboo subject into the open. We have even achieved another level of openness with the introduction of a hotline for battered husbands in South London. The problem was in the past severely underestimated;

now, perhaps, there is the danger of overestimation, with loose definitions of violence. Some studies, for instance, include verbal violence, which, while distressing, is hardly an abnormal occurrence in domestic circumstances.

Explanations of violence in the family have almost all been of a social and environmental nature – after all, what stronger social focus is there than the family, what more intense environment? But there's another bias against suggestions of an underlying biological cause for family violence: the idea that, once accepted, those explanations will somehow excuse the misery that such violence inflicts upon the family. There is a fear that seeing marital aggression as a product of endocrine or neurological dysfunction will remove the guilt of the assailant, whether moral or legal. We would suggest two arguments against this. First, if something is true, but open to abuse, that is no reason for covering it up – the malevolent will discover the truth one way or another, and it is better that people of goodwill should be forearmed with knowledge. Second, there is no excuse for those who will say, 'Don't blame me, blame my biology': knowing the cause of something is no justification for it ('I know my drunkenness will increase the danger of my driving'), just as ignorance of the law is no defence.

Those working in this area feel strongly that biological factors have to be taken into account. Without derogating from the importance of social and environmental factors, says one, since the brain is the organ of thought, emotion and behaviour, to discuss the topic of interfamilial violence and aggression in isolation from brain biology 'is like considering a car's performance without reference to the efficiency of its engine, steering and brakes'. He continues:

we must be aware of the potential for misuse of this information; however it may be even more reckless to ignore the potential contributions of biological factors, both to our understanding of this phenomenon and to our treatment and prevention efforts. It is unlikely that we will find biological factors alone to be responsible for marital aggression and equally unlikely that we will find them to be completely uninvolved.[1]

After all, society has been tacitly sanctioning family violence for centuries. Patriarchal societies upheld the right of a husband to chastise his wife with a whip. Even in Victorian times, the precise size of stick was specified as an acceptable instrument of punishment. All adultery laws are remarkably consistent: un-authorized sexual contact with a married woman is a crime, and the victim is the husband, who is commonly entitled to damages, to violent revenge, or to divorce with refund of bride price.

Sexual jealousy, on this explanation, was an evolutionary survival mechanism, to protect paternity, avoid the chore of protecting another man's child or prevent accidental incest and in-breeding. So, while adultery is generally now criminalized, jealous rage on the part of the husband has been to a large extent tolerated in legal circles. Jurists have stipulated that cuckoldry justifies, or at least mitigates, responsibility for otherwise criminal behaviour.

Today, sexual jealousy is the overwhelming reason given for wife-beating. More than half of the battered wives canvassed in a women's hostel in Ontario reported that the reason for the assault was jealousy. The other most frequently cited reason was drink. Studies of court cases where husbands used violence upon wives confirm that at the core of nearly all of them was jealousy: the husband responds with frustration at being unable to control the wife, often accusing her of being a whore or having an affair. In another study of female victims of spousal violence, 52 per cent listed jealousy as the main incitement, and 94 per cent named it as a frequent cause.

There's a phenomenon known as morbid jealousy, where even such irrational causes as the woman leaving the house result in accusations of infidelity, and where violent assault results in 95 per cent of the cases. Husbands seek every means to keep their wives ignorant and isolated; friendships of any sort are discouraged or forbidden – husbands object to the continuation of old friendships and sometimes to wives having a social life at all, often refusing to let their wives go shopping unescorted. Work is strenuously opposed; if women do work, efforts are made to ensure that both husband and wife work at the same place, so that the wife's conduct can be minutely and continuously monitored. Although in some societies, especially fundamentalist cultures of the Middle East, some of this behaviour is considered laudable and normal, in Western societies it is seen as a condition of obsessive concern about suspected infidelity, either imagined or sustained by irrational evidence. It's been called the Othello syndrome: Shakespeare's Moor of Venice could not believe his luck in the love of the beautiful Desdemona, so it was easy for the villainous Iago to kindle his jealousy by placing little clues to his wife's supposed infidelity in Othello's path. In the end, of course, Othello smothered the (tragically faithful) Desdemona.

We are all capable of lashing out, our anger and frustration pushed beyond the limits of control. What we'll be discussing here is not the once-in-a-lifetime flare-up, but those whose innately violent minds find regular or explosive expression in the family arena, way beyond the normal ups and downs of family life. (Family life, incidentally, we will define broadly as permanent or semi-permanent relationships, not necessarily sanctified with marriage licences or cemented by 2.4 children.)

First of all, how many such people are there?

Family violence is estimated to affect one in three marriages in the US – indeed, it is the most common cause of injury in women. Approximately 10–15 per cent of women in the US will be victims of repeated and serious physical aggression from their partners. One in twelve homicides are of wife by husband, or vice versa. Total annual health costs for such violence exceed $100 million, making marital aggression a top national health care priority.

In Britain, there is still a degree of cultural resistance among women to reporting such incidents; an inner-city study of Islington in North London, however, indicates that of 1,000 women interviewed, nearly a quarter had experienced a violent assault of a domestic nature in the previous twelve months. In Leeds, about a fifth of women reported having experienced violent or threatening attacks in the home over the same time span.

As for battered men, apart from the perceived stigma of admitting the situation, men may be better able than women to seek private solutions, either legal or therapeutic – for instance, they tend to have more control over the purse strings. It's obviously the greater degree of physical damage to women which makes their victimization more clamant, and the reluctance of men to acknowledge abuse at the hands of their wives makes it apparent why the battered husband receives little attention. There's not much empirical data on the subject, although the educated guess of one observer is that the intention to use violence is equal between sparring marital partners.

We're not talking mere black eyes here. Some women are assaulted daily – financial circumstances prevent their agonized desire to leave. Weapons include fists, feet, rocks, bottles, iron bars, knives and guns. The attacks take the form of scratching, slapping, punching, throwing down and kicking, with face and breasts the most frequent areas of assaults which may lead to multiple bruising; fractured ribs, detached retinas, strangling and choking to the point of unconsciousness are also reported. Some women report increased physical abuse during pregnancy; this is often seen as a form of prenatal child abuse.

Sex is one of the weapons used in marital violence, and its expression is violent rape. The rape is the more traumatic for being committed not by a stranger, but by someone you once knew, loved and trusted – but now detest. Marital rape victims are said to suffer greater trauma than others, because they feel a sense of betrayal and entrapment. Further, because society places the burden of making marriages work on women, they blame themselves; and they feel isolated, friendless, unsupported, partly because of a public perception that rape within marriage is merely legitimate, if rough, sex. Male politicians – threatened, perhaps by the notion that women have the right to challenge their own sexual demands – are inclined to view the issue as another bothersome feminist issue.

Marital rape is not confined to the drunken, the feckless, the dregs of society; one study of wife rape in the US found that 14 per cent of the 930 women interviewed had been raped by a husband or ex-husband – suggesting that at least one out of every seven women had experienced at least one such incident in the course of her married life. This may be an underestimate; many women, obviously, find it difficult to discuss the issue of forced sex by spouses. Three types of rape have been identified. The most common are the so-called 'battering rapes' where sex is used to degrade and humiliate the wife; men consider anal rape the 'quintessential sexual act by which to humiliate a woman'. About 40 per cent of interviewed wives described 'force only rapes' which occur in an otherwise non-violent context, usually when husbands demand control over the frequency of their conjugal rights. The least common are 'obsessive rapes' which are intrinsically sadistic or fetishistic acts.

Research into this painful area shows that the closer the prior association of the rapist and the victim, the more violent the assault is likely to be. Marital rape is often accompanied by extreme violence, which includes mutilation and sometimes ends in murder. Women have been subjected to many types of abuse – bestiality, the insertion of foreign objects or defilement with urine or faeces, bondage and arranged gang rape. Sometimes this takes place in the presence of children, or the children are even involved in the rapes. Figures show that almost three out of four victims have been raped more than once; and 10 per cent claim that sex is always on demand and they feel that they have no choice but to submit. Many women who claimed that they had not been raped said that they had submitted to sexual demands in order to prevent beatings. There is also more than a suggestion that among the perpetrators, the psychopathic mind may be prevalent.

The second most common area of family violence involves child abuse. In 1983, when the phenomenon was much less widely confronted than it is today, nearly a million and a half American children from a million families were reported to be abused and/or neglected; of those, 45,000 were the subject of serious physical abuse, and it is here that we must look for the violent mind at work.

Once again, researchers are handicapped by the lack of precise definitions, and the fact that the abuse is inflicted upon those without a voice, and in private. One comforting fact may be that, in spite of the current wave of reported incidents, the further back in the history of childhood we go, the less adequate and caring child welfare seems to have been. More children were abused, abandoned and murdered in the supposedly good old days.

The definition of child abuse is generally determined by four things: the intentionality of the act, its effect on a given child, the value judgment made about the act and the standard on which the judgment is made. An obvious area where the judgment is problematic involves the African tradition of body scarring and genital mutilation in the female. Female circumcision is widely practised in Africa and some Muslim countries – about 85 million women are so affected. The practice is illegal in the UK. Again, how far is it reasonable to teach the child the danger of fire by exposing him or her to the flame – and to what degree? Child care clearly operates on a continuum from optimal to devastatingly bad, but that leaves a considerable grey area where experts can disagree. Legal definitions are typically vague and do not specify the degree of injury considered as abusive; the cruel home becomes, in legal terms, merely an 'unfit place'. Neither the police, nor professionals of the social, educational and medical services, use a single, universally accepted definition. The only consensus arises when the harm is direct, the injury severe, the intention deliberate. Not surprisingly, a good half of reported cases are closed after investigation. A disproportionate number of cases not proceeded with involve white, middle-class families – suggesting a relative lack of confidence among the social services, or a fear of losing patients among doctors. There is also an assumption that separation from parent and 'being taken into care' will be more traumatic for the middle-class child.

We should at once respect the environmental factors involved in domestic violence. Alcohol abuse, for instance, is a major factor. There is also a victimology which suggests that some women are attracted and addicted to violent relationships. There exists a high association between early lack of care and later marital violence. Women who have experienced lack of care in childhood are twice as likely to have experienced violence in marriage as those without such an experience. As for child abuse, there is evidence that people who were abused as children grow up to be abusive parents, although exposure to violence as a child does not necessarily make for a potentially abusive adult.

In this less tangible area of environmental or psychological factors, the figures do not tell us much, however. In a study of over 500 male wife-batterers, 42 per cent had not themselves witnessed physical violence between their parents, 61 per cent had not been physically abused in childhood, 59 per cent had not been neglected by their parents and 50 per cent had not had an alcoholic father. In child abuse, only one third of the studies suggests that abused children become, in turn, abusive parents.

Wife-batterers, marital rapists and child abusers – does the possibility lurk in all of us, or is there a special mind which perpetrates this sort of vile behaviour? For an area of such importance, surprisingly little research has been done, but what there is points to the involvement of a biological factor. There is no real distinction between the cards that make up the violent criminal mind which we have already examined, and those in the minds of wife-beaters and child abusers; the only difference, it seems, is that much of this violence stays secret, private, unreported, unpunished.

Principal among these cards of violence are the aggressive psychopathic mind, and the explosively disordered mind. Episodic dyscontrol may take the form of unpredictable attacks of rage in response to minor provocation; and persistent, callous brutality exactly fits the pattern of the psychopath. Environmental aspects have eclipsed the role of neurophysical and metabolic factors in family violence, but once it is studied in the light of what we now know about these disordered brains, we are sure that the understanding of this tragically misunderstood area of life will benefit.

So what, first, have the scientists discovered about the psychopath in the family?

The evidence that 'psychopaths constitute a significant proportion of persistent [wife] batterers'[2] has come from a group of men taking part either voluntarily or as part of a sentence in a treatment programme for wife assault. One in four were found to be psychopaths – roughly the same as the proportion of the prison population in general. We cannot tell the percentage of those who do not enter treatment programmes – but estimates are that if they were included, the proportion would double.

This should not surprise us, given what we know about the psychopathic mind. The life of the psychopath is characterized by casual and flagrant violations of social norms and expectations. Psychopathic violence is callous and without feelings of guilt or remorse. It is not the sort that springs from powerful emotion. Violence and threats are merely instrumental, tools to be used in calculated conjunction with anger, defiance or frustration, or for the gratification of pleasure. The reaction to other people's shock or horror is one of indifference, or perhaps a sense of power and satisfaction. There is no regret at the damage done.

A Mr Leblanc (cited by Hare) was convicted of assaulting his common law wife and ordered to attend group therapy. He completely dominated the group and, with his persuasive charm, maintained that it had been a minor incident, the result of an argument in which he had unfortunately lost his temper – the sort of thing that could happen to anyone. His background as a paratrooper in Vietnam had taught him what *real* violence was, and his MBA from Columbia University was a token of his middle-class reliability.

What Mr Leblanc did not admit to was the fact that this was one of a whole string of attacks; he had broken his wife's nose and blackened her eyes; he had convictions for fraud, theft and embezzlement. And you will already have guessed about those Vietnam and university 'credentials'. He left the group, in clear violation of the court order, and skipped town . . .

The danger of such men lies in their very plausibility.

Elyse, for instance, was dazzled by Jeffrey when he walked straight up to her and asked for her telephone number. He was a thoroughly engaging person, filled with grand ideas about what he was going to do with his life and what they would make of life together. One day he was arrested, and a whole string of previous convictions emerged. Elyse was no fool; yet such was the persuasive power of his letters from prison that, even by post, his charm managed to overcome her. When he emerged from prison he moved right in with Elyse at the apartment she shared; but before long it seemed that any of her roommates would do for Jeffrey. He crawled into the bed of one of them, and terrified another by pinning her beneath him in her bedroom one night, apparently delighting in the look of terror on her face. The other girls tried to warn Elyse, but she was still mesmerized by the man. Her parents warned her about his 'strange, flat eyes' but Elyse simply would not allow her faith to be shaken. Eventually, she did decide to break off the affair – but Jeffrey would hear nothing of it. He said he would kill her first. He broke into her apartment, and grabbed her by the hair – Elyse was saved only by the appearance of her brother. At this point, Jeffrey instantly became normal, bade them both a casual goodbye, and left.

Elyse has since studied the behaviour of psychopaths – 'For Jeffrey,' she says, 'the rules of behaviour were written in pencil, and he had a big eraser.' Jeffrey, like so many psychopaths in relationships with women, saw his girlfriend not as a companion in life but as a supplier of food, shelter, clothing, laundry, recreation and sex. The consequences to her of his actions didn't even enter his consciousness.

Rape is a classic example of the selfish, instrumental use of violence favoured by the psychopath – although of course not all rapists are psychopaths. Perhaps half of repeat rapists are psychopaths, fuelled by their sexual drives, driven by their fantasies and unbridled by any sense of social or moral inhibition.

We know that the violent mind is more vulnerable to the effects of alcohol than is the case with normal men. Some statistics suggest a 95 per cent association of wife-beating with alcohol. The combination of alcohol intoxication, poor impulse control and pathological jealousy is a lethal mix.

The nature of the aggressive psychopath makes it just as likely that children will be the victims. From early years of parenthood, psychopathic mothers or fathers often leave young children alone when there is no babysitter available. One mother and her husband left their one-month-old baby with an alcoholic friend, who got drunk and left, forgetting his responsibilities. The baby ended up in care, after neighbours alerted the authorities. When the parents returned, they were outraged by this violation of parental rights, even after the evident malnutrition of the baby was pointed out to them. When neighbours see children wandering aimlessly out of doors in the cold, with no winter clothes or shoes, hungry and emotionally starved, although the mother or father will profess to love their children, the callous indifference to their physical and emotional welfare gives those protestations the lie. This indifference to the welfare of children – their own, or those of the man or woman they happen to be living with – is frequently found in the literature of psychopathy. Psychopaths see children as an inconvenience.

Psychopathic mothers are as indifferent to suffering as are fathers – a powerful negation of maternal feelings. Female psychopaths routinely neglect their children, physically or emotionally, or simply abandon them as they move from one sexual encounter to the next. One, whose daughter was beaten to death by one of her many lovers, remarked to the social worker, 'I can always have another,' adding by way of explanation, 'I love children.'

Little research has been conducted into the actual structure of the brain of these people. Usually the hypothesis is that they are unusually reactive to stimuli, which in turn triggers aggression. Six studies have examined brain activity in response to stimuli relating to children – a child's cry, for instance. One examined the reactions in physically abusive and non-abusive mothers to videos of children crying, sleeping, laughing and so on. The abusive mothers reported significantly more annoyance engendered by the crying portrayed than the non-abusive mothers, and significantly less contagious pleasure – indeed indifference – from the pictures of babies smiling. It seems likely that the arousal of emotion counteracts normal aggressive feelings (the secret of patient motherhood?) and that when the milk of emotion does not come on stream, only the aggression remains – undiluted. Skin resistance tests on the groups – like the lie-detector tests – showed this same comparative lack of reaction, engagement or emotion in the abusive mothers, the same result as with the classic psychopath.

But family violence is by no means confined to the psychopath; the other principal offender is the subject who is cursed with an explosively violent mind.

Throughout high school, William J. suffered from temper tantrums – 'It felt like I was jumping through my skin.' The only way of coping with the sensation was to destroy something. The trigger mechanism always seemed to be if something didn't go as planned, or as he wanted it to. Even the simplest things. Most of the time he was a charming and loving husband, but his wife and children lived in terror of the outbursts. Hammers, knives and so on would be thrown with some force. Once he had released his explosion, however, he would return to normal very quickly.

His wife, Jane, was on the point of moving out when she read an article in a magazine about a doctor called

Frank Elliott, and how he had discovered that these rages were caused by an electrical explosion within the brain – and that these otherwise inexplicable rages could be controlled with drugs. William and his wife took the article to a doctor, who referred them for specialist treatment. Nothing turned up on the ordinary EEGs, but when deep-probe electrodes were inserted through his nasal passages and into his brain, doctors discovered the classic abnormalities of those who suffer from this hidden form of electrical brain storm. William was then prescribed Inderal (an anti-convulsant) and peace and happiness has returned to the family. William says, 'It saved our marriage – and maybe, who knows, our lives. It's a miracle.'

We have already met this explosively violent mind, and have located the epicentre of these mental earthquakes in the limbic system and temporal lobe. One study of wife-beaters discovered a history of temporal lobe epilepsy in 30 per cent of the sample, while another found that 50 per cent of temporal lobe epileptics were subject to paroxysms of violence. You have to look carefully – temporal lobe attacks can be slight, and may be masked by other mental symptoms; and temporal lobe epilepsy mimics a wide range of psychopathological symptoms. But taking the care to identify the condition pays dividends; after all, unlike many other mental conditions, the seizures which cause the violence are treatable.

The episodic violence associated with epilepsy appears in various forms; incidental attacks of anything from irritability to destructive rages directed at people, animals or things without any very obvious seizure, undirected and disorganized violence, followed by amnesia accompanied by a sudden seizure discharge recorded by deep electrodes, or a towering rage culminating in convulsions. Seizures great and small usually involve changes in consciousness – dreamy states, confusion, a sense of unreality – sometimes accompanied by inappropriate behaviour. Hallucinations, both visual and auditory, are not infrequent. Disturbances are often accompanied by a sense of fear, depression, hatred or anxiety – or sometimes pleasure and even a sense of ecstasy. The gender card, as ever, is present – men are much more likely to suffer from this syndrome, although some women do have it. The onset is often abrupt and without any evident or apparent provocation. It starts with verbal abuse – obscenities and profanities which are quite out of character, and which understandably terrify the uncomprehending children who are faced with this dramatic change of personality. It is often accompanied by snarling, baring of teeth and growling; when the physical violence comes it often takes the primitive form of kicking, gouging, scratching, spitting and biting. A wife is picked up bodily and thrown against a wall. A young woman bites her two-year-old daughter on the cheek, leaving a lifelong scar.

Unlike the case of the psychopath, the attacks, whether verbal or physical, are usually followed by remorse; suicide is not rare.

Ted B. suffered from seizures as a student, but tests could not identify the cause of the fits. Anti-convulsant drugs, however, seemed to control them. He completed his medical studies, did his internship and started in neurology. He then began to drink heavily – he was, indeed, an alcoholic. At the end of his residency, he began to exhibit extreme behaviour: if he wanted to congratulate someone, he would do it with great exuberance, if he got annoyed he would lash out. In addition there was a sexual aberration – satyriasis – a kind of insatiable, Don Juan approach to women. He would occasionally touch a female patient inappropriately. It would happen for a brief moment – a matter of seconds. He was aware of what he was doing and was dismayed and shocked. Also dismaying was a tendency towards the destruction of property and, later, physical assault towards people around him. He would destroy windows, doors, drawers; he wrecked his piano; he burned furniture in his fireplace. The bathroom was particularly vulnerable: he ripped the lavatory and handbasin out. He sought psychiatric help, but to no avail. He also did three years of group therapy. He got married in December 1981 and to his great dismay assaulted his wife, giving her a thorough beating. He can't remember what prompted the episode, at the end of which the police were called. His psychiatrist thought that the cause of his problem was his relationship with his mother.

Severe decline set in. His judgment became poor – he invested in the high-risk futures market and lost a lot of money. His eyesight was failing, and he lost his senses of smell and taste. In a queue at a check-out, a young boy was in front of him. Ted B. was in a hurry, told him to 'get out of the way' and hit the child. He would frequently pick fights with motorists. 'I could have killed somebody. I was clearly dangerous.' His wife couldn't take it any more and was afraid for her children, so she left him. He specialized in destroying typewriters and then word processors. Once he got a hammer and pulverised the wreckage of a word processor on his kitchen floor – there are scars on the lino to this day. There were pathetic reminders of the terrible state he had fallen into – a rotting, three-year-old Christmas tree still standing in his room, his filthy house.

Ted B. was eventually hospitalized – and at last a temporal lobe tumour was diagnosed and removed. He describes an amazing feeling after the fourteen-hour operation. When he woke up in the recovery room he knew immediately that he was back in contact with the real world. It was like an epiphany; everything was going to be all right. Unfortunately, the tumour had left lasting damage. His rages continued. Finally, he went to see Dr Elliott, who found that he also had electrical discharges in the limbic and temporal area of the brain. Inderal was again prescribed, and Ted B. now lives a normal life, taking the drug whenever he feels the rage coming on.

A study based on 286 patients, in which care was taken to exclude borderline psychotics, core psychopaths, mentally retarded individuals guilty of an isolated act of violence and those whose aggressive behaviour was triggered by drugs, concluded that episodic dyscontrol and minimal brain dysfunction were common among wife-batterers and child abusers. There was evidence of multiple defects, revealed by EEGs, CAT scans and neuropsychological tests in 90 per cent of them.

None of these individuals were aware that they had any brain abnormality; although many had sought help for their shortness of temper and the violent impulses which they recognized, never had their neurological damage been realized or diagnosed. It is a tragedy that such people may have sought and received psychotherapy, counselling or a whole range of help – except the one thing which was relevant.

Less dramatic forms of brain dysfunction play their part in creating family stress. Slowness of thought can be frustrating for all involved, and limited vocabulary can retard personal communication, again leading to frustration and anger. Others have brain limitations which affect their perception – they miss the cues which are so important to smooth social relations – facial expression, tone of voice and body language. As a result, they fail to take into the account the feelings of others and wires become disastrously crossed.

Very often, we can link family violence to the specific card of brain damage.

Child abusers register as poor on word recognition and memory tests – both shortcomings which suggest anterior dysfunction of either the temporal lobe or frontal lobe, which are also sites frequently associated with aggression. And almost 90 per cent of wife-batterers in one study reported significant head injuries, involving periods of unconsciousness. A blind test of 45 maritally satisfied and 32 maritally discordant men were examined on a number of criteria, including alcohol and drug use, education, occupation, police record, psychiatric history, childhood conduct disorders – and head injury. A history of head injury increased the likehood of marital aggression six-fold. Another series of tests in 1989 found significant head injury in more than 60 per cent of wife-batterers. Head injury may not of itself be a cause of aggression – but it may impair the ability to *control* aggression.

The fact that a high percentage of children who were abused become abusers may help us tie together the environmental and biological schools; children brought up in damaging environments often receive damage to their brains, which for physical, biological reasons will predispose them to violence.

Early research indicates that between 20 per cent and 50 per cent of children who have been physically abused suffer intellectual retardation, brain damage and other forms of central nervous system impairment – severe enough neurological damage to affect daily functioning. In the first year of infant life, child abuse comes second only to motor accidents as a cause of all head injury. And 95 per cent of all brain damage involving intercranial haemorrhage is the result of hitting children on the head. This goes some way to explain why abused infants score significantly lower than normal children on measures of infant development: they make slower intellectual progress, and have poorer social, cognitive and communication skills than normal children – and that's when disparities of income and class have been taken into account. Even among delinquent children themselves, physically abused delinquents committed more crimes involving assault than those who had not suffered physical abuse. A fascinating study correlates violent children, perinatal problems, head trauma and childhood abuse. The most violent boys had more frequently been physically abused. The severity of the abuse matched a higher resort to violence. The more violent boys exhibited 'loose, rambling and illogical thought processes', the result of central nervous system damage, contributing to impulsivity, attention disorders and learning disabilities.

One theory scientists are working on is that brain damage means that physically abused children are less able to put events into an internal language which they can understand; the resulting incomprehension, or lack of moral perspective, leads to damaged individuals abusing their own children. Early verbal development is central to the working of the mind and the regulation of behaviour. Verbal fluency and information processing are frontal lobe functions. Patients with frontal lobe damage cannot use information provided by verbal clues, and so fail to adapt their behaviour appropriately. Growing up – mentally speaking – is a process of absorbing information, processing it, metabolizing it, digesting it; if we are cut off from this function, we simply do not grow. And our children bear the brunt of our own failure. The brain-damaged child goes on to damage the brain of his own children and make them, in turn, impulsively violent.

Alcohol – involved in some 95 per cent of violent incidents in the home – adds an extra lethal chemical dimension to the organic damage. Some studies have found that 40 per cent of abusive husbands were alcoholic, although others suggest that alcohol may have a calming effect. Possibly; but, as we know, alcohol has more effect on both the psychopathic and the explosively violent mind. Its first action is to depress the cortical inhibitory systems – that is, cut us off from our control mechanisms. If these functions are already compromised through injury, the effect of alcohol is so much the worse.

There is also a specifically female card in this deck of Unhappy Families. Family violence can also have its roots in premenstrual syndrome, PMS; Nicola, who changed so abruptly from the ballet-loving girl to the violent mother-hater, was suffering from PMS. Sudden mood changes, with unexpected irritability and fury at an apparently innocent, chance remark are frequent among those with this condition. Women may become irrational, impatient, aggressive and violent, hurling objects at their nearest and (usually) dearest, be they husband or children – though there is no research specifically linking PMS to child abuse. Unlike the cases of the psychopathic abuser or the explosively violent person, in women with PMS syndrome the monthly danger can be tracked and predicted through the calendar; more importantly, the syndrome is treatable, and once recognized and treated means that their children may safely be left with their mother and do not have to be taken into care.

Another cause of child abuse with a clearly biological basis is postnatal depression. This occurs when the hormone levels change dramatically at delivery, and again when breastfeeding ceases. The Infants Act of 1939 acknowledges the problem – a mother cannot be found guilty of murdering her child within the first twelve months of its life; she can be charged only with manslaughter, allowing the courts a much wider discretion in sentences, which may range from custody to care, probation or even complete freedom. But the statute covers only the murder of the mother's own child, not that of another person.

What is frustrating about so many of these episodes of family violence is that they are supremely avoidable. As we have seen, episodic dyscontrol syndrome can be treated successfully with anticonvulsant drugs. Men with violent, irrational outbursts have been given the relevant drug and none have had a problem since. The same is true for women who suffer from the violent mind of PMS. Counselling and anger-management courses are valuable – but is it really so wrong to fix things with a pill, if and when they are fixable? The constant objection is that by focusing on the bio-technology, we will give politicians an excuse not to deal with the environment of despair – the bad housing, the low wages, the unemployment against which so much family violence is played out. That's nonsense; when scientists discovered penicillin, legislators did not abandon the pursuit of a less septic society. In the same way, we have in our hands the knowledge which we know can prevent certain tragic, social ills like family violence – which should leave us more free to pursue those matters of social justice to which science has no answer.

CHAPTER 11

Sexually Deviant Minds

HE IS YOUNG – probably between 16 and 25. He will commit his crime between the hours of dusk and the small hours. Saturday is his preferred day of the week, and he is most active between the months of May and November. He is likely to come from a low social or income group. There is a 25 per cent chance that he will have done the same thing before, and a one-in-three chance that he has a background of violent crime – and that he'll know his victim. If he's caught, the chances are that he'll do it again after release from prison. His victim is likely to be young – elderly victims are very rare – usually single, characteristically on a low income, unemployed, or a student. Black women are over-represented in the victim population. One in ten offences may involve more than one attacker. Weapons – usually guns or knives – are used in half the reported cases, and in a quarter the attacker demands sexual acts such as fellatio or buggery. The location of the crime is usually his place – or hers.

He is a rapist, and probably the safest thing we can say about him, beyond the raw statistics of his activities, is that he is male.

But does that mean – as the feminist slogan has it – that all men are rapists, that sexual violence is an inherent constituent of maleness? Are all men potential rapists – the vast majority restrained by the sanctions of society? Or is the rapist a sick man – is there something wrong with his brain, his hormones, his neural pathways – in which case should our horror at his crime be tempered with compassion for his condition?

On the whole, to that last question science says no. Most men who rape are not more hormonally supercharged than other men – with the exception of the rapist who adds extra violent physical assault to his sexual attack. Certainly we may find an incidence of low IQ, low serotonin levels and all the familiar cards dealt to those with a constitutional incapacity to delay gratification or imagine the consequences of their actions (albeit most rapes are planned), but there is not – with most rapists – a tell-tale area of the brain which glows a distinctive colour under a PET scan.

There is simply too much rape around to enable us to say that it's the action of a freakish fringe. *Evening Standard* columnist Allison Pearson wrote 'Have I been date-raped? Almost certainly. Have you? Certainly, madam ... that is what growing up is all about: we sleep with the wrong people – out of pity, timidity, ignorance; out of Bacardi and coke; because we have missed the last train ...' On a more serious level, one estimate is that among girls who are twelve today, 20–30 per cent will experience a violent sexual attack at some time in the future. If we are to say that the perpetrators of such acts are 'psychologically sick' then we have to redefine our definition of sickness. It would be more accurate to describe them simply as irresponsibly male.

Nevertheless, evidence is beginning to emerge that there are consistent patterns to the sexually deviant mind – and that differing forms of sexual deviancy may result from the combination of different sorts of damage. In summary, disruption in the temporal lobe can involve sexual deviancy; similar problems in the frontal lobe are associated with violence; and a combination of both may result in aggressive, and sometimes fatal, sexual attacks. The psychopathic sadist also has a disconnection between his emotional centres and his conscience centres. And a host of other irregularities, mostly involving the function of the amygdala, contribute to the complexity of human sexual offending.

Let us start by looking at some of the manifestations of the non-violent sexual mind.

Exhibitionism – an exposure of genitals from a distance to strangers of the opposite sex – is one of the commonest criminal offences, but one which, judging by the number of repeat convictions, is hard to control or to deter.

Raymond G. started to 'flash' at schoolgirls when he was seventeen. He would hide his face from them by holding his coat over his head, but everyone knew it was him; he was well known as a harmless exhibitionist – indeed, he would run away when challenged. (He was later wrongfully convicted of rape on the basis of disputed confessions – the police failing to appreciate that a flasher is usually an inadequate person, and that such inadequates are also prone to make admissions when they feel under threat.) For him excitement lay in displaying himself at a distance, often with an erection, and in shocking the victim.

Some cases of exhibitionism include masturbation, while others masturbate later, with the memory of the encounter serving to arouse them. Some exhibitionists are sexually inhibited, like Raymond G., but others are married and enjoy ordinary sexual relationships. While women see it as a shocking and insulting gesture, the main concern is over its effect on children. Exhibitionism among homosexuals is often used as an invitation to sexual intercourse, but true exhibitionism in this group is rare. Among women it is virtually non-existent.

Toucherism or frotteurism are closely related sexual anomalies. The former is characterized by a strong desire to touch the private parts of an unknown female, while the latter is the desire to approach an unknown female and press the penis against her body – often in a crowd, or a packed train compartment. There is no comparable pattern of behaviour seen in women.

Voyeurism, or the Peeping Tom syndrome, can take many forms.

Typical is the case of a thirty-year-old man who had an excessive preoccupation with sexual fantasies. He would stare at girls in a sexual way, trying to attract them. If the object of his attention encouraged him by crossing and uncrossing her legs, he would have an erection or sometimes masturbate. He went no further and was worried that he might become too excited and masturbate openly. His history is typical – he had been an only child in a sexually inhibited home. He would take fright if girls made advances and at sixteen years of age he was still ignorant of the facts of life. He first had intercourse at the age of twenty-three with his future wife; he could not communicate with her and if she complained he remained silent for fear that he would lose control and beat her.

Fetishists often hoard quantities of material that they collect, for instance underwear taken from a washing line. Some will go to great lengths to steal unwashed articles; others, at an extreme, need actually to take objects from a woman – a lock of her hair, a handkerchief – thus often occasioning an actual assault. In most cases fetishists present no social or personal problems, and shade into harmless ultra-romanticism; indeed, poets have always yearned for a line of her handwriting, or envied the coat that enfolded their love.

Throughout all this variety of bizarre sexual behaviour, a common thread is beginning to emerge. As scientists begin to unravel the tangled skein of the brain, they are discovering a consistent abnormality in the left temporal lobe. This is the area of the brain responsible for our view of ourselves, and for the sort of person we are attracted to. The hypothesis at present is this; while most 'normal' boys and young men will become attracted to a film star, a pop star or the nearest available stunning blonde, people with frontal lobe abnormality cannot make such a mental attachment. Unaroused, yet seeking arousal, they fasten their affections on something which they find can satisfy them. It could be anything; in the Second World War a group of men were turned on by their gas masks.

Another man found, at the age of eight, that he derived great pleasure from looking at a safety pin. He was married, but partially impotent, and experienced much more pleasure from observing his pin than he did from sexual congress. He also suffered from epileptic fits. But when he underwent surgical removal of part of the left temporal lobe, both the epilepsy and the fetishism vanished.

A disproportionate amount of people suffering from epilepsy also suffer a loss of libido and impaired potency; one theory now is that the search for unorthodox stimulation and specific brain damage may be linked.

When exhibitionists were studied, the pattern became even firmer; twenty-one flashers, with no other convictions, revealed severe impairment of the verbal memory – a function of the left temporal lobe. Another man with frontal lobe damage had developed into a fatuous, irresponsible person who got pleasure and excitement by touching women whilst they were shopping or in public places. He was charged with indecent assault.

An intriguingly similar pattern seems to be emerging in the case of paedophiles.

The recent explosion of awareness about child sex abuse has made us all aware that the guilty secret of paedophilia is more common than was feared. The current assessment – that up to 10–15 per cent of children have experienced sexual victimization – may well be an underestimate. For 60 per cent, it is a one-off ordeal, while for the rest it may be episodic or regular. The offence itself usually consists of genital fondling, using hand or mouth, although occasionally the child is encouraged to fondle the adult's genitals. Masturbation and exhibitionism frequently accompany the act, though sexual penetration is rare. This may be because of fear that the child may suffer injury, or, more likely, that the offender desires a child-like sexuality rather than an adult one. In the case of girl victims, a family relative is usually involved. With boys, the offences tend to take place outside the home, and when they are older (and thus able to be approached outside the home). Sexual contacts with strangers are twice as frequent among boys as among girls.

A paedophile is typically a middle-aged heterosexual, lonely, isolated and seeking affection and companionship. He is likely to be unable to fulfil an adult sex role, and is often socially incompetent in other areas of life. Such men are in many ways the polar opposite of those rapists and assaultive sex offenders who are aggressive, uninhibited and insensitive to victims' feelings. Most paedophiles are persuasive and gentle to children, although a minority resemble rapists by their bullying attitude. Psychological tests given to male volunteers of the Paedophile Information Exchange (now disbanded) revealed this group of offenders to be over-represented by professional men and by professions such as teaching or social work. A typical family background included a classic domineering mother and weak or absent father. Half the subjects described their mothers as suffocating, narrow-minded, prudish or very religious.

The story of Russell George is typical. In his home life affection was never expressed, sex was never mentioned and he was discouraged from making friends. He admired his sister and tried on her clothes, wishing that he was a girl so that his mother might love him more. He was inhibited about sex – and neither he nor his wife enjoyed sex. Although they had two sons they had intercourse rarely. Paedophile practices started a few years after he was married. At family gatherings he used to sit the female children of relatives on his knee, put his hand up their skirts and get them to pull down their knickers. After he was caught by a relative, all the family kept away from him and he began to haunt the toy departments of large stores where he would approach young girls. Some agreed to go with him. After ten minutes of talk and fondling he would ejaculate and then lose interest. He was reported and convicted several times but his habit persisted. His wife was loyal but insisted on moving to a new area. After her death and his own early retirement, his behaviour became more reckless and eventually he was imprisoned. He was intent on suicide, but eventually got probation and embarked upon psychotherapy. This was eventually successful. At the age of seventy he declared he was free from all urges.

This story exemplifies several common traits among paedophiles – including the conundrum of a man apparently lacking in normal sexual desire, yet driven to the point of suicide by his pursuit of the unorthodox.

Paedophiles who escape detection – and who do not answer questionnaires – are probably more self-confident, feel less guilt and are more skilled in seduction than those who are caught and charged. For example, a man answered an advertisement put in a contact magazine by a researcher. He was a successful, middle-aged, married businessman, and believed in all forms of sexual freedom. He was an only child, having had, in this case, an unusually liberal upbringing – he had learnt about sex by being encouraged to have intercourse with his mother. He introduced permissiveness into his own marriage by 'wife swapping' and occasional contacts with friends' children. His own children were brought up like him – his son had intercourse with his wife and he had intercourse with both his daughters. He believed that there were no adverse results from these practices – his son and one daughter were already married. He did not consider himself a paedophile, but thought age was no barrier if the girl consented and as long as the experience was mutually gratifying. Sex, he believed, was a natural expression of friendship. He was discreet and got into no trouble with the police, and his children were taught not to talk about their home life.

There is a well-rehearsed litany of justification for the paedophile:

1. Genital fondling is not really sex, so no harm is done.
2. Children don't tell because they enjoy the sex.
3. Sex enhances a relationship with the child.
4. Society will eventually see that sex with children is acceptable.

5. A child enquiring about sex means that he/she wants to experience sex.
6. Physical sex is a good means of teaching children about sex.
7. A lack of physical resistance means that the child wants sex.

There is an explanation for why paedophiles abuse children, and it goes much further to explaining – and indeed excusing – their activities than any of the mawkish excuses proffered above. The evidence is emerging that there is a biological underlay to sexual deviancy. Take a non-violent paedophile and expose his living brain to CT scans, and you will find that there are distinct and predictable brain abnormalities.

The neural system responsible for our sexual arousal lies deep inside the limbic system. This system houses the basic instinctual centres of the brain, involving the amygdala, hypothalamus and hippocampus. The internal nerve networks can be disrupted as the brain develops in the womb or as consequence of hormonal imbalance, accident or illness. If this happens, the blueprint for the emotional control centres in the limbic system gets damaged and in consequence the system is wrongly wired; as a result the ensuing adult is sexually aroused by inappropriate and abnormal stimuli. The abnormality is increased if the child learns the wrong cues from his parents – a distant father and domineering mother seem to be part of the pattern.

That's the theory. Dr Hucker at the Clarke Institute has actually identified the damaged area in a series of CT scans conducted on non-violent paedophiles. They revealed an abnormality in the hypothalamus. There was also a significantly greater incidence of left temporal lobe damage. 'Substantial numbers of paedophiles examined in this study showed neuropsychological impairment.'[1] Scientists are now increasingly convinced that 'cerebral impairment might contribute appreciably to the expression of sexual preference for children.'[2]

But there's another biological strand in the sexual tapestry of deviant paedophilia. It's a matter not just of the structure of the brain, but of the hormones which first form its structure and later interact with it. Other studies at the Clarke Institute have found abnormalities in the endocrine system. The hormonal balance that controls sexual arousal seems to be abnormal in the paedophile. A feedback mechanism which, in most people, damps down excessive sexual arousal is not operating normally and is turned on by inappropriate sexual stimuli such as young children. At least one researcher believes that 'these results present compelling evidence that at least one form of sexually aberrant behaviour in males, paedophilia, may be associated with pathological endocrine phenomena.'[3]

What's going on, it seems, is a cumulative disturbance in the way the brain reacts. What happens with most of us is that the left side of the brain is responsible for our sexual programme and our executive actions. The right side of the brain deals in perceptions and the expression of sexual response. Thus

> Right brain to left brain: 'This is an attractive person.'
> Left brain to right brain: 'Yes, I've checked, this person fits my sexual preference programme.'
> Right brain to genitals: 'I am aroused by this person.'

Damage in paedophiles to the left brain not only distorts their sexual preference, but damages their executive control.

All this seems a touch too comfortable an explanation for the sexually violent paedophile and the child-killer. In fact, such killings are often unpremeditated, and form no part of any sexual intent. Often they are the result of panic, when the poor child screams out. But there clearly is a sub-set of child-molesters for whom killing forms part of a sexual pleasure.

A 45-year-old lorry driver was sentenced to life imprisonment for murdering a four-year-old girl and burying her body in Epping Forest. He had a long history of convictions and imprisonment for sexual molestations. At the age of twenty-seven, recently married, he was fined for indecent assault on a two-year-old girl and a three-year-old boy. Four years later he was convicted for indecent assaults on children, including his own two-year-old daughter, and sentenced to ten years in prison. At thirty-nine, having been released, and again at forty-one he received prison sentences for offences against young girls. Upon release, the social services – ignorant of his past – allowed him to do babysitting jobs. One of the mothers became suspicious when he was seen out in his car with one of his charges. He was acquitted in spite of medical evidence that the child had been sexually abused. Not long after, a child was reported missing and her bloodstained clothes were found in the forest.

The lorry driver was arrested a few months later when on three separate occasions on one day he tried to entice small girls into his car. He confessed after photographs of the murder victim and other indecent pictures were found in his room. He had taken the girl into the forest to photograph her but hit her on the head after she started to cry. He stripped her, buried her and hid the clothes. When his pictures did not turn out satisfactorily he returned to the forest two days later, uncovered the body and took more pictures. He said there were days when he was unable to control his actions and desires.

This astonishing, not to say terrifying catalogue of crime is an example of the persistence of some paedophiles in the face of the virtual certainty of exposure and of imprisonment (and the treatment of sex offenders in prison by other inmates goes beyond what even the most vindictive person would wish or could imagine).

In the case of the violent paedophile, it seems that two cards are present: not only the familiar abnormality in the limbic system and temporal lobes but also an extra, fatal degree of disruption to the frontal lobes. Damage in this area, we know, adds an extra dimension of violence and aggression.

What, then, will we find in the mind of the rapist?

The basic fact of rape, as of most crime, is biological, in

that it is committed by men. Rape occurs at a time in the male life cycle when testosterone levels are at their highest. But high testosterone levels are also seen in men who do not rape.

It's wrong, anyway, to think of the male hormone simply as sexual rocket fuel. Hormones act in two ways: once before we are born, by laying down the blueprint of our brains, and then from puberty onwards, when they energize that blueprint. While men may be bubbling with the male hormone at a certain age, a lot of the effect may be neutralized by the fact that it is operating on a relatively unresponsive mechanism. The shy, male librarian may have abnormally high testosterone levels; but his shyness, his sense of reserve are innate, a pattern laid down by hormones in the womb, and no excess of male hormone in later life is going to turn him into a sex maniac.

There is one, definably hormonal influence in rape – and that's in excessively violent rape. (We accept that all rape is violence, and all violence is excessive, but trust that the reader will understand this distinction.) Studies show that rapists who have used drastic degrees of violence have higher testosterone levels than rapists whose violence is restricted to the sexual act alone. A cycle of hormonal violence may be involved here, because sexual arousal and aggression can themselves heighten testosterone levels. Could it be, indeed, that some men prefer aggressive sex because they find it the most hormonally arousing form of sexual gratification? Does the rapist need the kick of aggression to release the energy of sex?

There is one area where we can make a definitive, chemical causal link between hormones and sexual crime. We have already touched on the impact of anabolic steroids, and their effect of enhancing natural hormone levels by up to 100 times. With two million Americans habitually taking anabolic steroids, some scientists believe that such abuse has actually changed the criminal climate of the country; that steroid abuse 'may contribute to an increased incidence of general aggression, unprovoked violence, and rape.'[4] The prevalence in adolescents is particularly disturbing, given the estimate that some 500,000 teenage boys are using – or misusing – steroids. 'This has become a national problem not only because of the personal health hazards. Individuals taking exogenous steroids appear to be more reactive to stimuli that elicit violent behaviour. While there is no proof at this time, it may be expected that a significant proportion of date rapes and other rapes may be from steroid self medication.'[5]

There is already evidence, if not proof, of the link between steroid abuse and rape.

In London, the Hanger Lane rapist terrorized the neighbourhood for over a year. He sexually assaulted eight women in broad daylight in the underpass beneath this busy intersection of the inner ring road and the main thoroughfare from London to the West. The police arrested him and discovered that he had an addiction to anabolic steroids, and established that it was the drugs that were altering his behaviour. There was not enough evidence to convict but they persuaded him to undergo treatment and co-operate with the police. He is now back to normal and deeply regrets what happened.

This is one of a number of cases studied by a Metropolitan Police officer seconded by the Home Office to study the effects of steroid abuse. The rapist was the youngest of four, from a good family. A tall, but skinny individual, he was encouraged to join a gym at the age of sixteen. After eighteen months, he started to take anabolic steroids. They made him feel good, and he began to build up his body. At the age of eighteen he – uncharacteristically – committed criminal damage by smashing up the windows of a bus when the driver did not have enough change.

The courts did not deal so compassionately with John Steed, the M4 murder rapist.

John Steed was a mild and gentle individual before he became a body-builder and started taking anabolic steroids. He did have a history of theft – but not of violence.

After embarking on a course of steroids, Steed picked up prostitutes and horrifically mutilated them. His entire defence was anabolic steroid addiction, but, blinded, perhaps, by the horror of the crimes, the court refused to accept that there was a chemical explanation for the carnage for which Steed was responsible.

In the past, the use of illicit androgenic agents was rare, restricted in the main to highly trained athletes. Now, steroid use has become a recognized part of the present-day obsession with health, fitness and the body beautiful. There is now habitual use of large doses of steroidal sex hormones for cosmetic and 'life-enhancing' purposes. The black-market steroid economy in America runs at $100m a week. A quarter of a million high school seniors are reckoned to be active users. The effects of anabolic steroids on sexual functioning are dramatic. In the first five years of dependence, libido soars. Even ejaculation fails to satisfy. It is becoming clear that apparently normal people can experience a mind-altering effect from steroids – and the alteration is one that instigates irrational and criminal behaviour. What sort of a time bomb is ticking away here?

Rape cannot, of course, be ascribed to any single chemical source. Studies have shown that there are many different kinds of rape, all of which have different causes. A study of 500 rapists has identified three broad categories of the crime. There's 'anger rape': rapists described their rage following arguments, sexual jealousies and social rejection. There was a sense of being wronged, and needing to get even. In these cases, rapists use far more force than is necessary to ensure compliance. The aim appears to be to inflict physical injury, with rape almost an afterthought, an additional way of inflicting pain. Such an anger rapist – and it is reckoned that they constitute 40 per cent of all offenders – may be men with low impulse control, or with a low arousal threshold. A second category, so-called 'power rape', accounted for a further 55 per cent; the goal here is conquest, and the satisfaction of dominance, physical force exercised to procure compliance. The final 5 per cent is the stuff of tabloid headlines – 'sadistic rape'. Here, sexuality and aggression feed upon each other. The victim is made to suffer extra agonies, typically by being tied, tormented and often tortured. The victim's humiliation and pain is sexually exciting, while the action of the rape itself increases the anguish, thus creating a spiral of malicious pleasure. As we will see, it is in this area that most progress is being made in the search for a specifically damaged mind.

There are further categories, such as the revenge rapist, whose victim has usually provided no actual cause for revenge; it is enough that she is a woman, and so bears a collective responsibility, in her attacker's mind, for the sins of any or all of her sex. So if a man has been insulted, demeaned or denied by any particular woman, all women will be at risk of his punitive, sexual wrath. This explains why an apparently unconnected flare-up so often precedes incidents of rape; usually, the cause of the row is a perceived sexual indiscretion on the part of the woman, a deviation from a strict and rigid standard of sexual conduct set, though not necessarily respected, by the man. For instance, she is accused, after a party, of having flirted outrageously with so-and-so. The row explodes when they get home. He storms out and, by some strange logic of fury, 'gets even' by attacking a stranger. Such revenge rapes are among the most brutal, including beatings, serious injury and even murder.

In one case, quoted from a study of 114 rapists, a young man thought he had a fairytale romance with his girlfriend, and expected total fidelity from her. When she went away to college and became involved with another man, his revenge lasted for eighteen months and involved the rape and murder of five women, all strangers who lived in his community. 'I wanted to take my revenge and anger out on a stranger . . . I wanted to use and abuse someone the way I had been used and abused. During the rapes and murders I would think of my girlfriend . . . I hated the victims because they probably messed men over. I hated women because they were deceitful, and I was getting revenge for what had happened to me.'

Some rapists admit that their motive was to get even not with the victim, or with womankind, but vicariously with the victim's male partners. One woman was raped because her partner owed the assailant money and was reneging on the debt. From the attacker's viewpoint, he is increasing the sense of his own manhood by the theft of another male's property. Many rapists felt that men had the right to discipline and punish women. Rape was used to 'put women in their place' and to 'prove their manhood' by displaying dominance over a female.

Another category emerged from this study – 'incidental rape'. Appalling as it may seem to the victim that her violation may simply be an opportunistic afterthought, rape and robbery often go together. Sometimes, the intention was to rape, with the theft of the victim's property as an afterthought. But a significant number of offenders said that the reverse was true: the decision to rape was made after the execution of the robbery or burglary. One man told researchers that he was robbing a home when he saw his victim asleep, and he saw it as 'an opportunity to go to bed with a white woman to see if it was different'. For some, the decision to rape was intimately bound up in the power situation presented by the robbery; they were 'in control' of a submissive woman – so the question was 'why not?' Rape was an erotic bonus to another criminal act.

For many rapists, the assault was seen simply as a response to the fact that sex was a right which, if denied, had to be acquired by forcible means. The goods were in the shop window but were not for sale, so they had to be stolen. The rape is often justified in these impersonal, commercial terms. A Scottish solicitor, for instance, had taken a girl out to an expensive St Andrew's night ball in London. Tickets for the evening's event, and other expenses, ran into hundreds of pounds. The couple danced most of the night away, but had a few hours to kill before the train back home, and spent it at the home of a friend. The woman went to sleep, but woke to the sight of the man dressed only in his Scottish evening-dress lace cuffs and a condom. The solicitor – who was sentenced to imprisonment for attempted rape – told the arresting officers that he felt entitled to do what he wanted with her, having spent so much money on her that evening. Again, if a woman is picked up in a bar, or while hitchhiking, or wears a provocatively short skirt, and subsequently resists sexual advances, the offenders consider rape to be justified.

Rape is sex as a commodity, in which people are seen as objects – and it is this very aspect of the crime which appeals to some offenders: 'Rape gave me the power to do what I wanted without feeling I had to please a partner or respond to a partner. I felt in control, dominant.' 'Rape was the ability to have sex without caring about the woman's response.' Wholesome sex involves a mutual surrender, a losing of self in each other – something many rapists cannot conceive of, or indeed of which they are fearful. That fear can be overcome only through the sense of power and control which rape provided. This combination of power and depersonalization is a common thread running through such crimes. Only 2 of the 114 rapists interviewed admitted to any concern for the victim. A common justification was that the women enjoyed the experience.

So the answer to the question 'Why do men rape?' is both a complex and a simple one; they rape for a variety of reasons, but common to all of them is the fact that they want to. Rape is described, by rapists themselves, as a challenge, an adventure. When asked to describe how they felt after an attack, only 8 per cent admitted to any sense of regret or guilt.

While biology cannot explain all these kinds of rape, it can offer some clues to the range of behaviour we have described. In its extreme manifestations, much of this fits, then, what we know about the mind of the psychopath – this sense of disconnection from the sense of another's suffering, this insistent priority on self-gratification. And indeed of those who repeatedly rape, one estimate is that half are psychopaths, their crimes a terrible mix of sexual drive, desire for power and control, and a view of their victims as pleasurable commodities − a mind which has no sense of right and wrong, a mind which sees people as objects, a mind with no apprehension of the agony and humiliation involved for the victim. This is an important distinction when it comes to releasing sex offenders; almost a third of rapists released on parole rape again, and the repeat rapists are the ones that score high on the psychopathy checklist.

As for those rapists who cannot be defined as psychopathic, new research is beginning to give us a more sophisticated glimpse into the make-up of the minds of some of them. Groups of men have been videotaped in conversation on early dates with women, to see how they interpret the signals and cues transmitted by their partners. Those with a record of date-rape proved to be short on conversational skills, but, more significantly, to be hopelessly inaccurate in recognizing the implicit messages of their partners. Tested on whether she was emitting 'bad mood' as opposed to 'romantic' signals, through facial expressions, body language or intonation, the rape-prone men consistently got the message wrong, when compared with a sample of non-rapists. It may not simply be a question of 'not taking no for an answer': men who rape may not hear the answer 'no'. Interestingly, this finding seems to be tied in quite specifically with sexual aggression; men who were merely aggressive read the signals better.

In two particular categories of rape we are beginning to distinguish specific mental abnormality. They have been identified by a machine which measures their sexual arousal − or to be more precise the size and rate of their erection − when confronted with pictures or narratives of various sexual situations.

The first is a class of rapists for whom the very reluctance of the victim is what makes her an object of desire. These men often have histories of voyeurism and exhibitionism. They are loners. They have experienced few, if any, normal sexual relationships. It is common for them to follow women and just watch ... until their fantasies develop to beyond the point at which mere observation is enough. Such men have much in common with other violent criminals – the same hand of cards which includes low levels of the neurotransmitter serotonin, and a high level of impulsiveness. But they have extra cards, so that their biological make-up tilts their criminality into the sexual arena.

The extra card, in their case, is described as a 'courtship disorder'. In most men, one of the functions of courtship is to neutralize their innate aggression. Men are programmed to defend territory and to scare off intruders. Clearly this is not a recipe for a happy relationship, so nature – and nurture – lay down a pattern whereby attraction to a putative partner switches off the normal territorial male attitudes. The exact extent to which these 'love maps', as they have been described, are the result of nature or nurture is difficult to define; maybe the wiring diagrams are laid down in the womb like so much of our other innate behaviour, maybe it is as the result of observation of parental behaviour or of imbibing romantic fairy stories. But the love map may be faulty – again, either because of hormonal interference in the womb, or because of confusions as the child grows up; for instance, a mother who beats her child and then cuddles him afterwards to show forgiveness may distort the map by implanting the idea that love and beating go together. In an extreme case, there may be a fundamental flaw in the love map; instead of the map providing a bypass around the man's aggression in order to attain the object of his desire, the map shows that he can reach fulfilment only through aggression. These men actually want their partners to be frightened, to want to run away. Coy courtship does not work. They need a woman's terror to arouse them.

There is evidence of a different type of underlying brain abnormality in the second class, that of the non-psychopathic violent rapist. Dr Roy Langevin's studies indicate that violent rapists have inappropriate emotions which are intermixed with their sexual programme. They show brain abnormalities in both the temporal lobe and in the limbic system. Aggressive responses fuse together with sexual responses, with the result that sex is only possible in an aggressive situation. This occurs because of the geography of the brain. Very near the amygdala, which controls aggression and the attacking/fleeing response, is the area responsible for sexual arousal. Both nuclei of these separate structures share the same exit system. Information travels down the same road, like signals down the same fibre optic cable. But in some men, especially during hyperarousal of the brain, the signals get mixed. Sex and aggression become inextricably entwined. The violent rapist's sexual arousal system is interwoven with the aggressive area of his brain.

Langevin believes that some are born with this abnormality, while others can become rapists after the brain is damaged in this area.

> One of his case histories involves a young man who was born into a wealthy family with servants. He went to a private school, and had a good relationship with his parents who were loving and caring. He did well in school and went on to university. He completed one year and had to leave to go abroad. When he returned, he fell in love and got married. One night, he was in a car when a drunk driver in another car smashed into him, rendering him unconscious. He woke up in hospital days later needing brain surgery. The doctors put a steel plate in his head to support his skull. Although he was not intellectually impaired, his character changed dramatically. He became impulsively violent and sexually obsessed. He eventually raped the fourteen-year-old daughter of a friend and was sentenced to eight years in prison. Studies of his brain indicated the same pattern of damage as seen in other rapists.

Indeed, let us look at an actual study of the brain of a non-psychopathic rapist.

> For seven months Bobby Jo Long, a man from Tampa, Florida, went on a wild spree of rape and murder. His method was to pick up women in bars, drive them to a lonely spot, tie them up, rape and strangle them. His sex

urge was compulsive. After each murder, he would sleep deeply and when he woke up would wonder, with great self-disgust, whether he had dreamt it all, confirming his own fears by buying the newspapers to read the details. By November 1983 Long had killed eight times.

His last intended victim was different. He found out from her that she had been abused as a child. He drove her around for hours, raped her but then set her free – in the full knowledge that she could identify him.

Long had led a traumatic childhood; his parents were divorced, his mother worked long hours and saw many different men. Long and his mother shared the same bed until he was twelve years old. Long married Cindy, who was very like his mother in looks and temperament – both were aggressive and manipulative. He enlisted into the army as an apprentice electrician, and six months into his training he had a severe motorcycle accident. He fractured his skull and remained semicomatose for weeks. He had severe headaches, but neither his X-rays nor his EEG were properly evaluated.

Long's view of the motorcycle accident was that it changed his life. He started thinking about sex all the time: he went from having sex two or three times a week to two or three times a day, as well as masturbating. The most disturbing change was his violent reaction to anything which stood in his way – although he could never recall clearly the resultant fit of fury.

He left the army and worked occasionally as an X-ray technician but was fired for making advances to female patients. From 1980 to 1983 he committed more than 50 rapes in Florida; he would call numbers listed in classified advertisements, and when he met a lone woman in the house he would tie her up, rape her and rob her. But he never murdered them and was seldom violent. All the time he appreciated the moral implications of what he was doing. In 1985 a psychological evaluation found him competent to stand trial.

The case came to the attention of Dr Otnow Lewis. Dr Lewis also discovered that Long had experienced other head trauma, such as falling off a swing and being knocked unconscious by a car. She reported that the overall result of these injuries was a significant level of damage to the left temporal lobe. A PET scan discovered the same story as Dr Lewis had suspected. But it also uncovered an abnormality in the amygdala – that area of the brain which generated emotions – and especially in that area of the amygdala known to be involved in the sexual drive, which, in Long's case, was hyperactive.

The significant thing – and what differentiates Long from the psychopathic rapist – is the fact that he was capable of feeling remorse. He had the normal connection between his 'feeling' centre in the limbic system and his 'moral' centre in the frontal lobes.

Long's appeal against the death sentence has so far failed.

There is another category of sex criminal, the psychopathic sadist.

The sensational publicity accorded to sadistic sex murderers (and as we will see the publicity can form part of the gratification) is in inverse proportion to the frequency of such occurrences. There's not, mercifully, a great deal of sadistic sex murder around. Murders after sexual assaults are no more than a small percentage of total murders in England. A Home Office research study in 1961 found that of 140 men convicted for murders between 1957 and 1960 11.4 per cent were sexually motivated. A certain percentage were not sentenced as they were classed as mentally insane, but interestingly this classification was less frequent among sexually motivated killers.

Robert Brittain, a forensic pathologist and psychiatrist, published a profile of sadistic sex murderers based on a lifetime of clinical experience. He paints a typical portrait of a man under thirty-five years of age, an introverted day-dreamer with a rich fantasy life, thought of as a loner by his acquaintances. He has a close attachment to his mother and a bad relationship with a distant father. He is vain and very sensitive to threats to his self-esteem, as well as being concerned about his sex potency.

He is attracted to accounts of cruelty and fascinated by knives and guns; he is drawn to Nazism and militaria. He was probably cruel to animals as a child. His deviant sex interest would have started early. He kills by throttling or strangling in the course of the sexual assault. Asphyxia is a common method of sadistic sexual killing, since by this means the victim's suffering may be prolonged; the killer repeatedly revives his victim from unconsciousness, in order to inflict further pain. Some studies suggest that such assaults actually are a substitute for the sexual act. These offenders may insert objects such as torch, milk bottle or pole with great force into the victim's rectum or vagina. The prognosis for such offenders is not good: many repeat the offences even after years of imprisonment. He may masturbate beside his victim, although sexual intercourse does not necessarily occur. At the time he is in a frenzy of excitement but immediately afterwards he returns to his normal routine. He is rational about hiding the body and covering his tracks – he may have planned his crime very carefully. His emotional response to the crime is superficial. He is not insane, although he may feel that he is under the influence of impulses such as voices encouraging him to do it or not.

Philip Atherton, a young man who abducted, sexually assaulted and murdered a young schoolboy in Nottingham in the mid-1980s, fits this profile exactly. He had planned his night's excursion carefully. He would entice his young victim on a cycle ride. Atherton had an almost magical sway over younger children – he was inept in his own peer group – which he maintained by bloodthirsty cruelty inflicted upon animals. While babysitting, it was later revealed, he had locked his charges in his car boot. He poured bleach into a tank of tropical fish. Having persuaded his victim to accompany him on a fictitious raid on a fizzy-drink depot, he strangled the child and attempted to bugger him. When he returned home, however, he was careful to put in place an alibi, should one be needed. In the event, he was arrested almost immediately, and confessed – but he then used his alibi to implicate another youth called Mark Cleary. The two young men were both found guilty and sentenced to life imprisonment. Cleary was completely innocent, and was freed only after evidence was gathered by Channel 4's *Trial and Error* programme. Atherton seems entirely unrepentant about the damage he has done to both victims – the child and Cleary.

Representing as they do the nightmare extreme of masculine violence, it is intriguing to find that researchers have identified a definite trace of the feminine in a significant proportion of such killers. One in six, for instance, reach orgasm while engaged in transvestism. Sadists seem relatively indifferent to their own sexuality, and many have been identified as having an effeminate tinge and feminine longings. A small number actually show a desire to change sex – causing in one case in a self-administered castration. There is also a pronounced narcissism among sexual sadists. The mass sex killers on the whole enjoyed the publicity surrounding the horror of their deeds.

Such behaviour gives every indication of a hormonal dimension to this area of rape, and research supports the thesis. The hormonal profiles of some forty-nine cases of extreme sexual aggression were studied, and surprisingly high levels of luteinizing hormone – a pattern that is more feminine than masculine – were discovered. Could their crazed cruelty be in part at least a result of their own gender confusion, or perhaps their frustration and envy of the women which they cannot be?

One should always be cautious about generalizations, and a psychological profile is a generalization writ large. For example, police investigating the Boston Strangler were directed to make enquiries among the gay community; they were fruitless, for the killer was, in fact, heterosexual. Worse still, a man was charged in 1994 with a brutal murder on Wimbledon Common largely because he matched Brittain's putative profile – the police even tried to bribe him to confess by offering the prospect of sex, but they failed, and the judge very properly threw the case out. Nevertheless, with those caveats the following case history represents a typical pattern.

Peter was raised in a stable middle-class family. His fantasies of killing women started when he was aged ten. These fantasies carried on throughout his teenage years, but he did nothing about them. He started stealing at a very young age from neighbours. His parents were horrified and tried to stop him. He showed no guilt or remorse. When he won a place at university, his parents were relieved. They hoped that this would occupy their strange boy's talents. But things grew worse. He started to break into peoples' homes just for kicks and would occasionally steal things. He would stalk women who lived on their own. Loitering around shopping centres, Peter would watch women to see if they had a husband meeting them. Once he made sure that they were single, he would follow them home and then break into their flats. He would sometimes stalk up to 4 or 5 women a day. This lasted about a year. As he thought about breaking and entering, he would get an erection. On one occasion, his erection got caught on the window-sill of a flat he was trying to burgle. In his excitement, he gagged the woman, beat her up and masturbated over her.

Peter's sexual system was being activated by his aggression system. As he learnt to inhibit his masturbation, this led to more violence. He began to kill his victims. Finally he was caught and sentenced. His fantasies did not change in prison, but he was a model prisoner. The authorities released him after ten years due to his good behaviour. On the day of his release, he took a plane into a new town. As he walked out of the airport a taxi cab pulled up, with a female driver. He jumped in. She was found a few hours later, dead. Her body was tied up to a tree and brutally beaten up. He had masturbated and urinated on her corpse.

For people like Peter, sexual arousal is possible only in the context of domination, control, entrapment, terror and injury. Power takes the place of foreplay; the victim has no alternative but to do his sexual bidding. Her very pleading for mercy is sexually stimulating. The actual killing may not produce a sexual climax, but it is sexually exciting in itself. For other psychopath sadists, the death of the victim is a prelude to their sexual activity, which may involve necrophiliac intercourse and oral sex. The victim's body may be mutilated in the frenzy of excitement – genitals are sometimes removed and cases of cannibalism have been reported.

Although too few have been conducted for a consistent and reliable pattern to emerge, brain scan studies have revealed abnormalities in a number of sadists. What's strange is that not only the sex-centres of the left temporal lobe, but also the aggression-control areas of the right – which we have already seen to be damaged in epileptics and some sexual deviations such as paedophilia – showed abnormalities. EEG studies suggest that extreme sexual aggression is the result of more specific damage than the defects responsible for aggression generally: men who were simply aggressive had generalized damage, but in sexual sadists there was specific damage to the right temporal lobe – an area which is also responsible for the control of aggression.

Apart from gross abnormalities of the right temporal lobe, in the small number of cases that have been examined using sophisticated deep-brain scans the amygdala is abnormal. Peter's case (above) was the result of specific brain damage – whether caused in the womb or as a result of a later trauma we do not know. The doctors examined his amygdala (the area of the limbic system involved in the expression of emotions) and found that this area was experiencing periodic fits, little explosions akin to epileptic seizures. The EEGs had not picked these up, being able to monitor only the electrical activity of the cortex – but they were like an electrical storm at the centre of the brain.

In these cases the right side of the amygdala seems to be overactive, which researchers interpret as the reason for the sexually obsessive behaviour. People like Peter also share the abnormality of other psychopathic types in that the guilt, or conscience, area of the brain is disconnected from the limbic system.

Karl X maintains that he is innocent of the murder of sixteen men – although he probably killed many more. He became known as the score-card killer, because of the record he kept of his young victims. He would drug them, mutilate them – one victim had his eyes burnt out and his genitals cut off – and then dump their bodies at the side of the highway, always nude and always in a sexual pose. He behaves in classic psychopathic manner, displaying neither remorse nor responsibility.

When he was submitted to a PET scan, the outer area of the frontal lobes – the home of intelligence – showed the same activity as a normal individual, reflecting what is found among other psychopathic types; they are not stupid, and do not kill in hot blood. But there was a difference in the area of the frontal lobe where the conscience abides, as well as temporal lobe abnormalities where damage, as we know, is associated with sexual deviancy. There was also low activity between the area of the limbic system which subserves memory and the frontal lobes – similar, though not identical, to the disconnection we have often observed between these two areas in psychopaths.

These, then, are brains where damage makes the emotions too strong, where inappropriate anger and aggression is confused with sexuality, and where there is little connection with ideas of guilt, conscience or remorse. At the moment, the findings are based on too few cases to be conclusive – but what should medicine and science do, if we discover a consistent constellation of factors in the brain of the sadistic killer rapist?

It is a question worth thinking about, before the guards attach the sponge and metal headset, attach the electrode to the shaven leg, pull the switch and terminally damage an already disordered brain.

CHAPTER 12

The Murderous Mind

THE PARAMEDICS UNPACK the bloody stretcher with rehearsed efficiency, as the blades of the Royal London Hospital's orange emergency helicopter still clatter above them. They wheel the trolley down the rooftop ramps of the helicopter pad, into the lifts which lead straight to the trauma room. But they're too late. 'She was leaking like a sieve,' says the surgeon apologetically. 'We did everything, but with more than twenty stab wounds there's only so much you can do.' Another day, another murder; a domestic flare-up which got out of control. It's the commonest form of murder in the UK: in as many as four fifths of murders the murderer and victim are known to each other or related to each other. When a wife dies in suspicious circumstances, let the husband beware.

As with the violent mind, there is not one murderous brain pattern; if we cut open, measured and distilled the contents, we would not find a recipe for murder. There are many different factors which, in different arrangements, may tilt the balance. But there are some killers who have specific mind patterns which have a direct, causal influence on their killing. By now, they may be becoming familiar, as our picture of the potentially criminal mind begins to emerge – although the pattern is subtly different in the mind of a killer.

Murder is, of course, the world's favourite crime. True crime was the fastest-expanding literary genre of recent years; initial sales of a monthly partwork specifically devoted to murder exceeded half a million in the UK – one in forty of the entire adult population read it. A typical television viewer will have absorbed 18,000 fictional murders by the age of eighteen.

We know more about the incidence and breakdown of

murder than of other crimes. Murder has a much higher rate of detection than any other crime (those suspicious spouses, we suppose). The average American runs a 1 in 10,000 risk of being murdered in any single year. The peak was in 1980, since when the rates have begun to dip and level off. Over a lifetime, the probability rises to 1 in 133. In the US and in the UK, it's not the stranger lurking in the dark alley we should fear most – it's our friends, relatives and acquaintances we need to worry about. Homicide is also the most frequently solved of all crimes: usually everything is in place for the police – the evidence, the weapon, the motive – and 75 per cent of homicides are cleared by arrest.

The law, of course, distinguishes between murder and manslaughter: murder needs the additional element of intention. In the US different degrees of killing are acknowledged. The first degree, favoured in fiction, is deliberate, premeditated and committed with malice; first degree murders include those committed during the course of rapes, robberies, burglaries, arson and kidnapping. Second degree murder is less obvious and less precise. It often involves a crime of passion; malice and intent may be present, but deliberation and premeditation are generally not. For instance, a wife becomes enraged on learning that her husband has blown the family savings on a gamble, grabs the bread knife and kills him. There is another category of non-negligent or voluntary manslaughter, where there is an intent to do bodily harm but not to kill – such as the jealous husband who decides to 'teach his wife a lesson' and smashes her head against a wall.

Definitions of degree of murder are difficult in the US because of the practice of plea-bargaining, in which the accused is persuaded to plead guilty in exchange for a lesser charge. But murder is predominantly a crime by the young against the somewhat older. In 1985, in the US 60 per cent of arrested offenders were aged 15–29, while 47 per cent of the victims were in the 20–34 age range. In the US, murder is the second leading cause of death (after automobile accidents) in males between 15 and 24.

It won't surprise the reader that the gender card counts strongly here. Most murder is by male upon male. In 1985 in the US 88 per cent of arrested offenders and 74 per cent of their victims were male. Given that males constitute 49 per cent of the general population, they are clearly over-represented in the figures. Ninety per cent of female victims were killed by males. Racially speaking, most murder is intra-ethnic; 94 per cent of US black victims are killed by blacks, and 88 per cent of whites by whites.

Murder is often characterized as an amateur's crime – the Cosa Nostra hits of New York's lower East Side are very much the exception. In the US, some 59 per cent of killings involve friends and relations, and close on 40 per cent of killings arise not as a result of rapes, arson, kidnapping or robberies but out of arguments, about money, sex, what television channel to watch or whose turn it is to put the cat out. According to one study of police records, 35 per cent of murders occurred in the course of an 'altercation of relatively trivial origin, insult, jostling, curse etc.'. 'Ostensible reasons for disagreement are usually trivial, indicating that many homicides are spontaneous acts of passion, not products of a single determination to kill.' An analysis of murder in Philadelphia confirms the findings; 37 per cent followed a relatively trivial event, in most cases the parties knew each other, 87 per cent were of the same race, and 94 per cent were male. The murders most frequently happened in a domestic setting during the summer months, most often between the hours of 8 p.m. on Saturday and 2 a.m. on Sunday morning. Alcohol is involved in about 90 per cent of all homicides in the US. UK figures, while smaller, are similar in that they show that we have more to fear from our friends than from our neighbours. These statistics suggest that we are probably all capable of murder. The provocations are mundane, the weapons are to hand and we don't even have to leave home to commit the crime. Those we have studied who are repetitively violent, or violently explosive as a result of their brain chemistry or damage may murder too – indeed, they are more likely to –

but most of us are capable of a one-off aberrant extreme of behaviour involving the gravest crime in the calendar.

Dan worked as a packer in a factory. The boss was always picking on him, for no very clear reason. His time-keeping and productivity were second to none, but for some reason the two men grated upon each other. Over the years, this mutual dislike began to fester. Dan used to rage, internally, about his employer. His work involved the use of a sharp knife. One day, he used it to stab his boss through the heart. His friend tried to separate the two – and he too got stabbed. Dan got a light sentence; he was a man of impeccable character, unlikely to repeat the crime, who had simply been driven beyond endurance.

We do, in fact, have something of an evolutionary investment in aggression and in defending our patch of territory. In some societies killing increases status. Blood revenge is one of the most commonly cited causes of violence and warfare in tribal societies. Studies of the Yanomamo Indians of Amazonas during the past 23 years show that 44 per cent of males over the age of 25 have participated in the killing of someone, that approximately 30 per cent of adult male deaths are due to violence and that nearly 70 per cent of all adults over 40 years of age have lost a close relative due to violence. In these societies most fights start over sexual issues: infidelity, attempts to seduce another man's wife, sexual jealousy and (rarely) rape. Raids motivated by revenge may seem counter-productive but swift retaliation serves as an effective long-term deterrent; family groups which retaliate swiftly are themselves attacked less frequently, and suffer a lower rate of mortality and abduction. And men who have killed have more wives and children than men who have not killed.

Our own societies constrain these primitive attitudes and behaviours, however close to the surface they lurk. But how much of the underlying motives for murder persists in spite of our modern rules, mores and penalties?

What we know about killers comes from studies of those in prison and in special hospitals for mentally disturbed offenders. What we find is that – for all that any of us can and do kill – there is a high proportion of mentally disordered minds. The disorders involve the same disturbances as we have identified in the violent mind, such as schizophrenia, depression and mood disorders. We also find the aggressive psychopath, deemed by the law and medicine to be sane, and those with episodic dyscontrol – an epilepsy-type explosion in the key control centres of the brain. But there is a smaller proportion of such disordered minds among those convicted for murder than among violent criminals, because so many murderers are, indeed, ordinary people who have, just once in their life, been driven to commit this extraordinary crime.

One study of men sentenced to life imprisonment rated nearly half the sample as 'highly disturbed' – and these were the men in prison who did not qualify for transfer to a mental hospital. Other reports support the view of probation officers that the rate of psychiatric disorder may be high among lifers. In a review of 183 lifers supervised by the Inner London Probation Service, over two thirds appeared to have some form of psychiatric disorder; as many as 10 per cent were assessed as psychotic, almost certainly schizophrenic; 11 per cent manifested depressive/affective disorder. There was little or no overlap between the two groups, because schizophrenia and depression spring from two very separate disorders. There was more overlap between those diagnosed as having antisocial personality disorder, which was often accompanied by a history of alcoholism and/or depression. Virtually all these conditions had been recognized as present at the time of the offence, and had not been brought on by the fact of imprisonment. Depression was more common in those prisoners convicted of manslaughter on the grounds of diminished responsibility.

Studies of murderers committed to special hospitals – that is, those murderers the court has classified as mentally ill –

show that the idea that murderers are uniformly violent and antisocial is a myth. Few murderers appear to be hardened criminals, and many have no history of antisocial behaviour.

Results of the most systematic attempt to relate personality to homicide come up with a choice of pictures. One is the so-called 'undercontrolled personality', with few inhibitions against aggression; we are familiar with this sort of mind from Chapters 8 and 9 on the violent mind. The aggressive psychopath is the main type. Then there are the 'overcontrolled personality' types. This sort of mind has strong inhibitions against aggression, but may respond with an aggressive outburst under conditions of severe frustration. The over-controlled personality will turn violent only when the provocation reaches a high level – but when the volcano blows, it blows, in the form of an extreme assault of homicidal proportions.

The assessment of fifty-six convicted killers who had been sent to Broadmoor came up with a more precise picture. A group of one third were assessed as over-controlled personalities. They didn't give any impression of mental illness in any conventional sense. The suggestion is that extreme events trigger an abnormal change in brain chemistry. They tended to be older, married and of high intelligence. Most people who had killed their own children fell into this group. The rest were under-controlled, divided into several groups.

In another third, anxiety and hostility were very apparent. There was much impulsive, acted-out behaviour. Since clinical experience suggests that patients with severe personality disorders also produce a similar pattern, patients with this profile are often diagnosed wrongly as paranoid schizophrenics. Some researchers would prefer to categorize them as secondary psychopaths. Members of this group were younger, tended to be unmarried, had a previous criminal record and were the least intelligent. Their victims were mostly strangers or casual acquaintances, and more than half the killings in this group had a sexual component.

A smaller, third group was characterized by strong impulse control, but abnormally high levels of introversion and social anxiety. The usual diagnosis was of schizophrenia. A fourth group, even smaller, combined characteristics of impulsiveness, extroversion, lack of social anxiety and high levels of hostility. In all cases, their victim was a family member. They conformed closely to clinical descriptions of the primary psychopath – indeed the group was labelled 'psychopathic type'. What's interesting already is that we find many fewer psychopaths among murderers than we do, proportionately, among non-homicidal violent criminals.

This study provides intriguing support for the theory that murder is different – that the murderous mind is unlike others we have seen; the fact that the largest group consisted of the over-controlled, otherwise well-behaved, mild-mannered people should make us think harder about the nature of the crime. The same pattern has been replicated in other studies and has also been found in prisons, as opposed to special hospitals.

What is fascinating is that the different groups commit different types of murder. Other studies also suggest that murderers have different characteristics, according to the kinds of murders they commit. Although there are overlaps, because diagnosis is not an exact science, a definite pattern emerges.

Those who kill strangers make up at least 14 per cent of known murders, and among them there seems to be a disproportionate number of people with intermittent explosive dyscontrol problems. This shouldn't surprise us – after all, almost by definition the murder of a total stranger is more likely to be an act of random rage than a slow-burning, long-planned, deliberate act. A study of 280 homicidal offenders whose acts had been characterized by impulsiveness found that 100 suffered specifically from this disorder (a fatal electrical brainstorm affecting control over their impulses). Alcohol, particularly, induced violence among them, for reasons we have already discovered – it acts as a chemical trigger for the electrical explosion.

A particularly valuable insight into this sort of murderous mind comes from a study of nine young men *before* they killed. These future murderers displayed a constellation of psychotic symptoms, major neurological impairment, a close relative who could be diagnosed as psychotic, violent acts during childhood and severe physical abuse – the full flush of cards held by those predisposed to violent crime. But what's the extra card, which leads them to kill people they have never known?

All nine murderers-to-be had manifested extreme violence as children and adolescents. All started young – one had choked a bird at the age of two, and threw a dog out of the window two years later; another threatened a teacher with a razor at the age of ten. (We remember the British youth Philip Atherton, who used to strangle pigeons, shoot squirrels and put bleach in the tanks of tropical fish. He was later to entice a small boy to accompany him on a late-night bicycle ride and then, for no discernible motive, strangle and drown him. Atherton was an enthusiast of CB – a way of communicating with strangers.) All were found to be severely neuropsychiatrically impaired; three had a history of seizures, one had abnormal EEGs and three more had a variety of psychomotor epileptic symptoms. In most cases, a close relative had been diagnosed as suffering from a psychiatric disorder. Much has been written about the association of parental brutality and homicidally aggressive behaviour. Parental abuse and violence were all too evident in the households of most of the boys, eight of whom had been severely abused. Some of all these factors can be found among the simply violent offenders; but in the mind of those who kill strangers, the whole lot are present – severe dysfunction of the central nervous system, and a family history of exposure to violence and psychotic behaviour.

These findings are confirmed by another study conducted on fourteen juveniles who had been sentenced to death for murder in the US – they had killed while under the age deemed acceptable for execution, but the authorities had ordained that they should live until suitable to be killed. Their ages at the time of the offence ranged from 15 to 17; 6 of them were black, 7 white, and 1 Hispanic. The evaluations consisted of psychiatric, neurological and EEG examinations. The same sorry picture of mental and psychiatric disturbance emerges: 9 had major neurological damage; two thirds indicated episodic dyscontrol or intermittent explosive disorder; 7 were psychotic at the time of their evaluation, or had been diagnosed as such earlier in their childhood; 4 of the subjects had histories of consistent and severe mood disorders. The 3 remaining subjects experienced periodic paranoid sensations, at which times they often assaulted people they believed were their enemies. Only two had IQs above 90. All displayed poor verbal skills – in fact three of them learned to read only while on death row. Drug abuse, alcoholism and psychiatric hospitalization were prevalent in the histories of the parents. Twelve had been brutally physically abused, 8 had suffered injuries that needed hospitalization and 5 had been sodomized by relatives.

To those who believe the question 'What makes a murderer?' is a vain one, here is at least part of the answer.

And for those who still cling to the belief that there is no functional difference in the mind of those who kill strangers, perhaps photographic evidence will help. Today, PET scans allow us literally to look into the brains of such people. In one project, forty-two American killers, all of whom had killed strangers, were taken under armed guard to various hospitals around the country. The scans themselves were analysed and compared by Professor Adrian Raine, a leading researcher in the field of violence and the mind. Most of them were single murderers of the impulsive type, or had committed two murders in quick succession. All were entering an insanity defence, in an attempt to avoid execution, but had, at trial, been judged to be sane. Six of the group were schizophrenics. Although there are some questions over how representative the group was, the findings of this state-of-the-art technology were marked, specific and significant. The murderers were character-ized by dysfunction in one particular area, the prefrontal area of the brain. The PET scans are dramatic: they show clearly that a specific part of the brain in this type of murderer is virtually inactive compared with the brains of normal people.

Since this is the area responsible for making plans and strategies, and for governing and controlling our behaviour, it would seem that this sort of impulsive murderer lacks a critical braking mechanism which the frontal lobe usually applies to control the limbic system – which, as it were, has a mind of its own, and an emotional one at that.

Findings from these PET scans show that other areas of the brain also do not function in a normal manner; there is lower activity in the left (but not right) side of the angular gyrus, an area involved with the three Rs – reading, writing and arithmetic. The link which we have seen between violent offenders and learning difficulties in school is consistent with damage in this area. Another interesting finding is that there is lower-than-normal activity in the corpus callosum, the bundle of nerve fibres which connect the two hemispheres of the brain, and which act as a central telephone exchange. In these murderers, the two halves of the brain were not communicating as well as they should – so once again the 'brakes' of left brain, with its sense of logic and control, are not able to exert their influence over the emotional right brain.

The amygdala, that anger and emotional generating centre, also seems to be different in murderers. In a normal, control group, the left side of the amygdala is more active than the right, but the reverse was true with the murderers. The right, and more active, side is the area associated with violence.

So it is clear that there is quite a complex and powerful array of brain cards in the hand of the impulsive, murderous mind that kills strangers.

Relevant to our understanding of those who kill strangers is an analysis of schizophrenics. It is wrong to say that the schizophrenic mind is necessarily a murderous, or even a violent mind – other factors are necessary to make it so; nevertheless schizophrenia characterizes many of those killers who fall into the legal category of mentally disturbed murderers. We have already met the various mentally ill minds of violence; but there is a higher proportion of the mentally disordered among murderers than among simply violent offenders. The studies show that they form the largest group of killers in the category of stranger or motiveless killings, and among that group schizophrenia is the main diagnosis. Those afflicted by depression are more likely to kill friends, acquaintances, or relations.

Among 205 hospitalized male schizophrenics surveyed in 1977, 59 had made homicidal threats or attacks; all had been in an active phase of the illness at the time. Among a group of mentally abnormal killers studied in 1958, 25 per cent were considered to have been principally motivated by delusional phenomena. The schizophrenic kills under the direction of internal 'voices'. The killer Edward Gein – the model for the infamous Hannibal Lecter in the novel *Silence of the Lambs* – who ate his victims, using their skin to make lampshades, was a chronic schizophrenic driven by his voices to kill. Lawyers at his trial agreed that he was mentally ill, and he was sent to a hospital for the criminally insane.

Herbert Mullin claimed to have killed his estimated eleven victims on instructions from a variety of 'voices' – God's, Einstein's and his father's. Described by his lawyer as 'nutty as a tree full of fish', Mullin came of a good middle-class family in Santa Cruz, California. He made friends easily and gained good grades at school. In 1969, at the age of twenty-two, after becoming heavily involved with drugs, Mullin began mindlessly to mimic the gestures and actions of others. The condition, known as echopraxia, is a common symptom of schizophrenia. He told doctors that he was controlled by 'secret voices' and 'cosmic emanations'. Believing (in fact wrongly) that he and Einstein shared a birthday, which was also the same day of the year that San Francisco was destroyed by earthquake, he acted on instructions from Einstein that people should be sacrificed in order to save the city from another seismic destruction.

A comparison of violent and non-violent schizophrenics provided an intriguing – if by now predictable – result. Both types shared a degree of damage – but the violent offenders had an extra card – a highly inactive area of the prefrontal lobe, as with the non-schizophrenic impulsive murderers.

The recent policy of discharging schizophrenics into the care of the community has had some disastrous and widely-publicized results; Jane Zito, whose husband was picked out at random and killed on a London suburban railway station by a discharged schizophrenic, has made the point that care in the community demands a community that cares, and can afford to care. The problem is that the discharged schizophrenic needs to be maintained on his medication – and that demands supervision. It is an impossible responsibility to lay upon the patient, and we do so at our own risk.

Of kinds of minds that kill strangers, impulsive killers commit what are known as 'trivial cause' killings; it's a misnomer, because there are clearly deeper causes which are simply precipitated by comparatively trivial factors. It's hardly surprising, knowing what we do of the pathology of the violent mind, that the primary or aggressive psychopath is well represented in this area of apparently unprovoked killing. A recent FBI study found that 44 per cent of those offenders who had killed a law enforcement officer on duty were aggressive psychopaths. When murder seems haphazard, random and motiveless, the correlation of a higher incidence of abnormal EEGs is virtually guaranteed. We already know that the greater the abnormality, the more violent the individual – habitually violent criminals having EEGs five times more abnormal than those of non-violent offenders. Equally, the more the brain damage, the more likely that the impulsive aggression will take a homicidal turn. For the aggressive psychopath, after all, the step to murder is not such a quantum leap; he has no inhibitions about using violence – it is merely a tool to achieve what he wants, or remove any obstacle to his demands. When he is angered, defied or frustrated, he gives no thought to the pain and humiliation experienced by the victim. His reaction is one of indifference, mixed with a sense of power, pleasure or satisfaction. No regret. Most normal, non-criminal people who have killed – soldiers, policemen, train drivers – suffer emotional flashbacks or traumatic stress disorder. Some police forces stipulate that the officer involved must receive psychiatric counselling. Such efforts would be wasted on psychopaths. Even case-hardened professionals find it unnerving to witness the psychopath's indifference to the devastating human havoc he can wreak.

The psychopath is well represented in stranger killings, because any stranger may get in his way; well represented in trivial cause murder, because to him murder itself is relatively trivial.

If there is one thing we can teach our children to make them safer, it is to avoid becoming the casual focus of dispassionately lethal attacks. Many murders result from the interaction between assailant and victim. The victim may annoy the attacker by some action, or even some offensive remark. This is interpreted as a challenge. He retaliates. The victim strikes back. An audience may have gathered, raising the stakes for both in terms of face-saving. Matters may escalate to the use of weapons – beer glasses, knives, lumps of wood. Both participants are now committed to a violent outcome. One study found that in 63 per cent of the cases examined, the victim initiated this interplay, contributing significantly to his own death.

So don't get involved; and the moral is the stronger when a psychopath is concerned, where impulse control is negligible. Submit to the stranger in the station waiting-room who spits in your face; let the burglar get on with his nefarious job – many are the courageous householders who have been kicked to death by the psychopathic burglars whom they have inconveniently sought to obstruct.

These impulsive, apparently motiveless murders are often intimately connected with alcohol. A study in Philadelphia found alcohol involved in 64 per cent of homicidal situations – either the killer or the victim or both had been drinking. Drink can make the victim more reckless in his provocation, just as it can lower the threshold of violent explosive disorder in the assailant. Other studies – including one which found an 83 per cent involvement – suggest that alcohol looms even larger as a contributory cause. As we have seen, those individuals who have impairment to the neurological braking systems of behaviour are more sensitive to the effects of alcohol, which lowers their already low serotonin levels, so making the expression of violence more likely. In those with episodic dyscontrol the smallest amount of alcohol can be enough to bring on the electrical storm that erupts when the limbic system takes on an uncontrolled life of its own.

One – admittedly small – sample of convicts on death row found that two thirds were prone to these episodic explosions in the mind. Another finding is that about a third of murderers are thus affected – 100 out of 280 killers studied. Typical among such cases – though rare in terms of gender – was a woman of 21. She had been a prostitute since the age of 12, and suddenly murdered 4 other prostitutes by stripping them bare and stabbing them in the neck. The psychologists will have much to say about the symbolism and motivation of the woman; but it should also be recognized that she was discovered to have severe abnormalities of the left temporal lobe and limbic area. This sort of abnormality is found in those who are subject to episodic rage. A 14-year-old killed the children she was babysitting in an episodic fit of rage caused by their crying. EEGs taken by monitors on the scalp revealed nothing; but electrodes inserted deep into the brain disclosed hitherto hidden, but critical, epileptic discharges in the temporal lobes which were specifically induced by the sound of crying.

There can be few greater breaches of trust than for a babysitter to murder a child, and few less attractive individuals than the mindless killer in a pub brawl. They will get little sympathy from the public, or from the law (which in the latter case will not look beyond the effect of alcohol, which may not be pleaded as a legal defence). But if we knew that such people were to some extent – scientists may argue later about the degree – trapped into their actions by the internal wirings of their brain, ought we not to comprehend rather than simply condemn?

A subject for whom it may be even harder to elicit sympathy is the mass killer – the man who takes a machine gun into McDonald's – or the serial killer, in both of which cases the victims are strangers. The hypothesis, when a lone killer suddenly goes on the rampage, is that the man suffers from a disturbance in that part of the brain which controls rage; his anger is, literally, ungovernable and undirected. Similar to those with episodic dyscontrol or intermittent explosive syndrome, in this case the whole explosion occurs as a great and tragic seismic one-off. Such crimes, although the stuff of screaming headlines, are mercifully rare. The case of Charles Whitman has been carefully studied to see what clues it may yield.

Whitman, of Austin, Texas, had recurrent fantasies about killing – in particular, the murder of his wife. He even went to see his family doctor and a psychiatrist, but they failed to acknowledge the severity of his problems. Eventually, Whitman's impulses gathered to a head and exploded. He went out and shot thirteen people. Whitman had left a note which said, 'Find me and stop me . . . Look at my brain . . . It is not normal.'

Indeed it was not. The explosion occurred in the amygdala, the seat of the emotional brain. Normally, it is the task of the left brain to control the emotions – but Whitman had a tumour on the left temporal lobe. His high intellectual functions could not control the storm. Compulsive thoughts, which are then given free rein, have been encountered in other cases of temporal lobe tumour as well as in temporal lobe epileptics, and following head injury or illness.

While we are familiar with the names of Bundy, Brady and Nilsen – for, like the mass killer, the serial killer gets the headlines – such people are also very rare: 'probably fewer than one hundred in North America' is one not altogether cheering estimate, in contrast to the estimated two to three million aggressive psychopaths. Because of this merciful scarcity, it is not easy to draw general conclusions about the make-up of serial killers' minds. There is clearly an overlap with the mind of the sexually deviant and sadistic murderers whom we met in the last chapter. What studies have been done suggest a deficit in the frontal lobe of the brain, which, as we know, means that the area of conscience is disconnected from the centre of feelings. Almost without exception, there is a sexual motivation in serial killing, so it comes within the orbit of the sexually-deviant minds which we have already discussed.

The serial killer typically selects his victims over a period of time and subjects them to torture, mutilation or sexual assault before murdering them. Some of them have been defined as secondary psychopaths: they have the characteristics of coldness and lack of guilt, but because they are introverts and loners they seem to lack the outwardly directed, aggressively violent traits of the main psychopathic type.

Although what they do severely tests our view of what sanity is, they are often not classified as mentally ill, deranged or psychotic. They simply lack the inner policeman, the voice of conscience which patrols the thoughts of most of us and prevents us indulging our wilder, nightmarish fantasies – and which Bobby Jo Long and Karl X in the previous chapter simply did not have.

Twenty-nine bodies were recovered from the Chicago home of John Wayne Gacy in 1978, who killed a total of thirty-three young men and boys. Police also found a cache of homosexual and pederastic books and videos, a pair of handcuffs and a nylon rope. Gacy was once interrupted in mid-murder by a telephone call. He sounded perfectly normal and self-controlled – even as a boy lay handcuffed and choking on his bed. Intriguingly, in the light of what we now know, he had suffered a severe head injury when he was eleven, from which he suffered blackouts over the course of the next five years. At Gacy's trial, the issue was whether he was sane or not. One doctor observed, 'I don't believe you can have thirty-three cases of temporary insanity.' The argument that he was evil rather than mad prevailed and Gacy was sentenced to death. The jury were clearly upset by Gacy's demeanour in court; he showed no remorse, adopting a sneering and contemptuous attitude as the relatives of his victims gave their evidence.

Because of a constitutional inability to appreciate the feelings of others, serial killers often do things that normal people find baffling and horrifying. As Dr Hare says, 'they can torture and mutilate their victims with about the same sense of concern that we feel when we carve the turkey for Thanksgiving dinner.' Before his execution the serial killer Ted Bundy admitted, 'I'm the most cold-blooded sonofabitch that you'll ever meet.' He is reckoned to have killed 100 young women, often posing as temporarily disabled in order to elicit the sympathy of his victims. Guilt, he claimed, was an illusion, an unhealthy social mechanism used to control people.

The serial killer can survive undetected because he is able to conceal the guiltless violence in his mind. They all appear to be more 'normal': they are much more successful at hiding their minds than aggressive psychopaths. Denis Nilsen, for example, passed among his colleagues as a rather drab individual.

Denis Nilsen is the biggest multiple killer in British criminal history. His murders of young men were discovered only when the drains at his North London flat became clogged with their remains. A homosexual minor civil servant, and a shy and totally insignificant personality, Nilsen says he killed for company. He would keep the bodies of the young men – 'rent boys', drifters and drunks – whom he enticed to his flat, sometimes propping them up in front of the television set. Others he would dismember, dispose of in dustbins, gardens and bonfires or render down in cooking cauldrons.

Nilsen was the son of an alcoholic Norwegian soldier who neglected the family. The marriage broke up when Nilsen was very young. He was a lonely youth, preferring reading and drawing to the company of friends. He joined the army for ten years, leaving to become first a trainee policeman and later a civil service clerk. He went to great lengths to cover up his homosexuality. He clearly had an obsession with death – he used to masturbate in front of a mirror with his body dusted with powder in order to look like a corpse. He would stare at his victims' bodies, put their underwear on and off and masturbate over them.

When asked by his defence solicitor 'Why?' Nilsen replied, 'I was hoping you would tell me that.' At trial it was contended that no one with a diminished sense of responsibility could have planned such an elaborate series of fatal seductions. Nilsen himself shows no remorse – 'I don't lose sleep over what I have done or have nightmares about it,' he says as he serves a recommended minimum of twenty-five years in prison. He will almost certainly never be released.

Gary Gilmour, whose request for execution re-opened the matter of capital punishment in the US after a ten-year moratorium, saw himself as a dispassionate killing machine. Asked if he would have killed if he had not been caught, he replied that he would have carried on killing 'until I got caught or shot to death by the police or something like that. I wasn't thinking, I wasn't planning, I was just doing. I'm just saying murder vents rage. Rage is not reason. The murders were without reason.'

Almost invariably, the serial killer has shown signs of deviancy early in life.

The English sex murderer Ian Brady, who with Myra Hindley chose victims of either sex, was, like Nilsen, a loner, and rather skinny and feeble as a young man. He had a reputation among his schoolmates for torturing cats – impaling them on railings or burying them alive. He progressed to tying up and bullying other children. He was fascinated by the Nazis. He began a career of petty crime, and was sent to Borstal until he was twenty. On his release, he worked as a clerk where he met Hindley. They both shared an interest in things German, laughing together over horror stories. She found that she could stimulate him by wearing kinky clothes, and she collaborated in Brady's sexual fantasies by letting herself be photographed in obscene poses holding whips and other instruments of domination. The tape he and Hindley made of a girl begging vainly for mercy has been described by those who heard it as the most harrowing experience of their lives. It certainly ensured the conviction of both.

The evidence, then, is that those who kill strangers *are* different, that they have a constellation of different but abnormal factors in the brain which makes such behaviour more likely. But when it comes to killing those we know, there is again a different pattern. Although of course the mentally deranged killer, the aggressive psychopath and those with explosive disorder can just as often kill family members as strangers, murder among friends does seem to involve more 'normal' people as well – including a greater proportion of women than is to be found among those who kill people they do not know. In fact, it's one of the few areas of crime where the gender card is conspicuous by its absence. A roughly equal number of wives kill their husbands as husbands kill their wives. Both have equal potential for marital violence, initiate similar acts of violence and, when the difference of physical strength is equalized by the carving knife or the poison bottle, both commit similar amounts of spousal homicide.

Revenge and jealousy often play a role, especially when relationships are on the verge of breakdown, as in this typical case.

Jane left her husband at the age of forty, and took another lover. Her husband went round one evening to try to talk things through, but Jane told him that it was all over, and that there was no chance of a reconciliation. A fight began. The husband went to a drawer in the room next door and took from it a gun. He shot her dead.

A recent study of family violence found that in more than one quarter (28 per cent) of all marriages there is at least one 'violent episode', an act intended to cause physical harm to a partner, ranging from slapping to beating up. About 5 per cent of all couples have been involved with beating and nearly 4 per cent of spouses have used a knife or a gun in attacking their husband or wife. There is the same amount of violence in middle-class and lower-class families alike. We are much more likely to murder the people we marry than our own blood relatives. Relatives have never been found to exceed one third of US homicides; spouses, as victims, outnumber all other relatives combined. Even living under the same roof, a genetic relative is eleven times less likely to be killed than someone not related by blood.

According to one researcher, the sad truth is that 'with the exception of the police and the military, the family is perhaps the most violent social group, and the home the most violent social setting, in our society. A person is more likely to be hit or killed in his or her home by another family member than anywhere else, or by anyone else.'[1]

The majority of family killings are different from the assaults of violent minds, in that they are often single events, committed by people with no history of violence. There are none of the familiar violent cards, and the assailant almost invariably expresses remorse. They occur when emotions run high, particularly the emotion of 'male sexual proprietariness', or jealousy. This sense that the husband somehow owns the woman and controls her means that women are highly at risk at times when the husband feels that the relationship is in danger of ending. There is a remarkable proportion of recently estranged wives among homicide victims; in an Australian study of murders by spouses, out of 217 women killed by their husbands 98 (45 per cent) were separated or in the process of separating, compared to 3 of 79 (4 per cent) men slain by their wives. Interviews with American men and women who had murdered their partner showed that in the overwhelming number of cases what led to the fatal fight were concerns with the wife's fidelity or her intention to leave the marriage. This was so whether it was the husband or wife who ended up dead. There is a strong social dimension to this – almost a dimension of gender politics. Men strive to control women by various means, while women strive to resist compulsion and maintain their freedom of choice. Each side indulges in brinkmanship. Sometimes one or the other falls over the edge. The following case illustrates how one incident can tip someone over into totally abnormal behaviour.

Michael Talling was gaoled for life in 1984 for the manslaughter of his wife Monika. He was a young man, with a marked inability to control his impulses and emotions. His wife taunted him about his sexual inadequacy and her own sexual ambitions. He shot her. Talling moved the body around the house, talking to it, for five months. Finally he took it to Devon and tried to bury it. The ground was too hard, so he cut off her head and dumped the rest of the body in the River Exe. His final act of proprietorship was to take his wife's head with him in the boot of his car, which is where it was when the police caught up with him.

We find again the Othello syndrome which we met in Chapter 10 – the exclusively male characteristic of fixed and irrational belief in the systematic infidelity of the partner. Such people can appear otherwise sane, purposeful and intelligent and rational, but at home they are obsessive and tyrannical, not allowing their wives to go out alone or have any sort of independent life of their own. A morbid jealousy is at work here, although it seems to be a distinctly one-sided emotion; an analysis of insane male murderers found that 12 per cent were diagnosed as morbidly jealous, compared to 3 per cent of insane female murderers. The same seems to hold true in studies of sane spouse killers – the woman just isn't as jealous.

We do not know the exact biological underpinning of jealousy – perhaps it serves some evolutionary purpose; as, for instance, when the male is constitutionally jealous because he does not want to invest energy in his spouse's child if it is not his own. The Othello syndrome is a compulsive obsessive disorder and, while no specific PET scans have been undertaken to uncover the seat of jealousy, one would suspect that one would find abnormalities in the emotional areas of the brain.

The case of Ruth Ellis is a rarity, in that it is a woman's murder conducted with both passion and planning.

Ellis waited outside a pub in Hampstead during the Easter holidays of 1955. She had a .38 Smith and Wesson. David Blakely was in the pub. He had failed to keep a date the previous evening, and had been avoiding her calls all day. When he emerged, she shot him twice. As he stumbled away, bleeding, she felled him with three more shots. The last she fired at point-blank range. Her defence tried in vain to find a precedent for a killing motivated by jealousy, and Ellis herself refused to accept that she was 'demented' by jealousy, saying that she was merely upset. She was the last woman to be hanged in Britain.

We know a little about women who kill their partners. Most women who kill do not have previous records, although according to one study 30 per cent of them had records of violent crimes such as assault, battery and weapon charges. They are likely to turn murderous later in life than men, and tend not to plan the crime, acting alone. The motive given most frequently for domestic homicide is self-defence – accounting for nearly 60 per cent of such cases.

A thirty-year-old Puerto Rican woman killed her spouse

in a domestic argument. The man was drunk. He began to break up the household furniture, and at one point threatened her with a chair. She shot him in the back of the head six times with his .38 pistol and successfully claimed self-defence.

The most frequent sentencing charge in a Miami study was voluntary manslaughter. Only 37 per cent of the women received prison sentences, of which the most common was ten years, often halved as a result of good behaviour.

With the killing of children, it is difficult to remain non-judgmental. Can there be any explanation beyond mere evil? One in six of the 500 homicides a year recorded for England and Wales involve the death of children under 16. Most are killed by their own parents. One third are in their first year of life, and most of the rest are between the ages of one and five. Less than 10 per cent – about six a year – are sex murders. Infanticide was common in antiquity – one remembers the stories of Spartan newborns left exposed to the elements, as an experiment in the literal survival of the fittest. Before Rome abolished the practice in 374 AD, in order to promote an increase in population, it was socially acceptable to discard children in rivers or by the roadside. Girls were more likely to be abandoned than boys, illegitimate children more than legitimate children and later born more than firstborn. In China today, with its rule of only one child per family (ironically to *prevent* a population increase), newborn girls are still frequently killed or abandoned.

Many of these practices are recorded into the nineteenth century in Europe. The bodies of German children were interred in walls and foundations of new buildings to give them greater structural strength, as late as 1843. Before 1750 only 25 per cent of children born in London lived to 5 years of age, the rest dying mostly as a result of disease and neglect but some inevitably as the victims of murder. Foundling homes established in Britain by Thomas Coram for deserted children did little to solve the problem of infant death.

Even the imagined horrors of the wicked step-parent seem to have a basis in fact across time and culture. In a study of 67 children of the Ache Indians of Paraguay, raised by mother and stepfather after the father's death, 43 per cent had died of various causes before their fifteenth birthday, compared with 19 per cent of those raised by natural parents. Children in step-parent families are disproportionately more often injured in modern industrial nations too, regardless of socio-economic status. Abusive parents discriminate – sparing their own children within the same household. In an English study of fatally battered babies, 15 per cent were killed by a step-parent. According to a 1976 study, a child living with one or more substitute parents in the US was massively more likely to be fatally abused than any child living with genetic parents.

Among these offenders, how many of our familiar violent minds can we distinguish? It seems that the aggressive psychopath is represented here. Here is one such case.

Diane Downs displayed a typically irresponsible pattern of parenthood found frequently among psychopaths. She would leave her young children – some as young as fifteen months – on their own if she couldn't find a babysitter. The children went ragged and underfed, even though Downs protested that she was a loving mother. The truth is that she saw her own children as an inconvenience. They got in the way of the life she wanted to live. In the end she shot them dead on an isolated country road. Throughout her trial, Downs protested her innocence, maintaining, with all the psychopath's plausibility, that her children (aged 9, 7 and 4) were shot by a 'shaggy-haired stranger' after he flagged her car down. At McKenzie-Willamette Hospital, the doctor on duty testi-fied that Downs was 'a woman who was very calm, very self-assured ... not tearful, not angry, occasionally smil-ing, occasionally chuckling'. She was found guilty and sentenced to life plus fifty years for murder and attempted murder. She protests her innocence: 'I will abide by the decision of the court, and when I am set free, I will try to find their killer.' The trial, which rocked America, hinged on the poignant irony that in 1982, barely a year before the killings, Downs, as a surrogate mother, had given birth to a baby for another couple. For this she was paid $10,000.

Society has found it hard to accept that the psychopathic mind could turn its cruelty upon its own family, and this is an area where definitions are difficult. What should we make, for instance, of this American mother?

Alice Crimmins was originally convicted of the murder and manslaughter of her five-year-old son Eddie and four-year-old daughter Missie. The verdict was subsequently reversed. Crimmins frequently left her children in the care of others as she pursued, singlemindedly, a phenomenally diverse sexual life; naked men were repeatedly ejected from her apartment by her long-suffering husband, and there was talk of sex in a car with the children's hair-dresser and nude swimming in another lover's pool when she might more reasonably have been grieving for her missing children.

We do not know whether such apparent total egotism was a manifestation of an underlying psychopathy, or merely of an intensely selfish person. There are no firm figures, anyway, in this area of child-killing, and we suspect that the psychopath is more involved in the killing of strangers and in non-homicidal violence.

There is a similar dearth of statistics on child-killers with intermittent explosive disorder, although there are cases which are clearly linked to episodic dyscontrol, including a case of a child murdering his parents.

The young man was fifteen, and had been asked to do the dishes. He took out a gun and murdered his mother, father and two sisters. He dragged his mother's body to the family van and took her to the other side of town. He was caught speeding by the police and is now serving a life sentence in prison. Before this incident he had been shy and introverted. His home environment seemed perfectly stable and normal. But tests showed that he had abnormal EEGs and that he had a left temporal lobe abnormality. He is, say the doctors, untreatable.

The chemical card of the female hormone is strong when it comes to family murders. In 1983 a research project on aggressive behaviour in women was conducted at a Massachusetts prison. Six women had killed, between them, three husbands, two children and one lover. In the case of all six women, the killings had occurred on the day before the first day of menstruation. All were described as 'quiet, mildmannered housewives' – suggesting that there is some truth to the observation that 'a murderess is only an ordinary woman with a temper'. The unpredictability resulting from hormonal upsets is well chronicled by the leading authority on premenstrual syndrome, Katharina Dalton. Here are two of her cases.

A young barmaid fatally stabbed her colleague to death. A few minutes earlier, both had been on the receiving end of harsh words from a third party, and the two had left together, apparently the best of friends and united by the shared experience of being harangued. Suddenly, however, the barmaid turned on the other. She was found, dazedly walking the streets of London, incoherent and unable to explain what had provoked her attack.

A student of eighteen killed her mother with a hammer in 1986. She told police, 'I felt I was going to pieces' and was diagnosed as suffering from a combination of depression and premenstrual tension.

Dalton believes that a premenstrual hallucination had triggered a terrible violence in her.

The hormonal imbalances which occur during pregnancy and at menopause can also be seen as mitigating circumstances, and have been acknowledged as such in child-killing cases; the law, we have seen, acknowledges postnatal depression in the killing of a child by its mother in the first year of its life (she can be charged only with manslaughter). We have seen that lack of food, and resulting low blood sugar, is a particularly powerful contributor to violent acts in PMS women.

In 1981 a 33-year-old mother of two children drowned her three-month-old baby and then took a massive overdose. She was resuscitated, but the baby died. The incident happened the day before menstruation, and the woman had not eaten for nine hours. She was freed on probation and, with subsequent progesterone treatment, has become a mother again. Mother and new baby are in excellent health, and their names have been removed from the social services' At Risk register.

The mentally ill commit their share of family killings, and in parent killing schizophrenia looms large; a study of special hospital inmates found that 74 per cent of 58 men who had killed their mothers were acting on the instructions of their 'voices'. A man who doused his wife and two sons with petrol and set them alight – they died of their burns – believed that God had directed him to do so. Although a schizophrenic is just as likely, if not more so, to kill strangers, those with affective disorders such as depression tended to select family members or girlfriends for their one, single act of despair. These are the people described as overly conforming, strongly controlled and lacking in hostile or aggressive tendencies. Those who commit one exceedingly violent crime, like the family man who kills his own family, do not have the same uninhibited aggression pattern typical of the psychopath. They do not seem to be mentally ill in any obvious sense, but seem to have a moment of overwhelming depression triggered by life's events – and the family provides many such stressful moments. A father in the throes of divorce may be tipped over the edge and kill his children on the grounds that if he cannot have them, then no one else will. There is a familiar and tragic association between such acts and subsequent suicide; a study of 78 such cases revealed that more than a third were suffering from acute depression.

Researchers have even identified another familiar card, low serotonin levels, in the minds of those who kill partners, and then attempt to kill themselves. This was also found in three cases where a parent killed a child before committing suicide.

A 29-year-old married mother of three was admitted to hospital after drowning her four-month-old son. A few years earlier she had tried to strangle another of her children and then thrown herself down the stairs.

A 36-year-old man stabbed his ten-year-old son, his wife and then himself. The son died but the wife survived.

A 38-year-old man tried to gas himself and his four-year-old daughter for whom he was caring in the middle of a divorce.

None had any previous history of violent behaviour. All had low serotonin levels. Studies all over the world have begun to identify the same link, suggesting that there may be a common biological input to murder/suicide regardless of different culture and race. Certainly the links between depression and low serotonin levels will continue to provide a fruitful area for research. Could it be that stress lowers serotonin levels, leading to depression in a vicious and fatal spiral of despair?

Whatever the answer, it now seems beyond doubt that the murderous mind, in all its many manifestations, is often itself an injured one. As we'll see, however, the law – with blithe disregard for the medical evidence which accumulates every day – rarely shares that view.

CHAPTER 13

Good, Bad, Evil or Mad?
Treatment and the Law

IT WAS NOT so very long ago in our history that we locked away the mentally ill and kept them in chains. We know better now, of course – that mental illness is not a God-given sign of evil and turpitude, and that the mentally ill are not the convenient scapegoats for our own original sin.

But if crime is – to any extent – the result of neurophysical or chemical factors beyond our control, just as is the case with the mentally ill, it is illogical for us to deal with whole classes of criminal in the way that we do. Will future generations stand aghast at the thought that some people were subjected to the whole panoply of our judicial and penal system – all those solemn arguments conducted in front of people wearing robes and wigs, the grim transport to the high-walled gaol, the clanging of gates and cell doors, the demeaning treatment and the meagre diet, the belief that a time spent suffering somehow purges the sin of the crime – when a simple diagnosis and treatment were all that was necessary or deserved. Will there come a time when, if criminologists heed the lessons of science, this will seem as ritualistic and nonsensical a cultivated barbarism as the drowning of witches?

We have presented a whole plethora of damaged minds – and damaged they are, whatever the moral or penal viewpoint. Low serotonin levels, damage to temporal lobes, disconnections between the cortex and the limbic system – such dysfunctions are not so much an undercurrent but a major tide in the analysis of crime. But where does that leave the issue of guilt – and, for that matter, theories of correction and rehabilitation? Should those with such neurophysical disadvantages simply have tried harder to resist temptation, even though they are no more able to do so than a two-month-old who soils his nappies, or the ninety-year-old who repeats himself? Or does the abnormal constitution of the mind make that ability to resist temptation a biological issue rather than a moral one? Can the will truly be free if it is channelled along physically predetermined grooves? We must face these issues.

Most of us – unless we had been bilked of our pensions by his fraud – wouldn't necessarily want to hang the fraudulent conman, who steals millions without the slightest pang of conscience. Yet we would reserve the worst penalty imaginable for someone like a child murderer, a 'monster of depravity', who shows no regret. Yet both are psychopaths; it's just that one of them has an extra brain card of violence in his mental make-up. So we are punishing him, are we not, for the crime of expressing the same dysfunction in a violent form? Some-times, the less terrible the crime, the more we are able to persuade ourselves that the perpetrator is merely bad, not mad. The persistent burglar, for instance, does not arouse our understanding in the same way as the serial killer might – yet the evidence is that there are many of the same, essential dysfunctions, chemical and neurological failure, as those which are also at work in the thieving mind.

The fact is that scientists do not always make very good moralists, and moralists, like social and psychological theorists, seem strangely disinclined to examine the scientific facts which underpin, explain and sometimes contradict their judgments. (It has taken the mighty science of Gender Studies a reluctant eternity to accept the findings that the brains of men and women are different and operate differently; they needed to see it all spelled out in differential, colour-coded PET scans before tentatively accepting the hypothesis.) And another fact is that there is a punitive imperative in most societies, a need to punish, to show disapproval, as a means either to deter or to define their values by setting limits to acceptable behaviour. This penal factor seems somewhat cyclical; the disappointment with the liberal experiments of the sixties has brought us a *fin-de-siècle* sternness which leads to the killing of the clearly mad in the US, the sentencing of children to death in other fundamentalist parts of the world, and a policy on crime in the UK, for instance, which consists principally of building more prisons for men, women and children alike. Biological facts will cut no ice with the world's present crop of legislators. Never have we needed more to remember Goethe's advice not to trust those whose desire to punish is strong . . .

Yet, such little political hiccoughs apart, the world does, in time, absorb truths and metabolize them into understanding. We have the legal concept of *mens rea*, the principle that the crime must have been intended. We have accepted that there must be some proportionality in punishment – we no longer hang people for sheep-stealing. The police and the courts are allowed a certain discretion. Mercy still has a place in justice. We allow, with variable amounts of reluctance, the idea that children are not responsible for their actions, and to some extent that those with the mind of a child may also have their responsibility diminished. We accept the principle that some people may be unfit to plead, in other words that the legal and penal process is irrelevant to them. Or we accept that they are not guilty by reason of insanity – a diagnosis which well predates our understanding of its organic basis.

Such is the way our legal system is arranged, however, that these diagnoses are usually the subject of forensic competition between expert medical witnesses. Lawyers referee the conflicting arguments about mental fitness, a process we would find difficult to accept in any other sphere – should accountants decide what pictures should hang in the Royal Academy, or dentists pronounce on the existence (or otherwise) of the paranormal? The sense in which legal systems are less a search for the truth than a competition between arguments was very evident in the case of the Yorkshire Ripper, Peter Sutcliffe, who, as we have seen, was judged sane, sentenced to a series of life sentences for his multiple killings, and then discreetly moved to a mental hospital. Perhaps prison life drove him mad. But it takes more than usual legal sophistry to argue that when he stabbed, slashed and mutilated his victims he was as normal as you or I but that the experience of confinement finally tipped the tender balance of his mind.

On the whole, however, we have accepted that abnormality of mind – whether arising from disease, injury, arrested or retarded development – does impair responsibility for the acts or omissions of a killer, and that such a person should not be convicted of murder. So the general principle exists – that mental impairment to some extent reduces the burden of guilt. But as we have seen, there is ample evidence that the various other minds to crime are also damaged or disturbed; they are all cursed with a biological hand of cards that influences their reactions and their responses in a way that is critically different from those of us with intact brains. But the law does not yet fully acknowledge them.

Society may, in time, come to regard recidivist crime as a disorder; for the moment, the medico-legal wrangling continues to centre on the concept of the offender's sanity at the precise time of the offence. Under English law, we are all held to be responsible for our actions, providing that we are sane and not acting under compulsion. We can argue that we do not have a guilty mind by claiming that we have an 'innocent' mind (this would include mental subnormality), that we suffer a diseased mind (through an identifiable mental illness) and are not aware of the nature of our actions, or by the defence of automatism, sane or insane. Sane automatism is judged to occur when some outside incident prompts a reflex action which causes the offending behaviour – an inappropriate injection, for instance – and, when proved, results in a full acquittal. Insane automatism is due to internal factors causing a disease of the mind, and until recently has led to mandatory confinement in hospital.

A brain tumour has been judged as a disease of the brain rather than an affliction of the mind, thus counting as an absolute defence of sane automatism. So should our new knowledge about neurotransmitter deficits be judged in the same light? Should the psychopathic disconnections be judged to be a brain disease, and a reason to acquit? Should we free the paedophile, because we know his problems lie in a malfunction of the temporal lobe, and be merciful to the rapist because he suffers the additional trauma of frontal lobe damage? If we now have three categories – mad, bad and 'can't help it' – with hospital for the first, and prison for the second, where does the third category go?

The law is made of sterner stuff, and even when defendants have suffered from severe, early environmental and biological handicaps, they are usually judged to have had a choice in their decision whether or not to commit their crime. But the – hypothetical – case of Luke, cited by Adrian Raine, illustrates the dilemma.

Luke was born of a prostitute mother and an alcoholic father. His birth involved brain damage which manifested itself in hyperactivity. Separated from his mother at two, and left to grow up in a crime-ridden inner city, he was abused by foster parents whose blows to Luke's head exacerbated brain dysfunction. Hyperactivity and low IQ resulted in a spiral of under-achievement at school and continued in fruitless efforts to gain qualifications or skills for work. Delinquency developed into a pattern of crime, which culminated in the shooting of an off-licence proprietor.

Raine asks, 'Are we right in taking Luke's life when in reality his biological and social predispositions (none of which he had any influence over) were virtually destined to lead him to a life of crime?'[1] The law, it is argued, takes too black and white a view of the matter of free will, conscious choice, *mens rea*.

The issue is particularly pertinent in the case of the link between premenstrual syndrome and crime, for crime demands a conscious intent, yet all the evidence suggests that is not the case for that 'minute proportion of women whose mood swings prior to menstruation are so violent that for a short time each month they are no longer responsible for their actions.'[2] The symptoms can range to the extreme of 'severe psychological changes including confusion, violence, delusions and hallucinations over which they have no control'.[2] Dalton believes such a woman is literally powerless to act rationally, consciously and coherently, without any insight into her condition, or any awareness of her condition; 'it is in that nightmare state that violence can erupt and endow the women with phenomenal physical strength, although she will have no idea of the damage she may be doing with it. It is an irresistible impulse that directs the action.'[3]

Diminished responsibility arising from premenstrual syndrome is now accepted as a mitigating factor not only on major charges such as murder, but on other charges and in civil matters. In 1991, Agnes Buchan killed a 'bullying thug' by stabbing him to death when he attacked her friend. The judge, Mr Justice Ognall, accepted the plea that her premenstrual tension had made her excitable and volatile: 'I can see no public interest in locking you up.'

But if PMS is a disease – and one for which there seems to be a perfectly effective cure, with progesterone being able to restore those women afflicted by it to the condition of normal, law-abiding members of the community – how can the law treat the consequences of PMS as a crime? Why should genuine sufferers of a disease, under which they lose control of their actions – actions of which they are often not aware – and who therefore lack the necessary *mens rea* or guilty intent, be stained with the guilt of a criminal record?

The case of *R. v. Craddock* shows the ludicrous impotence of the law when confronted with the obvious. The accused had committed 45 offences since puberty, had appeared in court 28 times, attempted suicide 20 times and been seen by 23 different psychiatrists, all of whom reported to the court that she had no psychiatric disorder and was fit to attend trial. Her defence plea that her criminal acts had been 'irresistible impulses' caused by hormonal imbalance fell on deaf ears. At appeal, their Lordships ruled that it was more important to protect society than to prevent a woman being unfairly branded as a criminal. All that would be conceded was that PMS could provide an argument for a plea of 'guilty by reason of insanity'. Such a plea, however, even when defined as temporary insanity, may involve a term of corrective detention in a grim institution such as Broadmoor. An insanity plea is therefore not one that a PMS sufferer would lightly choose. The specific PMS plea has been more successful in France and other European countries. In America the term is 'dyscontrol syndrome' – but there is reluctance to employ it in major, and possibly capital, cases, because of doubt over the validity of test results linking hormone levels to behaviour; if the results do not show a conclusive cure, then PMS cannot be branded a disease, and so the defence would fail.

Other bio-legal defences are developing. As we have seen, this chemical imbalance of the mind results in extraordinary and uncharacteristic behaviour, over which the subject seems to have very little control or even awareness. Recognized as a factor during the last century, it is now accepted as a cause for diminished responsibility in murder, and as a mitigating factor in lesser crimes and civil offences. But the criminal record exists; only the punishment is tempered. In some countries, particularly France, it has become an acceptable defence. Another hormonal upset, resulting in postnatal depression, is also recognized in most countries as a mitigating factor.

In the US, the postnatal depression defence has had mixed success in the courts. Postpartum psychosis of a severe nature is rare, but it can involve loss of sense of reality, delusions, extreme agitation, feelings of persecution or hallucinations. Typically it affects women who have no history of previous crime or history of serious mental illness. The defence was first used in 1951, in the case of a woman found guilty of murdering her six-day-old child. But the Illinois Supreme Court reversed the conviction after hearing psychiatric evidence about the defendant's sanity at the time that she suffocated the child. In 1987, a woman who drowned her eight-day-old daughter in the kitchen sink was acquitted of first degree murder, and the following year, a woman who shot her baby son and then tried to kill herself was found not guilty of first degree murder on the same grounds.

The dread hand of political correctness militates against hormonal defences as degrading to women, especially in the US. There are clear problems for women's career advancement if they are legally judged as occasional cyclical inadequates. Lawyers tie themselves up in knots by arguing that postnatal depression is a 'controversial diagnosis'; in the proper name of equality between the sexes they pretend that there is no difference between them.

It's a moral, biological and legal minefield. Husbands, as we have seen, come under intense pressure from their PMS-afflicted wives – it's a condition where understanding, sympathy and support seem to do no good; at least one divorcing father has cited his spouse's PMS as a factor allowing him custody of the children of the marriage, albeit unsuccessfully. And some have suggested that PMS could be used in mitigation when a husband murders his wife.

There have been several efforts, particularly in the US, to run the gene defence. For instance, men who are members of that small band who are genetically XYY, have cited their own biology to excuse their resort to violence, blaming their excessive aggression on the extra male chromosome, which can lower overall serotonin levels; they can hardly be held responsible, they argue, for their genetic biology. It has been tried, although so far without success, in four cases; on no occasion was the court convinced that a causal link had been established between XYY syndrome and criminal conduct. One complicating factor is the small number of XYY men, making it difficult to conduct any very telling research into links with criminality, and particularly with violent crime. In *People vs. Yuki* the ruling was that a medically certain link needed to be made between mental capacity and genetic condition, and that chromosomal abnormality must interfere substantially with the capacity to distinguish right from wrong. Lawyers have now virtually abandoned consideration of the XYY condition as a legal defence.

Stephen Mobley, whom we met in Chapter 8, relied on a gene defence to save him from the barbarities of the electric chair. It was accepted that he comes from a long line of robbers, rapists and killers – but his argument, of a genetic build-up over the generations leading to an inevitable and irresistible propensity for crime, did not prevail and he now awaits execution.

So far the neuro-genetic argument, that low serotonin is inherited, and that therefore some of us are born without the normal mechanisms for control, has not succeeded; but according to experts it is only a matter of time before the full flush of biochemical cards is played in the defence of certain types of criminal behaviour.

There has been more success by men relying on the defence of high testosterone levels, although the hormonal abnormality has usually been taken as subsidiary to a general defence of mental disturbance or insanity. Again, no direct link has been established between high testosterone levels and crime, at least not to the courts' satisfaction. The so-called 'boys will be boys' defence has also had a chequered history. In the case of the sexual assault of a mentally defective seventeen-year-old by four young men, it was argued that the victim was a temptress who 'craved sex', and that the defendants behaved as any red-blooded, opportunist male would in similar circumstances. This hormonal stereotyping of men was ridiculed. The defence was also attempted more successfully in the so-called 'Spur Posse' case, in which nine high school students were charged with molesting and raping girls as young as ten years old. The leader of the gang claimed sixty-six conquests and was described by his father as a 'virile specimen'. Only one of the boys was actively prosecuted and he was sent to a juvenile facility for less than a year. Usually, the biological defence succeeds only because of the occasional quirkiness of judges; in Maryland, a judge gave a sentence of probation to a middle-aged man who had raped his unconscious former employee, a teenage girl. The judge said that the girl was 'contributorily negligent', and noted that intercourse with an unconscious partner was 'the dream of quite a lot of males, quite honestly'

– which says more, perhaps, about the judge than it does about men in general, as well as much about the law's confusion when it collides with biology.

The effects of anabolic steroids have been raised in a number of court cases. The mild-mannered Horace Williams, the man whose character went through a violent and murderous transformation, was the first such case to be tested in the courts in Florida. The character change was put forward as a mitigating circumstance in an attempt to reduce Williams's death sentence to a life sentence. At trial, his defence was one of legal insanity: that under the influence of the drugs he had become psychotic and 'unable to appreciate the wrongfulness of his acts or the consequences of what he was doing'. The jury were convinced that he should not be given the death sentence, and gave him life on the basis of the steroid evidence. This seems somewhat to avoid the issue – Williams is either bad or mad, and whether or not he should be punished, rather than the degree or nature of the punishment, should be at the centre of the debate.

One of the researchers who undertook a major steroid study gave evidence at the trial. His belief was that 'on the basis of this research, it seems likely that there are many cases nationwide in which violent acts are committed by people who would not have been violent had they not been taking steroids'; '. . . there are unquestionably crimes for which steroids are a necessary if not primary factor in the criminal or violent behaviour.'[4]

Glenn Wollstrum is another example of the awesome effects of steroids. He worked as a prison security officer, a model employee with an outstanding performance record over many years. Then, inexplicably, he abducted and shot a young woman. The jury were sceptical about his defence of steroid-induced insanity. But those who have studied such cases are convinced that

in each of these cases that we have examined in detail, the individual involved had been a normal person with a normal psychiatric history, and no history of violence. Under the influence of steroids that person became uncharacteristically aggressive, and in some instances was not aware of how he had changed. In the course of events, that individual then committed a violent crime in a manner totally uncharacteristic of his previous behaviour.[5]

In other cases the defence has been argued with greater success. After a US navy mechanic began to take heavy doses of steroids, he went on a two-day burglary and arson spree, before he turned himself in to the police. In this case the judge instructed the jury that 'toxic levels of anabolic steroids have impaired his [the defendant's] ability to appreciate the criminality of his acts.'[6] He was acquitted.

The plea of brain dysfunction is likely to be more common, too, now that the courts have available to them graphic and tangible evidence in the form of PET scans, rather than the approximate and conflicting opinions of psychiatrists. A person known to be suffering from functional brain abnormality who commits an offence can already claim the condition in mitigation. This is especially true of people whose behaviour changes after an injury to the brain. The other well-studied brain abnormalities associated with epilepsy, such as explosive dyscontrol syndrome, have also been applied, with varying success – helped by the fact that we can now identify electrical brain flashes, or spikes, which last for only a fraction of a second, observable not just in epileptics, but also in depressives and those suffering from schizophrenia.

One man, a solicitor, was accused of fraud, after claiming to have witnessed and signed a legal document written by a man who did not exist. He was known to have epilepsy, and had indeed gone to the doctor on the very day of the supposed crime. EEG records had shown the presence of 'spikes', accounting for his irrational behaviour; the case was dropped.

Another case centring on brain damage concerned an adolescent schoolboy who carried out an unprovoked and vicious stabbing on a young woman. As soon as he had committed the act, he realized what he had done and summoned help. A scan revealed abnormalities in the right temporal lobe. The young man pleaded guilty, and he was put under medical care. The likelihood is that at the time of the attack the activity in the right limbic system was disordered.

Mrs D., a respectable housewife, killed her friend by stabbing her thirty times. She said she could remember nothing. A scan revealed abnormalities in the right temporal and frontal lobes – there was a structural brain lesion which had caused the aggression. Her plea of diminished responsibility was accepted.

M. was an eighteen-year-old with no record of any wrong-doing, who strangled a pub barmaid when she asked him not to eat his fish and chips on the premises. The attack was unpremeditated, vicious and frenzied. A scan revealed the results of early brain damage in the left hemisphere as well as damage to the amygdala. In the weeks before the attack M. had taken to hitting his head against a wall as a result of depression; it is likely that there is a link between his impulsiveness and his brain damage. He pleaded diminished responsibility, and, although the prosecution took the view that M. was a normal eighteen-year-old and was responsible for the assault, the jury accepted the plea.

A problem for a deeply human system like the law is that people are less likely to extend sympathy and understanding to those who deny their actions or show no remorse. And that is, indeed, a challenge in the case of the psychopath. But we have seen that the medical evidence is that the psychopath suffers a disconnection between the thinking and moral areas of the brain and those that create our emotions and feelings, causing an inability to comprehend moral concepts such as right and wrong – a key criterion ever since the McNaghten Rules, which established insanity as a defence. A psychopath therefore suffers the same diminution of responsibility as any of the above cases.

Robert Hare, the man who has spent his lifetime studying psychopaths, has sympathy with the law's dilemma. He is dreading the day that he has to stand in court, face the victim's family, and argue that a brutal killer could not help himself – but in the end that is what he believes to be the case. Others, however, believe that since the psychopath 'knows' intellectually what he is going to do and what he has done – even though he is incapable of caring about it – he should take the due punishment for it.

The law may claim to be above public opinion, but it cannot and should not ignore it. At the same time, it should review the evidence dispassionately, even when the crimes are of a nature which appals society at large. In cases of mass killers, if you strip away the sensationalism from even the most notorious of them you will probably find a classic pattern of brain abnormality. The Russian serial sex murderer Andrei Chikatilo murdered 21 boys aged between 8 and 16, 14 girls between 9 and 17 and seventeen older women. Chikatilo was keen to undergo psychiatric evaluation. He understood that his mind was not his own. He would tell people that 'the more I've thought about it, the more I've come to the conclusion that I suffer from a kind of sickness. I am a mistake of nature, a mad beast.'[7] In August 1991 he was seen by psychiatrist Dr Andrei Tkachenko. After two months of examination he diagnosed Chikatilo as 'Psychopathic, with organic dementia and a thwarted sex drive confused with sadistic mania'.[7] Tkachenko found abnormal patterns in Chikatilo's EEGs indicating that the brain was severely malfunctioning. The method of examination used, however, was not sophisticated enough to pick up the lower ranges of brain activity, so we do not know if the classic pattern of the sexually deviant killer was present.

Tkachenko did not consider that these abnormalities irretrievably compromised Chikatilo's free will. He concluded that

'Chikatilo suffered from his pathology, but he was conscious of his crimes and must be punished.'[7] As a result of his report, on 16 February 1994 Chikatilo the 'Rostov Ripper' was executed in Novocherkassk, near Rostov-on-Don. The executioner's bullet in the brain has now destroyed the evidence.

America's most celebrated sex killer, Ted Bundy, was executed on 24 January 1994 for murdering three women. He confessed to taking the lives of at least a hundred others across the whole continent – we will never know the terrible total. Bundy, too, was found to have the same classic brain abnormalities. But, again, in the eyes of the law he was able to exert his own free will and so was guilty of murder.

The law finds itself in a dreadful tangle when it comes to dealing with the sadistic killer. Again, although guilt and responsibility depend on the concept that the accused knew what he was doing and knew that it was wrong, and therefore could and should have acted to control himself, the law takes no account of the revolutionary discoveries of the workings of the damaged brain. Take the case of Denis Nilsen, for instance, who, as we described in Chapter 12, picked up 'rent boys', drifters and drunks, offered them a bed at his flat, where he strangled them, dismembered the bodies and disposed of them in dustbins, gardens, bonfires and latterly boiled the flesh down and flushed it down the drain. We can identify him in hindsight as a man incapable of conscience, and with classic deformation of his sex/aggression brain centres. His behaviour fits the pattern that researchers would associate with the damaged and sexually deviant mind, coupled with the frontal brain damage and resultant lack of conventional 'conscience'. The same could be said of Peter Kurten, the 'Monster of Düsseldorf', who murdered more than forty people.

> Kurten had sexual contacts with his sisters and animals when he was a boy. He also got special enjoyment out of stabbing the animals. (Cruelty to animals, as we have seen with Atherton's case and many others in previous chapters, is a strong indicator of violent behaviour and

293

low serotonin levels with the resultant poor control over aggressive impulses.) His first murder was at the age of sixteen when he strangled a girl. Kurten was vain about his appearance. He could appear pleasant and persuasive, and even women whom he had abused during sexual intercourse would return to him. His final killings began with a sexual assault on a nine-year-old girl whom he stabbed repeatedly. According to his confessions, which many people confirmed, he had attacked or killed more than 30 women and children in his final rampage. At his trial he was found guilty of 9 murders and 7 attempted murders. He admitted, candidly, that he killed for sexual pleasure; sometimes grabbing a victim by the throat led to orgasm. He ejaculated during stabbings and drank the blood of his victims. Killing became more important than intercourse and was a prerequisite of achieving orgasm. He was executed in 1931 at the age of forty-seven.

Mad or bad? Execute, treat or imprison? What we know today about the mind of such killers raises basic problems of justice. There is no point at all in sending them to prison for punishment or deterrence or rehabilitation – all impossible to achieve with a man with a damaged brain. The only function of imprisonment is to protect society. To that extent, such people present a powerful argument to the proponents of capital punishment. Treatment? We have reached a stage when we can tentatively explain the brain damage which has caused these problems, but we are still a long way from knowing how, if at all, we can repair the damage. Psychosurgery has been attempted, but with little reliable success.

Whatever the problems which acknowledgment of the biological basis of crime brings, is every criminal entitled, if the biological basis can be proved, to claim, 'It wasn't me, it's my prenatal hormonal imbalance, or my temporal lobe deficits, or a bit of trouble with the old limbic system'? Well, yes. If we are interested in the truth of the matter, that is precisely what is the matter. In cases where the accused has a provable hand of biological criminal cards, it is fatuous for judges to gaze over their half-moon spectacles and insist that the accused should have been better able to control himself; such judgments apply a jurassic morality to what ought to be a space-age state of knowledge. Right and wrong are absolutes, but they are only absolute against a background of understanding. The law, however, has always been pragmatic and political. A compassionate, liberal and affluent society should seek to identify and treat the damaged sex-offender, while properly punishing the man who rapes for mere pleasure, revenge or sense of entitlement. A sour, poor, vindictive community will seek a simpler expedient.

For those countries with death penalties the issue is, or should be, especially acute. Killing is society's ultimate statement of the offender's irredeemable evil. But what if PET scans were conducted on every man on death row and revealed a consistent defect? Would we claim to have discovered the root of evil – or simply the reason for wrongdoing? Should such offenders still receive the death penalty? Is killing such people philosophically akin to the racial cleansing policies of totalitarian cultures? How severe would the brain defect have to be to rescue it from immolation, from the volts of the electric chair? Who would decide? Certainly the interpretation of such defect scans would be less problematical than the present subjective and empty wrangles between psychiatrists. As one study concludes,

the psychiatrist . . . is manipulated by the system to serve the intentions of the court and jury . . . What happens currently involves less the merits of the psychiatrist's interpretation and evaluation and more the persuasiveness of his personality in the court room. New technologies, by providing clear and specific data, should minimize some potential abuses that result from persuasion rather than scientific validity.[8]

Studies on convicted murderers are scarce, but they do show a consistent pattern. The work of Dorothy Otnow Lewis on nine juveniles on death row showed that all nine had major neurological impairments and seven showed evidence of significant organic dysfunction. Yet this evidence was not raised at their trials, even though the central argument before the jury was whether or not they could distinguish between right and wrong, good and evil. The juveniles themselves had frequently told the examiner, 'I'm not crazy', 'I'm not retarded.' It took Lewis's specialized study to highlight the fact that they had multiple neurological handicaps.

During Lewis's study thirty-seven juveniles were awaiting execution. She raises another important point:

We seem to have inherited a paradoxical justice system that recognizes emotional and intellectual immaturity of juveniles and holds them less culpable than adults; at the same time, in the case of certain kinds of serious offences, juveniles are tried in the criminal justice system and their punishment for these offences, including execution, is meted out as though the juveniles were as responsible as adults.[9]

Another major study of murderers using PET scans revealed the same consistency. All forty-four murderers scanned revealed marked and specific prefrontal dysfunction – damage in the very area nature has ordained to help mankind distinguish right from wrong.

So if great swathes of crime are a biological disorder, how should it be treated if not by killing or incarceration? Perhaps we can make things easier for ourselves by not seeking to acquit or pardon such individuals, but by confining them for the protection of society. With the introduction of PET scans we should be able more easily to identify those with, for instance, dysfunctional control mechanisms. Identifying the cause, however, loads us with the responsibility of doing something about it – treating the offender. It is easier simply to condemn and lock away – although of course more expensive when the offender re-emerges from prison and inevitably offends again. Naturally, given the existing climate and the low financial priority accorded to the convicted, nothing will be done. Perhaps our best hope, paradoxically enough, is that where the crime does have treatable biological roots, criminals themselves will recognize their need for treatment and seek it – although it is something of an indictment of our normal, law-abiding society that we place the onus of seeking help upon the handicapped themselves.

Free will is not a simple, crossroads choice for people with a hand of many biological criminal cards; it is a dimension in which they are alien, alone, blind.

In any case, if crime is a symptom of a biological disorder, concepts of deterrence and punishment are largely irrelevant. Punishment cannot fit the crime if the crime is the result of an innate failing; no punishment actually fits red-headedness, stammering or measles. So should not the inmates of our prisons join the schizophrenics, psychotics and other mentally disturbed individuals whom we already treat in hospitals, or join the queue at the day surgery for extra doses of neurotransmitters? Should we end the fatuous search for the answer to crime by admitting that we have been asking the wrong questions all this time?

A recent academic treatise concludes that we now have enough evidence about the biological nature of persistent criminals to argue that 'many instances of repeated criminal behaviour, including theft and burglary, may represent a disorder or psychopathy in much the same way that depression or schizophrenia or other conditions currently recognized as mental disorders represent psychopathologies.'[10]

A brave and rare scientist who spells out the implications of his research; and while he admits that the public and the politicians will find this a difficult notion to accept, and that we have a need to punish, he believes that accepting the idea that crime may not be the malign choice of free will should set us on the path of looking for cures rather than responses. After all, the nostrums and remedies of the past have not been conspicuously successful in reducing crime. And if this view seems a little extreme, 'we must not forget that extreme views can be appropriate and that moderate views can be erroneous. During the days of the Spanish inquisition a moderate view would have been not to burn heretics; an extreme view not to burn any heretics.'[11]

So what's the alternative? We need to know what we do – as electors, lawmakers, jurors, doctors, citizens – with the growing knowledge that crime is as much a function of biology as anything else. Evil may be something no more sinister than a matter of loose connections. The devil may be the term for an accumulation of cerebral wounds. Perhaps the theologians, too, need to think again. Is it practically possible to discard the traditional concept of justice based on guilt and punishment and replace it with a 'medical model' based on prevention, diagnosis and treatment? Do we have the medical tools at hand to treat what has been diagnosed? (The question of prevention we will come on to later.)

A number of the syndromes described in earlier chapters are open to treatment. Drugs exist, and have been successfully used, to control the Jekyll-and-Hyde rages of episodic dyscontrol such as those endured by Ted B., the man who suffered extreme bouts of rage which lasted only a few seconds but during which he would inflict terrible damage. He knew that he could easily have killed his wife, and his remorse after the attacks was extreme and severe. He did not know until much later that he suffered from a hidden form of epilepsy, hard to diagnose, but eminently treatable with an anticonvulsant drug. How many such people with a secret epicentre of explosive rage are in our prisons undiagnosed?

The non-psychopathic and non-violent sex offender has been successfully treated with drugs for over a decade. Before that, the answer to what we now know lies in the brain has been to attack the genitals. Surgical castration has been the norm for thousands of years – though whether as a treatment or a punishment is open to question. Castration was first used 'therapeutically' in Europe in 1892. Denmark legalized this form of treatment for sex offenders in 1929. Northern Europe followed, but the southern, Catholic countries did not, regarding castration as dangerously close to a form of contraception. Unsurprisingly, the operation reduces fantasies and the sex drive, although in the long term sexual activity after castration is not unusual.

Chemistry has since taken the place of the surgical shears. In Germany and Switzerland, the drug Cyproterone, usually in the form of Cyproterone Acetate (CA), competes with androgens in binding to the brain synapses, and generally damps down the effects of testosterone. In the USA Medoxyprogesterone Acetate, MPA, has been offered as a substitute for imprisonment. It is a synthetic steroid which counteracts testosterone. The physiological effects over a period of weeks are a reduction in blood testosterone levels, loss of erection and orgasm and elimination of semen production. The drug treatment seems to have some success in both men and women – one woman who was clinically hypersexual found that her problems ceased with chemotherapy. It has also proved an effective treatment for paedophilia and exhibitionism – at least among volunteers with no other history of offending. Normal sex, apparently, is still possible.

Ethical problems abound. But the problems and potential solutions that scientific knowledge is delivering to us are not confined to the realm of sexual offending.

Treating the violent mind is now much more of a possibility, too. There is a whole range of drugs which increase the levels of serotonin in the brain, Prozac being the most common. These sorts of drugs are now being used to control those people who are diagnosed as APD – antisocial personality disordered – but who suffer from a brain deficit which leaves them without adequate brakes on their behaviour. Anger which explodes into maiming and killing can be curbed. Other tweaks to the serotonin levels have been tried – active serotonin or 5-HT has been administered to supplement low levels. The early results are mixed, but in most cases they seem to be encouraging; they seem to show a marked reduction in aggression, without making the subject sleepy. But a major problem is that many such people have other cards in their make-up, and may not be capable of maintaining themselves on the necessary medication. As one American expert says, 'In the US, the really big problem is that there is no penalty for failure to take the drug that prevents the violent outbursts. So they get arrested, are found to be insane, get put back on the drug, get sane, get released, spend their money on fun drugs, get violent – over and over again.'[12]

As ever, it is a matter of resources as well as ethics: it may be cheaper to punish than to treat and monitor the treatment. But at least we know that the means exist to control what hitherto we have seen as uncontrollable offending behaviour.

A few doctors and clinical psychologists, dealing with real patients rather than esoteric research, have begun to use drugs in children and young adults. While their results are not major clinical trials, they tell us that for some individuals drug treatment can change not only behaviour but also the very brain pattern which was a likely cause of their offending.

A particular case that comes from a Canadian neuropsychologist, Lorne Yeudall, concerns the young man called Mark.

Mark was born into a stable middle-class family in a small rural community just outside Edmonton. He had been a good student until he was twelve years old, achieving near honours grades. But he behaved badly at home, and at the age of thirteen his aggressive behaviour escalated. He was quite a tall boy and would intimidate and bully other class members. His grades dropped dramatically. About this time, he began to draw pictures of violent figures, with knives, depicting bodies being disembowelled and then hanged. Mark was picked up by the police at school with a loaded .357mm magnum pistol. He had stolen it from neighbours. He took the gun to school and stuffed it under his shirt and started to threaten the older boys in the school yard, saying he would blow their heads off. When Mark's parents were called down to the police station, they couldn't believe what he had done.

Mark's parents took him to see Yeudall, who did an EEG that gives a measure of the electrical activity in the cortex, or thinking areas of the brain, and he conducted more sophisticated tests known as evoked potentials, which elicit information about the deeper areas of the brain. Mark's 'brain map' showed that the connections between the thinking, executive part of the brain and the limbic emotional rage area were not working. The uninhibited brain was not being talked to by the rational brain. It also showed that the right side of the brain was not working properly either.

Yeudall prescribed a drug which raised the activity in this area of the brain – it can act like a kick-start, reactivating systems which are not working properly. After four weeks, Mark started to respond to the treatment. When he was reassessed, the clinicians found that his brain had normalized, and the aggressive fantasies had gone. The school was persuaded to let Mark re-sit his examinations; he achieved 90 per cent and jumped up a grade. When he looked at the pictures he used to draw he couldn't understand what he had been thinking.

There is no reason for women any longer to suffer the rages of severe premenstrual syndrome, which can be treated with a similar compound. A Swedish scientist had theorized that if the sex hormones are intimately involved in controlling the serotonin levels, things would work in reverse – a drug that increased the levels of neurotransmitters would cure the symptoms of PMS. In a careful study that took into account the various criticisms of other projects, he selected a number of women who suffered from severe PMS, but who had no underlying psychiatric problems. He then split them into two groups and gave one group Clompramine, while the other received a placebo. Clompramine is a drug that increases the level of active serotonin in the brain by preventing the neurons from removing serotonin from synapses, and so keeping the electricity flowing through the nerve network. The chemical brakes are kept on by the drug. The treatment worked.

Any biological intervention in trying to understand the roots of crime, and minimize the chances of future offending, has to take serotonin levels into account. It raises, of course, vast medical, ethical and political problems. But crime is a fairly big problem itself. If we have a means to affect the incidence of crime, and to lessen the chances of an individual developing into systematic criminality, we ought to discuss it. To discuss it, we ought to know about it. There must surely be room, among all the political rhetoric and sociological theory, for a bit of clinical science.

There is a deeper problem with the psychopath, be he violent or non-violent. There is no known drug which reconnects the conscience. Studies on psychopaths in prison show that they are less capable of learning from unpleasant experiences; if they have an autonomic nervous system which makes them relatively immune to electric shocks, is it likely that the shock of prison will help them mend their ways any more than it will deter them? Neither sticks nor carrots, the standbys of social training, have any effect: psychopaths have been found to show little enthusiasm for tasks that earned praise or approval. The persistent criminal's deficient sense of guilt flows from the same source as his lack of interest in society's conventions of approval. And of course by definition the psychopath does not feel the need to change – he doesn't feel that he has psychological or emotional problems and sees no reason to change this behaviour to conform to social standards with which he does not agree.

The psychopath is well satisfied with himself, however his fate may seem to outside observers. He feels no regret or remorse, only the gratification – his action seems quite logical. If anything, he sees himself as superior to the world with its petty conventions and little decencies. This superiority gives him the right to manipulate and exploit the little people around him. Psychotherapy – the method whereby we learn afresh about ourselves, our personal interactions and the language of emotional intimacy – is not a fruitful area for psychopaths. Anyway, by the time they might reach formal treatment their attitudes are well entrenched. Why change, when many simply enjoy their way of life? Indeed, psychotherapy may provide a further instruction manual in manipulation.

If we accept that repeated, serious crime is a disorder, the implication is that such offenders should not be punished as severely for their actions, that more freedoms should be restored to incarcerated prisoners, that new vigorous attempts should be made to increase new research and clinical efforts to understand and treat crime, and that the criminal justice system requires revision in order to take into account the consequent practical implications.[13]

What stands out from literally hundreds of papers and studies of the various types of criminal is widespread and cogent evidence of disordered minds resulting from dysfunctional brains. The real crime of many such people is the incapacity to comprehend the nature of guilt. If they had a more recognized learning disability, we would rush to help them with therapy and extra resources. But we do not recognize; we merely condemn. Incarceration is an expensive and wasteful reaction, which does very little good apart from providing a secure hotel facility for a limited amount of time.

We have no answers – except, perhaps, the earlier identification of those at risk of offending (which we will be addressing). What we present is a catalogue of independent research findings, reviewed in advance by a leading researcher in the field. Problematic it may be, but our legislators cannot claim it to be untrue. Law and ethics have always evolved in the light of knowledge. And this knowledge is too vital, and holds too much promise, to ignore.

We all have a vital interest in preventing crime. That effort and commitment defines the quality of our society. We know that many approaches have been tried to deter and reform the recidivist offender or nip criminality in the juvenile bud – but with the best will in the world, all such approaches have signally failed. Should we continue these futile efforts – now that we have a whole new seam of hope to quarry?

The fact is that we are better equipped than ever before to identify those who are at risk, to do something about crime before it happens. If we can identify neurological impairment, or constitutionally abnormal brain chemistry, and a developing pattern of low IQ, poor impulse control, violent delinquency – the familiar constellation of predictive criminality – is there not an obligation, as well as an investment, in developing programmes to recognize and treat these multiply handicapped children?

And that's what we will deal with next. Because, whatever the legal and moral confusion, there is hope.

CHAPTER 14

The Dangerous Few

LOOKED AT IN the light of what we now know, what about those case histories with which we began in Chapter 2?

Rick, the son of an alcoholic father, living on a run-down council estate, was sixteen when he got into trouble with the law – he was drunk, and, with a group of friends, smashed up the local playground because 'we were bored.' Rick is now nineteen. He has not seen his alcoholic father for two years. When he walked out, peace returned and mother and son got on well. The incident with the police was now a distant memory. Rick had been shocked by his arrest and decided it was time to curb his own drinking. He has just passed the mechanics exams too. A job at the big local garage looked as if it might come his way. But Rick knew that one more brush with the police would put an end to that chance. He never offended again.

Then there was James, the adopted child brought up in the criminal household. Again, you would have thought that the criminal odds were stacked against him. But James survived, because of a genetic make-up and a personality which protected him from his foster parents' influence. His biological parents, both eminently solid citizens, had been killed in a car crash. Their genes were James's sword and buckler against the social adversity he faced.

Simon, the pampered middle-class lad, has an outcome that could be predicted by his early problematic behaviour. His parents have long despaired of him. His criminal activities, far from decreasing as he got older, actually increased. The range and variety of his misdeeds numbed his parents. Simon did not care. When he reached the age where the police could lock him away, they did. Simon, too, is now nineteen, and under 'rehabilitative care' in one of the few secure units for young offenders.

Mary, the eight-year-old with a cruel streak, continued to behave in a disquieting manner. Her mother became worried by the lack of remorse Mary showed over the pain she had inflicted. The pattern of cruelty to animals became a part of Mary's life. It became impossible to have a family pet – no one would trust Mary with an animal. Her parents took her to the psychiatrist. It did no good. When Mary reached thirteen her troubles intensified. She refused to obey her parents, staying out all night, regularly truanting from school where her school reports, not surprisingly, went from bad to worse. Much worse was to come. Mary regularly baby-sat for the neighbours. One night she strangled the one-year-old she was looking after because he would not stop crying. Mary had a disturbed mind – but one whose actions could be predicted, and one that could be controlled.

Now that we are familiar with all the cards which make up the differing minds to crime in adult criminals, can we identify them in childhood? Can we identify, for instance, low arousal, poor verbal IQ, hormonal irregularities, genetic influences, malfunctions in the limbic system, poor neurotransmitter systems, functional damage in the temporal or frontal lobes, poor connections between the centres of feeling and of reason? And can we link these deficits to the small, hard core of persistent criminals?

The answer is, to a large extent, yes. Perhaps the most startling conclusion from the latest investigations into crime and the brain is that we may be able to predict which children are at risk of growing up to join the small hard core of persistent offenders. We have touched on this earlier in the book; now let us examine it further.

Virtually all adolescent males participate in antisocial behaviour, and the vast majority turn out to be sober citizens with careers, marriages and mortgages by their mid twenties. The fact is that most young men with weird personalities and low IQs don't go on to become persistent criminals. Which is just as well, given the natural preponderance of such characteristics in the young male.

The figures show that the vast majority of those committing crimes commit only a small number. But there is a small percentage that commit most of the crimes. Could it be that this hard core of offenders has a dysfunction which is so severe that, unlike the majority of their peers, they simply cannot 'grow out of it'? And is it possible to identify them at an early stage?

An American study of young male street criminals shows that nearly half of the sample – 46 per cent – had committed only one offence. Nearly all the robberies – 95 per cent – had been committed by a smaller, tighter, harder group. In a British study, 411 boys from poor London backgrounds were studied over a period of twenty years. Of these, a mere 6 per cent were responsible for 71 per cent of the homicides, 73 per cent of the rapes, 70 per cent of the robberies and 69 per cent of the aggravated assaults. In other studies, a kernel of some 12 per cent of youngsters convicted of serious crimes has been identified as the ones who commit a disproportionate amount of the crime. About half of this 12 per cent go on to become adult career criminals. On the basis of this study, then, of 100 young men who get themselves into trouble, 6 run the serious statistical risk of embarking upon a life of crime and the 'six-at-risk' will already have distinguished themselves by having committed a fairly comprehensive catalogue of crime.

A French study of 470 boys echoes the theme of prolific juvenile crime, declining in frequency as time goes on, but with the actual crimes committed becoming more serious in nature. The boys were assessed as being at a high risk of chronic criminality. Their careers showed how they sampled, and discarded, various forms of offending. Between the ages of 8 and 10, a range of petty misdemeanours were committed. In the next couple of years, from 10 to 12, there was a vogue for vandalism and shoplifting. But by the age of thirteen this 'kids'-stuff' was given up in favour of an explosion of more serious offending – principally in the areas of public disorder, theft and burglary. By the age of 15, the focus of offending had shifted to drug-trafficking, motor vehicle theft, mugging and armed robbery. By mid-adolescence, virtually the entire gamut of crimes had been experienced – with the exception of homicide and fraud.

What's clear is that there is not an inevitable progression from one sort of delinquent behaviour to the next level as the children get older. The children can either abandon one sort of crime for a more serious range of offending, or do what most of them do – give up offending altogether.

But which of the hundreds of thousands of our young people who do break the law will go on to be the persistent criminals?

Everyone has strong opinions on the causes of crime. Society's usually to blame, for being either too soft or too repressive. Or it could be the baby boom, the permissive revolution, broken homes, single-parent families, incompetent schools, racial discrimination, lenient judges, the decline of organized religion, TV violence, drug addiction, unemployment, capitalism or something they put in the drinking water.

One of the most comprehensive surveys of crime, Herrnstein and Wilson's *Crime and Human Nature*, shows correlations with crime and – virtually – *all* the above. Crime has multiple causes. But for all the plethora of criminological theories, there is not a single well-accepted theory of the cause of crime. The economic link alone doesn't quite work: there was less crime during the depression than later, when the economy boomed, but there was less public sensitivity about policemen giving a cautionary box on the ears to any juvenile malefactors they discovered. Most children raised in broken homes do not become serious offenders. Cain was busy inventing murder a considerable time before the advent of television.

Even so, in many hundreds of studies of those juveniles whose criminal behaviour may persist into adulthood, it is clearly possible to distinguish those at the greatest risk. Many researchers with the experience know that this type of child can be identified and distinguished from the mere adolescent hell-raiser, long before he matures into an adult criminal career. The fact is that this small, hard core who develop from childhood mischief, through teenage delinquency, to adult crime differ, in a whole range of characteristics, from those who have never committed a crime and from those who committed just a small number. It isn't simply a question of the majority successfully going through a delinquent phase and emerging the other end, while a few fail to develop and stay for ever enmeshed in habits of offending; researchers now think that they can distinguish the dangerous few from the normal impulsive, reckless and mischievous young lads well before they reach puberty. Here is the report card of a six-year-old (whose name has been changed):

Jonathan has not had a good term. He has found it difficult to settle in class, where he is fidgety and disruptive. He frequently spoils his own work by writing obscene words on it, or rips up the work of others. He is at his most disruptive in the art class, where he wrecked the class's joint project. He is verbally abusive, and prone to temper tantrums. He finds it hard to form friendships, and those that he does are short-lived, given his tendency to physical violence. Without constant supervision Jonathan is liable to get himself into all sorts of trouble, but he adopts a universally negative approach to efforts by his teachers to coax him into more acceptable behaviour. I am afraid to say that he runs rings round the staff. He has taken to exposing himself to the girls in the playground, and there have also been incidents of stealing where Jonathan has fallen under suspicion. I regret to say

that Jonathan does not have a clear sense of the consequences of his actions, nor an adequately developed sense
of right and wrong.

Jonathan is clearly the pre-school pupil from hell. He is
already the despair of his teachers, and his parents don't feel
too good about it, either. Is this a phase he'll grow out of – or
is there something fundamentally wrong? And what about
those other youngsters we have identified, such as the six-year-
old girl who tried to kill her father by running him over with
the jeep?

There are a number of childhood disorders that go under a
myriad of names – names that keep changing as the nature of
each disorder becomes better understood. 'Minimal brain dysfunction', 'hyperkinesis', 'attention deficit disorder', and 'conduct disorder' are all attempts to identify particular behaviours.
But whatever the diagnosis of childhood, the prognosis is
worrying.

The common factor in such disorders is aggression, either
verbal or physical, whose manifestations include fighting, lashing out, temper tantrums, disruptions, interruptions, negative
attitudes, hyperactivity, failure to concentrate, stealing, lying,
restlessness, noisiness and irritability. Again, the odds are
stacked against the male. Boys are much more likely than girls
to be diagnosed as having an intellectual disorder. In terms of
aggressive behaviour the sex difference is estimated to be 3:1
when associated with conduct disorder and up to 9:1 for
attention deficit disorders.

The diagnostic bible of the American medical establishment,
defining the diagnosis of antisocial personality disorders in
adults, states that it is detectable in early life: 'the essential
feature of this disorder is the pattern of irresponsible and
antisocial behaviour beginning in childhood or early adolescence and continuing into adulthood.'[1] Without exception, the
studies give a bad prognosis for children with conduct disorder;
and those with an actual record of delinquency have the worst
outlook. In childhood the significant behaviours are truancy,

running away from home, initiation of physical fights using weapons, forcing sexual relations on others, physical cruelty to animals or people, vandalism, fire-setting, lying and stealing with or without violent confrontation. The greater the variety and number of these types of behaviour, the more likely the subsequent emergence of criminal behaviour in adulthood and the diagnosis of an adult personality disorder. Equally, the earlier in a child's development that he gets into trouble with the law, the more likely he is to be convicted as an adult. Some studies indicate that 80 per cent of adult criminals had early childhood convictions – a virtual absence of adult problems in people who had no serious problems in childhood, according to one report – while others regard childhood wrongdoing as a prerequisite of adult criminal behaviour.

So adults with APD were all once APD children, but the reverse is not true: not all those afflicted by childhood conduct disorders are condemned to a life of adult criminality. There is a constant interplay between the tide of personality and the wind of environment. Even so, the finding that antisocial adult behaviour virtually requires a history of child behavioural problems is well enough documented to be beyond debate.

The relationship is particularly clear in the area of conduct disorders – anything from tantrums to bullying and childish arson. A study which began in 1978 followed the life histories of children in St Louis, Missouri, over a period of more than twenty years. Researchers found that in *every* case of adult personality disorder there had been evidence of antisocial behaviour before the age of 18. In 84 per cent of the cases antisocial behaviour was established by the age of 13, and 58 per cent had manifested this psychopathology by the age of 8. In a smaller sample of adult female psychopaths the behaviour usually became apparent between the ages of 14 and 18. The best predictor of post-adolescent antisocial personality disorder was the number of antisocial symptoms which had been displayed in childhood. All other factors – such as social class and parental attitude – were secondary to a child's own behavioural history and came a poor second when it came to predicting the outcome in adult life.

All children are naughty, all over the world – but somehow we haven't ended up with a totally criminal adult world. What makes the difference? And how does it manifest itself? Partly, it's a matter of degree – the number of those antisocial traits, and the force with which they are acted out. A child may steal, but be otherwise free of the factors which contribute to an antisocial personality. But other childhood behaviour betrays evidence of factors which may lead to problems in adult life.

Hyperactivity may be a precursor of adult personality disorders. Many of the antisocial personality group report problems which began at school, and which centre on restlessness, boredom and passivity. This attitude does not endear them to the teaching staff, and so a spiral of mutual alienation gets set in motion. School becomes, almost literally, a gaol for such children.

A psychologist and an expert in hyperactivity, Jim Satterfield, conducted a study following children in Los Angeles and comparing a hyperactive sample with a normal sample. The first stage examined behaviour among those from 6 to 12 years of age, while there was a follow-up at 14–20 years of age. The researchers found, disturbingly, that hyperactivity among children 'presents a remarkably immutable syndrome that forecasts an ominous picture for the future. The clinical picture often worsens as the child gets older, with resulting adolescent problems of academic failure and serious antisocial behaviour.'[2]

The significance of Satterfield's study lies in its dimensions. He carried out a large battery of tests to identify behaviour problems and detect brain deficiencies. What's important is that he kept a large sample under review for a period of eight years – the first longitudinal study to examine such a broad-based set of areas. He wasn't looking simply at hyperactivity and attention deficit disorders; the second major feature involved looking for clues in the children's neuropsychology which would help to predict serious antisocial behaviour.

Satterfield looked at 150 hyperactive children, with a control group of 88 normal young children from Los Angeles. All the hyperactive children had been referred to outpatient clinics for learning or behavioural problems.

The (male-only) hyperactive group tested normal for vision and hearing, all had IQ above 80 – above the cut-off point where they would be recognized as mentally subnormal, and were diagnosed by a psychiatrist as having all the symptoms of hyperactivity – inattention and impulsiveness as reported by parents and teachers. At the time the study began, the diagnosis of attention deficit disorder, or ADD, had not been coined, but the clinical criteria of the children in the study were similar to those currently recognized by the American Medical Association's assessment for attention deficit disorder. Five factors were rated – hyperactive, antisocial, withdrawn and impulsive behaviour and inattention. Satterfield asked parents to rate the children from 1 (or just a little), through 2 (pretty much) to 3 (very much) on each of the five factors. Teachers were given a scale too, though they were asked to assess irritability instead of withdrawn behaviour.

Satterfield then followed up these children when they were older, using official arrest data which classified them into non-serious and serious offenders. Non-serious offences included alcohol intoxication, vandalism, use of marijuana and petty theft. Serious offences encompassed robbery, burglary, car theft and assault with a deadly weapon.

The results were intriguing. Those who had been hyperactive as children committed 6 times more serious offences than the 'normal' control group. When it came to multiple offences, the hyperactive group outperformed – if that is the word – the control by a factor of 28:1. Offences that lead to institutionalization were 25 times more common among the hyperactive group.

Satterfield had gone to considerable lengths to eliminate biases of age and social class, and concluded that conduct disorder is a greater predictor of criminal behaviour than social background. And there's more evidence for this view from a specifically class-based study in the UK. It looked at the link from the opposite perspective – those, in the same working-class group, who were and were not hyperactive. When the sample was followed up, it was found that those who had not gone on to acquire a criminal record were distinguished at the age of 8–10 by being less daring, less troublesome and easier to discipline than their comparatively hyperactive peers. This was a group brought up in exactly the same adverse environmental climate of poverty, parental conflict and criminality. Yet these psychologically milder children, quiet, reflective and with low levels of sensation-seeking, did not go on to pursue criminal careers, while their more extroverted, aggressive colleagues did. Life, of course, would be dull without the aggressive, daring extroverts of this world – all the more reason for taking special and active care to keep them on the straight and narrow.

The whole question of concentration and attention is emerging as central to the question of delinquency. A study in Denmark looked at a group of children, grading them on their teachers' assessment of how well, or badly, they could concentrate on a given subject. As compared with normal children, a significant number of those 10–13-year-olds who scored poorly on the attention scale were found, eight years later, to have been arrested for various misdemeanours. That large British study of 411 children came up with the same success in predicting delinquency on the basis of poor attention – although the picture is confused, because of the different terminologies varying scientists give to the problem of attention deficits, and the different age ranges surveyed. For instance, the British study came out with similar predictive qualities; measures of hyperactivity and conduct problems (CP) among children between the ages of 8 and 10 significantly predicted juvenile convictions between the ages of 10 and 16. The results also suggest that hyperactivity and CP may both assist in predicting the extent of future criminal career at the time of first conviction. Children unafflicted with either hyperactivity or conduct disorder were particularly unlikely to become chronic offenders, while all measures of hyperactivity along with conduct disorder significantly predicted juvenile convictions. We must never lose sight of other predictors, such as low income, large family size, poor houses, poor parental guidance, poor supervision, convicted parents or delinquent brothers; but the fact is that hyperactivity or conduct disorder predicted as well as, or better than, all of the above. The only social factor to rival hyperactivity was whether or not the parents had themselves been convicted of crimes.

What seems to be becoming clear, through this plethora of definitions of disorders, is that a combination of inattention, hyperactivity and general bloody-mindedness – as expressed in Jonathan's report – is a severe warning of trouble to come.

The picture is becoming clearer, like a photograph emerging from the chemicals in the darkroom. The image is of psychological and intellectual damage, predisposing a child to subsequent adult wrongdoing. What we still need to know is the nature of this damage, and how redeemable it is.

Lennie P. is twenty-three, and is well established on a criminal career. He has already been convicted of ten offences. This is his life story, from notes on a survey of young criminals.

Subject had the most extensive offence history in the sample. Twenty-seven offences as a juvenile. First recorded offence for truancy was at age ten. As a juvenile his police contacts increased every year and included assaults and robberies, burglaries, disorderly conducts and possession of marijuana. Low scores on intelligence and achievement tests. Had very severe speech problem at a very early age – no medical intervention taken to eliminate the problem. The mother stated that as a child he knew about seven words that were spoken plainly. Examiner described the speech as unintelligible. At an early age the child showed cognitive and neurological disorders as well as symptoms of attention deficit disorders. Starting at age seven months, the subject banged his head against the side of his crib and rocked before going to sleep each night. Evidenced rocking periods during play with other children and often rocked and banged his head when he was angry ... Although subject did not experience major illnesses, there was mention of a head injury due to a fall at eighteen months – child fell out of couch and hit his head, after which he developed a fever and became groggy ... Mother separated three years after the child's birth and has not worked, family live on welfare. Family had a history of moving frequently and housing situation was continually deprived. Mother had little control over her children's behaviour and evidence indicated that she physically neglected her children sometimes. The subject was fearful of his mother as a child and the mother indicated that she often had to beat him to make him obey. There are many factors in the subject's background that could start and perpetuate criminal behaviour – borderline intellectual ability and low school achievement, severe articulation problems, neurological disorders, lack of co-ordination, bed wetting, serious head injury, large family size, middle birth order, frequent house moves, poor housing conditions, welfare status, ineffective and intellectually dull mother, neglectful and abusive mother, father who was absent and a criminal.

What's familiar here is the progression from minor delinquency – truancy – through to more serious offending. It wasn't, sadly, a phase he went through; he went from bad to worse. We've also recognized the low verbal IQ – he is virtually incoherent at the age of seven. We know that he's a borderline intelligence case. But what about all the other material, about his family background, his head injury, his lack of motor skills and so on? Are they part of our familiar hand of criminal cards?

Many of these 'difficult' children are referred to psychologists; and the principal reason for their referral is not delinquency, but problems with learning at school, typically a high rate of absenteeism, fatigue, inability to attend and concentrate, poor motivation for work, inability to follow directions, slow learning and infantile speech patterns. Learning disability or minimal brain dysfunction, as defined by the standard psychological measures, puts boys significantly below average in all areas. Most referrals, by a factor of 11:1, are indeed of boys.

It is now well established that children who suffer from these disorders have an underlying brain abnormality. More specifically, that apparent deficit in verbal IQ is a sure sign of damage to the left side of the brain, where the language centres are based. It is also accepted that males are more likely to suffer prenatal damage in brain development, and so to develop the brain abnormalities that make them prone to behavioural problems – contributing to that overwhelming male bias in crime. And we know by now that these temperamental problems in childhood are likely to be echoed, more severely, later in life.

Nearly fifty published reports have endeavoured to find the precise link between brain damage and maladaptive behaviour. The problem with such a plethora of studies is that many of them use different measures and different definitions of delinquency. Nevertheless, the findings are consistent. All find delinquency related to what are described as 'cognitive deficits', problems in the manner of thinking. All delinquents score poorly on the tests. In all studies the functions most consistently cited as impaired have been verbal, language-based skills and executive or frontal lobe functions (the frontal lobes of the brain being those areas controlling actions and planning later behaviour). We have already had clues of this in discussing the problem of low IQ – performance IQ was normal, but IQ as measured on the verbal level was poor.

Practical tests confirm the distinction. Assessments based on visuo-spatial skills – hand-eye co-ordination, for instance – show normal levels of intelligence; but when a test involves a verbal rather than a spatial task, and demands an oral rather than a manual solution, the deficit becomes apparent – 'an impressively replicable finding that warrants explanation'.[3]

One battery of tests assessed abstract reasoning, rhythmic sequencing and language skills to evaluate the functional integrity of the brain as whole; the tests showed evident impairment of the left, language-controlling part of the brain among delinquent children, while, interestingly, another study showed that non-delinquent children who also had learning difficulties had no such verbal impairment.

Long-term self-report studies reveal an even stronger link between delinquency and language problems. For eighteen years a team of scientists in New Zealand collated repeated examinations of neuropsychological impairment, neurological symptoms, behaviour problems, educational achievement, intelligence, delinquency and family factors in a complete sample of children born in 1972 from all social backgrounds. These so-called longitudinal and prospective studies represent the safest type of research, in that they are examining children 'blind', with no advance knowledge of what will befall them, and the symptoms are recorded contemporaneously, with no risk of poor recall or faulty memories about a child's behaviour.

When the children were older, they were divided into delinquent and non-delinquent groups, according to how much trouble they had subsequently got into. Working back to the original data, it was discovered that the greatest difference between the two groups, as children, lay in the field of speaking and hearing memory skills; in skills such as hand-eye co-ordination and mental flexibility functions (rotating a three-dimensional image in the mind's eye) the two groups had been indistinguishable.

The link with aggression was the next thing the New Zealand group studied; was there any correlation between those children who had gone on to commit crimes of violence and a low verbal IQ? When they compared the aggression scores of those individuals who showed high discrepancies between verbal and spatial scores, they found that subjects with high discrepancies had aggressive scales twice as high as those measured as having a more balanced intelligence. In a sub-group of delinquents with attention deficit disorder – ADD – they found especially poor performance in verbal and memory factors. Again, children who merely had learning problems but who were non-delinquent had much less severe verbal deficits.

So, to hyperactivity, we can add poor language skills as a strong predictor of future offending behaviour.

The study also confirms something we must always remember: the diversity of factors involved in creating a criminal mindset. The New Zealand studies showed up a significant interaction between low verbal IQ and poor home environment; taken together, these two handicaps seemed to result in a degree of aggressive behaviour some four times greater than could be found resulting from any other set of circumstances. Which explains a lot about Lennie P., as well as underlining the interplay between social and biological factors.

What it also explains is that there are, in a sense, protective factors for those with a poor start in life; children brought up in the most adverse family environment, yet who had strong and fluent communication skills, did not turn out to show such aggressive behaviour. Could this mean that a facility with language skills somehow acts as 'a buffer against the development of aggressive behaviour'?[4] It would certainly explain why so few girls show up in the delinquency statistics – girls having better verbal skills from the very outset.

So there's a statistical link between verbal skills and delinquency. But why should this be – apart from an advantage in talking yourself out of trouble? Why should language deficits lead to antisocial behaviour? There are various theories. One is that poor language ability makes it difficult for the child to follow verbal instructions, so they don't learn. Speech also seems to be central to the process of learning self-control. Simple instructions like 'no' to a two-year-old are not taken in; more importantly, while an adult is capable of thinking in a non-verbal shorthand, the child has to work things out through words, a process of mental verbalization – a sort of spelling out in the mind. So children fail to make the connections between verbal instructions and later events; they cannot see the consequences of disobeying an instruction. A study of boys with low socialization scores on the CPI (California Psychological Inventory) showed that they benefited less from the experimenter's approval in the laboratory conditioning study than boys with high scores. This suggests that things that motivate most of us, like the desire for praise and the need to avoid disapproval, both of which tend to make most of us amend our behaviour, don't seem to have the same effect on those with low verbal skills – perhaps because words simply don't mean as much. Without an internal monologue time horizons shrink; behaviour appears more connected to its immediate consequences. Maybe that was the problem with Jonathan, the terror of the playground; he did not have the vocabulary, grammar or syntax to communicate with himself.

But if the link between IQ and delinquency is valid, surely it's good news if, by repairing the verbal damage, we can help neutralize one of the factors – one of those aces or jacks or queens – which put the individual at risk? Can corrective educational measures be taken to repair the deficit? Is the deficit, indeed, the product of poor teaching, poor family or social circumstances, or is the damage innate? The New Zealand study set out to find out, using a battery of neuropsychological tests to determine the existence of brain problems, and again comparing delinquents with non-offenders. Their study concluded that the verbal deficit manifested itself comparatively early – before the children had learnt to read. A detailed study of children in Philadelphia over a period of thirty years shows that since the verbal deficits are to be found before they are taught to read, the verbal problems cannot be the result of poor teaching. The study confirmed the growing suspicion that poor reading achievement in school is a strong predictor of later delinquency.

The children were tested for levels of speech development at the age of four; from these results, predictions could be made as to who would learn to read, when, and at what degree of skill. This, in turn, was found to predict delinquency. Other studies have found that deficits in 4–5-year-olds predicted difficulties with reading: 'the conclusion that delinquents have lower IQs than non-delinquents is firmly established ... especially verbal IQ. They are not the causes of crime ... but should be regarded as symptoms.'[5]

So not only can we predict which children are at risk – we can probably identify them at the age of 4–5, and do something to remedy the deficit. The least we can do is to read to our children more.

So, with the help of experts, we must look deeper into the physical nature of a handicap which results in first verbal, and then social damage. The research in this area points to brain damage of a specific kind in the persistent juvenile criminal. Significantly, the damage occurs in the same area of the brain which governs language and self-control. The findings of at least one researcher, who examined 500 criminals in a 6-year study, have indicated a 'consistently high incidence of abnormal neuropsychological profiles in the persistent criminal'.[6] Evidence of these abnormal brain patterns has been supported by a further 11 studies.

And these patterns are the same as those we have discerned in the adult offender. The damage is consistently found in the frontal lobes (which play a decisive role in helping us to make plans and form intentions, regulate and verify complex behaviour, and enable us to plan an action, assess what's needed to execute it, assess its outcome and change or abandon the plan if necessary). Damage in this area may result in a mosaic of symptoms – we confuse tactics with strategy, we don't see inherent contradictions in our plan, we don't see the logical conclusion of what might happen. Concentration and motivation suffer, too; damage also diminishes control over our impulsiveness and our control of unsuccessful, inappropriate or impulsive behaviours, as well as the effective self-monitoring of behaviour and social awareness: 'lack of self-control, emotional outbursts, dramatic changes in personality, lack of or indifference to emotional feelings or conflicts (loss of normal guilt, shame, remorse), decrease in inhibition of sexual and aggressive behaviour and increased sensitivity to alcohol'.[7]

What we are describing here is the action of the 'mindless' vandal, the drunken football hooligan; it is also poor Jonathan's playgroup behaviour, translated onwards by a few years.

What tests now reveal, in the light of our new understanding of the brain, is that the classic symptoms of early trouble which show up as attention deficit disorders (ADD) or conduct disorder (CD) have an underlying cause within the brain. A mass of research highlights a widespread and typical incidence of frontal lobe dysfunction in delinquent groups. Sixteen studies specifically devoted to measuring planning and impulsiveness indicated that delinquents are constitutionally worse equipped to work actions out in advance and to put a brake on impetuous behaviour. The New Zealand study also found that ADD, which we have already identified as a delinquent trait, was accompanied by impairment of certain executive functions, strongly suggesting that ADD in particular may be related to frontal lobe function. EEGs and neurochemical evidence confirm that the frontal lobes are vital to the whole process of concentration and attention. And PET scans of a series of ADD patients show, graphically, that compared to normal controls, they have an inadequate blood flow in the tissues connecting the frontal lobes to the rest of the brain.

More evidence that delinquents suffer damage to executive functions such as concentration comes from their especially poor performance on an arithmetic subtest. The test appears at first to be a simple assessment of calculating skills, but, crucially, it's an oral, not a written task. The subject has to read a complex arithmetical problem, and must attend and concentrate while simultaneously recalling the problem and solving it mentally. The test measures how easily the subject resists distractions and is capable of sustained concentration. Whereas some frontal lobe damaged patients can solve arithmetical problems with a paper and pencil – relying on their mathematical skills – the task becomes impossible when they have to rely entirely on their – verbally deficient – mental faculties. Delinquents perform especially badly on this test.

As we've come to expect, the problem becomes more complex the more we examine it. What about all those children with ADD who *don't* go on to become delinquent – and most of them, of course, do not. Yet another research project looked at two groups, delinquent and non-delinquent, who both had attention deficit disorders. It was only among the delinquent ADD children that executive dysfunction of the frontal lobes was found.

Going further down the path of brain deficits, various studies have looked at juvenile and adult criminals with a history of violent offending. The peak age for such offences is the early twenties. Sixty males with at least one initial violent offence were tested; not only was the same brain deficit discovered, but the presence of this damage could predict future violent offending. Another study compared 40 violent adolescents with 40 non-violent delinquents at the same training school; the researchers found, using neuropsychological tests to assess dysfunction, that they could correctly discriminate between the violent and non-violent offenders in 83 per cent of the cases.

Children who go on to become serious offenders very often, then, have the sort of damage to their brains which – because of the verbal deficit – makes it hard for them to distinguish right from wrong, as well as the normal sticks and carrots of behaviour. And there is also an inherent problem in the brain which means they are less able to restrain their impulses, and more likely to be violent. Such children arrive at puberty with far less of a moral code in place than we would find in a normal young person.

The right sort of tests can identify which children are most at risk – in well-attested and clinical trials free from sociological or subjective compromise. Such tests are also likely to be able to discriminate between casual and long-term, violent offending. Whatever label is given to seriously disruptive behaviour – HIA or CD or ADD – it can be detected before the age of five in 95 per cent of cases. One study finds that at an average age of 2.9 years such symptoms may be detectable. Intervention, then, at this age could change the child's history.

Other studies show that brain abnormalities can be seen well before the child even gets in trouble with the law. We remember Mednick's study of 600 young Swedish children, in which he found this. The boys and girls were given waking and sleeping EEGs several times before the age of seventeen. Twelve years later the Swedish police records were examined; the average offender had a distinctive EEG at the original testing, even though over six years separated the test from the crime.

The EEGs showed that these children had low arousal levels, one of the most common cards to adult criminal behaviour that has been found in adults. A British study which followed a group of schoolboys in York came up with the same finding – low arousal is predictive of later criminal behaviour. (What was interesting in this study was that those antisocial boys who did not become criminal also did not show the pattern of low arousal. They were boys being boys – their behaviour alone, and of itself, was not predictive of future problems.)

The study of children in Los Angeles found that the at-risk hyperactive boys could be distinguished from ordinary children, and that children who were simply hyperactive and who would *not* go on to commit crimes could also be distinguished. 'From the clinical point of view the selection of subgroups of hyperactive children, most of whom can be predicted to have a poor outcome, is useful for delinquency prevention, because it is more economical to treat only those children who one can be reasonably sure will have a bad outcome without treatment.'[8]

So tests predicting future criminal behaviour are available. But with them comes a moral dilemma, posed by a recent article in *Scientific American*: 'Scientists are homing in on social and biological risk factors that they believe predispose individuals to criminal behaviour. The knowledge could be ripe with promise – or rife with danger.'[9]

So – do we try to fulfil the promise – or shrink from the danger? What, after all, are we to do with the predictions?

One of the leading researchers in the field put the problem to us in direct, human terms:

Imagine you are the parent of an eight-year-old child and you have been told that the prediction is that within twenty years he will become extremely violent, and are offered a series of programmes that will reduce the risk. What do you do? Do you place your boy in those programmes and risk stigmatizing him as a violent criminal, even though there is a real possibility that he is innocent? Or do you say no to the treatment and run an 80 per cent chance that your child will grow up to a) destroy his life b) destroy your life c) destroy the lives of his brothers and sisters and most important d) destroy the lives of the innocent victims who suffer at his hands?[10]

Many scientists worry that society may make premature and inappropriate use of such knowledge. The history of science is scarred by such instances – for example, by 1931, twenty-seven US states had passed laws allowing compulsory sterilization of the 'feeble minded', the insane and the habitually criminal.

What do we do about the dangerous few? Should society intervene? When and how should we? And how can we, without putting our population of children to the test in a manner which would appal most people's sense of civil liberty? Wouldn't such tests merely be a forensic reiteration of the gloomy prognosis, 'He was born to be hanged'? And yet if we are serious about our concern about crime – and about the offender and the victim, too – should we blithely discard the key that may unlock so much of the puzzle? If we can separate the dangerous few from the millions who commit one-off crimes, we may have a tool at hand to stop those millions of potential criminals from festering into regular criminals – a vast social saving in terms of damage prevented, a great financial saving in terms of imprisonment avoided, so releasing funds which could be diverted to helping to remedy these newly-recognized sources of crime. As Adrian Raine observes, 'for every 1 per cent that we reduce violence we save the country $1.2 billion.'[11]

There is a now a small but growing body of evidence that if we take a child who is showing all the at-risk signals when he or she is 4–5 years old, and treat the family alongside the child, we can actually in many cases change, neutralize or even successfully trump the biological hand of cards. A few people are now attempting to treat and change the behaviour of these children. They believe that if we concentrate on the small percentage likely to commit most of the crimes, and if we identify, early enough, the available clinical markers, we can achieve a significant reduction in crime. But we must be prepared to think of these children as disabled, as having a moral learning difficulty.

The Oregon Social Learning Centre has monitored and treated more than 250 families with antisocial children for the past ten years. The treatment amounts to 'remedial parenting': parents are taught more effective ways of monitoring their child's behaviour with a points system to reward good behaviour and to punish the breaking of rules. A brain which, for all the reasons we have explained, finds it hard to put together the concept of a moral code, needs – and benefits from – this extra encouragement.

At Johns Hopkins University, too, they have developed a 'good behaviour game' to reinforce the moral learning of those at risk. They have also developed a 'mastery' technique to prevent slower children becoming more isolated by the educational process, by ensuring that each pupil has mastered each lesson before moving on to the next – a system which is now being used by more than 30 million students in 3,000 schools around the world and which educators claim has helped to reduce truancy and behaviour problems.

If the children still go off the rails, another American scheme has found a means of remedying the problem. It has found that among those who experiment with delinquency, only those who develop bonds to a peer group made up of other antisocial children are likely to remain involved in crime. The obvious solution is to try to put them into groups that are mainly prosocial. In a study doing just that, 700 boys were divided into groups of about 40, some groups of bad, and some groups of good and bad together. The results were that the boys in totally antisocial groups showed no decline in their offending, but 91 per cent of antisocial boys in the mixed groups showed a reduction in their offending behaviour of nearly 50 per cent.

Another approach involves the preschool targeting of at-risk children in Michigan. A study offers evidence that early intervention through a high-quality preschool programme can alter a child's life. In a study of 123 disadvantaged children, the detention and arrest rates for the 58 children who had attended the programme was 31 per cent compared with 51 per cent for the 65 who did not. Also those in the preschool programme were more likely to go on to graduate from high school, enrol in secondary education and get jobs – as well as less likely to become pregnant as teenagers.

But the most successful approach uses both parent training and child training and drugs to alter the behaviour of the potentially criminal child. Jim Satterfield and his wife have pioneered the method, which they call multimodality therapy. And it works. The original intention was not to prevent delinquency, but to help children with hyperactivity. But a ten-year follow up of these hyperactive children revealed an unexpected bonus. Satterfield found that only 8 per cent of those who received the multimodality therapy had been arrested for three or more crimes, as compared with 19 per cent of hyperactives who had only been treated with drugs; 25 per cent of those treated solely with medication had eventually been imprisoned compared with 11 per cent of those receiving the combined treatment. Satterfield's programme can cut a hyperactive child's chances of becoming a criminal in half.

This is a wonderful example of the success of combining the biological and psychological sciences. In this treatment parents, who feel at a total loss when confronted with their children's behaviour, are taught about its causes, and how it is a childhood disease like the familiar ones of measles or mumps. Knowledge about the disorder means that they get less angry and feel less impotent. The drug Ritalin is also prescribed to control the hyperactivity – or rather to raise arousal level, so that the children do not seek such extreme sensations. The children are not verbally fluent – it's almost as if they lack an internal language – so they are actively encouraged and trained to talk about their problems. By this form of mental physiotherapy, the connections are strengthened to help link behaviour and its consequences. Satterfield's centre can play it rough – if a child has threatened to kill its parents, the therapists will simulate the threat, which usually upsets the child; empathy, the ability to conceive of someone else's pain, is thus inculcated into a brain which is less than naturally adapted to the notion.

The centre believes that the behaviour is not the result of deep-seated psychological problems, it's seen as a brain problem, an action resulting from raw biological causes. The children smash the 'Mummy' doll not because of a psychological problem with Mummy, but because they like to smash things. There is nothing symbolic in their actions – the hitting of people or breaking of things are just an expression of uncontrolled anger and rage.

Drug intervention can neutralize the effect of brain dysfunction. We remember the case of Mark, the model pupil who went off the rails at the age of thirteen; his grades collapsed and he began indulging in macabre and brutal fantasies, before taking a magnum pistol to school. Mercifully, damage was identified in the right temporal and frontal lobes, which could be treated through anti-depressive tablets. Not everyone will be susceptible to this sort of miracle salvage; but the point about Mark is that someone knew where to look, and that once that effort had been made, the solution itself was relatively simple. Psychotherapy might have been able to describe his problem, but not to diagnose it.

That's not to say that treatment is simple, easy or quick. There's a lot of natural damage to reverse. And that's particularly true in the case of the juvenile psychopath, such as Else and Michael, whom we met in Chapter 8.

Michael's verbal and physical violence, even at the age of three, deeply upset his mother. He was constitutionally restless, a bully, had a violent temper, tantrums, and was precociously sexually active. Attempts to discipline the child were futile, since disapproval went ignored. His mother had to watch him every minute, because he was prone to torture both his sister and his little brother.

In desperation, the family turned to the Satterfield multi-modal treatment. Part of it was to remedy Michael's failure to connect actions with consequences. He was rewarded with tokens, or chips, when he had done something good – the chips could be traded for otherwise forbidden treats. The chip system has to be in constant operation, and is basic, positive training for children with a need far greater than in normal youngsters to be told and told again and again and again. Drugs are used to calm the rages – and the calm helps them to concentrate more on the lessons. Michael, too, was given the shock treatment of seeing puppets act out the threat to kill his brother and sister – he was confronted with the concept of another person's pain, and was helped to make the connection with his own misdeeds. There is constant and regular dialogue with parent or therapist, but this is not psychotherapy – everything is conducted on a simple, pragmatic level. It is like teaching someone to walk again, after a car accident: one step, slowly, at a time. Children like Michael never knew how to feel, how to connect, how to empathize: it is an experience they have to acquire.

No one would say Michael is an angel, but the progress so far has been remarkable. Any child, of course, blitzed with such attention, would improve; the fact is that a structural brain fault was discerned early enough in his life, and action taken to repair it.

Else was the angelic youngster with a taste for running her father down with the family jeep, who tried to amputate the fingers of her classmates with a cigar cutter. She was also fascinated by fire, and had set fire to previous pets, seriously injuring two of them.

She, and her parents, have all undergone the gruelling and varied Satterfield regime. Now, Else has apparently acquired, by dogged coaching, the normal sense of right and wrong, guilt and conscience, that most children acquire at the age of 4 or 5. It's common sense: catch the child early before the grooves of criminal behaviour are formed and there is a chance of getting the child out of the offending rut. The difference is that this is being done before the child has become enmeshed in the criminal justice system. And that's possible only by identifying the symptoms of the developing mind to crime.

Once the basic acknowledgment of the link between crime and brain abnormality has been made, the way is open for a wide range of practical, positive interventions. We have already mentioned, during the course of the book, several ways forward, but two others deserve a mention.

The first place we should look for help is the delivery room. Drugs and alcohol cause damage to the growing foetus, and during birth the child can be starved of oxygen if the umbilical cord becomes entangled. Although less than 5 per cent of the population suffered from birth complications and early childhood rejection, these cases account for nearly one fifth of all violent crime. We can argue as long as we like about what matters more, the birth trauma or the rejection – the likelihood is that one is linked to the other – but at least two of the leading specialists in the field believe that the simplest and most effective method to cut crime would be to improve prenatal and perinatal care.

A second approach is developing as we write. We have shown the consistent results linking crime to low arousal levels in the brain. This has the double effect of making the subject hungry for ever more extreme sensations, and of failing to awaken him to the dangers of what he is doing. We have already mentioned the possibility of drug treatment, and the raising of levels of the neurotransmitter, serotonin. Now, it seems, there may be a drug-free route to the enhancement of the arousal system.

Described as 'aerobics for the mind', biofeedback is one of those therapies which cause the raising of conventional eyebrows. Yet there is no doubt that individuals can be taught to control various functions such as heart rate and relaxation by hooking themselves up to a monitor which measures these specific brain activities. It's rather like a video game, except that it is controlled not by the hands but by the very power of the brain.

Researchers now believe that just as biofeedback can help people lower their heart rate and increase their relaxation, it can also be used to raise arousal levels. In a very small number of pilot studies, children have been monitored by machines which measure the theta waves in the brain. Children with low arousal demonstrate greater theta activity and drowsiness. What the children see is a traditional, Packman video game. They learn that the more they concentrate, the more they reduce their own theta waves and the faster they can complete the game. After an average of thirty sessions, at two sessions a week, there is a discernible improvement in concentration and school performance. The US prison service is currently testing the method at one of its juvenile correction centres. It is too early yet to assess the results, but the case of Cary suggests that there may be good reason for optimism.

Cary was different – and difficult – from the moment he was born. Aggressive and violent, he would return from the birthday parties of other infants with his pockets bulging with stolen toys. At first his mother, a successful businesswoman, and his father, an attorney, hoped that it was merely a childhood phase, but Cary's behaviour grew more extreme. He was a grade F pupil at school, which he rarely attended. At the age of 9, he would stay out all night until apprehended by the police. At the age of 14 he stole a car. He took, and sold, drugs. Cary was locked up for twelve months in a detention centre in Utah. His parents tried every psychotherapeutic remedy available, but in vain.

It was only when the correction centre identified low arousal levels that hope began to dawn for Cary. He began the biofeedback course to aid his concentration and raise his arousal levels. Before long, he found that he could concentrate on books and school work. He was no longer bored, as he had been, at school. His grades improved dramatically. Doctors have established that Cary's theta waves are now 100 per cent normal.

Cary's mother says that the change is 'like a miracle'. All delinquent behaviour has now ceased. Cary has a machine at home, and does his mental workout three times a week. He is now getting straight As and is going to college.

Not every case of delinquency is going to respond in such a fairy-tale fashion as it has with Cary. And the whole issue of intervention remains a moral minefield. But the evidence is overwhelming that crime is in large part due to problems in the brain, that these problems are what distinguish the criminal few from the mischievous many and that they can be identified early on and, to an as yet unknown degree, treated. Many will protest that our new understanding of the brain's biology takes a drably determinist view of human nature. It doesn't. The human spirit, the human genius, can conquer the disabilities of the body. Biology dictates destiny only if it is ignored. And to do that would be a criminal waste of opportunity.

NOTES

CHAPTER ONE

1. Hoyenga, Katharine Blick, and Hoyenga, Kermit T., *Gender-related Differences, Origins and Outcomes*, Allyn & Bacon, Boston and London (1993).
2. Siegal, Larry, 'Introduction', *Crime in Biological, Social and Moral Contexts*, Ellis, L., and Hoffman, H. (eds.), Praeger, New York (1991), pp. i–xiii.
3. Ibid.

CHAPTER TWO

1. Jones, Ann, *Women Who Kill*, Victor Gollancz Ltd., London (1991), pp. xiv–xxi.
2. Daly, Martin, and Wilson, Margo, *Homicide: Foundations of Human Behaviour*, Aldine de Gruyter, New York (1988).
3. Hoyenga, Katharine Blick, and Hoyenga, Kermit T., op.cit.
4. Datesman, Susan, and Scarpitti, Frank, *Women, Crime and Justice*, Oxford University Press, New York and Oxford (1980), 'Introduction'.
5. Steffensmeier, Darrell, and Streifel, Cathy, 'Age, Gender, and Crime Across Three Historical Periods: 1935, 1960, and 1985', *Social Forces*, Vol. 69, No. 3, University of Carolina Press, Pennsylvania (1991), p. 886.
6. Jones, Ann, op.cit., p. 2.
7. Wilson, James, and Herrnstein, Richard J., *Crime and Human Nature*, Simon & Schuster Inc., New York (1985), p. 26.
8. Ibid., p. 130.
9. Ibid., p. 158.
10. Ibid., p. 159.
11. Ibid., p. 159.
12. Ibid., p. 186.
13. Ibid., p. 191.

CHAPTER THREE

1. Ellis, Lee, 'Evidence of Neuroandrogenic Etiology of Sex Roles from a Combined Analysis of Human, Nonhuman, Primate, Nonprimate

Mammalian Studies', *Personal Individual Differences*, Vol. 7, No. 4, Pergamon Journals Ltd., Great Britain (1986), p. 527.

2. Olweus, Dan, *et al.*, 'Circulating Testosterone Levels and Aggression in Adolescent Males: a Causal Analysis', *Psychosomatic Medicine*, Vol. 50, Elsevier Science Publishing Co., New York (1988), p. 261.

3. Ibid., p. 270.

4. Staub, Ervin, 'A Conception of the Determinants and Development of Altruism and Aggression Motives, the Self and the Environment', *Altruism and Aggression*, Zahn-Waxler, Carolyn, *et al.* (eds.), Cambridge University Press, Cambridge (1986).

5. Dalton, Katharina, *Premenstrual Syndrome Goes to Court*, Peter Andrew Publishing Co., (1990), p. 75.

CHAPTER FOUR

1. Hoyenga, Katharine Blick, and Hoyenga, Kermit T., *Psychobiology: the Neuron and Behavior*, Brooks/Cole Publishing Co., California (1988), p. 3.

2. Ibid., p. 1.

3. Ellis, Lee, and Coontz, Phyllis D., 'Androgens, Brain Functioning and Criminality: the Neurohormonal Foundation of Antisociality', *Crime in Biological, Social and Moral Contexts*, Praeger, New York (1991), p. 26.

4. Ellis, Lee, 'Monoamine Oxidase and Criminality: Identifying an Apparent Biological Marker for Antisocial Behaviour', *Journal of Research in Crime and Delinquency*, Vol. 28, No. 2, Sage Publications Inc., Beverley Hills, CA (1991), p. 229.

5. Ibid., p. 231.

6. Hoyenga, Katharine Blick, and Hoyenga, Kermit T., op. cit.

7. Farringdon, David P., 'Implications of Biological Findings for Criminological Research', *The Causes of Crime*, Mednick, Sarnoff, *et al.* (eds.), Cambridge University Press, Cambridge (1987), p. 58.

8. Ellis, Lee, and Coontz, Phyllis D., op. cit., p. 175.

CHAPTER FIVE

1. Yeudall, Lorne, *et al.*, 'A Neuropsychosocial Theory of Persistent Criminality: Implications for Assessment and Treatment', *Advances in Forensic Psychology and Psychiatry*, Rieber, Robert W. (ed.), Vol. 2, Ablex Publishing Co., New Jersey (1987), p. 120.

CHAPTER SIX

1. Mednick, Sarnoff, Moffitt, Terrie, Gabrielli, William jr., and Hutchings, Barry, 'Genetic Factors in the Etiology of Criminal Behaviour', *The*

Causes of Crime, Mednick, Sarnoff, *et al.* (eds.), Cambridge University Press, Cambridge (1987), p. 74.

2. Mednick, Sarnoff, 'Crime in the Family Tree', *Psychology Today* (1985), p. 60.
3. Mednick, Sarnoff, *et al.* (eds.), *The Causes of Crime*, op. cit., p. 80.
4. Hollin, Clive R., *The Psychology of Crime*, Routledge, London and New York (1989), p. 30.
5. Lewis, Dorothy Otnow, *et al.*, 'Perinatal Difficulties: Head and Face Trauma and Child Abuse in the Medical History of Seriously Delinquent Children', *American Journal of Psychiatry*, 136.4A (1979), p. 422.
6. Ibid.
7. Lewis, Dorothy Otnow, *et al.*, 'The Medical Assessment of Seriously Delinquent Boys: a Comparison of Pediatric Psychiatric Neurological Records', *Journal of Advanced Health Care*, Vol. 3 (1982), p. 160.

CHAPTER SEVEN

1. Mednick, Sarnoff, *et al.* (eds.), *The Causes of Crime*, op. cit., p. 80.
2. Hare, Dr. Robert D., *Without Conscience*, Warner Books, London and Boston (1993), p. xi.
3. Ibid.
4. Ibid., p. 147.
5. Ibid., p. 130.

CHAPTER EIGHT

1. Ibid., p. 3.
2. Ibid., p. 52.
3. Ibid., p. 61.
4. Ibid., p. 36.
5. Ibid., p. 68.
6. Ibid., p. 207.
7. Yeudall, Lorne, personal communication.
8. Hare, Dr. Robert D., op. cit., p. 190.
9. Ibid., p. 191.
10. Ibid., p. 210.
11. Hare, Dr. Robert D., op. cit., p. 72.
12. Raine, Adrian, and Scerbo, Angela, 'Biological Theories of Violence', *Neurophysiology of Aggression*, Milner, Joel (ed.), Kluwer Academic, Boston (1991), p. 8.

CHAPTER NINE

1. Dalton, Katharina, op. cit.
2. Ibid.

3. Ibid.
4. Ibid.

CHAPTER TEN

1. Rosenbaum, A., 'Neuropsychology of Marital Aggression', *Neuropsychology of Aggression*, op. cit. (1991).
2. Hare, Dr. Robert D., op. cit., p. 113.

CHAPTER ELEVEN

1. Hucker, S., *et al.*, 'Neuropsychological Impairment in Pedophiles', *Canadian Journal Behav. Sci./Rev. Canadian Sci. Comp.*, 18(4), (1986), p. 446.
2. Ibid., p. 446.
3. Bain, J. (M.D.), 'Sex Hormones in Pedophiles', *Annals of Sex Research*, Vol. 1 (1988), p. 452.
4. Hucker, S., *et al.*, op. cit., p. 445.
5. Thiessen, Del, 'Hormonal Correlates of Sexual Aggression', *Crime in Biological, Social and Moral Contexts*, op. cit., p. 155.

CHAPTER TWELVE

1. Gelles, Richard J., and Straus, Murray A., 'Violence in the American Family', *Journal of Social Issues*, Vol. 35, No. 2 (1979).

CHAPTER THIRTEEN

1. Raine, Adrian, op. cit., p. 311.
2. Dalton, Katharina, op. cit., p. 1.
3. Ibid., p. 90.
4. Lubell, Adele, 'Does Steroid Abuse Cause—or Excuse—Violence?', *The Physician and Sports Medicine*, Vol. 17, No. 2 (1989), p. 176.
5. Ibid., p. 180.
6. Ibid., p. 178.
7. Cullen, Robert, *The Killer Department*, Orion, London (1993).
8. Tancredi, Laurence R., and Volkow, Nora, 'Neural Substrates of Violent Behaviour: Implications for Having a Public Policy', *Int. J. of Law and Psychiatry*, Vol. 11 (1988), p. 47.
9. Lewis, Dorothy Otnow, *et al.*, 'Neuropsychiatric, Psychoeducational and Family Characteristics of 14 Juveniles Condemned to Death in the United States', *Am. J. of Psychiatry*, 145:5 (1988), p. 588.
10. Raine, Adrian, *The Psychopathology of Crime*, Academic Press Inc., San Diego and New York (1993), p. 2.
11. Ibid., p. 315.

12. Hoyenga, Katharine Blick, personal communication.
13. Raine, Adrian, op. cit., p. 315.

CHAPTER FOURTEEN

1. Zuckerman, Marvin, *Psychobiology of Personality*, Cambridge University Press, Cambridge (1991), p. 360.
2. Satterfield, James, 'Childhood Diagnostic and Neurophysiological Predictors of Teenage Arrest Rates: an Eight Year Prospective Study', *The Causes of Crime*, op. cit., p. 146.
3. Moffitt, Terrie, and Henry, Bill, 'Neuropsychological Studies of Juvenile Delinquency and Juvenile Violence', *Neuropsychology of Aggression*, op. cit., p. 69.
4. Ibid., p. 73.
5. Buikhuisen, W., 'Cerebral Dysfunction and Persistent Juvenile Delinquency', *The Causes of Crime*, op. cit., p. 186.
6. Ibid., p. 170.
7. Ibid., p. 173.
8. Satterfield, James, *The Causes of Crime*, op. cit., p. 163.
9. Wayt Gibbs, W., 'Seeking The Criminal Element', *Scientific American* (1995), p. 77.
10. Ibid., p. 77.
11. Ibid., p. 78.

REFERENCES

General References

Chusid, Joseph G. (M.D.), *Correlative Neuroanatomy and Functional Neurology*, 18th edn., Lange Medical Publications (1982).

Daly, Martin, and Wilson, Margo, *Homicide: Foundations of Human Behavior*, Aldine de Gruyter, New York (1988).

Datesman, Susan K., and Scarpitti, Frank R. (eds.), 'Female Delinquency and Broken Homes: a Reassessment', *Women, Crime and Justice*, Oxford University Press, New York and Oxford (1980), pp. 129–49.

Denno, Deborah W., *Biology and Violence*, Cambridge University Press, Cambridge (1990).

Denno, Deborah W., *Biology, Crime, and Violence: New Evidence*, University of Pennsylvania (1986).

Ellis, Lee, and Hoffman, Harry (eds.), *Crime in Biological, Social, and Moral Contexts*, Praeger, New York (1991).

Eysenck, H. J., 'Personality Theory and the Problem of Criminality', *The Inequality of Man*, Temple Smith, London (1973), pp. 30–80.

Faulk, Malcolm, *Basic Forensic Psychiatry*, Blackwell Scientific Publications, Oxford (1988).

Flor-Henry, Pierre, 'Cerebral Basis of Psychopathology', *Influence of Gender on Psychopathology*, John Wright, Boston and Bristol (1983), pp. 97–116.

Grove, William M., and Cicchetti, Dante (eds.), *Thinking Clearly about Psychology, Vol. 2: Personality and Psychopathology*, University of Minnesota Press (1991).

Hollin, Clive R., *Psychology and Crime: an Introduction to Criminological Psychology*, Routledge, London and New York (1989).

Hoyenga, Katharine Blick, and Hoyenga, Kermit T., *Gender-related Differences, Origins and Outcomes*, Allyn & Bacon, Boston and London (1993).

—— *Psychobiology: the Neuron and Behaviour*, Brooks/Cole Publishing Co., California (1988).

Lamb, Michael E., Brown, Ann L., and Rogoff, Barbara (eds.), *Advances in Developmental Psychology*, Vol. 4, Lawrence Erlbaum Assoc., New Jersey (1986).

Liebman, Jeffrey M., and Cooper, Steven J., *The Neuropharmacological Basis of Reward*, Clarendon Press, Oxford (1989).

Lumsden, Charles J., and Wilson, Edward O., *Genes, Mind, and Culture: the Coevolutionary Process*, Harvard University Press, Cambridge, Massachusetts (1981).

Mednick, Sarnoff A., Moffitt, Terrie E., and Stack, Susan A. (eds.), *The Causes of Crime*, Cambridge University Press, Cambridge (1987).

Milner, Joel S., *Neuropsychology of Aggression*, Kluwer Academic Publishers, Boston (1991).

Panksepp, Jaak, 'The Neurochemistry of Behavior', *Ann. Rev. Psychol.*, Vol. 37 (1986), pp. 77–107.

Plomin, Robert, *Genes, Brain, and Behavior*, McHugh, Paul, and McCusick, Victor (eds.), Raven Press, New York, Vol. 69, Association for Research in Nervous and Mental Disease.

Prins, H., *Criminal Behaviour: an Introduction to Criminology and the Penal System*, Tavistock, London (1982).

Raine, Adrian, *The Psychopathology of Crime: Criminal Behavior as a Clinical Disorder*, Academic Press, Inc., New York (1993).

Raine, Adrian, and Scerbo, Angela, 'Biological Theories of Violence', *Neuropsychology of Aggression*, Kluwer Academic Publishers, Boston (1991), pp. 1–25.

Rieber, Robert W. (ed.), *Advances in Forensic Psychology and Psychiatry*, Vol. 2, Ablex Publishers Co., New Jersey (1987).

Rutter, Michael, and Casaer, Paul (eds.), *Biological Risk Factors for Psychosocial Disorders*, Cambridge University Press, Cambridge (1991).

Taylor, Lawrence, *Born to Crime: the Genetic Causes of Criminal behavior*, Greenwood Press, Westport, Connecticut (1984).

Wilson, Glenn, 'Aggression and Crime', *The Great Sex Divide*, Peter Owen, London (1989), pp. 115–31.

Wilson, James Q., and Herrnstein, Richard J., *Crime and Human Nature*, Simon & Schuster, Inc., New York (1985).

Wolfgang, Marvin E., and Weiner, Neil Alan (eds.), *Criminal Violence*, Sage Publications, Beverly Hills, CA (1982).

Yeudall, L. T., *et al.*, 'A Neuropsychosocial Theory of Persistent Criminality: Implications for Assessment and Treatment', *Advances in Forensic Psychology and Psychiatry*, Vol. 2, Ablex Publishers Co., New Jersey (1987), pp. 119–91.

Yochelson, Samuel, and Samenow, Stanton E., *The Criminal Personality – Vol. 1: a Profile for Change*, Jason Aronson, New York (1976).

Yochelson, Samuel, and Samenow, Stanton E., *The Criminal Personality – Vol. 2: the Change Process*, Jason Aronson, New York (1977).

Yochelson, Samuel, and Samenow, Stanton E., *The Criminal Personality – Vol. 3: the Drug User*, Jason Aronson, New York (1986).

Zuckerman, Marvin, *Psychobiology of Personality*, Cambridge University Press, Cambridge (1991).

Chapter References

CHAPTER ONE

Barlow, George W., 'Nature-nurture and the Debates Surrounding Ethnology and Sociobiology', *American Zoology*, Vol. 31 (1991), pp. 286–96.

Bayer, Ronald, 'Crime, Punishment and the Decline of Liberal Optimism', *Crime and Delinquency* (1981), p. 169.

Cullen, Robert, *The Killer Department*, Orion, London (1993).

Ellis, Lee, 'Universal Behavioral and Demographic Correlates of Criminal Behavior: Toward Common Ground in the Assessment of Criminological Theories', *Crime in Biological, Social and Moral Contexts*, Ellis, Lee, and Hoffman, Harry (eds.), Praeger, New York (1991), pp. 38–49.

—— 'Introduction: the Nature of the Biosocial Perspective', *Crime in Biological, Social and Moral Contexts*, Ellis, Lee, and Hoffman, Harry (eds.), Praeger, New York (1991), pp. 3–17.

—— 'Conceptualizing Criminal and Related Behavior from a Biosocial Perspective', *Crime in Biological, Social and Moral Contexts*, Ellis, Lee, and Hoffman, Harry (eds.), Praeger, New York (1991) (a), pp. 18–35.

—— and Hoffman, Harry, 'Views of Contemporary Criminologists on Causes and Theories of Crime', *Crime in Biological, Social and Moral Contexts*, Ellis, Lee, and Hoffman, Harry (eds.), Praeger, New York (1991) (b), pp. 52–8.

—— 'The Evolution of Violent Criminal Behavior and its Non-legal Equivalent', *Crime in Biological, Social and Moral Contexts*, Ellis, Lee, and Hoffman, Harry (eds.), Praeger, New York (1991) (c), pp. 61–79.

—— 'The Evolution of Collective Counter Strategies to Crime: from the Primate Control Role to the Criminal Justice System', 'Evolutionary and Genetic Aspects', *Crime in Biological, Social and Moral Contexts*, Ellis, Lee, and Hoffman, Harry (eds.), Praeger, New York (1991) (d), pp. 81–99.

Gelles, Richard J., and Straus, Murray A., 'Violence in the American Family', *Journal of Social Issues*, Vol. 35, No. 2 (1979), pp. 15–39.

Gordon, Robert A., 'Research on IQ, Race, and Delinquency: Taboo or Not Taboo?', *Taboos in Criminology*, Sagarin, Edward (ed.), Sage, Beverly Hills, CA (1980), p. 37.

Jeffery, Ray C., 'Sociobiology and Criminology: the Long Lean Years of the Unthinkable and the Unmentionable', *Taboos in Criminology*, Sagarin, Edward (ed.), Sage, Beverly Hills, CA (1980), pp. 115–23.

Levin, Michael E., 'Science with Taboos: an Inherent Contradiction', *Taboos in Criminology*, Sagarin, Edward (ed.), Sage, Beverly Hills, CA (1980), pp. 23–35.

Prins, Herschel A., 'Diminished Responsibility and the Sutcliffe Case: Legal, Psychiatric and Social Aspects (A 'Layman's' View)', *Med. Sci. Law*, Vol. 23, No. 1 (1983), pp. 17–24.

Sagarin, E. (ed.), *Taboos in Criminology*, Sage, Beverly Hills, CA (1980).

Siegal, Larry, 'Foreword', *Crime in Biological, Social and Moral Contexts*, Ellis, Lee, and Hoffman, Harry (eds.), Praeger, New York (1991), pp. i–xiii.

Straus, M., and Gelles, J., 'Societal Change and Change in Family Violence from 1975–1985 as Revealed by Two National Surveys', *Journal of Marriage and Family*, Vol. 48 (1986), pp. 465–79.

CHAPTER TWO

Adler, Freda, 'The Interaction between Women's Emancipation and Female Criminology: a Cross Cultural Perspective', *Women, Crime, and Justice*, Datesman, Susan K. and Scarpitti, Frank R. (eds.), Oxford University Press, New York and Oxford (1980), pp. 150–65.

Arch, Elizabeth C., 'Risk-taking: a Motivational Basis for Sex Differences', *Psychological Reports*, Vol. 73, Lewis and Clark College, Portland, Oregon (1993).

Baldwin, John D., 'The Role of Sensory Stimulation in Criminal Behavior, with Special Attention to the Age Peak in Crime', Introduction, *Crime in Biological, Social and Moral Contexts*, Ellis, Lee, and Hoffman, Harry (eds.), Praeger, New York (1991).

Berch, Daniel B., and Bender, Bruce G. (eds.), 'Sex Chromosome Abnormalities and Human Behavior', *AAAS Selected Symposium*, Westview Press, Inc., Colorado (1990).

Buikhuisen, W., 'Cerebral Dysfunction and Persistent Juvenile Delinquency', *The Causes of Crime*, Mednick, Sarnoff, Moffitt, Terrie, and Stack, Susan (eds.), Cambridge University Press, Cambridge (1987).

Cairns, Robert B., 'An Evolutionary and Developmental Perspective on Aggressive Patterns', *Altruism and Aggression*, by Zahn-Waxler, C., Academic Press, New York (1986), pp. 58–87.

Cameron, Mary Owen, *The Booster and the Snitch*, Collier-Macmillan Ltd., London (1964).

Campbell, Anne, *The Girls in the Gang*, Basil Blackwell, Oxford (1984).

Chesney-Lind, Meda, 'Women and Crime: the Female Offender', *Journal of Women in Culture and Society*, Vol. 12, No. 1 (1986).

Coontz, Phyllis D., 'Androgens, Brain Functioning and Criminality: the Neurohormonal Foundations of Antisociality', *Crime in Biological, Social and Moral Contexts*, Ellis, Lee, and Hoffman, Harry (eds.), Praeger, New York (1991), pp. 162–93.

Daly, Martin, and Wilson, Margo, *Homicide: Foundations of Human Behavior*, Aldine De Gruyter, New York (1988).

Datesman, Susan K., and Scarpitti, Frank R. (eds.), 'Patterns of Female Crime', *Women, Crime, and Justice*, Oxford University Press, New York and Oxford (1980) (a), pp. 167–91.

—— 'The Extent and Nature of Female Crime', *Women, Crime, and Justice*, Oxford University Press, New York and Oxford (1980), pp. 3–53.

—— 'Unequal Protection for Males and Females in the Juvenile Court', *Women, Crime, and Justice*, Oxford University Press, New York and Oxford (1980) (b), pp. 300–19.

—— 'Women's Crime and Women's Emancipation', *Women, Crime, and Justice*, Oxford University Press, New York and Oxford (1980), pp. 355–76.

—— 'Female Delinquency and Broken Homes: a Reassessment', *Women, Crime, and Justice*, Oxford University Press, New York and Oxford (1980) (c), pp. 129–49.

Davis, Anthony T., and Kosky, Robert J., 'Attempted Suicide in Adelaide and Perth: Changing Rates for Males and Females, 1971-1987', *Medical Journal of Australia*, Vol. 154 (1991), pp. 666–70.

Davis, Simon, 'Men as Success Objects and Women as Sex Objects: a Study of Personal Advertisements', *Sex Roles*, Vol. 23, Nos. 1–2, Plenum Publishing Co., New York and London (1980), pp. 43–51.

Denno, Deborah W., 'Gender, Crime, and the Criminal Law Defences', *Journal of Criminal Law and Criminology*, Vol. 85, No. 1 (1994) (a).

—— 'Gender, Crime, and the Defenses', *Legal Implications of Genetics*, Vol. 85, No. 1 (1994)(b).

—— 'Early Cognitive Functioning: Sex and Race Differences', *International Journal of Neuroscience*, Vol. 16 (1982), Gordon and Breach Science Publishers, Great Britain, pp. 159–72.

Dinitz, Simon, and Conrad, John P., 'The Dangerous Two Per Cent', *Critical Issues in Juvenile Delinquency*, David Schichor (ed.), (1980), pp. 139–55.

Dodge, Kenneth A., 'Social Information-processing Variables in the Development of Aggression and Altruism in Children', *Altruism and aggression*, Zahn-Waxler, C. *et al.* (eds.), Cambridge University Press, Cambridge (1986), pp. 280–302.

Doyle, *et al.*, *The Painthouse: Words from an East End Gang*, Penguin Books, Harmondsworth (1972).

Ebbe, Obi N. I., 'The Correlates of Female Criminality in Nigeria', *International Journal of Comparative and Applied Criminal Justice*, Vol. 9, No. 1 (1993).

Eisenberg, Nancy, and Miller, Paul A., 'Empathy, Sympathy, and Altruism: Empirical and Conceptual Links', *Critical Issues in the Study of Empathy*, Cambridge University Press, Cambridge (1987)(b), pp. 1–13.

—— and Fabes, Richard A., Bustamante, Denise, and Mathy, Robin M., 'Physiological Indices of Empathy', *Empathy and its Development*, Cambridge University Press, Cambridge (1987) (a), pp. 380–5.

—— and Mussen, Paul H., 'Biology and Prosocial Behavior', *The Roots of Prosocial Behavior in Children*, Cambridge University Press, Cambridge (1989).

—— and Fabes, Richard A., and Miller, Paul A., 'The Evolutionary and Neurological Roots of Prosocial Behavior', *Crime in Biological, Social and Moral Contexts*, Ellis, Lee, and Hoffman, Harry (eds.), Praeger, New York (1991), pp. 247–51.

Ellis, Lee, 'Sex Differences in Criminality: an Explanation Based on the Concept of R/K Selection', *Mankind Quarterly*, Vol. 30 (1989), pp. 17–37.

—— 'Evidence of Neuroandrogenic Etiology of Sex Roles from a Combined Analysis of Human, Nonhuman, Primate and Nonprimate Mammalian Studies', *Personal Individual Differences*, Vol. 7, No. 4, Pergamon Journals Ltd. (1986), pp. 519–52.

—— see reference for Chapter One (1991) (a).

—— see reference for Chapter One (1991) (c).

—— and Coontz, Phyllis D., 'Androgens, Brain Functioning, and Criminality: the Neurohormonal Foundations of Antisociality', *Crime in Biological, Social and Moral Contexts*, Ellis, Lee, and Hoffman, Harry (eds.), Praeger, New York (1991), pp. 162–93.

—— and Hoffman, Harry: see reference for Chapter One (1991) (b).

Eme, Robert F., 'Sex-role Stereotypes and the Epidemiology of Child Psychopathology', *Sex Roles and Psychopathology*, Widom, Cathy Spatz (ed.), Plenum Press, New York (1984).

—— 'Sex Differences in Childhood Psychopathology: a Review', *Psychological Bulletin*, Vol. 86, No. 3 (1979), pp. 574–95.

Eron, Leonard D., and Huesmann, L. Rowell, 'The Role of Television in the Development of Prosocial and Antisocial Behavior', *Development of Antisocial and Prosocial Behavior*, Olweus, Dan, Block, Jack, and Radke-Yarrow, Marian (eds.), Academic Press, Inc., New York (1986), pp. 285–314.

Eysenck, S. B. G., 'Social Class, Sex, and Response to a Five-part Personality Inventory', *Educational and Psychological Measurement*, Vol. XX, No. 1 (1960), p. 47.

Farley, F., 'The Big T in Personality', *Psychology Today*, (1986), pp. 44–52.

Farringdon, David P., 'Implications of Biological Findings for Criminological Research', *The Causes of Crime*, Mednick, Sarnoff, Moffitt, Terrie, and Stack, Susan (eds.), Cambridge University Press, Cambridge (1994), pp. 43–63.

—— 'Longitudinal Analyses of Criminal Violence', *Criminal Violence*, Wolfgang, Marvin (ed.), Sage Publications, Beverly Hills, CA (1982), p. 171.

—— 'Stepping Stones to Adult Criminal Careers', *Development of Antisocial and Prosocial Behaviour*, Olweus, Dan, Block, Jack, and Radke-Yarrow, Marian (eds.), Academic Press, New York (1986), pp. 359–84.

—— and Loeber, Rolf, and Van Kammen, Welmoet B., 'Long-term Criminal Outcome of Hyperactivity – Impulsivity – Attention Deficit and Conduct Problems in Childhood', *Straight and Devious Pathways from Childhood to Adulthood*, Robins, Lee N., and Rutter, Michael (eds.), Cambridge University Press, Cambridge (1990), pp. 63–81.

Feiring, Candice, and Lewis, Michael, 'The Transition from Middle Child-hood to Early Adolescence: Sex Differences in the Social Network and Perceived Self-competence', *Sex Roles*, Vol. 24, Nos. 7-8, Plenum Publishing Co., New York (1991), pp. 489–509.

Feshbach, Seymour, and Feshbach, Norma Deitch, 'Aggression and Altruism: a Personality Perspective', *Altruism and Aggression – Biological and Social Origins*, Zahn-Waxler, Carolyn, and Cummings, E. Mark, and Iannotti, Ronald (eds.), Cambridge University Press, Cambridge (1986), pp. 189–217.

Fingerhut, Lois A. (M.A.), and Kleinman, Joel C. (Ph.D.), 'International and Interstate Comparisons of Homicide among Young Males', *JAMA*, Vol. 263, No. 24 (1990), pp. 3292–95.

Flor-Henry, P., 'Gender, Hemispheric Specialization and Psychopathology', *Social Science and Medicine*, Vol. 12B, Pergamon Press Ltd. (1978), pp. 155–62.

Frost, L. A., Moffitt, T. E., and McGee, R., 'Neuropsychological Correlates of Early Adolescent Psychopathology', *Abstracts*.

Gandelman, Ronald, 'Gonadal Hormones and Sensory Function', *Neuroscience and Biobehavioral Reviews*, Vol. 7, Ankho International Inc., U.S.A. (1983), pp. 1–17.

Geschwind, N., and Galaburda, A., 'Cerebral Lateralisation, Biological Mechanisms, Associations, Pathology', *Archives of Neurology*, Vol. 42 (1985), pp. 521–52.

Giallombardo, Rose, 'Female Delinquency', *Critical Issues in Juvenile Delinquency*, by David Schichor (1980), pp. 63–82.

Gladue, Brian A., 'Aggressive Behavioral Characteristics, Hormones, and Sexual Orientation in Men and Women', *Aggressive Behavior*, Vol. 17, Wiley-Liss, Inc., U.S.A. (1991), pp. 314–26.

Glover, John H., 'A Case of Kleptomania by Covert Sensitization', *British Journal of Clinical Psychology*, 24 (1985), pp. 213–6

Gordon, Robert A.: see reference for Chapter One.

Gove, Walter R., 'The Effect of Age and Gender on Deviant Behavior: a Biopsychosocial Perspective', *Gender and the Life Course*, Rossi, Alice S. (ed.), Aldine (1985), pp. 115–43.

—— and Wilmoth, Charles., 'Risk, Crime, and Neurophysiologic Highs: a Consideration of Brain Processes that May Reinforce Delinquent and Criminal Behavior', *Crime in Biological, Social and Moral Contexts*, Ellis, Lee, and Hoffman, Harry (eds.), Praeger, New York (1991), pp. 143–145.

Haft, Marilyn G., 'Women in Prison: Discriminatory Practices and Some Legal Solutions', *Women, Crime, and Justice*, Datesman, Susan, and Scarpitti, Frank (eds.), Oxford University Press, New York and Oxford (1980), pp. 320–37.

Haley, Kathleen, 'Mothers Behind Bars: a Look at their Parental Rights', *Women, Crime, and Justice*, Datesman, Susan, and Scarpitti, Frank (eds.), Oxford University Press, New York and Oxford (1980), pp. 339–53.

Hanson, R. A., *et al.*, 'Age and Gender Differences in Empathy and Moral Reasoning among Adolescents', *Child Study Journal*, Vol. 15 (1985), pp. 181–8.

Hartnagel, Timothy F., 'Modernization, Female Social Roles, and Female Crime: a Cross-national Investigation', *The Sociological Quarterly*, Vol. 23 (1982), pp. 477–90.

Helleday, Jan, *et al.*, 'Personality Characteristics and Platelet MAO Activity in Women with Congenital Adrenal Hyperplasia (CAH)', *Psychoneuroendocrinology*, Vol. 18, Nos. 5–6, Pergamon Press, U.S.A. (1993), pp. 343–54.

Hill, Gary D., and Crawford, Elizabeth M., 'Women, Race, and Crime', *Criminology*, Vol. 28, No. 4 (1990), p. 601.

Hills, Stuart L., 'Crime and Deviance on a College Campus: the Privilege of Class', *Humanity and Society*, Vol. 6 (1982), pp. 257–66.

Hinde, Robert A., 'Some Implications of Evolutionary Theory and Comparative Data for the Study of Human Prosocial and Aggressive Behaviour', *Development of Antisocial and Prosocial Behaviour*, Olweus, Dan, Block, Jack, and Radke-Yarrow, Marian (eds.), Academc Press, New York (1986).

Hines, Melissa, 'Prenatal Gonadal Hormones and Sex Differences in Human Behaviour', *Psychological Bulletin*, Vol. 92, No 1 (1982), pp. 56–80.

Hinshaw, Stephen P., 'On the Distinction Between Attentional Deficits/Hyperactivity and Conduct Problems/Aggression in Child Psychopathology', *Psychological Bulletin*, Vol. 101, No. 3 (1987), pp. 443–63.

Hoffman, Martin L., 'The Contribution of Empathy to Justice and Moral Judgment', *Empathy and its Development*, Eisenberg, Nancy (ed.), Cambridge University Press, Cambridge (1987), pp. 47–79.

Houston, H. G., and McClelland, R. J., 'Age and Gender Contributions to Intersubject Variability of the Auditory Brainstem Potentials', *Biol. Psychiatry*, Vol. 20 (1985), pp. 419–30.

Hoyenga, Katharine Blick, and Hoyenga, Kermit T., *Gender-related Differences, Origins and Outcomes*, Allyn & Bacon, Boston and London (1993).

Hoyenga, Katharine Blick, *Sex Differences in Human Stratification: a Biosocial Approach*, Praeger, New York (1993), pp. 139–55.

Inciardi, James A., 'Women, Heroin and Property Crime', *Women, Crime and Justice*, Datesman, Susan, and Scarpitti, Frank (eds.), Oxford University Press, New York and Oxford (1980), pp. 214–21.

Jacobs, Lucia F. *et al.*, 'Evolution of Spatial Cognition: Sex-specific Patterns of Spatial Behavior Predict Hippocampal Size', *Proc. Natl. Acad. Sci.*, Vol. 87 (1990), pp. 6349–52.

Jones, Ann, *Women Who Kill*, Victor Gollancz Ltd., London (1991), pp. xiv–xxix.

Kandel, Elizabeth, and Mednick, Sarnoff A., 'IQ as a Protective Factor for Subjects at High Risk for Antisocial Behavior', *Journal of Consulting and Clinical Psychology*, Vol. 56, No. 2 (1988), pp. 224–6.

345

Katz, David L. (M.D.), *et al.*, 'Brief Communication', *Journal of Nervous and Mental Disease*, Vol. 175, No. 5, Williams & Wilkins Co., U.S.A. (1987), pp. 306–8.

Katz, Jack, *Seductions of Crime*, Basic Books, Inc., New York (1988).

Kerns, Kimberly A., and Berenbaum, Sheri A., 'Sex Differences in Spatial Ability in Children', *Behavior Genetics*, Vol. 21, No. 4, Plenum Publishing, New York (1991), pp. 383–96.

Klein, Dorie, 'The Etiology of Female Crime: a Review of the Literature', *Women, Crime and Justice*, Datesman, Susan, and Scarpitti, Frank (eds.), Oxford University Press, New York and Oxford (1980), pp. 70–105.

Klein, Malcolm W., 'Watch Out for that Last Variable', *The Causes of Crime*, Mednick, Sarnoff, Moffitt, Terrie, and Stack, Susan (eds.), Cambridge University Press, Cambridge (1987), pp. 25–41.

Klemke, Lloyd W., 'Exploring Juvenile Shoplifting', *Sociology and Social Research*, Vol. 67, No. 1 (1982), pp. 59–72.

Kupke, T., 'Sex Differences in the Neuropsychological Functioning of Epileptics', *Journal of Consulting and Clinical Psychology*, Vol. 47 (1979), pp. 1128–30.

Le Blanc, Marc, 'Family Dynamics, Adolescent Delinquency, and Adult Criminality', *Psychiatry* (United States), Vol. 55, No. 4 (1992), pp. 336–53.

—— 'Two Processes of the Development of Persistent Offending: Activation and Escalation', *Straight and Devious Pathways from Childhood to Adulthood*, Robins, Lee N., and Rutter, Michael (eds.), Cambridge University Press, Cambridge (1990), pp. 83–100.

Lehmann, Dietrich, 'Mapping, Spatial Analysis, and Adaptive Time Segmentation of EEG/ERP Data', *Brain Electrical Potentials and Psychopathology*, Shaglass, C. *et al.* (eds.), Elsevier Pub. Co. Inc. (1986), p. 27.

—— 'A Clinical Follow-up of Delinquent Males: Ignored Vulnerabilities, Unmet Needs, and the Perpetuation of Violence', *J. Am. Acad. Child Adolesc. Psychiatry*, Vol. 33, No. 4 (1994), pp. 518–28.

—— 'A Follow-up of Female Delinquents: Maternal Contributions to the Perpetuation of Deviance', *J. Am. Acad. Child Adolesc. Psychiatry*, Vol. 30, No. 2 (1991), pp. 197–201.

—— 'Special Article: from Abuse to Violence: Psychophysiological Consequences of Maltreatment', *J. Am. Acad. Child Adolesc. Psychiatry*, Vol. 31, No. 3 (1992), pp. 383–91.

Lewis, Richard S., and Harris, Lauren Julius, 'The Relationship between Cerebral Lateralization and Cognitive Ability: Suggested Criteria for Empirical Tests', *Brain and Cognition*, Vol. 8, Academic Press, New York (1988), pp. 275–90.

—— and Kampiner, N. Laura, 'Sex Differences in Spatial Task Performance of Patients With and Without Unilateral Cerebral Lesions', *Brain and Cognition*, Vol. 6, Academic Press, New York (1987), pp. 142–52.

Lykken, David T., 'Fearlessness, its Carefree Charm and Deadly Risks', *Psychology Today* (1982), pp. 20–8.

Maccoby, Eleanor E., 'Gender and Relationships', *American Psychologist*, Vol. 45, No. 4, American Psychological Assocation, Inc. (1990), pp. 513–20.

—— 'Social Groupings in Childhood: their Relationship to Prosocial and Antisocial Behavior in Boys and Girls', *Development of Antisocial and Prosocial Behavior*, Olweus, Dan, Block, Jack, and Radke-Yarrow, Marian (eds.), Academic Press, New York (1986), pp. 263–84.

Macdonald, Eileen, *Shoot the Women First*, Fourth Estate, London (1991).

Magnusson, David, and Bergman, L. R., 'A Pattern Approach to the Study of Pathways from Childhood to Adulthood', *Straight and Devious Pathways from Childhood to Adulthood*, Robins, Lee N., and Rutter, Michael (eds.), Cambridge University Press, Cambridge (1980), pp. 101–15.

Mannuzza, Salvatore, *et al.*, 'Childhood Predictors of Psychiatric Status in the Young Adulthood of Hyperactive Boys: a Study Controlling for Chance Associations', *Straight and Devious Pathways from Childhood to Adulthood*, Robins, Lee N., and Rutter, Michael (eds.), Cambridge University Press, Cambridge (1990), p. 279.

Marcus, Robert F., 'Naturalistic Observation of Cooperation, Helping, and Sharing and their Associations with Empathy and Affect', *Altruism and Aggression*, Zahn-Waxler, Carolyn, and Cummings, E. Mark, and Iannotti, Ronald (eds.), Cambridge University Press, Cambridge (1986), pp. 256–79.

Maughan, Barbara, and Pickles, Andrew, 'Adopted and Illegitimate Children Growing Up', *Straight and Devious Pathways from Childhood to Adulthood*, Robins, Lee N., & Rutter, Michael (eds.), Cambridge University Press, Cambridge (1990), pp. 36–7.

McCaghy, Charles H., and Cernkovich, Stephen A., *In American Society*, Macmillan Publishing Co., New York (1987).

McCord, Joan, 'Long-term Perspectives on Parental Absence', *Straight and Devious Pathways from Childhood to Adulthood*, Robins, Lee N., and Rutter, Michael (eds.), Cambridge University Press, Cambridge (1990), pp. 117–34

McCord, Joan, 'A Thirty-year Follow-up of Treatment Effects', *American Psychologist*, American Psychological Association, Inc., U.S.A. (1978), pp. 284–9.

McGuinness, Diane, *When Children Don't Learn, Basic Books, Inc.*, New York (1985).

Mednick, Sarnoff A., 'Primary Prevention of Juvenile Delinquency', *Critical Issues in Juvenile Deliquency* (1980), pp. 263–77.

—— *et al.*, 'EEG as a Predictor of Antisocial Behavior', *Criminology*, Vol. 19, No. 2 (1981), pp. 219–29.

Meyer-Bahlburg, Heino F. L., and Ehrhardt, Anke A., 'Prenatal Sex Hormones and Human Aggression: a Review, and New Data on Progestogen Effects', *Aggressive Behavior*, Vol. 8, Alan R. Liss, Inc., New York (1982), pp. 39–62.

Meyer-Bahlburg, Heino F. L., 'Aggression, Androgens, and the XYY Syndrome', *Sex Differences in Behavior*, John Wiley & Sons, London (1974).

Miller, Walter B., 'Lower Class Culture as a Generating Milieu of Gang Delinquency', *Journal of Social Issues*, Vol. 14 (1958), pp. 5–19.

—— 'The Molls', published by permission of Transaction Society, Inc., Vol. 11 (1973), *Women, Crime and Justice*, Datesman, Susan, and Scarpitti, Frank (eds.), Oxford University Press, New York and Oxford (1980).

Moffitt, Terrie E., 'Juvenile Delinquency and Attention Deficit Disorder: Boys' Developmental Trajectories from Age 3 to Age 15', *Child Development*, Vol. 61, Society for Research in Child Development, Inc., U.S.A. (1990), pp. 893–910.

—— 'Neuropsychological Assessment of Executive Function in Self-reported Delinquents', *Development and Psychopathology*, Vol. 1 (1989), pp. 105–18.

—— and Henry, Bill, 'Neuropsychological Studies of Juvenile Delinquency and Juvenile Violence', *Neuropsychology of Aggression*, Kluwer Academic Publishers, Boston (1991), pp. 67–91.

Moore, Joan, Vigil, Diego, and Garcia, Robert, 'Residence and Territoriality in Chicano Gangs', *Social Problems*, Vol. 31, No. 2 (1983), pp. 182–94.

Moyer, Carole, 'Sex Differences in Behavior', *Sex Differences in Aggression*, John Wiley & Sons, New York/London (1974), pp. 335–72.

Munro, Pam, and Govier, Ernest, 'Dynamic Gender-Related Differences in Dichotic Listening Performance', *Neuropsychologia*, Vol. 31, No. 4, Pergamon Press Ltd., Great Britain (1993), pp. 347–53.

Mussen, Paul, 'Commentary on Part II', *Empathy and its Development*, Cambridge University Press, Cambridge (1987), pp. 185–91.

Naylor, Cecile E., Wood, Frank B., and Flowers, D. Lynn, 'Physiological Correlates of Reading Disability', *Perspectives on Dyslexia*, Vol. 1, John Wiley & Sons Ltd. (1990), pp. 141–62.

Noller, P., 'Sex Differences in Non Verbal Communication: Advantages Lost or Supremacy Regained', *Australian Journal of Psychology*, Vol. 38 (1986), pp. 23–32.

Nunney, L., 'Group Selection, Altruism and Structured Demi Models', *The American Naturalist*, Vol. 126 (1985), pp. 212–30.

Nyborg, Helmuth, 'The Neuropsychology of Sex-related Differences in Brain and Specific Abilities', *The Neuropsychology of Individual Differences*, Vernon, Philip A. (ed.), Academic Press, Inc., New York (1994), pp. 59–113.

Olweus, Dan, *et al.*, *Development of Antisocial and Prosocial Behavior*, Academic Press, Inc., Orlando (1986).

—— 'Bullying at School, What We Know and What We Can Do', *Understanding Children's Worlds*, Blackwell, U.S.A. (1993).

—— 'Circulating Testosterone Levels and Aggression in Adolescent Males: a Causal Analysis', *Psychosomatic Medicine*, Vol. 50, Elsevier Science Publishers Co., Inc., New York (1988), pp. 261–72.

Opolot, James S. E., 'Analysis of Crime in Africa by the Mass Media in the 1960s and 1970s', *International Journal of Comparative and Applied Criminal Justice*, Vol. IV, No. 1 (1980).

Otnow Lewis, D., 'The Development of the Symptom of Violence', *Child and Adolescent Psychiatry*, Lewis, Melvin (ed.), Williams & Wilkins Co., Baltimore, pp. 331–40

Panksepp, Jaak, 'The Psychobiology of Prosocial Behaviors: Separation Distress, Play, and Altruism', *Altruism and Aggression, Biological and Social Origins*, Zahn-Waxler, Carolyn, and Cummings, E. Mark, and Iannotti, Ronald, Cambridge University Press, Cambridge (1986), pp. 19–57.

Rahav, Giora, and Ellis, Lee, 'International Crime Rates and Evolutionary Theory: an Application of the R/K Selection Concept to Human Populations', *Crime in Biological, Social, and Moral Contexts*, Ellis, Lee, and Hoffman, Harry (eds.), Praeger, New York (1991).

Reinisch, June Machover, 'Prenatal Exposure to Synthetic Progestins Increases Potential for Aggression in Humans', *Science*, Vol. 211, American Association for the Advancement of Science (1981), pp. 1171–73.

—— and Sanders, Stephanie A., 'A Test of Sex Differences in Aggressive Response to Hypothetical Conflict Situations', *Journal of Personality and Social Psychology*, Vol. 50, No. 5, American Psychological Association, Inc. (1986), pp. 1045–49.

—— et al., 'Hormonal Contributions to Sexually Dimorphic Behaviour: Development in Humans', *Psychoneuroendocrinology*, Vol. 16, Pts 1–3 (1991), pp. 213–78.

Remillard, G. M., 'Sexualictal Manifestations Predominate in Women with Temporal Lobe Epilepsy', *Neurology*, Vol. 33 (1983), pp. 323–30.

Resnick, S. M., et al., 'Sensation Seeking in Opposite Sex Twins: an Effect of Prenatal Hormones', *Behavior Genetics*, Vol. 23, No. 4 (1993), pp. 323–29.

Rivera, Beverly, and Widom, Cathy Spatz, 'Childhood Victimization and Violent Offending', *Violence and Victims*, Vol. 5, No. 1, Springer Publ. Co., U.S.A. (1990), pp. 19–35.

Robins, Lee N., 'The Consequences of Conduct Disorder in Girls', *Development of Antisocial and Prosocial Behavior*, Olweus, Dan, Block, Jack, and Radke-Yarrow, Marian (eds.), Academic Press, Inc., London (1986).

—— and Rutter, Michael, *Straight and Devious Pathways from Childhood to Adulthood*, Cambridge University Press, Cambridge (1990).

Rockett, Ian R. H., and Smith, Gordon S., 'Homicide, Suicide, Motor

Vehicle Crash, and Fall Mortality: United States' Experience in Comparative Perspective', *American Journal of Public Health*, Vol. 79, No. 10 (1989), pp. 1396–1400.

Rodin, Ernst A. (M.D.), 'Psychomotor Epilepsy and Aggressive Behavior', *Journal of Arch. Gen. Psychiatry*, Vol. 28 (1973), pp. 210–4.

Rowe, David C., 'Inherited Dispositions Toward Learning Delinquent and Criminal Behavior: New Evidence', *Crime in Biological, Social, and Moral Contexts*, Ellis, Lee, and Hoffman, Harry (eds.), Praeger, New York (1991), pp. 121–33.

Rutter, Michael, 'Resilience in the Face of Adversity: Protective Factors and Resistance to Psychiatric Disorder', *British Journal of Psychiatry*, Vol. 147 (1985), pp. 598–611.

—— 'Temperament, Personality and Personality Disorder', *British Journal of Psychiatry*, Vol. 150 (1987), pp. 443–58.

—— *et al.*, 'Adult Outcome of Institution-reared Children: Males and Females Compared', *Straight and Devious Pathways from Childhood to Adulthood*, Robins, Lee N., and Rutter, Michael (eds.), Cambridge University Press, Cambridge (1990), pp. 135–57.

Satterfield, James H., 'Childhood Diagnostic and Neurophysiological Predictors of Teenage Arrest Rates: an Eight-year Prospective Study', *The Causes of Crime*, Mednick, Sarnoff, Moffitt, Terrie, Stack, Susan (1987)(a)

—— and Schell, Anne M., 'Childhood Brain Function Differences in Delinquent and Non-delinquent Hyperactive Boys', *Electroencephalography and Clinical Neurophysiology*, Vol. 57, Elsevier Scientific Publishers, Ireland, Ltd. (1984), pp. 199–207.

—— *et al.*, 'A Prospective Study of Delinquency in 110 Adolescent Boys with Attention Deficit Disorder and 88 Normal Adolescent Boys', *American Journal of Psychiatry*, Vol. 139, No. 6 (1982), pp. 795–8.

—— *et al.*, 'Multimodality Treatment', *Journal of Arch. Gen. Psychiatry*, Vol. 36 (1979), pp. 965–74.

—— *et al.*, 'Prediction of Antisocial Behavior in Attention-deficit Hyperactivity Disorder Boys from Aggression/defiance Scores', *Journal of Am. Acad. Child Adolesc. Psychiatry*, Vol. 33, No. 2 (1994)(a), pp. 185–90.

—— *et al.*, 'Preferential Neural Processing of Attended Stimuli in Attention-deficit Hyperactivity Disorder and Normal Boys', *Psychophysiology*, Vol. 31, Cambridge University Press, U.S.A. (1994) (b), pp. 1–10.

—— *et al.*, *Therapeutic Interventions to Prevent Delinquency in Hyperactive Boys*, American Academy of Child and Adolescent Psychiatry (1987) (b), pp. 56–64.

—— *et al.*, 'Three-year Multimodality Treatment Study of 100 Hyperactive Boys', *Journal of Pediatrics*, Vol. 98, No. 4 (1981), pp. 650–5.

Schellenbach, Cynthia J., 'Biological Correlates of Gender Differences in

Violence', *Neuropsychology of Aggression*, Kluwer Academic Publishers, Boston (1991), p. 117.

Simpson, Sall S., 'Caste, Class and Violent Crime: Explaining Differences in Female Offending', *Criminology*, Vol. 29, Pt. 1 (1991), pp. 115–35.

Smith, David James, *The Sleep of Reason*, Century, London (1994).

Sommers, Ira, and Baskin, Deborah, 'Sex, Race, Age, and Violent Offending', *Violence and Victims*, Vol. 7, No. 3, Springer Publishers Co. (1992), pp. 191–201.

South, Scott J., and Messner, Steven F., 'The Sex Ration and Women's Involvement in Crime: a Cross-national Analysis', *Sociological Quarterly*, Vol. 28, No. 2, JAI Press, Inc., U.S.A. (1986), pp. 171–88.

Steffensmeier, Darrell J., and Allan, Emilie Andersen, 'Sex Disparities in Arrests by Residence, Race, and Age: an Assessment of the Gender Convergence/Crime Hypothesis', *Justice Quarterly*, Vol. 5, No. 1, Academy of Criminal Justice Sciences (1988), pp. 54–80.

Steffensmeier, Darrell, *et al.*, 'Development and Female Crime: a Cross-national Test of Alternative Explanations', *Social Forces*, Vol. 68, No. 1, University of North Carolina Press, Pennsylvania (1989), pp. 262–83.

Steffensmeier, Darrell, and Streifel, Cathy, 'Age, Gender, and Crime across Three Historical Periods: 1935, 1960, and 1985', *Social Forces*, Vol. 69, No. 3, University of North Carolina Press (1991), pp. 869–94.

Strayer, F. F., and Noel, J. M., 'The Prosocial and Antisocial Functions of Preschool Aggression: an Ethological Study of Triadic Conflict Among Young Children', *Altruism and Aggression*, Zahn-Waxler, Carolyn, *et al.* (eds.), Cambridge University Press, Cambridge (1986), pp. 107–31.

Thoma, Stephen J., 'Estimating Gender Differences in the Comprehension and Preference of Moral Issues', *Developmental Review*, Vol. 6, Academic Press, Inc. (1986), pp. 165–80.

Thomas, Mark, *Every Mother's Nightmare: the Killing of James Bulger*, Pan Books Ltd., London (1993).

Trivers, Robert, *Social Evolution*, The Benjamin/Cummings Publishing Co. Inc., California (1985).

Widom, Cathy Spatz (ed.), *Sex Roles and Psychopathology*, Plenum Press, New York/London (1984).

Wiggins, Jerry S., and Pincus, Aaron L., 'Personality: Structure and Assessment', *Annual Review of Psychology*, Vol. 43 (1992), pp. 473–504.

Wilson, William Julius, 'Studying Inner-city Social Dislocations: the Challenge of Public Agenda Research', *American Sociological Review*, Vol. 56 (1991), pp. 1–14.

Wong, Maria Mei-ha, and Csikszentmihalyi, Mihaly, 'Affiliation Motivation and Daily Experience: Some Issues on Gender Differences', *Journal of Personality and Social Psychology*, Vol. 60, No. 1 (1991), pp. 154–64.

Youniss, James, 'Development in Reciprocity through Friendship', *Altruism and Aggression – Biological and Social Origins*, Zahn-Waxler, Carolyn, Cummings, E. Mark, and Iannotti, Ronald (eds.), Cambridge University Press, Cambridge (1986), pp. 88–106.

Zahn-Waxler, Carolyn, 'Conclusions: Lessons from the Past and a Look to the Future', *Altruism and Aggression – Biological and Social Origins*, Zahn-Waxler, Carolyn, Cummings, E. Mark, and Iannotti, Ronald (eds.), Cambridge University Press, Cambridge (1986), pp. 303–24.

Zaslow, Martha J., and Hayes, Cheryl D., 'Sex Differences in Children's Response to Psychosocial Stress: Toward a Cross-context Analysis', *Advances in Developmental Psychology*, Lamb, Michael E., *et al.* (eds.), (1986), pp. 285–337.

Zeitlin, H., *The Natural History of Psychiatric Disorder in Children*, Oxford University Press, Oxford (1986).

Zuckerman, Marvin, 'Sensation Seeking and its Biological Correlates', *Psychological Bulletin*, Vol. 88, No. 1 (1980), pp. 187–214.

CHAPTER THREE

Bancroft, John, 'Reproductive Hormones', *Biological Factors for Psychosocial Disorders*, Rutter, Michael, and Casaer, Paul, Cambridge University Press, Edinburgh (1991), pp. 260–310.

Baucom, Donald H., 'Relation Between Testosterone Concentration, Sex Role Identity, and Personality Among Females', *Journal of Personality and Social Psychology*, Vol. 48 (1985), pp. 1218–26.

Becker, Jill B., *et al.*, *Behavioral Endocrinology*, The MIT Press, Massachusetts and London (1992).

Blumenthal, Susan J. (M.D., M.P.A.), and Nadelson, Carol C. (M.D.), 'Late Luteal Phase Dysphoric Disorder (Premenstrual Syndromes): Clinical Implications', *Journal of Clinical Psychiatry*, Vol. 49, No. 12 (1988), pp. 469–74.

Bremner, Charles, 'Hormone Count at Root of Lawyers' Machismo', *Times Tribune* Nov. (1990), p. 9.

Buchanan, Christy Miller, 'Are Adolescents the Victims of Raging Hormones: Evidence for Activational Effects of Hormones on Moods and Behavior at Adolescence', *Psychological Bulletin*, Vol. 111, No. 1 (1992), pp. 62–107.

Buss, Arnold H., *Aggression Pays*, Singer, J. (ed.), Academic Press, New York and London (1971), pp. 7–24.

Cairns, Robert B.: see reference for Chapter Two.

Carriere, Elizabeth, 'Young Trial Lawyers are Especially High in Testosterone', Dept. of Psychology, Atlanta, Georgia.

Casper, Robert F. (M.D.), Graves, Gillian R. (M.D.), and Reid, Robert L. (M.D.), 'Objective Measurement of Hot Flushes Associated with the Premenstrual Syndrome', *Fertility and Sterility*, Vol. 47, No. 2 (1987).

Casper, Robert F. (M.D.), and Hearn, Margaret T. (Ph.D.), 'The Effect of Hysterectomy and Bilateral Oophorectomy in Women with Severe Premenstrual Syndrome', *Ovariectomy for PMS,* Vol. 162, No. 1, Medical Research Council Group (1989), pp. 105–9.

Casson, P. (M.D.), Hahn, P. M. (M.Sc.), Van Vugt, D. A. (Ph.D.), and Reid, R. L. (M.D.), 'Lasting Response to Ovariectomy in Severe Intractable Premenstrual Syndrome', Division of Reproductive Endocrinology, Queen's University, Ontario, Canada (1990), pp. 99–106.

Choi, Precilla Y. L. (Ph.D.), and Pope, Harrison G. jr. (M.D.), 'Violence Toward Women and Illicit Androgenic-anabolic Steroid Use', *Annals of Clinical Psychiatry,* Vol. 6, No. 1 (1994), pp. 21–5.

Christiansen, Kerrin, and Winkler, Eike-Meinrad, 'Hormonal, Anthropo-metrical, and Behavioral Correlates of Physical Aggression in !Kung San Men of Namibia', *Aggressive Behavior,* Vol. 18, Wiley-Liss, Inc. (1992), pp. 271–80.

Coontz, Phyllis D.: see reference for Chapter Two.

Cummings, Mark E., Hollenbeck, Barbara, Iannotti, Ronald, Radke-Yarrow, Marian, and Zahn-Waxler, Carolyn, 'Early Organization of Altruism and Aggression: Developmental Patterns and Individual Differences', *Altruism and Aggression – Biological and Social Origins,* Zahn-Waxler, Carolyn, Cummings, Mark E., and Iannotti, Ronald (eds.), Cambridge University Press, Cambridge (1986), pp. 165–88.

Dabbs, James M. jr., *Testosterone and Facial Expressions of Affect and Dominance,* Georgia State University, Atlanta (1990).

—— 'Age and Seasonal Variation in Serum Testosterone Concentration Among Men', *Chronobiology International,*Vol. 7, No. 3, Dept. of Psychology, Georgia State University, Atlanta, Pergamon Press, Great Britain (1990), pp. 245–9.

—— 'Testosterone and Occupational Achievement', Dept. of Psychology, Georgia State University, Atlanta.

—— and de la Rue, Denise, and Williams, Paula M., 'Testosterone and Occupational Choice: Actors, Ministers, and Other Men', *Journal of Personality and Social Psychology,* Vol. 59, No. 6, Dept. of Psychology, Georgia State University, Atlanta (1990), pp. 1261–5.

—— and Hopper, Charles H., and Jurkovic, Gregory J., 'Testosterone and Personality among College Students and Military Veterans', *Personal Individual Differences,* Vol. 11, No. 12, Dept. of Psychology, Georgia State University, Atlanta, Pergamon Press (1990), pp. 1263–9.

—— 'Salivary Testosterone Measurements: Reliability Across Hours, Days, and Weeks', *Physiology and Behavior,* Vol. 48 (1990), Pergamon Press, Great Britain, pp. 83–6.

—— and Frady, Robert L. (Ph.D.), Carr, Timothy S. (Ph.D.), and Besch, Norma F. (Ph.D.), 'Saliva Testosterone and Criminal Violence in Young Adult Prison Inmates', *Psychosomatic Medicine,* Vol. 49, No. 2, Dept. of Psychology, Georgia State University, Atlanta (1987), pp. 175–82.

—— and Ruback, Barry R., Frady, Robert L., Hopper, Charles H., and Sgoutas, Demetrios S., 'Saliva Testosterone and Criminal Violence Among Women', *Personal Individual Differences*, Vol. 9, No. 2, Dept. of Psychology, Georgia State University, Atlanta, Pergamon Press, Great Britain (1988), pp. 269–74.

Dalton, Katharina, *Premenstrual Syndrome Goes to Court*, Peter Andrew Publishing Co. Ltd., Great Britain (1990).

Dittman, R. W., *et al.*, 'Congenital Adrenal Hyperplasia I: Gender Related Behaviour and Attitudes in Female Patients and Sisters', *Psychoneuroendocrinology*, Vol. 15, Pergamon Press, Oxford (1990), pp. 401–20.

—— *et al.*, 'Congenital Adrenal Hyperplasia II: Gender-related Behavior and Attitudes in Female Salt-wasting and Simple-virilizing Patients', *Psychoneuroendocrinology*, Vol. 15, Pergamon Press, Oxford (1990), pp. 421–35.

Ellis, Lee: see reference for Chapter Two (1986).

—— and Coontz, Phyllis D.: see reference for Chapter Two.

Ellison Rodgers, Joann, 'Brain Triggers, Biochemistry and Behavior', *Science Digest* (1983), pp. 60–6.

Eriksson, Elias, 'Effect of Clomipramine on Premenstrual Syndrome', *Acta Psychiatrica Scandinavia*, Vol. 81 (1990), pp. 87–8.

—— 'Serotonergic Agents in the Treatment of Disorders of Anxiety and Impulse Control', *Clinical Neuropharmacology*, Vol. 15, Suppl. 1, Pt. A (1992), pp. 108–346.

—— and Humble, Mats, 'Serotonin in Psychiatric Pathophysiology', *Programme Basic Clinical Pharmacology*, Vol. 3, Karger, Basle, Switzerland (1990), pp. 66–119.

—— *et al.*,'Serum Levels of Androgens are Higher in Women with Premenstrual Irritability and Dysphoria than in Controls', *Psychoneuroendocrinology*, Vol. 17, No. 2/3 (1992), pp. 195–204.

Fraile, I. G., McEwen, B. S., and Pfaff, D. W., 'Comparative Effects of Progesterone and Alphaxalone on Aggressive, Reproductive and Locomotor Behaviors', *Pharmacology, Biochemistry and Behavior*, Vol. 30, Pergamon Press, U.S.A. (1988), pp. 729–35.

Freeman, Ellen (Ph.D.), Rickels, Karl (M.D.), Sondheimer, Steven J. (M.D.), and Polansky, Marcia (Sc.D.), 'Ineffectiveness of Progesterone Suppository Treatment for Premenstrual Syndrome', *JAMA*, Vol. 264, No. 3 (1990), pp. 349–53.

Gandelman, Ronald: see reference for Chapter Two.

Gladue, Brian A., 'Aggressive Behavioral Characteristics, Hormones, and Sexual Orientation in Men and Women', *Aggressive Behavior*, Vol. 17, Wiley-Liss, Inc. (1991), pp. 314–26.

Goleman, Daniel, 'When the Tough Get Going, Maybe It's Time to Check Those Raging Hormones', *Herald Tribune* 18 July (1990).

Gove, Walter R.: see reference for Chapter Two.

Grant, Ellen C. G., and Pryse-Davies, John, 'Effect of Oral Contraceptives on Depressive Mood Changes and on Endometrial Monoamine Oxidase and Phosphatases', *British Medical Journal*, Vol. 3 (1968), pp. 777–80.

Gray, Anna (Ph.D.), Jackson, Douglas (Ph.D.), and McKinlay, John B. (Ph.D.), 'The Relation between Dominance, Anger, and Hormones in Normally Aging Men: Results from the Massachusetts Male Aging Study', *Psychosomatic Medicine*, Vol. 53 (1991), pp. 375–85.

Gunnar, Megan R., 'Human Developmental Psychoneuroendocrinology: a Review of Research on Neuroendocrine Responses to Challenge and Threat in Infancy and Childhood', *Advances in Developmental Psychology*, Lawrence Erlbaum Associates, New Jersey (1986), p. 51.

Hammarbäck, Stefan, *et al.*, 'Cyclical Mood Changes as in the Premenstrual Tension Syndrome During Sequential Estrogen-progestagen Postmenopausal Replacement Therapy', *Acta Obstet. Gynecol. Scand.*, Vol. 64 (1985), pp. 393–7.

Hannan, Charles J., *et al.*, 'Psychological and Serum Homovanillic Acid Changes in Men Administered Androgenic Steroids', *Psychoneuroendocrinology*, Vol. 16, No. 4, Pergamon Press, Great Britain (1991), pp. 335–43.

Harrison, Wilma M. (M.D.), Endicott, Jean (Ph.D.), and Nee, John (Ph.D.), 'Treatment of Premenstrual Dysphoria with Alprazolam', *Arch. Gen. Psychiatry*, Vol. 47 (1990), pp. 270–5.

Hassler, Marianne, 'Testosterone and Artistic Talents', *International Journal of Neuroscience*, Vol. 56, Gordon and Breach Science Publishers, U.K. (1991), pp. 25–38.

Hines, Melissa: see reference for Chapter Two.

Howard, Rick, Gifford, Mervyn, and Lumsden, John, 'Changes in an Electrocortical Measure of Impulsivity During the Menstrual Cycle', *Personal Individual Differences*, Vol. 9, No. 5, Pergamon Press, Great Britain (1988), pp. 917–8.

Huntingford, Felicity A., and Turner, Angela K., *Animal Conflict*, Chapman and Hall, Great Britain (1987).

Kashkin, Kenneth B. (M.D.), and Kleber, Herbert D. (M.D.), 'Hooked on Hormones? An Anabolic Steroid Addiction Hypothesis', *JAMA*, Vol. 262, No. 22 (1989), pp. 3166–70.

Key, Timothy J. A., 'Testosterone, Sex Hormone-binding Globulin, Calculated Free Testosterone, and Oestradiol in Male Vegans and Omnivores', *British Journal of Nutrition*, Vol. 64 (1990), pp. 111–9.

Logue, Camille M. (Ph.D.), and Moos, Rudolf H. (Ph.D.), 'Perimenstrual Symptoms: Prevalence and Risk Factors', *Psychosomatic Medicine*, Vol. 48, No. 6, Elsevier Science Publ. Co., New York (1986), pp. 388–414.

Michael, Richard P. (M.D., Ph.D.), *et al.*, 'Sexual Violence in the United States and the Role of Reason', *American Journal of Psychiatry*, Vol. 140, No. 7 (1983), pp. 883–6.

Miller, Walter B.: see reference for Chapter Two (1980).

Moore, Joan, Vigil, Diego, and Garcia, Robert: see reference for Chapter Two.

Moyer, Carole: see reference for Chapter Two.

Moyer, K. E., 'The Physiology of Aggression and the Implications for Aggression Control', *The Control of Aggression and Violence*, Academic Press, New York/London (1971), pp. 61–92.

Nass, R., and Baker, S., 'Androgen Effects on Cognition: Congenital Adrenal Hyperplasia', *Psychoneuroendocrinology*, Vol. 16 (1991), pp. 189–201.

Nyborg, Helmuth: see reference for Chapter Two.

Olweus, Dan, *et al.*: see reference for Chapter Two (1988).

d'Orban, P. T., and Dalton, J., 'Violent Crime and the Menstrual Cycle', *Psychological Medicine*, Vol. 10, Cambridge University Press, Cambridge (1980), pp. 353–9.

Paikoff, Roberta J., *et al.*, 'Effects of Girls' Hormonal Status on Depressive and Aggressive Symptoms over the Course of One Year', *Journal of Youth and Adolescence*, Vol. 20, No. 2, Plenum Publishing Corporation, New York (1991), pp. 191–215.

Parlee, Mary Brown, 'Menstrual Rhythms in Sensory Processes: a Review of Fluctuations in Vision, Olfaction, Audition, Taste, and Touch', *Psychological Bulletin*, Vol. 93, No. 3 (1983), pp. 539–49.

Persky, Harold, *et al.*, 'Relation of Psychologic Measures of Aggression and Hostility to Testosterone Production in Man', *Psychosomatic Medicine*, Vol. 33, No. 3 (1971), pp. 265–77.

Pope, Harrison G. jr. (M.D.), 'Anabolic-androgenic Steroid Use Among 1,010 College Men', *The Physician and Sports Medicine*, Vol. 16, No. 7 (1988)(a), pp. 75–81.

—— 'Affective and Psychotic Symptoms Associated with Anabolic Steroid Use', *American Journal of Psychiatry*, Vol. 145 (1988)(b), pp. 487–90.

—— and Katz, David L. (M.D.), 'Psychiatric and Medical Effects of Anabolic-androgenic Steroid Use, a Controlled Study of 160 Athletes', *Arch. Gen. Psychiatry*, Vol. 51 (1994), pp. 375–82.

—— and Katz, David L., 'Bodybuilder's Psychosis', *The Lancet* 11 April (1987).

Rada, Richard, *et al.*, 'Plasma Androgens in Violent and Non Violent Offenders', *American Academy of Psychiatry*, Vol. 11 (1983), pp. 149–58.

Rausch, Jeffrey L., and Janowsky, David S., 'Premenstrual Tension: Etiology', *Behavior and the Menstrual Cycle*, Marcel Dekker, Inc., New York (1982), pp. 397–427.

Reinisch, June Machover, and Sanders, Stephanie A.: see reference for Chapter Two (1986).

—— and Sanders, S. A., 'Effects of Prenatal Exposure to Diothystilbestrol (DES) on Hemispheric Laterality in Human Males', *Hormones and Behavior*, Vol. 26 (1992), pp. 62–75.

—— *et al.*: see reference for Chapter Two (1991).

Resnick, S. M.: see reference for Chapter Two.

Rivera-Tovar, Ana D. (Ph.D.), and Frank, Ellen (Ph.D.), 'Late Luteal Phase

Dysphoric Disorder in Young Women', *American Journal of Psychiatry*, 147:12 (1990), pp. 1634–7.

Rubin, Robert T., *et al.*, 'Postnatal Gonadal Steroid Effects on Human Behavior', *Science*, Vol. 211, American Association for the Advancement of Science (1981), pp. 1318–24.

Rubinow, David R., and Schmidt, Peter, 'Mood Disorders and the Menstrual Cycle', *Journal of Reproductive Medicine*, Vol. 32 (1987), pp. 389–94.

—— and Roy-Byrne, Peter (M.D.), 'Premenstrual Syndromes: Overview from a Methodologic Perspective', *American Journal of Psychiatry*, Vol. 141, No. 2 (1984), pp. 163–72.

Sherwin, Barbara B., and Gelfand, Morrie M., 'Sex Steroids and Affect in the Surgical Menopause: a Double-blind, Cross-over Study', *Psychoneuroendocrinology*, Vol. 10, No. 3, Pergamon Press, U.K. (1985), pp. 325–35.

Shute, Valeria J., *et al.*, 'The Relationship Between Androgen Levels and Human Spatial Abilities', *Bulletin of the Psychonomic Society*, Vol. 21, No. 6 (1983), pp. 465–8.

Singer, Jerome L. (ed.), *The Control of Aggression and Violence: Cognitive and Physiological Factors*, Academic Press, New York (1971), pp. 1–5.

—— 'The Psychological Study of Aggression', *The Control of Aggression and Violence: Cognitive and Physiological Factors*, Academic Press, New York (1971).

Stattin, Håkan, and Magnusson, David, *Pubertal Maturation in Female Development*, Lawrence Erlbaum Associates, Publishers, Hove/London (1990).

Staub, Ervin, 'A Conception of the Determinants and Development of Altruism and Aggression Motives, the Self and the Environment', *Altruism and Aggression*, Zahn-Waxler, Carolyn, *et al.* (eds.), Cambridge University Press, Cambridge (1986), pp. 135–164.

Sundblad, C., *et al.*, 'Clomipramine Effectively Reduces Premenstrual Irritability and Dysphoria: a Placebo-controlled Trial', *Acta Psychiatr. Scand.*, Vol. 85 (1992), pp. 38–47.

—— 'Clomipramine Administered During the Luteal Phase Reduces the Symptoms of Premenstrual Syndrome: a Placebo-controlled Trial', *Neuropsychopharmacology*, Vol. 9, No. 2 (1993), pp. 133–45.

—— 'Effect of Clomipramine on Premenstrual Syndrome', *Acta Psychiatr. Scand.*, Vol. 81 (1990), pp. 87–8.

Susman, Elizabeth J., *et al.*, 'Hormones, Emotional Dispositions, and Aggressive Attributes in Young Adolescents', *Child Development*, Vol. 58 (1987), pp. 1114–34.

Tallal, Paula, 'Hormonal Influences in Developmental Learning Disabilities', *Psychoneuroendocrinology*, Vol. 16, Nos. 1–3, Pergamon Press, Great Britain (1991), pp. 203–11.

Thiessen, Del, 'Hormonal Correlates of Sexual Aggression', *Crime in*

Biological, Social and Moral Contexts, Ellis, Lee, and Hoffman, Harry (eds.), Praeger, New York (1991), pp. 153–61.

Thompson, Wendy M., *et al.*, 'Changes in Saliva Testosterone Levels during a 90-day Shock Incarceration Program', *Criminal Justice and Behavior*, Vol. 17, No. 2 (1990), pp. 246–51.

Warren, Michelle P., and Brooks-Gunn, J., 'Mood and Behavior at Adolescence: Evidence for Hormonal Factors', *Journal of Clinical Endocrinology and Metabolism*, Vol. 69, No. 1 (1989), pp. 77–83.

Yates, William R., *et al.*, 'Aggression and Hostility in Anabolic Steroid Users', *Biol. Psychiatry*, Vol. 31 (1992), pp. 1232–4.

CHAPTER FOUR

Arch, Elizabeth C.: see reference for Chapter Two.

Baldwin, John D.: see reference for Chapter Two.

Blaszczynski, Alexander P., 'A Winning Bet: Treatment for Compulsive Gambling', *Psychology Today* (1985), pp. 38–46.

—— and Winter, Simon W., and McConaghy, Neil, 'Plasma Endorphin Levels in Pathological Gambling', *Journal of Gambling Behavior*, Vol. 2 (1), Human Sciences Press, U.S.A. (1986), pp. 3–14.

Bloom, Floyd E., and Lazerson, Arlyne, *Brain, Mind, and Behavior*, W. H. Freeman and Company, New York (1985).

Bourgeois, M., 'Serotonin, Impulsivity and Suicide', *Human Psychopharmacology*, Vol. 6, John Wiley & Sons Ltd., Great Britain (1991), pp. 31–6.

Bridge, T. P., *et al.*, 'Platelet Monoamine Oxidase Activity: Demographic Characteristics' Contribution to Enzyme Activity Variability', *Journal of Gerontology*, Vol. 40 (1985), pp. 23–8.

Brown, C. S., 'Blood Platelet Uptake of Serotonin in Episodic Aggression', *Psychiatry Research*, Vol. 27 (1989), pp. 5–12.

Brown, Gerald L. (M.D.), and Linnoila, Markku I. (M.D., Ph.D.), 'CSF Serotonin Metabolite (5-HIAA) Studies in Depression, Impulsivity, and Violence', *Journal of Clinical Psychiatry*, Vol. 51, Suppl. 4 (1990), pp. 31–41.

—— and Goodwin, F.K., 'Diagnostic, Clinical and Personality Characteristics of Aggressive Men with Low 5-HIAA', *Clinical Neuropharmacology*, Vol. 7, Suppl. 1 (1984), Raven Press, New York.

Brunner, Han G., 'Evidence Found for a Possible "Aggression Gene" ', *Science*, Vol. 260 (1993).

—— *et al.*, 'X-linked Borderline Mental Retardation with Prominent Behavioral Disturbance: Phenotype, Genetic Localization, and Evidence for Disturbed Monoamine Metabolism', *American Journal of Human Genetics*, Vol. 52 (1993), pp. 1032–9.

—— *et al.*, 'Abnormal Behavior Associated with a Point Mutation in the Structural Gene for Monoamine Oxidase A', *Science*, 22 October 1993.

Coccaro, Emil F., 'Central Serotonin and Impulsive Aggression', *British Journal of Psychiatry*, Vol. 155, Suppl. 8 (1989), pp. 52–62.

—— 'Impulsive Aggression and Central Serotonergic System Function in Humans: an Example of a Dimensional Brain–Behavior Relationship', *International Clinical Psychopharmacology*, Vol. 7 (1992), pp. 3–12.

—— and Kavoussi, Richard J., and Lesser, Juliet C., 'Self- and Other-directed Human Aggression: the Role of the Central Serotonergic System', *International Clinical Psychopharmacology*, Vol. 6, Suppl. 6 (1992), pp. 70–83.

—— *et al.*, 'Serotonergic Studies in Patients with Affective and Personality Disorders, *Archives of General Psychiatry*, Vol. 46 (1989), pp. 587–99.

Coontz, Phyllis D.: see reference for Chapter Two.

Coursey, Robert D., Buchsbaum, Monte S., and Murphy, Dennis L., '2-year Follow-up of Subjects and Their Families Defined as At Risk for Psychopathology on the Basis of Platelet MAO Activities', *Neuropsychobiology*, Vol. 8 (1982), pp. 51–6.

—— *et al.*, 'Psychological Characteristics of Subjects Identified by Platelet MAO Activity and Evoked Potentials as Biologically At Risk for Psychopathology', *Journal of Abnormal Psychology*, Vol. 89, No. 2 (1980), pp. 151–64.

Craig, Ian, 'Misbehaving Monoamine Oxidase Gene', *Psychiatric Genetics*, Vol. 4, No. 2 (1994).

Davis, Kenneth L., 'Impulsive Aggression in Personality Disorder: Evidence for Involvement of 5-HT-1 Receptors', *Biological Psychiatry*, Vol. 25 (1989), pp. 84A–89A.

Eisenberg, Nancy, Fabes, Richard A., and Miller, Paul A., 'The Evolutionary and Neurological Roots of Prosocial Behavior', *Crime in Biological, Social and Moral Contexts*, Ellis, Lee, and Hoffman, Harry (eds.), Praeger, New York (1991), pp. 247–51.

Ellis, Lee: see reference for Chapter Two (1986).

—— 'Monoamine Oxidase and Criminality: Identifying an Apparent Biological Marker for Antisocial Behavior', *Journal of Research in Crime and Delinquency*, Vol. 28, No. 2, Sage Publications, Inc., U.S.A. (1991), pp. 227–51.

—— and Coontz, Phyllis D.: see reference for Chapter Two.

Engelberg, Hyman, 'Low Serum Cholesterol and Suicide', *The Lancet*, Vol. 339 (1992), pp. 727–9.

Eriksson, Elias, 'Serotonergic Agents in the Treatment of Disorders of Anxiety and Impulse Control', *Clinical Neuropharmacology*, Vol. 15, Suppl. 1, Pt. A (1992), pp. 108–346.

—— and Humble, Mats, 'Serotonin in Psychiatric Pathophysiology', *Programme Basic Clinical Pharmacology*, Vol. 3, Karger, Basle, Switzerland (1990), pp. 66–119.

Flor-Henry, P., Tomer, R., Kumpula, I., Koles, Z. J., and Yeudall, L. T., 'Neurophysiological and Neuropsychological Study of Two Cases of

Multiple Personality Syndrome and Comparison with Chronic Hysteria', *International Journal of Psychophysiology*, Vol. 10, Elsevier Science Publishers, New York (1990), pp. 151–61.

Fowkes, F. G. R., Leng, G. C., Donnan, P. T., Deary, I. J., Riemersma, R. A., and Housley, E., 'Serum Cholesterol, Triglycerides, and Aggression in the General Population', *The Lancet*, Vol. 340 (1992), pp. 995–8.

Gove, Walter R.: see reference for Chapter Two.

—— and Wilmoth, Charles: see reference for Chapter Two.

Gunnar, Megan R.: see reference for Chapter Three.

Helleday, Jan, *et al.*: see reference for Chapter Two.

Hesselbrock, Michie N. (Ph.D.), and Hesselbrock, Victor M. (Ph.D.), 'Relationship of Family History, Antisocial Personality Disorder and Personality Traits in Young Men At Risk for Alcoholism', *Journal of the Study of Alcohol* (1992), pp. 619–25.

Hokanson, Jack E., Willers, K. R., and Koropsak, Elizabeth, 'The Modification of Autonomic Responses During Aggressive Interchange', pp. 386–91.

Howard, Rick, Gifford, Mervyn, and Lumsden, John: see reference for Chapter Three.

Hoyenga, Katharine Blick, and Hoyenga, Kermit T., *Gender-related Differences, Origins and Outcomes*, Allyn & Bacon, Boston and London (1993).

—— *Psychobiology: the Neuron and Behavior*, Brooks/Cole Publishing Co., California (1988).

Kaplan, 'The Effects of Fat and Cholesterol on Aggressive Behaviour in Monkeys', *Psychosomatic Medicine*, Vol. 52 (1990), pp. 226–7.

Kitahara, M., 'Dietary Tryptophan Ration and Homicide in Western and Southern Europe', *Journal of Orthomolecular Medicine*, Vol. 1 (1986), pp. 13–6.

Kolb, Bryan, and Whishaw, Ian Q., *Fundamentals of Human Neuropsychology*, W. H. Freeman & Co, New York (1990).

Kruesi, M. J. P., 'Cruelty to Animals and CSF', *Psychiatry Research*, Vol. 28 (1989), pp. 115–6.

—— *et al.*, 'Cerebrospinal Fluid Monoamine Metabolites, Aggression, and Impulsivity in Disruptive Behavior Disorders of Children and Adolescents', *Arch. Gen. Psychiatry*, Vol. 47 (1990), pp. 419–26.

Linnoila, Markku (M.D., Ph.D.), De Jong, Judith (Ph.D.), and Virkkunen, Matti (M.D.), 'Family History of Alcoholism in Violent Offenders and Impulsive Fire Setters', *Arch. Gen. Psychiatry*, Vol. 46 (1989), pp. 613–6.

—— and Virkkunen, Matti (M.D.), 'Aggression, Suicidality, and Serotonin', *Journal of Clinical Psychiatry*, Vol. 53, Suppl. 10 (1992), pp. 46–51.

—— *et al.*, 'Low Cerebrospinal Fluid 5-hydroxyindoleacetic Acid Concentration Differentiates Impulsive from Nonimpulsive Violent Behavior', *Life Sciences*, Vol. 33, Pergamon Press Ltd., U.S.A. (1983), pp. 2609–14.

—— *et al.*, 'Serotonin, Violent Behavior and Alcohol', *Toward a Molecular*

Basis of Alcohol Use and Abuse, Janssen, B. (ed.), Birkhausen Verlag, Basle (1994), pp. 155–63.

Luthar, Suniya S. (Ph.D.), and Rounsaville, Bruce J. (M.D.), 'Substance Misuse and Comorbid Psychopathology in a High-risk Group: a Study of Siblings of Cocaine Misusers', *The International Journal of the Addictions*, Vol. 28, No. 5, Marcel Dekker, Inc., U.S.A. (1993), pp. 414–34.

McCanne, Thomas R., 'Methodological and Measurement Issues in a Study of the Neuropsychology of Aggression', *Neuropsychology of Aggression*, Kluwer Academic Publishers, Boston (1991), pp. 27–45.

McKim, William A., *Drugs and Behavior: an Introduction to Behavioral Pharmacology*, Prentice Hall, New Jersey (1991).

McMillen, David L., *et al.*, 'Personality Traits and Behaviors of Alcohol-impaired Drivers: a Comparison of First and Multiple Offenders', *Addictive Behaviors*, Vol. 17, Pergamon Press Ltd., U.S.A. (1992), pp. 407–14.

Morgan, Ross E., *et al.*, 'Plasma Cholesterol and Depressive Symptoms in Older Men', *The Lancet*, Vol. 341 (1993), pp. 75–9.

Myslobodsky, Michael S., and Weiner, Murray, 'Pharmacopsychotherapy in Aberrant Brain Laterality', *Hemisyndromes*, Academic Press, New York (1983), pp. 448–78.

Newcomb, Michael D., and Bentler, Peter M., 'Antecedents and Consequences of Cocaine Use: an Eight-year Study from Early Adolescence to Young Adulthood', *Straight and Devious Pathways from Childhood to Adulthood*, Robin, Lee N., and Rutter, Michael (eds.), Cambridge University Press (1990), pp. 159–81.

Nielsen, David A., *et al.*, 'Suicidality and 5-hydroxyindoleacetic Acid Concentration Associated with a Tryptophan Hydroxylase Polymorphism', *Arch. Gen. Psychiatry*, Vol. 51 (1994).

Olweus, Dan: see reference for Chapter Two (1993).

Resnick, Susan M., *et al.*: see reference for Chapter Two.

Rubin, Robert T., 'The Neuroendocrinology and Neurochemistry of Antisocial Behavior', *The Causes of Crime*, Medenick, Sarnoff, Moffitt, Terrie, and Stack, Susan (eds.), Cambridge University Press, Cambridge (1987), pp. 239–62.

Schalling, D., *et al.*, 'Markers for Vulnerability to Psychopathology: Temperament Traits Associated with Platelet MAO Activity', *Acta Psychiatr. Scand.*, Vol. 76 (1987), pp. 172–82.

Siegal, Jerome M., 'Behavioral Functions of the Reticular Formation', *Brain Research Reviews*, Vol. 1 (1979), pp. 69–105.

Soubrie, P., 'Reconciling the Role of Serotonin Neurons in Human and Animal Behaviour', *Behavioural and Brain Sciences*, Vol. 9 (1986), pp. 319–63.

Swaab, D. F., 'Relation Between Maturation of Neurotransmitter Systems in the Human Brain and Psychosocial Disorders', *Biological Risk Factors for Psychosocial Disorders*, Rutter, Michael, and Casaer, Paul (eds.), Cambridge University Press, Cambridge (1991), pp. 51–66.

Vanyukov, Michael M., *et al.*, 'Antisocial Symptoms in Preadolescent Boys and in Their Parents: Associations with Cortisol', *Psychiatry Research*, Vol. 46, Elsevier Scientific Publishers Ltd., Ireland (1993), pp. 9–17.

Venables, P. H., 'Autonomic Nervous System Factors in Criminal Behavior', *The Causes of Crime*, Mednick, Sarnoff, Moffitt, Terrie, and Stack, Susan (eds.), Cambridge University Press, Cambridge (1987), pp. 110–35.

Virkkunen, Matti, 'Brain Serotonin and Violent Behaviour', *Journal of Forensic Psychiatry* (1992), pp. 171–4.

—— 'CSF Biochemistries, Glucose Metabolism, and Diurnal Activity Rhythms in Alcoholics, Violent Offenders, Fire Setters, and Healthy Volunteers', *Arch. Gen. Psychiatry*, Vol. 51 (1994), pp. 20–7.

—— 'Metabolic Dysfunctions Among Habitually Violent Offenders: Reactive Hypoglycemia and Cholesterol Levels', *The Causes of Crime*, Mednick, Sarnoff, Moffitt, Terrie, and Stack, Susan (eds.), Cambridge University Press, Cambridge (1987), pp. 292–311.

—— and Linnoila, Markku, 'Serotonin in Early Onset, Male Alcoholics with Violent Behaviour', *Annals of Medicine*, Vol. 22 (1990), pp. 327–31.

—— *et al.*, 'Relationship of Psychobiological Variables to Recidivism in Violent Offenders and Impulsive Fire Setters', *Arch. Gen. Psychiatry*, Vol. 46 (1989), pp. 600–1.

Von Knorring, L. L., *et al.*, 'Personality Traits Related to Monamine Oxidase Activity in Platelets', *Psychiatry Research*, Pt. 12 (1984), pp. 11–26.

Waksman, S. A., 'Diet and Children's Behaviour Disorders: a Review of Research', *Clinical Psychology Review*, Vol. 3 (1983), pp. 201–13.

Witten, Mark, 'Of Two Minds', *Saturday Night Science* (1987), pp. 13–16.

Yaryura-Tobias, J.A., *et al.*, 'Violent Behaviour Brain Dysrhythmia and Glucose Dysfunction: a New Syndrome', *Orthomolecular Psychiatry*, Vol. 4, Pt. 3 (1975), pp. 182–8.

Zuckerman, Marvin: see reference for Chapter Two.

CHAPTER FIVE

Bach-Y-Rita, George (M.D.), *et al.*, 'Episodic Dyscontrol: a Study of 130 Violent Patients', *American Journal of Psychiatry*, Vol. 127 (1971), p. 11.

Bloom, Floyd E., and Lazerson, Arlyne: see reference for Chapter Four.

Bryant, Ernest T., Scott, Monte L., and Golden, Charles J., 'Neuropsychological Deficits, Learning Disability, and Violent Behavior', *Journal of Consulting and Clinical Psychology*, Vol. 52, No. 2 (1984), pp. 323–4.

Buikhuisen, W., 'Cerebral Dysfunctions and Persistent Juvenile Delinquency', *The Causes of Crime*, Mednick, Sarnoff, Moffitt, Terrie, and Stack, Susan (eds.), Cambridge University Press, Cambridge (1987), pp. 169–83.

Cohen, P., 'Mechanisms of the Relationship Between Perinatal Problems, Early Childhood Illness and Psychopathology', *Child Development*, Vol. 60 (1989), pp. 701–9.

Eisenberg, N., and Lennon, R., 'Sex Differences in Empathy and Related Capacities', *Psychological Bulletin* (1994), pp. 100–31.

Elliott, Frank A. (M.D.), 'Neurological Findings in Adult Minimal Brain Dysfunction and the Dyscontrol Syndrome', *The Journal of Nervous and Mental Disease*, Vol. 170, No. 11 (1982), pp. 680–7.

Ellis, Lee: see reference for Chapter Two.

——— 'Left- and Mixed-handedness and Criminality: Explanations for a Probable Relationship', *Left-Handedness*, Elsevier Science Publishers B.V., New York (1990), pp. 485–506.

——— and Coontz, Phyllis D.: see reference for Chapter Two.

Flor-Henry, Pierre, 'Gender, Hemispheric Specialization and Psychopathology', *Social Science and Medicine*, Vol. 12B, Pergamon Press Ltd., Oxford (1978), pp. 155–62.

——— 'Sinistrality and Psychopathology', *Left-Handedness*, Elsevier Science Publishers, New York (1990), pp. 415–40.

——— and Koles, Z. J., 'EEG Characteristics of Normal Subjects: a Comparison of Men and Women and of Dextrals and Sinistrals', *Research Communications in Psychology, Psychiatry and Behavior*, Vol. 7, No. 1 (1982), pp. 21–37.

——— et al., 'Neurophysiological and Neuropsychological Study of Two Cases of Multiple Personality Syndrome and Comparison with Chronic Hysteria', *International Journal of Psychophysiology*, Vol. 10, Elsevier Science Publishers, New York (1990), pp. 151–61.

Frost, L. A., Moffitt, T. E., and McGee, R.: see reference for Chapter Two.

Gabrielli, William F. jr., and Mednick, Sarnoff A., 'Sinistrality and Delinquency', *Journal of Abnormal Psychology*, Vol. 89, No. 5 (1980), pp. 654–61.

Geschwind, N., and Galaburda, A.: see reference for Chapter Two.

Goodman, Robert, 'Developmental Disorders and Structural Brain Development', *Biological Risk Factors for Psychosocial Disorders*, Rutter, Michael, and Casaer, Paul (eds.), Cambridge University Press, Cambridge (1980), pp. 21–49.

Gunnar, Megan R.: see reference for Chapter Three.

Heinrichs, R., 'Frontal Cerebral Lesions and Violent Incidents in Chronic Neuropsychiatric Patients', *Biological Psychiatry*, Vol. 25 (1989), pp. 174–8.

Houston, H. G., and McClelland, R. J.: see reference for Chapter Two.

Hoyenga, Katharine Blick, and Hoyenga, Kermit T., *Psychobiology: the Neuron and Behavior*, Brooks/Cole Publishing Co., California (1988).

Kandel, Eric R., and Hawkins, Robert D., 'The Biological Basis of Learning and Individuality', *Scientific American* (1992), pp. 53–9.

Klein, Malcolm W.: see reference for Chapter Two.

Kolb, Bryan, and Whishaw, Ian Q.: see reference for Chapter Four.

Kruk, Menno R., et al., 'Comparison of Aggressive Behavior Induced by Electrical Stimulation in the Hypothalamus of Male and Female Rats',

Progress in Brain Research, Vol. 61, Elsevier Science Publishers, New York (1984), pp. 303–13.

Krynick, V. E., 'Cerebral Dysfunction in Repetitively Assaultive Adolescents', *Journal of Nervous and Mental Disease*, Vol. 166 (1978), pp. 59–67.

Langevin, Ron, *et al.*, 'Brain Damage, Diagnosis, and Substance Abuse Among Violent Offenders', *Behavioral Sciences and the Law*, Vol. 5, No. 1, John Wiley & Sons, U.S.A. (1987), pp. 78–94.

Lehmann, Dietrich: see reference for Chapter Two.

Lewis, Collins E. (M.D.), 'Neurochemical Mechanisms of Chronic Antisocial Behavior (Psychopathy)', *The Journal of Nervous and Mental Disease*, Vol. 179, No. 12, Williams & Wilkins, U.S.A. (1991), pp. 720–7.

Lewis, Richard S., and Kampiner, N. Laura: see reference for Chapter Two.

—— and Harris, Lauren Julius: see reference for Chapter Two.

Lubell, Adele, 'Does Steroid Abuse Cause – or Excuse – Violence?', *The Physician and Sports Medicine*, Vol. 17, No. 2 (1989), p. 176.

Maccoby, Eleanor E.: see reference for Chapter Two (1990).

Mednick, Sarnoff A., *et al.*: see reference for Chapter Two (1981).

Michalewski, Henry J., *et al.*, 'Sex Differences in the Amplitudes and Latencies of the Human Auditory Brain Stem Potential', *Electroencephalography and Clinical Neurophysiology*, Vol. 48, Elsevier/North-Holland Scientific Publishers, Ltd. (1980), pp. 351–6.

Miller, Laurence, 'Neuropsychology of the Aggressive Psychopath: an Integrative Review', *Aggressive Behavior*, Vol. 13, Alan R. Liss, Inc., U.S.A. (1987), pp. 119–40.

Mitchell, William, *et al.*, 'Epilepsy with Fetishism Relieved by Temporal Lobectomy', *The Lancet* (1954), pp. 626–30.

Mungas, Dan, 'Psychometric Correlates of Episodic Violent Behaviour', *British Journal of Psychiatry*, Vol. 152 (1988), pp. 180–7.

Munro, Pam, and Govier, Ernest: see reference for Chapter Two.

Myslobodsky, Michael S., and Weiner, Murray: see reference for Chapter Four.

Nachshon, Israel, 'Hemisphere Dysfunction in Psychopathy and Behavior Disorders', *Hemisyndromes: Psychobiology, Neurology, Psychiatry*, Myslobodsky, Michael (ed.), Academic Press, Inc., New York (1983), pp. 389–414.

—— 'Neurological Bases of Crime, Psychopathy, and Aggression', *Crime in Biological, Social and Moral Contexts*, Ellis, Lee, and Hoffman, Harry, Praeger, New York (1991)(a), pp. 194–203.

—— 'Neuropsychology of Violent Behavior: Controversial Issues and New Developments in the Study of Hemisphere Function', *Neuropsychology of Aggression*, Kluwer Academic Publ., Boston (1991)(b), pp. 93–116.

—— 'Toward Biosocial Approaches in Criminology', *Journal of Social Biological Structure*, Vol. 5, Academic Press Inc., London (1982), pp. 1–9.

—— and Denno, Deborah, 'Violent Behavior and Cerebral Hemisphere Function', *The Causes of Crime*, Mednick, Sarnoff, Moffitt, Terrie, and Stack, Susan (eds.), Cambridge University Press, Cambridge (1987).

Noller, P.: see reference for Chapter Two.

Norris, Joel, 'Bobby Joe Long', *Serial Killers – the Growing Menace*, Arrow Books, London (1990), pp. 186–202.

Nyborg, Helmuth: see reference for Chapter Two.

O'Callaghan, Mark A. J., and Carroll, Douglas, 'The Role of Psychosurgical Studies in the Control of Antisocial Behavior', *The Causes of Crime*, Mednick, Sarnoff, Moffitt, Terrie, and Stack, Susan (eds.), Cambridge University Press, Cambridge (1987), pp. 312–3.

Olweus, Dan: see reference for Chapter Two (1986).

—— 'The Medical Assessment of Seriously Delinquent Boys: a Comparison of Pediatric, Psychiatric, Neurological Records', *Journal of Adolescent Health Care*, Vol. 3 (1982), pp. 160–4.

Otnow Lewis, D., 'Neuropsychiatric, Psychoeducational, and Family Characteristics of 14 Juveniles Condemned to Death in the United States', *American Journal of Psychiatry*, Vol. 145, No. 5 (1988).

—— see reference for Chapter Two, pp. 331–40.

—— *et al.*, 'Biopsychosocial Characteristics of Children who Later Murder: a Prospective Study', *American Journal of Psychiatry*, Vol. 142, No. 10 (1985), pp. 1161–7.

—— 'The Medical Assessment of Seriously Delinquent Boys; a Comparison of Pediatric, Psychiatric, Neurological Records', *Journal of Adolescent Health Care*, Vol. 3 (1982), pp. 160–4.

—— 'Violent Juvenile Delinquents, Psychiatric, Neurological, Psychological, and Abuse Factors', *American Academy of Child Psychiatry*, pp. 307–19.

Piccirilli, Massimo, *et al.*, 'Individual Differences in Cerebral Organization: Influence of Sex and Familial Sinistrality in the Language Lateralization of Strongly Right-handed Subjects', *Functional Neurology*, Vol. 3, No. 3 (1988), p. 285.

Pipe, Margaret-Ellen, 'Atypical Laterality and Retardation', *Psychological Bulletin*, Vol. 104, No. 3 (1988), pp. 343–7.

Raine, Adrian, 'Biosocial Bases of Antisocial and Violent Behavior', *Western Psychological Association, 75th Annual Convention* (1995).

—— *et al.*, 'Selective Reductions in Prefrontal Glucose Metabolism in Murderers', *Society of Biological Psychiatry*, Vol. 36 (1994), pp. 365–73.

Rosenbaum, Alan, *et al.*, 'Head Injury in Partner-abusive Men', *Journal of Consulting and Clinical Psychology*.

Shagass, Charles, *et al.* (eds.), *Brain Electrical Potentials and Psychopathology*, Elsevier, New York (1988).

Siegal, J. M.: see reference for Chapter Four.

Stedman, J., 'Educational Underachievement and Epilepsy: a Study of Children from Normal Schools, Admitted to Special Hospital for Epilepsy', *Early Child Development and Care*, Vol. 9 (1981), pp. 65–82.

Surwillo, Walter W., 'The Electroencephalogram and Childhood Aggression',

Aggressive Behavior, Vol. 6, Alan R. Liss, Inc., U.S.A. (1980), pp. 9–18.

Vanyukov, Michael M., *et al.*: see reference for Chapter Four.

Venables, P. H.: see reference for Chapter Four.

Volavka, Jan, 'Electroencephalogram Among Criminals', *The Causes of Crime*, Medenick, Sarnoff, Moffitt, Terrie, and Stack, Susan (eds.), Cambridge University Press, Cambridge (1987), pp. 137–45.

Voyer, Daniel, and Bryden, M. P., 'Gender, Level of Spatial Ability, and Lateralization of Mental Rotation', *Brain and Cognition*, Vol. 13, Academic Press, Inc., New York (1990), pp. 18–29.

Weiner, Murray and Myslobodsky, Michael S., 'What, Where, and Why?', *Hemisyndromes*, (1983) pp. 448–78.

Wong, Maria Mei-ha, and Csikszentmihalyi, Mihaly: see reference for Chapter Two.

Yeudall, Lorne T., 'Neuropsychological Impairment of Persistent Delinquency', *Journal of Nervous and Mental Disease*, Vol. 170, No. 5 (1982), pp. 257–65.

Yeudall, Lorne T., 'The Neuropsychology of Aggression', prepared for Clarence M. Hincks Memorial Lectures, University of Western Ontario and Ontario Mental Health Foundation (1978).

CHAPTER SIX

Bouchard, Thomas J. jr., 'A Twice-told Tale: Twins Reared Apart', *Thinking Clearly About Psychology, Vol. 2: Personality and Psychology*, Grove, William M., and Cicchetti, Dante (eds.), University of Minnesota Press, Minneapolis (1991), pp. 188–215.

—— and McGue, Matthew, 'Genetic and Rearing Environmental Influences on Adult Personality: an Analysis of Adopted Twins Reared Apart', *Journal of Personality*, Vol. 58, No. 1 (1990), pp. 263–92.

Breakefield, Xandra O., and Cambi, Franca, 'Molecular Genetic Insights into Neurologic Disease', *Annual Review of Neuroscience*, Vol. 10 (1987), pp. 535–94.

Brennan, P. A., and Mednick, S. A., 'Genetic Perspectives on Crime', *Acta Psychiatr. Scand.*, Suppl. 370 (1993), pp. 19–26.

Brennan, P., Mednick, S., and John, Richard, 'Specialization in Violence: Evidence of a Criminal Subgroup', *Criminology*, Vol. 27, No. 3 (1989), pp. 437–53.

Brunner, Han G.: see reference for Chapter Four.

Cannon, Tyrone D., Mednick, Sarnoff A., and Parnas, Josef, 'Two Pathways to Schizophrenia in Children at Risk', *Straight and Devious Pathways from Childhood to Adulthood*, Robins, Lee N., and Rutter, Michael (eds.), Cambridge University Press, Cambridge (1990).

Coccaro, Emil F., Bergeman, C. S., and McClearn, Gerald E., 'Heritability of

Irritable Impulsiveness: a Study of Twins Reared Together and Apart', *Psychiatry Resarch*, Vol. 48, Elsevier Publications Ireland Ltd. (1993), pp. 229–42.

Cohen, P., 'Mechanisms of the Relationship Between Perinatal Problems, Early Childhood Illness and Psychopathology', *Child Development*, Vol. 60 (1989), pp. 701–9.

Coid, B., Lewis, S. W., and Reveley, A. M., 'A Twin Study of Psychosis and Criminality', *British Journal of Psychiatry*, Vol. 162 (1993), pp. 87–92.

Costa, Paul T. jr., and Widiger, Thomas A., 'Introduction', *'Personality Disorders and the Five-factor Model of Personality'*, American Psychological Association (1994), pp. 1–56.

Craig, Ian: see reference for Chapter Four.

Davis, Kenneth L., 'Impulsive Aggression in Personality Disorder: Evidence for Involvement of 5-HT-1 Receptors', *Biological Psychiatry*, Vol. 25 (1989), pp. 84A–89A.

Dawkins, Richard, *The Selfish Gene*, Oxford University Press, Oxford (1976).

Dawkins, Richard, *The Blind Watchmaker*, Penguin Books, Harmondsworth (1991).

Eaves, Lindon J., *et al.*, 'Analyzing Twin Resemblance in Multisymptom Data: Genetic Applications of a Latent Class Model for Symptoms of Conduct Disorder in Juvenile Boys', *Behavior Genetics*, Vol. 23, No. 1 (1993), pp. 5–19.

Ellis, Lee, 'A Biosocial Theory of Social Stratification Derived from the Concepts of Pro/antisociality and R/K Selection', *Politics and the Life Sciences*, Vol. 10 (1991), pp. 5–44.

—— and Coontz, Phyllis D.: see reference for Chapter Two.

Goodman, Robert: see reference for Chapter Five.

Gottesman, Irving I., and Goldsmith, H. Hill, 'Developmental Psychopathology of Antisocial Behavior: Inserting Genes into its Ontogenesis and Epigenesis', *Threats to Optimal Development: Integrating Biological, Psychological, and Social Risk Factors*, Nelson, C. A. (ed.), Lawrence Erlbaum Assoc., New Jersey (1994), pp. 69–104.

Gottfredson, M., 'The True Value of Lambda Would Appear to be Zero: an Essay on Career Criminals', *Criminology*, Vol. 24 (1986), pp. 213–34.

Grove, William M., *et al.*, 'Heritability of Substance Abuse and Antisocial Behavior: a Study of Monozygotic Twins Reared Apart', *Society of Biological Psychiatry*, Vol. 27 (1990), pp. 1293–1304.

Herrnstein, Richard J., and Murray, Charles, *The Bell Curve*, The Free Press, New York (1994).

Hesselbrock, Michie N. (Ph.D.), and Hesselbrock, Victor M. (Ph.D.), 'Relationship of Family History, Antisocial Personality Disorder and Personality Traits in Young Men At Risk for Alcoholism', *Journal Stud. Alcohol*, U.S.A. (1992), pp. 619–25.

Holden, Constance, 'Identical Twins Reared Apart', *Science*, Vol. 207 (1980), pp. 1323–8.

Hoyenga, Katharine Blick, and Hoyenga, Kermit T., *Gender-related Differences, Origins and Outcomes*, Allyn & Bacon, Boston and London (1993).

Lynton, D. T., 'Emergenesis: Genetic Traits That May Not Run in Families', *American Psychologist*, Vol. 47 (1992), pp. 1565–77.

McGue, M., 'A Comparison of Identical Twins Raised Apart', *Behaviour Genetics*, Vol. 6 (1981), pp. 607 *et seq.*

Mednick, Sarnoff, 'Crime in the Family Tree', *Psychology Today* (1985), p. 58.

—— 'Genetic Influences in Criminal Convictions: Evidence from an Adoption Cohort', *Psychology Today* (1984), p. 891.

—— and Gabrielli, William F., 'Genetic Influences in Criminal Convictions: Evidence from an Adoption Cohort', *Science*, Vol. 224 (1984), pp. 891–4.

—— 'Biological Factors in Crime Causation: the Reactions of Social Scientists', *The Causes of Crime*, Mednick, Sarnoff, Moffitt, Terrie, and Stack, Susan (eds.), Cambridge University Press, Cambridge (1987).

—— *et al.*, Genetic Factors in the Etiology of Criminal Behavior, *The Causes of Crime*, Mednick, Sarnoff, Moffitt, Terrie, and Stack, Susan (eds.), Cambridge University Press, Cambridge (1987).

—— *et al.*, 'Biology and Violence', *Criminal Violence*, Wolfgang, Marvin E., and Weiner, Neil Alan (eds.), Sage Publications, London (1982)

—— *et al.*, 'Genetic Factors in Criminal Behavior: a Review', *Development of Antisocial and Prosocial Behavior*, Olweus, Dan, Block, Jack, and Radke-Yarrow, Marian (eds.), Academic Press, New York (1986).

Morell, V., 'Evidence Found for a Possible Aggression Gene', *Science*, Vol. 260 (1993), pp. 1722–3.

Nyborg, Helmuth, 'Good, Bad, and Ugly Questions About Heredity', *Behavioral and Brain Sciences*, Vol. 13, No. 1 (1990), p. 142.

Otnow Lewis, Dorothy: see reference for Chapter Two (1991).

—— 'Perinatal Difficulties, Head and Face Trauma, and Child Abuse in the Medical Histories of Seriously Delinquent Children', *American Journal of Psychiatry*, Vol. 136, No. 4A (1979), pp. 419–23.

Plomin, Robert, 'Genetic Risk and Psychosocial Disorders: Links Between the Normal and Abnormal', *Biological Risk Factors for Psychosocial Disorders*, Rutter, Michael, and Casaer, Paul (eds.), Raven Press, Ltd., New York (1991).

Raine, Adrian, Brennan, Patricia, and Mednick, Sarnoff A., 'Birth Complications Combined with Early Maternal Rejection at Age One Year Predispose to Violent Crime at Age 18 Years', paper presented at the Annual meeting of the American Association for the Advancement of Science, San Francisco, February 1994.

Reid, William H. (M.D., M.P.H.), 'Genetic Correlates of Antisocial Syndromes', *The Psychopath*, Brunner/Mazel, New York (1978).

Reitsma-Street, Marge, *et al.*, 'Pairs of Same-sexed Siblings Discordant for

Antisocial Behaviour', *British Journal of Psychiatry*, Vol. 146 (1985), pp. 415–23.

Robins, Lee N.: see reference for Chapter Two (1986).

Rowe, David C.: see reference for Chapter Two.

Rowe, D. C., 'Genetic Components of Antisocial Behaviour: a Study of 265 Twin Pairs', *Criminology*, Vol. 24, Pt. 3, pp. 513–32.

Rushton, J. Philippe, *et al.*, 'Altruism and Aggression: the Heritability of Individual Differences', *Journal of Personality and Social Psychology*, Vol. 50, No. 6, American Psychological Association, Inc., Washington DC (1986), pp. 1192–8.

Stevenson, Jim, 'Evidence for a Genetic Etiology in Hyperactivity in Children', *Behavior Genetics*, Vol. 22, No. 3 (1992), pp. 338–44.

—— and Graham, Philip, 'Antisocial Behaviour and Spelling Disability in a Population Sample of 13-year-old Twins', *European Child and Adolescent Psychiatry*, Vol. 2, Issue 4, Hogrefe and Huber Publishers (1993)(a), pp. 179–191.

—— *et al.*, 'Hyperactivity and Spelling Disability: Testing for Shared Genetic Aetiology', *J. Child Psychol. Psychiat.*, Vol. 34, No. 7, Pergamon Press Ltd., Great Britain (1993)(b), pp. 1137–51.

Tellegen, Auke, *et al.*, 'Personality Similarity in Twins Reared Apart and Together', *Journal of Personality and Social Psychology*, Vol. 54, No. 6 (1988), pp. 1031–9.

Thapar, Anita, and McGuffin, Peter, 'Is Personality Disorder Inherited? an Overview of the Evidence', *Journal of Psychopathology and Behavioral Assessment*, Vol. 15, No. 4 (1993), pp. 325–45.

Whitney, Glayde, 'On Possible Genetic Bases of Race Differences in Criminality', *Crime in Biological, Social, and Moral Contexts*, Ellis, Lee, and Hoffman, Harry (eds.), Praeger, New York (1991), pp. 135–49.

Widiger, Thomas A., 'Introduction: Personality Disorders and the Five Factor Model of Personality', *Description of Personality Disorders in Personality Disorders*, American Psychological Association, Washington, DC (1994).

Wiggins, Jerry S., and Pincus, Aaron L.: see reference for Chapter Two.

CHAPTER SEVEN

Alexander, R., *The Biology of Moral Systems*, Aldine De Gruyter, New York (1987).

Alterman, Arthur, and Druley, Keith A., 'A Comparison of Moral Reasoning in Drug Addicts and Non Addicts', *Journal of Clinical Psychology* (1978), pp. 790–4.

Arbuthnot, Jack, and Gordon, Donald A., 'Behavioral and Cognitive Effects of Amoral Reasoning Development Intervention for High-risk Behavior-disordered Adolescents', *Journal of Consulting and Clinical Psychology*, Vol. 54, No. 2, Ohio University (1986), pp. 208–16.

Babiak, Paul, 'When Psychopaths Go To Work: a Case Study of an Industrial Psychopath', *Applied Psychology: an International Review*, Vol. 44 (2), Hopewell Junction, New York (1995), pp. 171–88.

Brennan, P. A., and Mednick, S. A.: see reference for Chapter Six.

Cairns, Robert B.: see reference for Chapter Two.

Cameron, Mary Owen: see reference for Chapter Two.

Chesney-Lind, Meda: see reference for Chapter Two.

Coleman, James William, 'Toward an Integrated Theory of White-collar Crime', *American Journal of Science*, Vol. 93, No. 2 (1987), pp. 406–39.

Cressey, D., 'The Criminal Violation of Financial Trust', *American Sociological Review* (1950), pp. 738–43.

Cummings, Mark E., *et al*.: see reference for Chapter Three.

Dodge, Kenneth A.: see reference for Chapter Two.

Eisenberg, N., and Lennon, R.: see reference for Chapter Five.

—— and Miller, Paul A.: see reference for Chapter Two (1987) (b).

—— and Mussen, Paul H.: see reference for Chapter Two.

—— and Fabes, Richard A., Bustamante, Denise, and Mathy, Robin M.: see reference for Chapter Two (1987) (a).

Ellis, Lee: see reference for Chapter Six.

—— see reference for Chapter One (1991) (c).

Feshbach, Seymour, and Feshbach, Norma Deitch: see reference for Chapter Two.

Gladue, Brian A., 'Aggressive Behavioral Characteristics, Hormones, and Sexual Orientation in Men and Women', *Aggressive Behavior*, Vol. 17, Wiley-Liss, Inc., U.S.A. (1991), pp. 314–26.

Glover, John H.: see reference for Chapter Two.

Gottfredson, M.: see reference for Chapter Six.

Gove, Walter R.: see reference for Chapter Two.

Hare, Robert D., 'Psychopathy: a Clinical Construct Whose Time Has Come', *Criminal Justice and Behavior*, 20th anniversary issue.

—— *Without Conscience*, Warner Books, U.S.A. (1993).

—— and Connolly, John F., 'Perceptual Asymmetries and Information Processing in Psychopaths', *The Causes of Crime*, Medenick, Sarnoff, Moffitt, Terrie, and Stack, Susan, Cambridge University Press (1987), pp. 219–37.

—— and Cox, David N. (Ph.D.), 'Psychophysiological Research on Psychopathy', *The Psychopath*, by Reid, William H., Brunner/Mazel, New York (1978).

——and Jutai, Jeffrey W., 'Psychopathy and Cerebral Asymmetry in Semantic Processing', *Personal Individual Differences*, Vol. 9, No. 2, Pergamon Press, Great Britain (1988), pp. 329–37.

Harpur, Timothy J., Hart, Stephen D., and Hare, Robert D., 'Personality of the Psychopath', American Psychological Association, Washington (1994), pp. 149–73.

Hills, Stuart L.: see reference for Chapter Two.

Hinde, Robert A.: see reference for Chapter Two.

Hoffman, Martin L.: see reference for Chapter Two.

Hokanson, Jack E., Willers, K.R., and Koropsak, Elizabeth: see reference for Chapter Four.

Hoyenga, Katharine Blick, *Sex Differences in Human Stratification: a Biosocial Approach*, Praeger, New York (1993), pp. 139–55.

Jaffa, Sam, *Maxwell Stories*, Robson Books, Great Britain (1992).

Klemke, Lloyd W.: see reference for Chapter Two.

Kruesi, M. J. P.: see reference for Chapter Four.

Maccoby, Eleanor E.: see reference for Chapter Two (1986).

Marcus, Robert F.: see reference for Chapter Two.

Maxwell, Betty, *A Mind of My Own: My Life with Robert Maxwell*, Pan Books, London (1994).

McCaghy, Charles H., and Cernkovich, Stephen A.: see reference for Chapter Two.

McCord, Joan, 'Instigation and Insulation: How Families Affect Antisocial Aggression', *Development of Antisocial and Prosocial Behaviour*, Olweus, Dan, Block, Jack, and Radke-Yarrow, Marian (eds.), Academic Press, New York (1986), pp. 343–56.

Mednick, Sarnoff: see reference for Chapter Six (1985).

—— *et al.*: see reference for Chapter Six (1982, 1986, 1987).

——and Gabrielli, William F.: see reference for Chapter Six.

Mussen, Paul: see reference for Chapter Two.

Noller, P.: see reference for Chapter Two.

Nunney, L.: see reference for Chapter Two.

Olweus, Dan: see reference for Chapter Two (1986).

Panksepp, Jaak: see references for Chapter Two (1985, 1986).

Pulkkinen, Lea, 'The Role of Impulse Control in the Development of Antisocial and Prosocial Behavior', *Development of Antisocial and Prosocial Behavior*, Olweus, Dan, Block, Jack, and Radke-Yarrow, Marian (eds.), Academic Press, Inc., New York (1986), pp. 149–206.

Rada, Richard, *et al.*: see reference for Chapter Three.

Radke-Yarrow, Marian, and Zahn-Waxler, Carolyn, 'The Role of Familial Factors in the Development of Prosocial Behavior: Research Findings and Questions', *Development of Antisocial and Prosocial Behavior*, Olweus, Dan, Block, Jack, and Radke-Yarrow, Marian (eds.), Academic Press, Inc., New York (1986), pp. 207–33.

Rahav, Giora, and Ellis, Lee: see reference for Chapter Two.

Reid, William H. (M.D., M.P.H.), *The Psychopath: a Comprehensive Study of Antisocial Disorders and Behaviors*, Brunner/Mazel, Publishers, New York (1978).

Reite, M., and Fields, T. (eds.), *The Biology of Social Attachments and Separation*, Academic Press Inc., New York (1985).

Rushton, J. Philippe, *et al.*: see reference for Chapter Six.

Simon, Herbert A., 'A Mechanism for Social Selection and Successful Altruism', *Science*, Vol. 250 (1990), pp. 1665–8.

Strayer, F. F., and Noel, J. M.: see reference for Chapter Two.

Thoma, Stephen J.: see reference for Chapter Two.

Thornton, David, and Reid, R. L., 'Moral Reasoning and Type of Criminal Offence', *British Journal of Social Psychology*, Vol. 21 (1982), pp. 231–8.

Trivers, Robert: see reference for Chapter Two.

Virkkunen, Matti, *et al.*: see reference for Chapter Four (1989).

Virkkunen, Matti: see reference for Chapter Four (1994).

Virkkunen, Matti, and Linnoila, Markku: see reference for Chapter Four (1990).

Whitney, Glayde: see reference for Chapter Six.

Yeudall, Lorne T.: see references for Chapter Five (1978, 1982).

Youniss, James: see reference for Chapter Two.

Zahn-Waxler, Carolyn: see reference for Chapter Two.

Zahn-Waxler, Carolyn, 'Introduction: Altruism and Aggression: Problems and Progress in Research', *Altruism and Aggression*, Zahn-Waxler, Carolyn, *et al.* (eds.), (1986), pp. 1–15.

Zaslow, Martha J., and Hayes, Cheryl D.: see reference for Chapter Two.

CHAPTER EIGHT

Becker, Jill B., *et al.*: see references for Chapter Three.

Black, D. A. (ed.), 'Division of Criminological and Legal Psychology', *Issues in Criminological and Legal Psychology*, No. 2 (1986).

Blackburn, Ronald, 'Patterns of Personality Deviation among Violent Offenders', *British Journal of Criminology*, Vol. 26, No. 3 (1986).

—— 'Personality Types Among Abnormal Homicides', *British Journal of Criminology*, Vol. 11 (1971), pp. 14–31.

Bourgeois, M.: see reference for Chapter Four.

Brennan, Patricia, Mednick, Sarnoff, and John, Richard: see reference for Chapter Six.

Brown, Gerald L. (M.D.), and Linnoila, Markku I. (M.D., Ph.D.): see reference for Chapter Four.

—— and Goodwin, F. K.: see reference for Chapter Four.

Brunner, Han G.: see reference for Chapter Four.

—— *et al.*: see reference for Chapter Four.

Bryant, Ernest T., Scott, Monte L., and Golden, Charles J.: see reference for Chapter Five.

Buss, Arnold, H.: see reference for Chapter Three.

Christiansen, Kerrin, and Winkler, Eike-Meinrad, 'Hormonal, Anthropometrical, and Behavioral Correlates of Physical Aggression in '!Kung San Men of Namibia', *Aggressive Behavior*, Vol. 18, Wiley-Liss, Inc., U.S.A. (1992), pp. 271–80.

Clark, Lee Anna, and Livesley, John W., 'Two Approaches to Identifying the Dimensions of Personality Disorder: Convergence on the Five-factor Model', *Personality Disorders and Five-Factor Model of Personality*, by Costa, Paul T. jr., and Widiger, Thomas A. (eds.), American Psychological Association, Washington DC (1994), pp. 261-77.

Coccaro, Emil F., Bergeman, C. S., and McClearn, Gerald E.: see reference for Chapter Six.

—— *et al.*: see reference for Chapter Four.

Coid, B., Lewis, S. W., and Reveley, A. M.: see reference for Chapter Six.

Coontz, Phyllis D.: see reference for Chapter Two.

Costa, Paul T. jr., and Widiger, Thomas A.: see reference for Chapter Six.

Craig, Ian: see reference for Chapter Four.

Dabbs, James M. jr. (Ph.D.), Frady, Robert L. (Ph.D.), Carr, Timothy S. (Ph.D.), and Besch, Norma F. (Ph.D.): see reference for Chapter Three.

—— Ruback, Barry R., Frady, Robert L., Hopper, Charles H., and Sgoutas, Demetrios S.: see reference for Chapter Three.

Dalton, Katharina, *Premenstrual Syndrome Goes to Court*, Peter Andrew Publishing Co. Ltd., Great Britain (1990).

Davis, Kenneth L., 'Impulsive Aggression in Personality Disorder: Evidence for Involvement of 5-HT-1 Receptors', *Biological Psychiatry*, Vol. 25 (1989), pp. 84A–89A.

Denno, Deborah W., 'Legal Implications of Genetics and Crime Research', *Genetics of Criminal and Antisocial Behaviour*, prepared for CIBA Foundation Symposium No. 194, February 1995.

Denno, Deborah W.: see reference for Chapter Two (1994) (b).

Deykin, Eva Y. (Dr. P.H.), Levy, Janice C. (M.D.), and Wells, Victoria (M.D., Dr. P.H.), 'Adolescent Depression, Alcohol and Drug Abuse', *American Journal of Public Health*, Vol. 77, No. 2 (1987), pp. 178–82.

Eaves, Lindon J., Silberg, Judy L., Hewitt, John K., Rutter, Michael, Meyer, Joanne M., Neale, Michael C., and Pickles, Andrew: see reference for Chapter Six.

Elliott, Frank A. (M.D.), 'Biological Roots of Violence', *Proceedings of the American Philosophical Society*, Vol. 127, No. 2 (1983), p. 84.

—— 'Neurological factors', *Handbook of Family Violence*, (ed.) Van Hasselt, Vincent B. (1988), Plenum Press, New York, pp. 359–82.

—— 'Violence, the Neurologic Contribution: an Overview', *Archives of Neurology*, Vol. 49 (1992), pp. 595–603.

Ellis, Lee: see reference for Chapter Four.

—— and Coontz, Phyllis D.: see reference for Chapter Two.

Eme, Robert F.: see reference for Chapter Two.

Engelberg, Hyman: see reference for Chapter Four.

Eriksson, E., 'Effect of Clomipramine on Premenstrual Syndrome', *Acta Psychiatrica Scandinavia*, Vol. 81 (1990), pp. 87-8.

—— and Humble, Mats, 'Serotonin in Psychiatric Pathophysiology', *Programme Basic Clinical Pharmacology*, Vol. 3, Karger, Basle, Switzerland (1990), pp. 66–119.

Fishbein, Diana H., and Pease, Susan E., 'Neurological Links between Substance Abuse and Crime', *Crime in Biological, Social and Moral Contexts*, Ellis, Lee, and Hoffman, Harry (eds.), Praeger, New York (1991), pp. 218–43.

Flor-Henry, P., 'Gender, Hemispheric Specialization and Psychopathology', *Social Science and Medicine*, Vol. 12B, Pergamon Press Ltd., Oxford (1978), pp. 155–62.

Fowkes, F. G. R., Leng, G. C., Donnan, P. T., Deary, I. J., Riemersma, R. A., and Housley, E., 'Serum Cholesterol, Triglycerides, and Aggression in the General Population', *The Lancet*, Vol. 340 (1992), pp. 995–8.

Gibbens, T. C. N., and Robertson, G., 'A Survey of the Criminal Careers of Restriction Order Patients', *British Journal of Psychiatry*, Vol. 143 (1983), pp. 370–5.

—— and Robertson, G., 'A Survey of the Criminal Careers of Hospital Order Patients', *British Journal of Psychiatry*, Vol. 143 (1983), pp. 362–9.

Gladue, Brian A.: see reference for Chapter Three.

Goleman, Daniel: see reference for Chapter Three.

Gottesman, Irving I., and Goldsmith, H. Hill: see reference for Chapter Six.

Gove, Walter R.: see reference for Chapter Two.

Greenwood, Peter W., 'The Violent Offender in the Criminal Justice System', *Criminal Violence*, Wolfgang, Martin E., and Weiner, Neil Alan (eds.), Sage Publications, London (1982), pp. 320–1.

Grinspoon, Lester (M.D.), and Bakalar, James B., 'Drug Abuse, Crime, and the Antisocial Personality: Some Conceptual Issues', *The Psychopath*, Reid, William (ed.) (1978), p. 234.

Hare, Robert D., 'Psychopathy: a Clinical Construct Whose Time has Come', *Criminal Justice and Behavior*, Brunner/Mazel, New York.

—— see reference for Chapter Seven (1993).

—— and Connolly, John F.: see reference for Chapter Seven (1987).

—— and Cox, David N. (Ph.D.): see reference for Chapter Seven (1978).

—— and Jutai, Jeffrey W.: see reference for Chapter Seven (1988).

Harpur, Timothy J., Hart, Stephen D., and Hare, Robert D.: see reference for Chapter Seven.

Henderson, Monika, 'An Empirical Typology of Violent Incidents Reported by Prison Inmates with Convictions for Violence', *Aggressive Behavior*, Vol. 12, Alan R. Liss, Inc., U.S.A. (1986), pp. 221–32.

—— *British Journal of Criminology*, Vol. 22, No. 1 (1982), pp. 1–20.

Hesselbrock, Michie N. (Ph.D.), and Hesselbrock, Victor M. (Ph.D.): see reference for Chapter Six.

Hokanson, Jack E., Willers, K. R., and Koropsak, Elizabeth: see reference for Chapter Four.

Horgan, J., 'Genes and Crime. A US Plan to Reduce Violence Rekindles an Old Controversy', *Scientific American*, Vol. 268, No. 2 (1993), pp. 24, 26 and 29.

Hoyenga, Katharine Blick, and Hoyenga, Kermit T., 'Psychobiology: the Neuron and Behavior', Brooks/Cole Publishing Co., California (1988).

Huizinga, David, 'Assessing Violent Behavior with Self-reports', *Neuropsychology of Aggression*, Kluwer Academic Publishers, U.S.A. (1991), pp. 47–67.

Jacobs, Lucia F., Gaulin, Steven J. C., Sherry, David F., and Hoffman, Gloria E., 'Evolution of Spatial Cognition: Sex-specific Patterns of Spatial Behavior Predict Hippocampal Size', *Proc. Natl. Acad. Sci.*, Vol. 87 (1990), pp. 6349–52.

Jutai, J. W., *et al.*, 'Psychopathy and Event-related Brain Potentials (ERPS) Associated with Attention to Speech Stimuli', *Personality and Individual Differences*, Vol. 8 (1987), pp. 175–84.

Kruesi, Markus J., *et al.*: see reference for Chapter Four.

Lafave, Hugh G. (M.D.), Pinkney, Annette A. (B.A.), and Gerber, Gary J. (Ph.D.), 'Criminal Activity by Psychiatric Clients after Hospital Discharge', *Hospital and Community Psychiatry*, Vol. 44, No. 2 (1993), p. 180.

Langevin, Ron, *et al*: see reference for Chapter Five.

Lewis, Collins E. (M.D.): see reference for Chapter Five.

Linnoila, Markku, *et al.*: see reference for Chapter Four (1994).

Linnoila, Markku (M.D., Ph.D.), De Jong, Judith (Ph.D.), and Virkkunen, Matti (M.D.): see reference for Chapter Four (1989).

Linnoila, M., *et al.*: see reference for Chapter Four (1983).

Linnoila, V. Markku I. (M.D., Ph.D.), and Virkkunen, Matti (M.D.): see reference for Chapter Four (1992).

Malmquist, Carl P., 'Depression and Extreme Violence in Adolescence', *Biological Risks for Psychosocial Disorders: Thinking Clearly about Psychology*, Rutter, Michael, and Casaer, Paul (eds.), Cambridge University Press, Cambridge (1991), pp. 378–9.

McCaghy, Charles H., and Cernkovich, Stephen A.: see reference for Chapter Two.

McCanne, Thomas R.: see reference for Chapter Four.

McMillen, David L., *et al.*: see reference for Chapter Four.

Mednick, Sarnoff A., *et al.*: see references for Chapter Six (1982, 1986, 1987).

Mednick, Sarnoff A., and Gabrielli, William F.: see reference for Chapter Six (1984).

Mednick, Sarnoff: see reference for Chapter Six (1985).

Miller, Laurence: see reference for Chapter Five.

Monroe, Russell R. (M.D.), 'The Medical Model in Psychopathy and Dyscontrol Syndromes', *The Psychopath*, Reid, William (ed.) (1978), pp. 190–1.

Morell, V.: see reference for Chapter Six.

Nachshon, Israel: see references for Chapter Five (1982, 1983, 1991 (a) (b)).

Nachshon, Israel and Denno, Deborah: see reference for Chapter Five (1987).

Otnow Lewis, Dorothy, *et al.*: see references for Chapter Five, pp. 307–19, and Chapter Six.

Otnow Lewis, Dorothy, *et al.*, 'Toward a Theory of the Genesis of Violence: a Follow-up Study of Delinquents', *American Academy of Child and Adolescent Psychiatry* (1989), pp. 431–6.

Plomin, Robert: see reference for Chapter Six.

Pollock, V. E., *et al.*, 'Childhood Antecedents of Antisocial Behavior: Parental Alcoholism and Physical Abusiveness', *American Journal of Psychiatry*, Vol. 147, No. 10 (1990), pp. 1290–3.

Pulkkinen, Lea: see reference for Chapter Seven.

Rada, Richard T. (M.D.), 'Sociopathy and Alcohol Abuse', *The Psychopath*, Reid, William (1978), p. 223.

Rada, Richard, *et al.*: see reference for Chapter Three.

Raine, Adrian, Brennan, Patricia, and Mednick, Sarnoff A.: see reference for Chapter Six.

Raine, Adrian: see references for Chapter Five (1994, 1995).

Reid, William H. (M.D., M.P.H.): see references for Chapters Six and Seven.

Reitsma-Street, Marge, *et al.*: see reference for Chapter Six.

Robins, Lee N., and Rutter, Michael: see reference for Chapter Two.

Rosenblum, Karen E., 'Female Deviance and the Female Sex Role: a Preliminary Investigation', *Women, Crime and Justice*, Datesman, Susan, and Scarpitti, Frank, Oxford University Press, New York (1980), pp. 106–27.

Rowe, D. C.: see reference for Chapter Six.

Rubin, Robert T.: see reference for Chapter Four.

Rueddel, H. (M.D.), *et al.*, 'Impact of Hostility on Blood Pressure', *Psychosomatic Medicine*, Vol. 52 (1990), pp. 222–46.

Rule, Ann, 'The Stranger Beside Me', Warner Books, U.S.A. (1989).

Rushton, J. Philippe, *et al.*: see reference for Chapter Six.

Sandifer, Paul H., 'Social and Medico-legal Problems of the Psychopath', *Medico-Legal Journal*, Vol. 60, No. 4 (1992), pp. 230–42.

Satterfield, James, *et al.*: see reference for Chapter Two (1994 (a)).

Schalling, D., *et al.*: see reference for Chapter Four.

Steinmetz, Suzanne K. (Ph.D.), 'Women and Violence: Victims and Perpetrators', *American Journal of Psychotherapy*, Vol. XXXIV, No. 3 (1980), pp. 334–50.

Susman, Elizabeth J., *et al.*: see reference for Chapter Three.

Swaab, D. F.: see reference for Chapter Four.

Tancredi, Laurence R., and Volkow, Nora, 'Neural Substrates of Violent Behavior: Implications for Law and Public Policy', *International Journal of Law and Psychiatry*, Vol. 11, Pergamon Press, U.S.A. (1988), pp. 13–49.

Taylor, Pamela J., and Gunn, John, 'Violence and Psychosis', *British Medical Journal*, Vol. 289 (1984), pp. 9–12.

Taylor, Pamela J., 'Psychiatric Disorder in London's Life-sentenced Offenders', *British Journal of Criminology*, Vol. 26, No. 1 (1986), pp. 63–78.

Taylor, Pamela J., 'Motives for Offending Among Violent and Psychotic Men', *British Journal of Psychiatry*, Vol. 147 (1985), pp. 491–8.

Thapar, Anita, and McGuffin, Peter: see reference for Chapter Six.

Thiessen, Del: see reference for Chapter Three.

Thompson, Wendy M., *et al.*: see reference for Chapter Three.

Vanyukov, Michael M., *et al.*: see reference for Chapter Four.

Venables, P. H.: see reference for Chapter Four.

Virkkunen, Matti: see references for Chapter Four (1987, 1992).

Virkkunen, Matti, *et al.*: see reference for Chapter Four (1989).

Virkkunen, Matti, and Linnoila, Markku: see reference for Chapter Four (1990).

Volavka, Jan: see reference for Chapter Five.

Whitney, Glayde: see reference for Chapter Six.

Widom, Cathy Spatz (ed.): see reference for Chapter Two.

Witten, Mark: see reference for Chapter Four.

Wolf, Proben, 'Definitions of Antisocial Behavior in Biosocial Research', *The Causes of Crime*, Cambridge University Press (1987), pp. 65–73.

Yaryura-Tobias, J.A., *et al.*: see reference for Chapter Four.

Yates, William R., *et al.*, 'Aggression and Hostility in Anabolic Steroid Users', *Biol. Psychiatry*, Vol. 31 (1992), pp. 1232–4.

Yeudall, Lorne T.: see reference for Chapter Five (1978).

Zubin, Joseph, *et al.*, 'Event-related Potential and Behavioral Methodology in Psychiatric Research', *Brain Electrical Potentials and Psychopathology*, Elsevier Science Publ. Co., Inc., New York (1986).

CHAPTER NINE

Bach-Y-Rita, George (M.D.), *et al.*: see references for Chapter Five.

Bancroft, John: see references for Chapter Three.

Baucom, Donald H.: see references for Chapter Three.

Becker, Jill B., *et al.*: see references for Chapter Three.

Blackburn, Ronald: see references for Chapter Eight.

Blumenthal, Susan J. (M.D., M.P.A.), and Nadelson, Carol C. (M.D.): see reference for Chapter Three.

Bourgeois, M.: see reference for Chapter Four.

Brennan, Patricia, Mednick, Sarnoff, John, Richard: see reference for Chapter Six.

Brooner, Robert K., Schmidt, Chester W. jr., and Herbst, Jeffrey H., 'Personality Trait Characteristics of Opioid Abusers With and Without Comorbid Personality Disorders', *Personality Disorders and the Five-Factor Model of Personality*, Costa, Paul, and Widiger, Thomas (eds.), American Psychological Association, Washington DC (1994), pp. 131–48.

Brown, C. S.: see reference for Chapter Four.

Brown, Gerald L. (M.D.), and Linnoila, Markku I. (M.D., Ph.D.): see reference for Chapter Four.

Brunner, Han G.: see reference for Chapter Four.

Brunner, H. G., *et al.*: see references for Chapter Four.

Bryant, Ernest T., Scott, Monte L., and Golden, Charles J.: see reference for Chapter Five.

Cadoret, Remi J., 'Early Life Psychosocial Events and Adult Affective Symptoms', *Straight and Devious Pathways from Childhood to Adulthood*, Robbins, Lee, and Rutter, Michael (eds.), Cambridge University Press, Cambridge (1990).

Cannon, Tyrone D., Mednick, Sarnoff A., and Parnas, Josef: see reference for Chapter Six.

Casper, Robert F. (M.D.), and Hearn, Margaret T. (Ph.D.): see reference for Chapter Three.

Casson, P. (M.D.), Hahn, P. M. (M.Sc.), Van Vugt, D. A. (Ph.D.), and Reid, R. L. (M.D.): see reference for Chapter Three.

Chesney-Lind, Meda: see reference for Chapter Two.

Choi, Precilla Y. L. (Ph.D.), and Pope, Harrison G. jr. (M.D.): see reference for Chapter Three.

Christiansen, Kerrin, and Winkler, Eike-Meinrad: see reference for Chapter Three.

Cirincione, C., *et al.*, 'Schizophrenia as a Conticent Factor for Criminal Violence', *Int. J. Law and Psychiatry*, Vol. 15, Pt 4 (1992), pp. 347–58.

Clark, Lee Anna, and Livesley, John W., 'Two Approaches to Identifying the Dimensions of Personality Disorder: Convergence on the Five-factor Model', *Personality Disorders and the Five-Factor Model of Personality*, Costa, Paul, and Widiger, Thomas (eds.), American Psychological Association, Washington DC (1994), pp. 262–77.

Coccaro, Emil F., Bergeman, C. S., and McClearn, Gerald E.: see reference for Chapter Six.

—— *et al.*: see reference for Chapter Four.

Coid, B., Lewis, S. W., and Reveley, A. M.: see reference for Chapter Six.

Coontz, Phyllis D.: see reference for Chapter Two.

Craig, Ian: see reference for Chapter Four.

Dabbs, James M. jr. (Ph.D.), Frady, Robert L. (Ph.D.), Carr, Timothy S. (Ph.D.), and Besch, Norma F. (Ph.D.): see reference for Chapter Three.

Dabbs, James M. jr., Ruback, Barry R., Frady, Robert L., Hopper, Charles H., and Sgoutas, Demetrios S.: see reference for Chapter Three.

Dalton, Katharina: see reference for Chapter Three.

Davis, Kenneth L., 'Impulsive Aggression in Personality Disorder: Evidence for Involvement of 5-HT-1 Receptors', *Biological Psychiatry*, Vol. 25 (1989), pp. 84A–89A.

Deykin, Eva Y. (Dr. P.H.), Levy, Janice C. (M.D.), and Wells, Victoria (M.D., Dr. P.H.), 'Adolescent Depression, Alcohol and Drug Abuse', *American Journal of Public Health*, Vol. 77, No. 2 (1987), pp. 178–82.

Eaves, Lindon J., *et al.*: see reference for Chapter Six.

Elliott, Frank A. (M.D.): see references for Chapters Five and Eight (1983, 1988, 1992).

Ellis, Lee, 'The Drive to Possess and Control as a Motivation for Sexual Behavior: Applications to the Study of Rape', *Social Science Information*, Vol. 30, No. 4 (1991), Sage Publications, London and New Delhi, pp. 663–75.

Ellis, Lee, 'A Synthesized (Biosocial) Theory of Rape', *Journal of Consulting and Clinical Psychology*, Vol. 59, No. 5 (1991), pp. 631–42.

Ellis, Lee: see reference for Chapter Four.

Ellis, Lee, and Coontz, Phyllis D.: see reference for Chapter Two.

Engelberg, Hyman: see reference for Chapter Four.

Eriksson, Elias, and Humble, Mats, 'Serotonin in Psychiatric Pathophysiology', *Programme Basic Clinical Pharmacology*, Vol. 3 (1990), Karger, Basle, Switzerland, pp. 66–119.

Eriksson, Elias, Sundblad, Charlotta, Lisjö, Pia, Modigh, Kjell, and Andersch, Björn, 'Serum Levels of Androgens are Higher in Women with Premenstrual Irritability and Dysphoria than in Controls', *Psychoneuroendocrinology*, Vol. 17, No. 2/3 (1992), pp. 195–204.

Eriksson, E., 'Effect of Clomipramine on Premenstrual Syndrome', *Acta Psychiatrica Scandinavia*, Vol. 81 (1990), pp. 87–8.

Fishbein, Diana H., and Pease, Susan E., 'Neurological Links between Substance Abuse and Crime', *Crime in Biological, Social and Moral Contexts*, Ellis, Lee and Hoffman, Harry (eds.), Praeger, New York (1991), pp. 218–43.

Flor-Henry, P., Tomer, R., Kumpula, I., Koles, Z. J., and Yeudall, L. T., 'Neurophysiological and Neuropsychological Study of Two Cases of Multiple Personality Syndrome and Comparison with Chronic Hysteria', *International Journal of Psychophysiology*, Vol. 10, Elsevier Science Publishers (Biomedical Division)(1990), pp. 151–61.

Fowkes, F.G.R., *et al.*: see reference for Chapter Eight.

Fraile, I. G., McEwen, B. S., and Pfaff, D. W.: see reference for Chapter Three.

Freeman, Ellen (Ph.D.), Rickels, Karl (M.D.), Sondheimer, Steven J. (M.D.), and Polansky, Marcia (Sc.D.): see reference for Chapter Three.

Gibbens, T. C. N., and Robertson, G., 'A Survey of the Criminal Careers of Restriction Order Patients', *British Journal of Psychiatry*, Vol. 143 (1983), pp. 370–5.

Gibbens, T. C. N., and Robertson, G., 'A Survey of the Criminal Careers of Hospital Order Patients', *British Journal of Psychiatry*, Vol. 143 (1983), pp. 362–9.

Gladue, Brian A.: see reference for Chapter Three.

Goleman, Daniel: see reference for Chapter Three.

Gottesman, Irving I., and Goldsmith, H. Hill: see reference for Chapter Six.

Gove, Walter R.: see reference for Chapter Two.

Greenwood, Peter W.: see reference for Chapter Eight.

Grove, William M., *et al.*: see reference for Chapter Six.

Harrison, Wilma M. (M.D.), Endicott, Jean (Ph.D.), and Nee, John (Ph.D.): see reference for Chapter Three.

Heinrichs, R.: see reference for Chapter Five.

Henderson, Monika, 'An Empirical Classification of Convicted Violent Offenders', *British Journal of Criminology*, Vol. 22, No. 1 (1982), pp. 1–20.

Henderson, Monika, 'An Empirical Typology of Violent Incidents Reported by Prison Inmates with Convictions for Violence', *Aggressive Behavior*, Vol. 12, Alan R. Liss, Inc. (1986), pp. 221–32.

Hesselbrock, Michie N. (Ph.D.), and Hesselbrock, Victor M. (Ph.D.): see reference for Chapter Six.

Hoyenga, Katharine Blick, and Hoyenga, Kermit T., *Psychobiology: the Neuron and Behavior*, Brooks/Cole Publishing Co., California (1988).

Huizinga, David: see reference for Chapter Eight.

Kupke, T.: see reference for Chapter Two.

Lafave, Hugh G. (M.D.), Pinkney, Annette A. (B.A.), and Gerber, Gary J. (Ph.D.): see reference for Chapter Eight.

Lindovist, Per, and Allebeck, Peter, 'Schizophrenia and Crime, a Longitudinal Follow-up of 644 Schizophrenics in Stockholm', *British Journal of Psychiatry*, Vol. 157 (1990), pp. 345–50.

Linnoila, V. Markku I. (M.D., Ph.D.), and Virkkunen, Matti (M.D.): see reference for Chapter Four (1992).

Linnoila, Markku (M.D., Ph.D.), De Jong, Judith (Ph.D.), and Virkkunen, Matti (M.D.): see reference for Chapter Four (1989).

Linnoila, M., *et al.*: see reference for Chapter Four (1983).

Logue, Camille M. (Ph.D.), and Moos, Rudolf H. (Ph.D.): see reference for Chapter Three.

Luthar, Suniya S. (Ph.D.), and Rounsaville, Bruce J. (M.D.): see reference for Chapter Four.

McGuffin, Peter, and Katz, Randy, 'The Genetics of Deppression and Manic-depressive Disorder', *British Journal of Psychiatry*, Vol. 155 (1989), pp. 294–304.

McKim, William A.: see reference for Chapter Four.

McMillen, David L., *et al.*: see reference for Chapter Four.

Menzies, Christopher J., *et al.*, 'At the Mercy of the Mad: Examining the

Relationship between Violence and Mental Illness', *Advances in Forensic Psychology* (1987), pp. 63–100.

Monroe, Russell R. (M.D.), 'The Medical Model in Psychopathy and Dyscontrol Syndromes', *The Psychopath*, Reid, William (ed.), pp. 190–1.

Mungas, Dan: see reference for Chapter Five.

Nachshon, Israel, and Denno, Deborah: see reference for Chapter Five (1987).

Nachshon, Israel: see references for Chapter Five (1983, 1991(a) (b)).

Newcomb, Michael D., and Bentler, Peter M.: see reference for Chapter Four.

d'Orban, P. T., and Dalton, J.: see reference for Chapter Three.

Pollock, V. E., *et al.*: see reference for Chapter Eight.

Pope, Harrison G. jr. (M.D.): see reference for Chapter Three (1988) (b).

Pope, Harrison G. jr. (M.D.), and Katz, David L. (M.D.): see references for Chapter Three (1987, 1994).

Post, Robert M. (M.D.), 'Transduction of Psychosocial Stress into the Neurobiology of Recurrent Affective Disorder', *American Journal of Psychiatry*, Vol. 149, No. 8 (1992), pp. 999–1009.

Prins, H., *Dangerous Behaviour, the Law and Mental Disorder*, Tavistock, London.

Quinton, David, Rutter, Michael, and Gulliver, Lesley, 'Continuities in Psychiatric Disorders from Childhood to Adulthood in the Children of Psychiatric Patients', *Straight and Devious Pathways from Childhood to Adulthood*, Robins, Lee N., and Rutter, Michael (eds.), Cambridge University Press, Cambridge (1990), pp. 259–78.

Reid, William H. (M.D., M.P.H.): see reference for Chapter Seven.

Rivera-Tovar, Ana D. (Ph.D.), and Frank, Ellen (Ph.D.): see reference for Chapter Three.

Robins, Lee N., and McEvoy, Lawrence, 'Conduct Problems in Predictors of Substance Abuse', *Straight and Devious Pathways from Childhood to Adulthood*, Robins, Lee N., and Rutter, Michael (eds.), Cambridge University Press, Cambridge (1990).

Rodgers, Bryan, 'Influences of Early-life and Recent Factors on Affective Disorder in Women: an Exploration of Vulnerability Models', *Straight and Devious Pathways from Childhood to Adulthood*, Robins, Lee N., and Rutter, Michael (eds.), Cambridge University Press, Cambridge (1990).

Rodin, Ernst A. (M.D.): see reference for Chapter Two.

Sherwin, Barbara B., and Gelfand, Morrie M.: see reference for Chapter Three.

Stedman, J., 'Educational Underachievement and Epilepsy: a Study of Children from Normal Schools Admitted to Special Hospital for Epilepsy', *Early Child Development and Care*, Vol. 9 (1981), pp. 65–82.

Steinhausen, H.-Ch., and Rauss-Mason, C., 'Epilepsy and Anticonvulsive Drugs', *Biological Risk Factors for Psychosocial Disorders*, Rutter, Michael, and Casaer, Paul (eds.), Cambridge University Press, Cambridge (1991).

Steinmetz, Suzanne K. (Ph.D.): see reference for Chapter Eight.

Sundblad, C., *et al.*: see references for Chapter Three (1992, 1993).

Susman, Elizabeth J., *et al.*: see reference for Chapter Three.

Swaab, D. F.: see reference for Chapter Four.

Targum, Steven D., *et al.*, 'Menstrual Cycle Phase and Psychiatric Admissions', *Journal of Affective Disorders*, Vol. 22 (1991), pp. 49–53.

Taylor, David C., 'Aggression and Epilepsy', *Journal of Psychosomatic Research*, Vol. 13, Pergamon Press, N. Ireland (1969), pp. 229–36.

Taylor, Pamela J., and Gunn, John: see reference for Chapter Eight.

Taylor, Pamela J.: see references for Chapter Eight (1985, 1986).

Thapar, Anita, and McGuffin, Peter, 'A Twin Study of Depressive Symptoms in Childhood', *British Journal of Psychiatry*, Vol. 165 (1994), pp. 259–65.

Tienari, Pekka, *et al.*, 'Schizophrenics and Controls: the Finnish Adoptive Family Study of Schizophrenia', *Straight and Devious Pathways from Childhood to Adulthood*, Robins, Lee N., and Rutter, Michael (eds.), Cambridge University Press, Cambridge (1990).

Tsuang, Ming T., *The Genetics of Mood Disorders*, The Johns Hopkins University Press, Baltimore and London (1990).

Virkkunen, Matti: see reference for Chapter Four (1992).

Volkow, Nora D., *et al.*, 'Cerebral Blood Flow in Chronic Cocaine Users: a Study with Positron Emission Tomography', *British Journal of Psychiatry*, Vol. 152 (1988), pp. 641–8.

Volkow, Nora D., *et al.*, 'Decreased Dopamine D_2 Receptor Availability is Associated with Reduced Frontal Metabolism in Cocaine Abusers', *Synapse*, Vol. 14, Wiley-Liss, Inc., U.S.A. (1993), pp. 169–77.

Volkow, Nora D., *et al.*, 'Long-term Frontal Brain Metabolic Changes in Cocaine Abusers', *Synapse*, Vol. 11, Wiley-Liss, Inc., U.S.A. (1992), pp. 185–90.

Volkow, Nora D., *et al.*, 'Use of Positron Emission Tomography to Investigate Cocaine', *Advances in the Biosciences*, Vol. 80, Pergamon Press, U.K. (1991), pp. 129–41.

Volkow, Nora D., *et al.*, 'Effects of Chronic Cocaine Abuse on Postsynaptic Dopamine Receptors', *American Journal of Psychiatry*, Vol. 147, No. 6 (1990), pp. 719–24.

Volkow, Nora D., *et al.*, 'Decreased Cerebral Response to Inhibitory Neurotransmission in Alcoholics', *American Journal of Psychiatry*, Vol. 150, No. 3 (1993), pp. 417–22.

Volkow, Nora D., *et al.*, 'Decreased Brain Metabolism in Neurologically Intact Healthy Alcoholics', *American Journal of Psychiatry*, Vol. 149, No. 8 (1992), pp. 1016–22.

Volkow, Nora D., *et al.*, 'Recovery of Brain Glucose Metabolism in Detoxified Alcoholics', *American Journal of Psychiatry*, Vol. 151, No. 2 (1994), pp. 178–83.

Volkow, Nora D., *et al.*, 'Changes in Brain Glucose Metabolism in Cocaine

Dependence and Withdrawal', *American Journal of Psychiatry*, Vol. 148, No. 5 (1991), pp. 621–6.

Wexler, Bruce E., *et al.*, 'Possible Subtypes of Affective Disorder Suggested by Differences in Cerebral Laterality and Testosterone', *Arch. Gen. Psychiatry*, Vol. 46 (1989), pp. 429–33.

Winokur, George, and Coryell, William, 'Familial Subtypes of Unipolar Depression: a Prospective Study of Familial Pure Depressive Disease Compared to Depression Spectrum Disease', *Biol. Psychiatry*, Vol. 32 (1992), pp. 1012–8.

Winokur, G., 'A Familial ("Genetic") Methodology for Determining Valid Types of Affective Illnesses', *Pharmacopsychiat.* Vol. 25 (1992), pp. 14–7.

Witten, Mark: see reference for Chapter Four.

CHAPTER TEN

Alter-Reid, *et al.*, 'Clinical Psychology – Sexual Abuse of Children: Review of the Empirical Findings', *Clinical Psychology Review*, Vol. 6 (1986), pp. 249–66.

Andrews, Bernice, and Brown, George W., 'Marital Violence in the Community: a Biographical Approach', *British Journal of Psychiatry*, Vol. 153 (1988),pp. 305–12

Bach-Y-Rita, George (M.D.), *et al.*: see reference for Chapter Five.

Becker, Jill B., *et al.*: see reference for Chapter Three.

Becker, Judith V., and Coleman, Emily M., 'Incest', *Handbook of Family Violence*, Van Hasselt, Vincent B. (ed.), Plenum Press, New York and London (1988), pp. 187–205.

Blaffer Hrdy, Sarah, and Hausfater, Glenn (eds.), *Comparative and Evolutionary Perspectives on Infanticide: Introduction and Overview*, Aldine Publishing Co., New York (1984), pp. xiii–xxxv.

Bowker, Lee H., 'The Effects of National Development on the Position of Married Women in the Third World: the Case of Wife-beating', *International Journal of Comparative and Applied Criminal Justice*, Vol. 9, No. 1 (1985), pp. 1–13.

Brennan, Patricia, Mednick, Sarnoff, and John, Richard: see reference for Chapter Six.

Browne, Angela, 'Family Homicide', *Handbook of Family Violence*, Van Hasselt, Vincent B. (ed.), Plenum Press, New York and London (1988).

Casanova, Gisele M., Domanic, Jodi, McCanne, Thomas R., and Milner, Joel S., 'Physiological Responses to Non-child-related Stressors in Mothers at Risk for Child Abuse', *Child Abuse and Neglect*, Vol. 16, Pergamon Press, U.S.A. (1992), pp. 31–44.

Chagnon, Napoleon A., 'Life Histories, Blood Revenge, and Warfare in a Tribal Population', *Articles*, Vol. 239 (1988), pp. 985–92.

Chesney-Lind, Meda: see reference for Chapter Two.

Christiansen, Kerrin, and Winkler, Eike-Meinrad, 'Hormonal, Anthropometrical, and Behavioral Correlates of Physical Aggression in !Kung San Men of Namibia', *Aggressive Behavior*, Vol. 18, Wiley-Liss, Inc., U.S.A. (1992), pp. 271–80.

Clark, Lee Anna, and Livesley, John W.: see reference for Chapter Eight.

Dabbs, James M. jr. (Ph.D.), Frady, Robert L. (Ph.D.), Carr, Timothy S. (Ph.D.), and Besch, Norma F. (Ph.D.): see reference for Chapter Three.

Dabbs, James M. jr., Ruback, Barry R., Frady, Robert L., Hopper, Charles H., and Sgoutas, Demetrios S.: see reference for Chapter Three.

Dalton, Katharina: see reference for Chapter Three.

Daly, Martin, and Wilson, Margo, 'Male Sexual Jealousy', *Ethology and Sociobiology*, Vol. 3, Elsevier Science Publishing Co. Inc., New York (1982)(a), pp. 11–27.

Daly, Martin, and Wilson, Margo, 'Evolutionary Social Psychology and Family Homicide', *Articles*, Vol. 242 (1988), pp. 519–40.

Daly, Martin, and Wilson, Margo, 'A Sociobiological Analysis of Human Infanticide', *Family Violence*, Aldine Publishing Co., New York (1984), pp. 487–502.

Daly, M., and Wilson, M., 'Homicide and Kinship', *American Anthropologist*, Vol. 84 (1982)(b), pp. 372–8.

Daly, M., and Wilson, M., 'Child Abuse and Other Risks of Not Living with Both Parents', *Ethology and Sociobiology*, Vol. 6 (1985), pp. 197–210.

Daly, M., and Wilson, M., 'Homicide and Kinship', *American Anthropologist*, Vol. 84 (1982), pp. 372–8.

Davis, Kenneth L., 'Impulsive Aggression in Personality Disorder: Evidence for Involvement of 5-HT-1 Receptors', *Biological Psychiatry*, Vol. 25 (1989), pp. 84A–89A.

Dickermann, Mildred, 'Concepts and Classification in the Study of Human Infanticide: Sectional Introduction and Some Cautionary Notes', *Infanticide, Comparative and Evolutionary Perspectives*, Hausfater, G. and Blafter Hrdy, S. (eds), Aldine Publishing Co. (1984), pp. 427–37.

Dobash, Emerson R., and Donash, Russell P., 'The Nature and Antecedents of Violent Events', *British Journal of Criminology*, Vol. 24, No. 3 (1984), pp. 269–89.

Elliott, Frank A. (M.D.): see references for Chapters Five and Eight (1983, 1988, 1992).

Eriksson, E, 'Effect of Clomipramine on Premenstrual Syndrome', *Acta Psychiatrica Scandinavia*, Vol 81 (1990), pp. 87–8.

Eriksson, Elias, Sundblad, Charlotta, Lisjö, Pia, Modigh, Kjell, and Andersch, Björn, 'Serum Levels of Androgens are Higher in Women with Premenstrual Irritability and Dysphoria Than in Controls', *Psychoneuroendocrinology*, Vol. 17, No. 2/3 (1992), pp. 195–204.

Feldman, Marilyn (M.A.), Mallouh, Katherine, and Otnow Lewis, Dorothy (M.D.), 'Filicidal Abuse in the Histories of 15 Condemned Murderers', *Bulletin of American Academic Psychiatry Law*, Vol. 14, No. 4 (1986), pp. 345–52.

Fraile, I. G., McEwen, B. S., and Pfaff, D. W.: see reference for Chapter Three.

Geffner, Robert, Rosenbaum, Alan, and Hughes, Honore, 'Research Issues Concerning Family Violence', *Handbook of Family Violence*, Van Hasselt, Vincent B. (ed.), Plenum Press, New York and London, (1988) pp. 457–81.

Gelles, Richard J., and Straus, Murray A.: see reference for Chapter One.

Haft, Marilyn G.: see reference for Chapter Two.

Haley, Kathleen: see reference for Chapter Two.

Hare, Robert D. (Dr.): see reference for Chapter Seven (1993).

Hausfater, Glenn, and Blaffer Hrdy, Sarah (eds.), *Infanticide, Comparative and Evolutionary Perspectives*, Aldine Publishing Co., New York (1984).

Hilberman, Elaine, and Munson, Kit, 'Sixty Battered Women', *Victimology: An International Journal*, Vol. 2, Nos. 3-4, Visage Press Inc., U.S.A. (1977–8), pp. 460–70.

Howard, Rick, Gifford, Mervyn, and Lumsden, John: see reference for Chapter Three.

Johansson, Sheila Ryan, 'Deferred Infanticide: Excess Female Mortality During Childhood', *Infanticide*, Hausfater, Glenn, and Blaffer Hrdy, Sarah (eds.), Aldine Publishing Co., New York (1984), pp. 463–85.

Lafave, Hugh G. (M.D.), Pinkney, Annette A. (B.A.), and Gerber, Gary J. (Ph.D.): see reference for Chapter Eight.

Leonard, Kenneth E., and Jacob, T., 'Alcohol, Alcoholism, and Family . Violence', *Handbook of Family Violence*, Van Hasselt, Vincent B. (ed.), Plenum Press, New York and London, pp. 383–406.

Linnoila, V. Markku I. (M.D., Ph.D.), and Virkkunen, Matti (M.D.).: see references for Chapter Four (1989, 1992).

Linnoila, M., *et al.*: see reference for Chapter Four (1983).

Margolin, Gayla Sibner, Linda, Gorin, and Gleberman, Lisa, 'Wife Battering', *Handbook of Family Violence*, Plenum Press, New York and London (1988), pp. 89–117.

McCaghy, Charles H., and Cernkovich, Stephen A.: see reference for Chapter Two.

McCanne, Thomas R., and Milner, Joel S., 'Physiological Reactivity of Physically Abusive and At-risk Subjects to Child-related Stimuli', *Neuropsychology of Aggression*, Milner, Joel (ed.), Kluwer Academic Publishers, Boston (1991), pp. 147–67.

McCord, Joan: see reference for Chapter Seven.

Milner, Joel S., and McCanne, Thomas R., 'Neuropsychological Correlates of Physical Child Abuse', *Neuropsychology of Aggression*, Kluwer Academic Publishers, Boston (1991), pp. 131–45.

Milner, Joel S., 'Social Information Processing and Physical Child Abuse', *Clinical Psychology Review*, Vol. 13, Pergamon Press Ltd., U.S.A. (1993), pp. 275–94.

Mussen, Paul: see reference for Chapter Two.

Nachshon, Isreal, and Denno, Deborah: see reference for Chapter Five (1987).

Nachshon, Israel: see references for Chapter Five (1983, 1991(a)(b)).

O'Leary, K. Daniel, 'Physical Aggression Between Spouses', *Handbook of Family Violence*, Plenum Press, New York/London (1988), pp. 31–55.

d'Orban, P. T., and Dalton, J.: see reference for Chapter Three.

Otnow Lewis, Dorothy: see reference for Chapter Two (1992).

Pleck, Elizabeth, *Domestic Tyranny: the Making of Social Policy Against Family Violence from Colonial Times to the Present*, Oxford University Press, New York/Oxford (1987).

Pollock, V. E., *et al.*: see reference for Chapter Eight.

Pope, Harrison G. jr. (M.D.): see reference for Chapter Three (1988)(a).

Raine, Adrian: see reference for Chapter Five (1995).

Reid, John B., 'Social-interactional Patterns in Families of Abused and Nonabused Children', *Altruism and Aggression*, Zahn-Waxler, Carolyn, *et al.* (eds.), Cambridge University Press (1986), pp. 238–55.

Reid, William H. (M.D., M.P.H.): see reference for Chapter Seven.

Remillard, G. M.: see reference for Chapter Two.

Rivera, Beverly, and Widom, Cathy Spatz: see reference for Chapter Two.

Rosenbaum, Alan, 'The Neuropsychology of Marital Aggression', *Neuropsychology of Aggression*, Milner, Joel (ed.), Kluwer Academic Publishers, Boston (1991)(a).

Rosenbaum, Alan, *et al.*, 'Partner-abusive Men: Current Research and Future Directions', presented at the Convention of the American Psychological Association, San Francisco, August 1991(b).

Rosenbaum, Alan, *et al.*, 'Head Injury in Partner-abusive Men', *Journal of Consulting and Clinical Psychology*.

Rosenblum, Karen E.: see reference for Chapter Eight.

Rounsaville, Bruce J., 'Theories in Marital Violence: Evidence from a Study of Battered Women', *Victimology: an International Journal*, Vol. 3, Nos. 1–2, Visage Press, Inc., U.S.A. (1978), pp. 11–31.

Rubinow, David R. (M.D.): see reference for Chapter Three (1987).

Rubinow, David R. (M.D.), and Roy-Byrne, Peter (M.D.): see reference for Chapter Three (1984).

Safilios-Rothschild, Constantina, '"Honour" Crimes in Contemporary Greece'. Revised version of paper read at Michigan Sociological Association in Michigan, 26 March 1964.

Salzinger, Suzanne, *et al.*, 'Risk for Physical Child Abuse and the Personal Consequences for its Victims', *Criminal Justice and Behavior*, Vol. 18, No. 1, American Association for Correctional Psychology (1991), pp. 64–81.

Shepher, Joseph, 'Incest, a Biosocial View', *Studies in Anthropology*, Academic Press, New York (1983).

Starr, Raymond H. jr., 'Physical Abuse of Children', *Handbook of Family Violence*, Plenum Press, New York/London (1988), pp. 119–55.

Steinmetz, Suzanne K. (Ph.D.): see reference for Chapter Eight.

Steinmetz, Suzanne K., and Lucca, Joseph S., 'Husband Battering', *Handbook of Family Violence*, Plenum Press, New York/London (1988), pp. 233–46.

Straus, M., and Gelles, J.: see reference for Chapter One.

Sundblad, C., *et al.*: see reference for Chapter Three (1993).

Swaab, D. F.: see reference for Chapter Four.

Trivers, Robert: see reference for Chapter Two.

Virkkunen, Matti: see reference for Chapter Four (1992).

Virkkunen, Matti, and Linnoila, Markku: see reference for Chapter Four (1990).

Waters, Everett, *et al.*, 'Infant–Parent Attachment and the Origins of Prosocial and Antisocial Behavior', *Development of Antisocial and Prosocial Behavior*, Olweus, Dan, *et al.* (eds.), Academic Press, Inc., New York (1986), pp. 97–125.

Whitehurst, Robert N., 'Violence Potential in Extramarital Sexual Responses', *Journal of Marriage and the Family*, Vol. 33 (1971), pp. 683–91.

Widom, Cathy Spatz: see reference for Chapter Two.

Wolfe, David A., *et al.*, 'Child Victims of Sexual Abuse', *Handbook of Family Violence*, Van Hasselt, Vincent B. (ed.), Plenum Press, New York/London (1988), pp. 157–85.

CHAPTER ELEVEN

Alder, Christine, 'The Convicted Rapist: a Sexual or a Violent Offender?', *Criminal Justice and Behaviour*, Vol. 11, No. 2, University of Melbourne (June 1984), pp. 157–77.

Bain, J. (M.D.), 'Sex Hormones in Pedophiles', *Annals of Sex Research*, Vol. 1 (1988), pp. 443–545.

Baxter, D. J., 'Sexual Responses to Consenting and Forced Sex in a Large Sample of Rapists and Nonrapists', *Behav. Res. Cheo*, Vol. 24, No. 5, Pergamon Journals Ltd., Great Britain (1986), pp. 513–20.

Becker, Judith V., and Coleman, Emily M.: see references for Chapter Ten.

Blair, David C., and Lanyon, Richard I., 'Exhibitionism: Etiology and Treatment', *Psychological Bulletin*, Vol. 89, No. 3 (1981), pp. 439–63.

Brittain, Robert P., 'The Sadistic Murderer', *Medical Science Law*, Vol. 10 (1970), pp. 198–207.

Cassens, G., Ford, M., Lothstein, L., and Gallenstein, T., 'Neuropsychological Dysfunction and Brain-imaging Studies in Paraphiles: Preliminary Studies', *Journal of Clinical and Experimental Neuropsychology*, Vol. 10 (1988), p. 73.

Croall, Hazel, *White Collar Crime: Criminal Justice and Criminology*, Open University Press, Buckingham, Philadelphia.

Cullen, Robert: see reference for Chapter One.

Ellis, L., and Ames, M. A., 'Neurohormonal Functioning and Sexual Orientation: a Theory of Homosexuality and Heterosexuality', *Psychological Bulletin*, Vol. 101 (1987), pp. 233–58.

Ellis, Lee (Ph.D.), *Theories of Rape: Inquiries into the Causes of Sexual Aggression*, Hemisphere Publishing Corporation, New York (1989).

Fagan, Peter J., 'Treatment Case: a Couple with Sexual Dysfunction and Paraphilia', *Personality Disorders and the Five-Factor Model of Personality*, Costa, Paul T., and Widiger, Thomas (eds.), American Psychological Association, Washington DC (1994), pp. 251–7.

Flor-Henry, P., Lang, R. A., Koles, Z. J., and Frenzel, R. R., 'Quantitative EEG Studies of Pedophilia', *International Journal of Psychophysiology*, Vol. 10 (1991), pp. 253–8.

Flor-Henry, P. (M.D.), and Lang, R. A. (Ph.D.), 'Quantitative EEG Investigations of Genital Exhibitionism', *Annals of Sex Research* (1988), pp. 47–62.

Flor-Henry, P., Kolest, Z. J., Reddon, J. R., and Baker, L., 'Neurophysiological Studies (EEG) of Exhibitionism', *Brain Electrical Potentials and Psychopathology*, Elsevier Science Publishing Co., Oxford (1986), pp. 279–303.

Flor-Henry, P., 'Cerebral Aspects of Sexual Deviation', *Genetic and Hormonal Factors*, p. 49.

Freeman, Ellen (Ph.D.), Rickels, Karl (M.D.), Sondheimer, Steven J. (M.D.), and Polansky, Marcia (Sc.D.), 'Ineffectiveness of Progesterone Suppository Treatment for Premenstrual Syndrome', *JAMA*, Vol. 264, No. 3 (1990), pp. 349–53.

Freund, Kurt, and Watson, Robin J., 'Assessment of the Sensitivity and Specificity of a Phallometric Test: an Update of Phallometric Diagnosis of Pedophilia', *A Journal of Consulting and Clinical Psychology*, Vol. 3, No. 2 (1991), pp. 254–60.

Freund, Kurt, 'Courtship Disorders: Toward a Biosocial Understanding of Voyeurism, Exhibitionism, Toucheurism, and the Preferential Rape Pattern', *Crime in Biological, Social and Moral Contexts*, pp. 100–12.

Hare, Robert D. (Dr.): see reference for Chapter Seven (1993).

Hellhammer, Dirk H., Hubert, Walter, and Schürmeyer, Thomas, 'Changes in Saliva Testosterone after Psychological Stimulation in Men', *Psychoneuroendocrinology*, Vol. 10, No. 1, Pergamon Press, Great Britain (1985), pp. 77–81.

Heim, W., and Hurch, C., 'Castration for Sex Offenders: Treatment or Punishment – a Review and Critique of Recent European Literature, *Archives of Sexual Behaviour*, Vol. 8 (1979), pp. 281–304.

Hucker, S., Langevin, R., Wortzman, G., Bain, J., Handy, L., Chambers, J., and Wright, S., 'Neuropsychological Impairment in Pedophiles', *Canad. J. Behav. Sci./Rev.*, Vol. 18, No. 4 (1986), pp. 440–8.

Langevin, Ron, *et al.*: see reference for Chapter Five (1987).

Langevin, Ron, *Sexual Strands*, Lawrence Erlbaum Associates, New Jersey (1983).

Langevin, R., *et al.*, 'Sexual Sadism: Brain, Blood, and Behavior', *Annals of the Academy of Sciences*, Vol. 528 (1988), pp. 163–71.

Langevin, Ron, *et al.*, 'Sexual Aggression: Constructing a Predictive Equation, a Controlled Pilot Study', *Erotic Preference, Gender Identity, and Aggression in Men: New Research Studies*, Lawrence Erlbaum Associates, New Jersey (1985), pp. 39–72.

Lawrence, Joan M., 'Case Report of a Female-to-male Transsexual Homicide Offender', *Australian and New Zealand Journal of Psychiatry*, Vol. 26 (1992), pp. 661–5.

Lehne, Gregory K., 'The Neo-PI and the MCMI in the Forensic Evaluation of Sex Offenders', *Personality Disorders and the Five-Factor Model of Personality*, Costa, Paul, T., and Widiger, Thomas A. (eds.), American Psychological Association, Washington DC (1994), p. 175.

McCaghy, Charles H., and Cernkovich, Stephen A.: see reference for Chapter two.

McLeod Petty, George jr., and Dawson, Brenda, 'Sexual Aggression in Normal Men: Incidence, Beliefs, and Personality Characteristics', *Personal Individual Differences*, Vol. 10, No. 3, Pergamon Press, Great Britain (1989), pp. 355–62.

Mitchell, William, *et al.*: see reference for Chapter Five.

Mohammed, Suzanne, 'Testosterone Concentrations Increase with Sexual Activity', paper written as student at Georgia State University.

Money, John, and Bennett, Richard G., 'Post Adolescent Paraphilic Sex Offenders: Antiandrogenic and Counseling Therapy Follow-up', *International Journal of Mental Health*, Vol. 10, Nos. 2–3, M. E. Sharpe, Inc., U.S.A. (1981), pp. 122–33.

Mosher, Donald L., and Anderson, Ronald D., 'Macho Personality, Sexual Aggression, and Reactions to Guided Imagery of Realistic Rape', *Journal of Research in Personality*, Vol. 20, Academic Press, Inc., New York (1986), pp. 77–94.

Muehlenhard, Charlene L., and Cook, Stephen W., 'Men's Self-reports of Unwanted Sexual Activity', *The Journal of Sex Research*, Vol. 24 (1988), pp. 58–72.

Neumann, F., and Kalmus, J., 'Cyproterone Acetate in the Treatment of Sexual Disorders: Pharmacological Base and Clinical Experience', *Exp. Clin. Endocrinol.*, Vol. 98, No. 2, J. A. Barth, Leipzig (1991), pp. 71–80.

Norris, Joel, *Serial Killers, the Growing Menace*, Arrow Books Ltd., London (1988).

Norris, Joel: see reference for Chapter Five.

Olweus, Dan, *et al.*: see reference for Chapter Two (1986).

Otnow Lewis, Dorothy, 'Special Article: From Abuse to Violence: Psychophysiological Consequences of Maltreatment', *J. Am. Acad. Child Adolesc. Psychiatry*, Vol. 31, No. 3 (1992), pp. 383–91.

Pagelow, Mildren Daley, 'Marital rape', *Handbook of Family Violence*, Plenum Press, New York/London (1988), pp. 207–32.

Pinta, Emil R., 'Treatment of Obsessive Homosexual Pedophilic Fantasies with Medroxyprogesterone Acetate', *Biological Psychiatry*, Vol. 13, No. 3 (1978), pp. 369–73.

Pope, Harrison, G. jr. (M.D.): see reference for Chapter Three (1988)(a).

Reeves Sanday, Peggy, 'The Socio-cultural Context of Rape: a Cross-cultural Study', *Journal of Social Issues*, Vol.37, No.4 (1981), p.5.

Remillard, G. M., *et al.*, 'Sexualictal Manifestations Predominate in Women with Temporal Lobe Epilepsy', *Neurology*, Vol. 33 (1983), pp. 323–33.

Romero, Joseph J., and Williams, Linda M. (Ph.D.), 'Group Psychotherapy and Intensive Probation Supervision with Sex Offenders', *Federal Probation*, Vol. 97 (1983), pp. 36–42.

Romero, Joseph J., and Williams, Linda Meyer, 'Recidivism Among Convicted Sex Offenders: a 10-year Follow Up Study', *Federal Probation*, Vol. 49 (1985), pp. 58–64.

Rowe, David C., *et al.*, 'Sexual Behavior and Nonsexual Deviance: a Sibling Study of Their Relationship', *Developmental Psychology*, Vol. 25, No. 1, American Psychological Association, Washington DC (1989), pp. 61–9.

Rubinstein, Mark (B.F.A.), *et al.*, 'Sexually Assaultive Male Juveniles: a Follow-up', *American Journal of Psychiatry*, 150:2 (1993), pp. 262–5.

Scully, Diana, and Marolla, Joseph, '"Riding the Bull at Gilley's": Convicted Rapists Describe the Rewards of Rape', *Social Problems*, Vol. 32, No. 3 (1985), pp. 251–63.

Shepher, Joseph: see reference for Chapter Ten.

Thiessen, Del: see reference for Chapter Three.

West, D. J., 'Sexual Crimes and Confrontations', *Cambridge Studies in Criminology*, Gower, Aldershot (1987).

Wolfe, David A.: see reference for Chapter Ten.

Wright, P. (M.A.), and Dickey, R. (M.D.), 'Hormonal Correlates of Human Sexual Arousal', *Annals of Sex Research*, Vol. 1, pp. 320–9.

Zaslow, Martha J.: see reference for Chapter Two.

Zucker, Kenneth J., and Green, Richard, 'Psychosexual Disorders in Children and Adolescents', *J. Child Psychol. Psychiat.*, Vol. 33, No. 1, Pergamon Press (1992), pp. 107–51.

CHAPTER TWELVE

Black, D. A. (ed.): see references for Chapter Eight.

Blackburn, Ronald: see references for Chapter Eight.

Bourgeois, M.: see reference for Chapter Four.

Bower, Tom, *Maxwell the Outsider*, Mandarin Paperbacks, London (1992).

Brittain, Robert P.: see reference for Chapter Eleven.

Brown, C. S.: see reference for Chapter Four.

Brown, Gerald L. (M.D.), and Linnoila, Markku I. (M.D., Ph.D.): see reference for Chapter Four.

Browne, Angela: see reference for Chapter Ten.

Chagnon, Napoleon A.: see reference for Chapter Ten.

Christiansen, Kerrin, and Winkler, Eike-Meinrad: see reference for Chapter Three.

Clark, Lee Anna, and Livesley, John W.: see reference for Chapter Eight.

Dalton, Katharina: see reference for Chapter Three.

Daly, Martin, and Wilson, Margo: see references for Chapters Two and Ten (1982 (a)(b), 1984, 1985, 1988).

Elliott, Frank A. (M.D.): see references for Chapters Five and Eight (1983, 1988, 1992).

Ellison Rodgers, Joann: see reference for Chapter Three.

Feldman, Marilyn (M.A.), Mallouh, Katherine, and Otnow Lewis, Dorothy (M.D.): see reference for Chapter Ten.

Fingerhut, Lois A. (M.A.), and Kleinman, Joel C. (Ph.D.): see reference for Chapter Two.

Geffner, Robert, Rosenbaum, Alan, and Hughes, Honore: see reference for Chapter Ten.

Gelles, Richard J., and Straus, Murray A.: see reference for Chapter One.

Gibbens, T. C. N., and Robertson, G., 'A Survey of the Criminal Careers of Restriction Order Patients', *British Journal of Psychiatry*, Vol. 143 (1983), pp. 370–5.

Gibbens, T. C. N., and Robertson, G., 'A Survey of the Criminal Careers of Hospital Order Patients', *British Journal of Psychiatry*, Vol. 143 (1983), pp. 362–9.

Hausfater, Glenn, and Blaffer Hrdy, Sarah: see reference for Chapter Ten.

Henderson, Monika, 'An Empirical Classification of Convicted Violent Offenders', *British Journal of Criminology*, Vol. 22, No. 1 (1982), pp. 1–20.

Henderson, Monika, 'An Empirical Typology of Violent Incidents Reported by Prison Inmates with Convictions for Violence', *Aggressive Behavior*, Vol. 12, Alan R. Liss, Inc. (1986), pp. 221–32.

Hesselbrock, Michie N. (Ph.D.), and Hesselbrock, Victor M. (Ph.D.): see reference for Chapter Six.

Johansson, Sheila Ryan: see reference for Chapter Ten.

Jones, Ann: see reference for Chapter Two.

Lafave, Hugh G. (M.D.), Pinkney, Annette A. (B.A.), and Gerber, Gary J. (Ph.D.): see reference for Chapter Eight.

Leonard, Kenneth E., and Jacob, T.: see reference for Chapter Ten.

Lidberg, Lars, *et al.*, '5-hydroxyindoleacetic Acid Levels in Attempted Suicides Who Have Killed their Children', *The Lancet*, 20 October 1984.

Linnoila, V. Markku I. (M.D., Ph.D.), and Virkkunen, Matti (M.D.): see reference for Chapter Four (1992).

Linnoila, Markku (M.D., Ph.D.), De Jong, Judith (Ph.D.), and Virkkunen, Matti (M.D.):see reference for Chapter Four (1989).

Linnoila, M., et al.: see reference for Chapter Four(1983).

Macdonald, Eileen: see reference for Chapter Two.

Mann, C., 'Getting Even? Women Who Kill in Domestic Encounters', *Justice Quarterly*, Vol. 5 (1988), pp. 33–51.

Maxon, Cheryl L., Gordon, Margaret A., and Klein, Malcolm W., 'Differences Between Gang and Nongang Homicides', *Criminology*, Vol. 23, No. 2 (1985), pp. 209–23.

McCaghy, Charles H., and Cernkovich, Stephen A.: see reference for Chapter Two.

McCanne, Thomas R., and Milner, Joel S.: see reference for Chapter Ten

Milner, Joel S., and McCanne, Thomas R.: see reference for Chapter Ten (1991).

Milner, Joel S.: see reference for Chapter Ten (1993).

Nachshon, Israel: see references for Chapter Five (1983, 1991)(a) and (b)).

Norris, Joel: see reference for Chapter Eleven.

d'Orban, P. T., and Dalton, J.: see reference for Chapter Three.

Otnow Lewis, Dorothy, et al.: see references for Chapters Five (1982, 1985, 1988, pp. 307–19) and Six.

Pleck, Elizabeth, :see reference for Chapter Ten.

Pope, Harrison G. jr. (M.D.), and Katz, David L. (M.D.), 'Homicide and Near-homicide by Anabolic Steroid Users', *Journal of Clinical Psychiatry*, Vol. 51, No. 1 (1990), pp. 28–31.

Raine, Adrian, et al.: see reference for Chapter Five (1994).

Reid, John B.: see reference for Chapter Ten.

Rosenbaum, Alan: see reference for Chapter Ten (1991)(a).

Rosenbaum, Alan, et al.: see reference for Chapter Ten (1991)(b).

Scrimshaw, Susan C. M., 'Infanticide in Human Populations: Societal and Individual Concerns', *Infanticide*, Aldine Publishing Co., New York (1984), pp. 439–62.

Straus, M., and Gelles, J.: see reference for Chapter One.

Taylor, Pamela J., and Gunn, John: see reference for Chapter Eight (1984).

Taylor, Pamela J.: see reference for Chapter Eight (1986).

Virkkunen, Matti: see reference for Chapter Four (1992).

Virkkunen, Matti, and Linnoila, Markku: see reference for Chapter Four (1990).

Wong, M., and Singer, K., 'Abnormal Homicide in Hong Kong', *British Journal of Psychiatry*, Vol. 123 (1973), pp. 295–8.

Bell, Rodney D., Alexander, Guillermo M., and Schwartzman, Robert J., 'Methylphenidate Decreases Local Glucose Metabolism in the Motor Cortex', *Pharmacology, Biochemistry and Behavior, U.S.A.*, Vol. 18 (1983), pp. 1–5.

Bentovim, Arnon (Dr.), Elton, Anne, and Tranter, Marianne, 'Prognosis for Rehabilitation After Abuse', *Adoption Fostering*, Vol. 11, No. 1 (1987), pp. 26–31.

Blair, David C., and Lanyon, Richard I.: see reference for Chapter Eleven.

Coccaro, Emil F. (M.D.), Gabriel, Steven (Ph.D.), and Siever, Larry J. (M.D.), 'Buspirone Challenge: Preliminary Evidence for a Role for Central 5-HT Receptor Function in Impulsive Aggressive Behavior in Humans', *Psychopharmacology Bulletin*, Vol. 26, No. 3 (1990), pp. 393–405.

Cooper, Alan J., 'Progestogens in the Treatment of Male Sex Offenders: a Review', *Canadian Journal of Psychiatry*, Vol. 31 (1986), pp. 73–9.

Cullen, Robert: see reference for Chapter One.

Dalton, Katharina: see reference for Chapter Three.

Daly, Martin, and Wilson, Margo: see reference for Chapter Two.

Datesman, Susan K., and Scarpitti, Frank R.(eds.): see reference for Chapter Two (1980)(a).

Denno, Deborah W.: see reference for Chapter Two (1994) (a) (b).

Denno, Deborah W., 'Legal Implications of Genetics and Crime Research', *Genetics of Criminal and Antisocial Behaviour*, February 1995.

Dwyer, Allen, *Historical Perspective*, Plenum Press, New York (1984).

Ebbe, N. I. (O.B.I.), 'Power and Criminal Law: Criminalization of Conduct Norms in a Colonial Regime', *International Journal of Comparative and Applied Criminal Justice*, Vol. 9, No. 2 (1993), pp. 114–21.

Eisenberg, Nancy, and Mussen, Paul H., *Biology and Prosocial Behavior*, Cambridge University Press, Cambridge (1989).

Eisenberg, Nancy, Fabes, Richard A., Bustamante, Denise, and Mathy, Robin M., 'Physiological Indices of Empathy', *Empathy and its Development*, Cambridge University Press, Cambridge (1987), pp. 380–5.

Eisenberg, Nancy, Fabes, Richard A., and Miller, Paul A., 'The Evolutionary and Neurological Roots of Prosocial Behavior', *Altruism and Aggression*, Zahn-Waxler, Carolyn, *et al.* (eds.), Cambridge University Press, Cambridge (1991), pp. 247–51.

Ellis, Lee: see reference for Chapter One (1991)(d).

Ellison Rodgers, Joann, 'Brain Triggers, Biochemistry and Behavior', *Science Digest* (1983), pp. 60–6.

Eriksson, Elias, 'Serotonergic Agents in the Treatment of Disorders of Anxiety and Impulse Control', *Clinical Neuropharmacology*, Vol. 15, Suppl. 1, Pt. A (1992), pp. 108–346.

Eriksson, E., 'Effect of Clomipramine on Premenstrual Syndrome', *Acta Psychiatrica Scandinavia*, Vol. 81 (1990), pp. 87–8.

Fagan, Peter J.: see reference for Chapter Eleven.

Farley, F.: see reference for Chapter Two.

Fenwick, Peter, 'Brain, Mind and Behaviour, Some Medico-legal Aspects', *Butron Journal of Psychiatry*, Vol. 163 (1993), pp. 565–73.

Fraile, I. G., McEwen, B. S., and Pfaff, D. W.: see reference for Chapter Three.

Freeman, Ellen (Ph.D.), Rickels, Karl (M.D.), Sondheimer, Steven J. (M.D.), and Polansky, Marcia (Sc.D.): see reference for Chapter Three.

Grant, Ellen C. G., and Pryse-Davies, John: see reference for Chapter Three.

Grossman, Linda S. (Ph.D.), 'Research Directions in the Evaluation and Treatment of Sex Offenders: an Analysis', *Behavioral Sciences and the Law*, Vol. 3, No. 4, John Wiley & Sons (1985), pp. 421–40.

Grusec, Joan E., and Dix, Theodore, 'The Socialization of Prosocial Behavior: Theory and Reality', *Crime in Biological, Social and Moral Contexts*, Ellis, Lee, and Hoffman, Harry (eds.), Praeger, New York (1989), pp. 218–37.

Hammarbäck, Stefan, Bäckström, Torbjörn, Holst, Juhani, von Schoultz, Bo, and Lyrenäs, Sven, 'Cyclical Mood Changes as in the Premenstrual Tension Syndrome during Sequential Estrogen-progestogen Postmenopausal Replacement Therapy', *Acta Obstet Gynecol Scand.*, Vol. 64 (1985) pp. 393–7.

Hanson, R. A., *et al.*: see reference for Chapter Two.

Hare, Robert D. (Dr.): see reference for Chapter Seven (1993).

Hare, Robert D., 'Psychopathy: a Clinical Construct whose Time has Come', *Criminal Justice and Behavior.*

Hare, Robert D., and Jutai, Jeffrey W.: see reference for Chapter Seven (1988).

Harpur, Timothy J., Hart, Stephen D., and Hare, Robert D.: see reference for Chapter Seven.

Harrison, Wilma M. (M.D.), Endicott, Jean (Ph.D.), Nee, John (Ph.D.): see reference for Chapter Three.

Hiem, W., and Hurch, C.: see reference for Chapter Eleven.

Hoffman, Martin L.: see reference for Chapter Two.

Horgan, J.: see reference for Chapter Eight.

Hoyenga, Katharine Blick, *Sex Differences in Human Stratification: a Biosocial Approach*, Praeger Publishers, New York (1993), pp. 139–55.

Kashkin, Kenneth B. (M.D.), and Kleber, Herbert D. (M.D.): see reference for Chapter Three.

Kramer, Peter D., *Listening to Prozac*, Fourth Estate, London (1994).

Kruesi, M. J. P.: see reference for Chapter Four.

Kruesi, Markus J., *et al.*: see reference for Chapter Four.

Langevin, Ron (Ph.D.), and Lang, Reuben A. (Ph.D.), 'Psychological Treatment of Pedophiles', *Behavioral Sciences and the Law*, Vol. 3, No. 4, John Wiley & Sons (1985), pp. 403–19.

Lubell, Adele: see reference for Chapter Five.

Maccoby, Eleanor E.: see reference for Chapter Two (1986).

Marcus, Robert F.: see reference for Chapter Two.

McGurk, Barry J., Thornton, David M., and Williams, Mark, *Applying Psychology to Imprisonment*, Her Majesty's Stationary Ofice, London (1987).

Meyer, Walter J., *et al.*, 'Physical, Metabolic, and Hormonal Effects on Men of Long-term Therapy with Medroxyprogesterone Acetate', *Fertility and Sterility*, Vol. 43, No. 1 (1985), pp. 102–8.

Money, John, and Bennett, Richard G.: see reference for Chapter Eleven.

Monroe, Russell R. (M.D.), 'The Medical Model in Psychopathy and Dyscontrol Syndromes', *The Psychopath*, Reid, William (ed.), pp. 190–1.

Neumann, F., and Kalmus, J.: see reference for Chapter Eleven.

Olweus, Dan, 'Bully/victim Problems Among Schoolchildren: Basic Facts and Effects of a School Based Intervention Program', *The Development and Treatment of Childhood Aggression*, Erlbaum, New Jersey (1991), pp. 411–48.

Olweus, Dan, 'Annotation: Bullying at School: Basic Facts and Effects of a School Based Intervention Program', *J. Child Psychol. Psychiat.*, Vol. 35, No. 7, Pergamon, Great Britain (1994), pp. 1171–89.

Olweus, Dan, 'Social Withdrawal, Inhibition, and Shyness', *Victimization by Peers: Antecedents and Long-Term Outcomes*, Erlbaum, New Jersey (1993), pp. 315–40.

Otnow Lewis, Dorothy: see reference for Chapter Five (1988).

Pinta, Emil R.: see reference for Chapter Eleven.

Pope, Harrison G. jr. (M.D.): see reference for Chapter Three (1988)(a).

Prins, H.: see reference for Chapter Nine.

Prins, Herschel A.: see reference for Chapter One.

Radke-Yarrow, Marian, and Zahn-Waxler, Carolyn: see reference for Chapter Seven.

Romero, Joseph J., and Williams, Linda M. (Ph.D.): see references for Chapter Eleven (1983, 1985).

Rule, Ann: see reference for Chapter Eight.

Rushton, J. Philippe, *et al.*: see reference for Chapter Six.

Sandifer, Paul H.: see reference for Chapter Eight.

Sherwin, Barbara B., and Gelfand, Morrie M., 'Sex Steroids and Affect in the Surgical Menopause: a Double-blind, Cross-over Study', *Psychoneuroendocrinology*, Vol. 10, No. 3, Pergamon Press, U.K. (1985), pp. 325–35.

Sherwin, Barbara B., and Gelfand, Morrie M.: see reference for Chapter Three.

Smith, David James: see reference for Chapter Two.

Steinhausen, H.-Ch., and Rauss-Mason, C.: see reference for Chapter Nine.

Stevenson, Jim, *et al.*: see reference for Chapter Six (1993)(b).

Sundblad, C., *et al.*: see references for Chapter Three (1990, 1992, 1993).

Tancredi, Laurence R., and Volkow, Nora: see reference for Chapter Eight.

Taylor, Pamela J.: see reference for Chapter Eight (1985).

CHAPTER FOURTEEN

Allan, E. A., and Steffensmeier, D. J., 'Youth, Underemployment, and Property Crime: Differential Effects of Job Availability and Job Quality on Juvenile and Young Adult Arrest Rates', *American Sociological Review*, Vol. 54 (1989), pp. 107–23.

Bailey, Walter C., 'Correctional Outcome: an Evaluation of 100 Reports', *Journal of Criminal Law*, Vol. 57, No. 2 (1966), pp. 153–61.

Bayer, Ronald: see reference for Chapter One.

Blakely, Craig H., 'Diversion of Juvenile Offenders: an Experimental Comparison', Vol. 55, No. 1 (1987), pp. 68–75.

Brennan, Patricia A., and Mednick, Sarnoff A., 'Learning Theory Approach to the Deterrence of Criminal Recidivism', *Journal of Abnormal Psychology*, Vol. 103, No. 3 (1994), pp. 430–40.

Brennan, Patricia, Mednick, Sarnoff, John, Richard: see reference for Chapter Six.

Bryant, Ernest T., Scott, Monte L., and Golden, Charles J.: see reference for Chapter Five.

Buikhuisen, W.: see reference for Chapter Five.

Cannon, Tyrone D., Mednick, Sarnoff A., and Parnas, Josef: see reference for Chapter Six.

Caspi, Avshalom, Elder, Glen H. jr., and Herbener, Ellen S., 'Childhood Personality and the Prediction of Life-course Patterns', *Straight and Devious Pathways from Childhood to Adulthood*, Robins, Lee, and Rutter, Michael (eds.), Cambridge University Press, Cambridge (1990), pp. 13–35.

Clarke, R. V. G., 'Delinquency, Environment and Intervention', Jack Tizard Memorial Lecture, *J. Child Psychol. Psychiat.*, Vol. 26, No. 4, Pergamon Press, Great Britain (1985), pp. 505–23.

Cohen, P.: see reference for Chapter Six.

Cullen, Francis T., Clark, Gregory A., and Wozniak, John F., 'Explaining the Get Tough Movement: Can the Public be Blamed?', *Federal Probation Journal*, Vol. 49 (1985), pp. 16–24.

Cullen, J. E., and Seddon, J. W., 'The Application of a Behavioural Regime to Disturbed Young Offenders', *Personal Individual Differences*, Vol. 2 (1981), pp. 285–92.

Datesman, Susan K., and Scarpitti, Frank R. (eds.): see reference for Chapter Two (1980)(b).

Davis, Kenneth L., 'Impulsive Aggression in Personality Disorder: Evidence for Involvement of 5-HT-1 Receptors', *Biological Psychiatry*, Vol. 25 (1989), pp. 84A–89A.

Dinitz, Simon, and Conrad, John P.: see reference for Chapter Two.

Elliott, Delbert S., 'Recurring Issues in the Evaluation of Delinquency Prevention and Treatment Programs', *Critical Issues in Juvenile Deliquency* (1980), pp. 237–61.

Eme, Robert F., 'Sex Role Stereotypes and the Epidemiology of Child Psychopathology', *Sex Roles and Psychopathology*, Widom, Cathy Spatz (ed.), Plenum Press, New York (1984).

Eme, Robert F., 'Sex Differences in Childhood Psychopathology: a Review', *Psychological Bulletin*, Vol. 86, No. 3 (1979), pp. 574–95.

Empey, LaMar T., 'Revolution and Counterrevolution: Current Trends in Juvenile Justice', *Critical Issues in Juvenile Delinquency*, Schichor, David (ed.) (1980), pp. 157–75.

Erickson, Maynard L., and Gibbs, Jack P., 'Punishment, Deterrence, and Juvenile Justice', *Critical Issues in Juvenile Delinquency*, pp. 183–200.

Erlenmeyer-Kimling, L., Cornblatt, Barbara A., Bassett, Anne S., Moldin, Steven O., Hilldoff-Adamo, Ulla, and Roberts, Simone, 'High-risk Children in Adolescence and Young Adulthood: Course of Global Adjustment', *Straight and Devious Pathways from Childhood to Adulthood*, Robins, Lee, and Rutter, Michael (eds.), Cambridge University Press, Cambridge (1990), p. 351.

Farringdon, David P.: see references for Chapter Two (1981, 1986, 1987).

Farringdon, David P., Loeber, Rolf, and Van Kammen, Welmoet B.: see reference for Chapter Two.

Farringdon, David P., and West, Donald J., 'Criminal, Penal and Life Histories of Chronic Offenders: Risk and Protective Factors and Early Identification', *Criminal Behaviour and Mental Health*, Vol. 3, Whurr Publishers Ltd., U.K. (1993), pp.492–523.

Frost, L. A., Moffitt, T. E., and McGee, R.: see reference for Chapter Two.

Gibbons, Don C., 'Explaining Juvenile Delinquency: Changing Theoretical Perspectives', *Critical Issues in Juvenile Delinquency* (1980), p. 9.

Gibbs, W. Wayt, 'Seeking the Criminal Element', *Trends in Behavioral Science, Scientific American* (1995), pp. 76–83.

Goodman, Robert: see reference for Chapter Five.

Gove, Walter R., and Wilmoth, Charles: see reference for Chapter Two.

Greenwood, Peter W.: see reference for Chapter Eight.

Gunnar, Megan R.: see reference for Chapter Three.

Hinshaw, Stephen P.: see reference for Chapter Two.

Hurley, Dan, 'Arresting Delinquency', *Psychology Today* (March 1985).

Kandel, Elizabeth, and Mednick, Sarnoff A.: see reference for Chapter Two.

Katz, Jack: see reference for Chapter Two.

Kazdin, Alan E., 'Treatment of Antisocial Behavior in Children: Current

Status and Future Directions', *Psychological Bulletin*, Vol. 102, No. 2 (1987), pp. 187–203.

Kobrin, Solomon, Hellum, Frank R., and Peterson, John W., 'Offense Patterns of Status Offenders', *Critical Issues in Juvenile Delinquency* (1980), pp. 203–35.

Kruesi, Markus J., *et al.*: see reference for Chapter Four.

Krynick, V. E.: see reference for Chapter Five.

Le Blanc, Marc: see references for Chapter Two (1990, 1992).

Lewis, Dorothy Otnow, *et al.*: see references for Chapters Two (1994), Five (pp. 307–19) and Eight.

Loeber, R., and Dishion, T., 'Early Predictors of Male Delinquency: a Review', *Psychological Bulletin*, Vol. 94, No. 1 (1983), pp. 68–99.

Lubar, Joel F., *et al.*, 'The Evaluation of the Effectiveness of EEG Neurofeedback Training for ADHD in a Clinical Setting as Measured by Changes in TOVA Scores, Behavioural Ratings, and WISC-R Performance', *Journal of Biofeedback and Self-regulation*, Vol. 20, No. 1 (1995).

Maccoby, Eleanor E.: see references for Chapter Two (1990).

Magnusson, David, and Bergman, L. R.: see reference for Chapter Two.

Mannuzza, Salvatore, *et al.*: see reference for Chapter Two.

Maughan, Barbara, and Pickles, Andrew: see reference for Chapter Two.

McCord, Joan: see references for Chapter Two (1978, 1990).

McGuinness, Diane: see reference for Chapter Two.

McGurk, Barry J., Thornton, David M., and Williams, Mark: see reference for Chapter Thirteen.

Mednick, Sarnoff A., *et al.*: see reference for Chapter Two (1981).

Mednick, Sarnoff: see references for Chapters Two (1980) and Six (1984, 1985).

Moffitt, Terrie E., and Henry, Bill: see reference for Chapter Two.

Moffitt, Terrie E.: see references for Chapter Two (1989, 1990).

Naylor, Cecile E., Wood, Frank B., and Flowers, D. Lynn: see reference for Chapter Two.

Olweus, Dan, *et al.*: see reference for Chapter Two (1988).

Olweus, Dan: see reference for Chapter Two (1993).

Otnow Lewis, D: see reference for Chapter Two (1992, pp. 331–40).

Palamara, Frances, Cullen, Francis T., and Gersten, Joanne C., 'The Effect of Police and Mental Health Intervention on Juvenile Deviance: Specifying Contingencies in the Impact of Formal Reaction', *Journal of Health and Social Behavior*, Vol. 27 (1986), pp. 90–105.

Pope, Harrison G. jr. (M.D.), and Katz, David L. (M.D.): see references for Chapters Three (1987, 1994) and Twelve.

Raine, Adrian, Brennan, Patricia, and Mednick, Sarnoff A.: see reference for Chapter Six.

Reid, I. D., *et al.*, 'The Shape Project for Young Offenders', *Journal of Offender Counseling, Services and Rehabilitation*, Vol. 4, No. 3, Haworth Press, U.K. (1980), pp. 233–46.

Rivera, Beverly, and Widom, Cathy Spatz: see reference for Chapter Two.

Robins, Lee N.: see reference for Chapter Two (1986).

Robins, Lee N., and Rutter, Michael: see reference for Chapter Two (1990).

Rowe, David C.: see reference for Chapter Two.

Rutter, Michael, and Mawhood, Lynn, 'The Long-term Psychosocial Sequelae of Specific Developmental Disorders of Speech and Language', *Biological Risk Factors for Psychosocial Disorders*, Cambridge University Press, Cambridge (1991), pp. 233–59.

Rutter, M.: see references for Chapter Two (1985, 1987).

Rutter, M., *et al.*: see reference for Chapter Two (1990).

Satterfield, James H.: see reference for Chapter Two (1987)(a).

Satterfield, James H., and Schell, Anne M.: see reference for Chapter Two (1984).

Satterfield, James H., *et al.*: see references for Chapter Two (1979, 1981, 1982, 1987(b), 1994(a)(b)).

Stevenson, Jim: see reference for Chapter Six (1992).

Stevenson, Jim, and Graham, Philip: see reference for Chapter Six (1993)(a).

Strayer, F. F., and Noel, J. M.: see reference for Chapter Two.

Surwillo, Walter W.: see reference for Chapter Five.

Tallal, Paula: see reference for Chapter Three.

Thomas, Mark: see reference for Chapter Two.

Tolan, Patrick, and Guerra, Nancy, *What Works in Reducing Adolescent Violence: an Empirical Review of the Field*, Center for the Study and Prevention of Violence, University of Illinois, Chicago (1994).

Trasler, Gordon, 'Some Cautions for the Biological Approach to Crime Causation', *The Causes of Crime*, Mednick, Sarnoff A., *et al.* (eds.), Cambridge University Press (1987), pp. 7–23.

Venables, P. H.: see reference for Chapter Four.

White, J., *et al.*, 'How Early Can We Tell Pre-School Predictors of Boys' Conduct Disorder and Delinquency?', *Criminology*, Vol. 28 (1990), pp. 507–33.

White, Jennifer L., and Moffitt, Terrie E., 'A Prospective Replication of the Protective Effects of IQ in Subjects at High Risk for Juvenile Delinquency', *Journal of Consulting and Clinical Psychology*, Vol. 57, No. 6 (1989), pp. 719–24.

Wiggins, Jerry S., and Pincus, Aaron L.: see reference for Chapter Two.

Wilson, William Julius: see reference for Chapter Two.

Yeudall, Lorne T.: see references for Chapter Five (1978, 1982).

Zeitlin, H., *The Natural History of Psychiatric Disorder in Children*, Oxford University Press, Oxford (1986).

Zoccolillo, Mark, *et al.*, 'The Outcome of Childhood Conduct Disorder: Implications for Defining Adult Personality Disorder and Conduct Disorder', *Psychological Medicine*, Vol. 22, Cambridge University Press, Cambridge (1992), pp. 971–86.

INDEX

Rubin, R.T. 130

sadistic killers 246–51, 293–4
Satterfield, Jim 313–4, 328–31
schizophrenia 7, 91, 98, 116, 138, 196–9, 256, 261–3, 278, 290
sensation-seeking 43, 61, 73–4, 76–7, 172–3, 178, 203
serial killers 3, 266–70
serotonin (5-hydroxytryptamine, 5-HT) 59–60, 72, 113, 130–1, 138, 140, 141, 177–8, 190–2, 193, 198, 200, 203, 279, 287, 288, 299, 301–2
sexual activity: early 168, 203
sexual deviation 3, 6, 9, 91, 226–51, 267, 292–3, 298–9
see also rape
Sheper, Ann 45
shoplifting 15, 16, 125, 126, 140
Siegal, Larry 8
single-parent families 120–1
skin conductivity 79–80, 157, 174, 218
sleep disorder 63, 68, 69
Snoswell, Amelia 45
spacing behaviour 35–6
SPECT 158
spousal murder 270–4, 279
'Spur Posse' case 288
Steed, John 237–8
Stohr, Oskar 106
stress 70–1, 79–80
suicidal behaviour 62, 64, 66, 279
Sutcliffe, Peter 195, 282–3
Sutherland, Edwin 143

Talling, Michael 272
temporal lobes 86–7, 94–5, 96–7, 103, 134, 179, 182, 186, 198, 219–21, 222, 227, 229, 233, 243, 246, 250, 251, 265, 266, 277

territory: defence of 35–6, 40
testosterone 28, 29, 35, 39, 40, 81, 113, 130, 138, 140, 145, 171–3, 191, 236, 288, 299
theft 15, 123–43
Tkachenko, Andrei 292–3
toucheurism 228
treatment of offenders 9–10, 294, 296–7, 298–302
twins 43, 104–5, 106–7, 109–10, 112–3, 117

verbal activity 18, 20–1, 22, 129, 135, 148, 171, 181–2, 223–4, 318, 319–22
violent offenders 3, 6, 9, 44–5, 68–9, 74–5, 98–9, 101–3, 130, 134–5, 160–83, 184–206, 234–5, 236, 243–6, 323
voyeurism 228–9, 242

Wechsler, D. 20–1
West, D.J. 19, 25, 120
white-collar crime 143–4, 146, 153
Whitman, Charles 6, 266
wife-beating 21, 209, 210–1, 217, 219, 222–3
Williams, Horace 48–9, 289
Wilson, James 20, 21, 308
Wiltshire, Willie 205
Wollstrum, Glenn 289
Woods, Frank 165

XXY males 33
XYY males 287

Yeudall, Lorne 96, 97, 300–1
Yufe, Jack 106
Yuki, People vs. 287

Zito, Jane 263